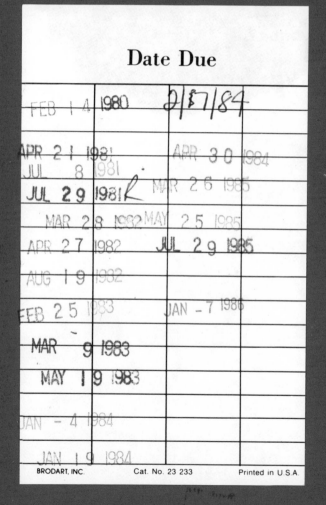

Date Due

FEB 1 4 1980	2/57/84	
APR 2 1 1981	APR 3 0 1984	
JUL 8 1981		
JUL 2 9 1981	MAR 2 6 1985	
MAR 2 8 1982	MAY 2 5 1985	
APR 2 7 1982	JUL 2 9 1985	
AUG 1 9 1982		
FEB 2 5 1983	JAN - 7 1986	
MAR 9 1983		
MAY 1 9 1983		
JAN - 4 1984		
JAN 1 9 1984		

BRODART, INC.   Cat. No. 23 233   Printed in U.S.A.

MELVILLE'S SHORT FICTION
1853–1856

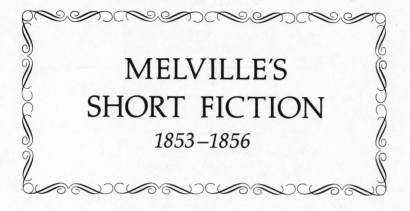

MELVILLE'S SHORT FICTION
1853–1856

William B. Dillingham

THE UNIVERSITY OF GEORGIA PRESS
ATHENS

The University of Georgia Press, Athens 30602

Set in 11 on 13 point Intertype Garamond
Printed in the United States of America

Library of Congress Cataloging in Publication Data

Dillingham, William B
  Melville's short fiction, 1853–1856.
  Includes index.
  CONTENTS: Unconscious duplicity: Bartleby,
the scrivener. — High-spirited revolt: Cock-a-
doodle-doo. — An hourglass run out: The encantadas. [etc.]
    1. Melville, Herman, 1819–1891—Criticism and
interpretation. I. Title.
PS2387.D53   813'.3   76-28922
        ISBN 0-8203-0411-5

TO ELIZABETH

patientia, integritate, benevolentia

CONTENTS

MELVILLE'S SHORT FICTION
1853–1856

INTRODUCTION

When in 1853 Herman Melville learned to his disappointment that he was not going to be appointed United States consul to the Sandwich Islands, he decided to become, at least for a time, a writer of magazine stories. It was perhaps a way of driving off the spleen. During the years 1853–1856 while living on a farm near Pittsfield, Massachusetts, he wrote sixteen short works of fiction which he published with two exceptions in *Harper's New Monthly Magazine* and *Putnam's Monthly Magazine,* seven in each. Coming as it does in the wake of *Moby-Dick,* his undisputed masterpiece, and *Pierre,* a dismal failure according to numerous contemporary reviewers, this period in Melville's life appears relatively calm, as if it were a time of withdrawal from the public eye. In fact it was the opposite, for these short works of fiction reached a surprisingly large audience because of the popularity of *Harper's* and *Putnam's* magazines.

Harper's was started in 1850 principally as an advertising medium for the books being published by the firm. It was an "eclectic" magazine, that is, one that included among other things pieces that had originally appeared elsewhere. Installments of the current work of Dickens, Bulwer, Thackeray, and other British writers filled its ample and attractive pages. By the time Melville began publishing stories there in December 1853,[1] *Harper's* had eased its original policy of concentrating heavily on British authors and was including more works by Americans. It became the most popular magazine of its type in America. Its success amazed the editors and perplexed the competition. Within six months after it was established its circulation rose to 50,000, and in the next few years it reached the phenomenal figure of 200,000.[2] Ironically Melville's fame continued to grow dimmer even as his audience expanded, for both *Harper's* and *Putnam's* did not as a rule include the names of their contributors. Therefore most readers would not have known that these stories were by Melville.

Putnam's originated as a patriotic challenge to *Harper's*. Its announced aim was to print materials by Americans and for Americans. Melville's invitation to write for the new magazine came in October 1852 in the form of a circular letter that was sent out to scores of other American authors. In addition to stories by Melville, the early numbers contained works by Longfellow, Lowell, and others of prominence. The circulation of *Putnam's* never equalled that of *Harper's,* but it was widely read and it paid its contributors well. Melville received at least five dollars a page, which added up to a substantial amount for long stories like "Bartleby" and "Benito Cereno."

Melville must have been acutely aware of this dramatic shift in his situation as an author. By the time reviewers had finished with *Pierre,* he might well have wondered if he would ever sell another work of fiction and—if he did—if anyone would bother to read it. Then, suddenly, he was a regular contributor to two highly successful periodicals. To remain so he had to conform in certain ways to the public tastes, for these two magazines were

---

1. A chapter from *Moby-Dick,* "The Town-Ho's Story," was published earlier in *Harper's* (October 1851).
2. Frank Luther Mott, *A History of American Magazines, 1850–1865* (Cambridge: Harvard University Press, 1938), p. 391.

the very mirrors of nineteenth-century middle-class American culture.

To begin with he had to find a way to avoid offending anyone. Hell-raising was definitely out. Both magazines were explicit about their determination to publish only those writings that were in good taste. In the "Advertisement" that concluded the third volume (1851) of Harper's, this policy is clearly stated: "The object of the Publishers is to combine the greatest possible Variety and Interest, with the greatest possible Utility. Special care will always be exercised in admitting nothing into the Magazine in the slightest degree offensive to the most sensitive delicacy; and there will be a steady aim to exert a healthy moral and intellectual influence, by the most attractive means."[3] This noble aim is restated in almost the same language at the end of the fourth volume. Putnam's was no less genteel and protective of the public's delicate feelings. "Care is taken," reads the statement that closes the fourth volume (1854), "that nothing in the remotest degree offensive to propriety or good taste defaces these pages."[4]

When Melville violated this code of nonoffensiveness, he found himself without a publisher. Only once did it happen, however. Putnam's rejected "The Two Temples" because the first part of the story came down hard on one of the most important churches in New York City and by implication condemned the hypocrisy of affluent church-goers all over the country. The editor of Putnam's wrote Melville that "my editorial experience compels me to be very cautious in offending the religious sensibilities of the public."[5] In the same letter the editor indicated that he had deleted "a few words" from the sketch of "The

3. *Harper's New Monthly Magazine* 3 (June–November 1851): ii.
4. *Putnam's Monthly Magazine* 4 (July–December 1854): iv.
5. Quoted in Jay Leyda, *The Melville Log: A Documentary Life of Herman Melville, 1819–1891* (New York: Harcourt, Brace, 1951), 1: 487.

Encantadas" that deals with the Chola widow to "improve" it. What these words were is not now known, but chances are that they, too, ran the risk of offending someone's delicate sensibilities.

Melville began his writing career by openly offending a large number of people with his sharp attacks on missionaries in *Typee* and *Omoo*. He stirred up more controversy with his criticism of flogging and other practices in the United States Navy in *White-Jacket*. By the time he wrote *Moby-Dick* he had learned much about the fine art of concealment. He took a special pleasure in writing what he called a "wicked" book that most people would not recognize as such. The methods Melville employed for concealing his deeper and more personal meanings in novels like *Moby-Dick,* *Pierre,* and *Billy Budd* have been the subject of numerous books and articles over the last twenty-five years. What has not been generally recognized is that in his short fiction he carried the technique of concealment even further. *Moby-Dick* and *Pierre* offended some readers who probably did not even glimpse the true depths of the works simply because of their wildness, their ravings, their stark incongruities. Many a genteel heart said, in effect, "I don't know what it is, but I know I don't like it."

Given the requirements for publishing in *Harper's* and *Putnam's,* therefore, it was not enough for Melville to camouflage his complicated meanings and submerge his attacks on the world; he must also—and this was perhaps a greater challenge than he had faced before—create a smooth, unrippled surface. He must *seem* congenial, amusing, and harmless. In a word, he must conceal his profundity in an illusion of vapidity. It is one thing to hide meanings; it is something else to hide the entire work. A reader may be easily impressed with *Mardi* or *Moby-Dick* if for no other reason than that of their sheer bulk. Conversely it is easy to dismiss as slight stories like "The Lightning-Rod Man" because of their extreme brevity. Melville seemed determined in some works to defy limitations imposed

on him, to say more and more in less and less space. In this sense
he resembled his own character Bartleby, who seeks wider freedom by placing himself behind walls.

Melville created the illusion of vapidity through several
means. Most of his stories are without much adventure or action. Some of them turn upon a single incident—a man tells
of his search for a rooster he wants to buy; a homeowner recounts a visit from a salesman; a husband describes an argument
with his wife about remodeling their house; a traveler tells of
his visits to a men's club in London and to a paper mill in
America. In all but two of the stories Melville used first-person
narrators. Generally they are older men, most of them reminiscing about some episode that happened years ago. They are as
a rule mild, domestic types, husbands and fathers or bachelors
who have settled down to a staid way of life. They offer no
offense, pose no threat. They are witty, humane, educated, congenial, a bit boring. Beneath these external similarities, however,
are great differences. Some of them are rebellious deep divers,
others shallow and hypocritical weaklings, but such differences
become evident only after careful scrutiny.

This then was Melville's basic formula: an older man remi-
nisces in urbane fashion about some episode in his life or some
eccentric character he has known or something he has once
seen. In the two stories that do not use a first-person narrator,
"The Bell-Tower" and "Benito Cereno," there is more violence
and more action. But these are smothered into inoffensiveness in
the one case by a heavy blanket of pseudomoralizing that appears
to be (but is not) straight out of Hawthorne and in the other
by what seems (but is not) the final triumph of order and jus-
tice and truth. Throughout most of the stories a sense of artistic ineptness prevails that is as deceptive as the unrippled
surface. "The Bell-Tower" seems overly didactic and derivative;
"Benito Cereno" appears horribly fragmented, as does "The
Encantadas." Other stories seem to start with too little and to
get nowhere. College students who read the much anthologized

"Bartleby" frequently consider the silent scrivener an intolerable bore. Jimmy Rose seems a nonentity. In story after story the reader looks up from "The Fiddler" or "The Happy Failure" or "The Piazza" with a sense of having read something very thin, a mere anecdote or slight sketch—some queer genre far removed from the traditional short story form with its five-part structure of situation, generating circumstance, rising action, climax, and dénouement.

So it is not surprising that some of Melville's staunchest admirers have evaluated many of these short works as the lapses of an exhausted genius. Newton Arvin speaks of them as potboilers, products of a "flagging vitality and depleted inventiveness." He believes that Melville was "sparing himself by attempting only short and unexacting flights."[6] Similarly Leon Howard sees the period of the short fiction as one in which Melville wrote "apparently without any strain," when "he was not going to attempt anything ambitious," when he made good money for "easily written sketches."[7] Even Richard Harter Fogle, in his book-length study of Melville's short fiction, is compelled to conclude his introductory chapter on an apologetic note in which he warns against overrating the stories, reiterates Melville's lack of craftsmanship in the shorter form of fiction, and points out weaknesses even in the stories often considered the best.[8] Although recently there have appeared a great number of articles that attempt to reassess and upgrade Melville's short fiction, and a refreshing book on the subject by R. Bruce Bickley, Jr.,[9] most of the stories still do not enjoy a high place

6. *Herman Melville* (New York: Sloane, 1950), p. 231.
7. *Herman Melville: A Biography* (Berkeley: University of California Press, 1951), pp. 208, 212.
8. *Melville's Shorter Tales* (Norman: University of Oklahoma Press, 1960).
9. *The Method of Melville's Short Fiction* (Durham: Duke University Press, 1975). Although my interpretations of individual works disagree almost consistently with those in Bickley's study (which appeared too late to be considered in detail in this book), I am in full agreement

in the Melville canon. "To respect these tales at their full value," Fogle concludes, "one must have respected Melville to begin with." [10]

Fogle's statement is true but not, I suspect, in the sense he intended. To respect Melville in the beginning means to expect the unexpected, to put aside all traditional rules of genre and form, to examine whatever he has written on its own terms and with the understanding that whatever is there may be revealed only after time and patience and meditation. If his short stories are not like other short stories, neither were his novels like other novels, nor his poems like other poetry. Almost everything he ever wrote was experimental in nature. He never found what he considered the perfect vehicle for his vision, but he knew that the ordinary and accepted forms were inadequate. Emerson and the other Transcendentalists may have been the official spokesmen for "organic form" in nineteenth-century America, but there never was a more genuine practitioner of that theory of writing than Melville.

He wrote as he did in these stories for two basic reasons: concealment and artistic experimentation. He camouflaged meanings because concealment had already become a characteristic of his nature as a writer, because the articulation of a private vision in coded language, as it were, served the ends of both therapy and art, and because the magazines he was writing for demanded palatable art for queasy minds. One motive furthered the other: greater concealment led to greater experimentation. What appear to be inoffensive and somewhat amateurish sketches com-

---

with his overall evaluation of Melville's short fiction: "In experimenting with short fiction in the middle 1850's, Melville found new artistic strength. Obliged by the form of the magazine tale to compress and focus his creative powers, he saw more clearly than he had before the effect of discipline on craftsmanship. As a result, there is very little wasted motion in the magazine stories, and some of the tales reveal a verbal facility unrivalled anywhere in his works" (p. 131).

10. Fogle, p. 13.

7

posed for the masses are in reality highly sophisticated and poetically compacted works often of unsurpassed originality.

Although little is known of Melville's thoughts and theories about the short work of fiction as an art form, he apparently wanted to create something radically different from the traditional story through the juxtaposition of opposing fictive integrals. He seems to have conceived his stories mostly in pairs rather than in independent units. The most obvious examples of pairing are the three works that consist in each case of two separate episodes, each with its own title: "The Two Temples," "Poor Man's Pudding and Rich Man's Crumbs," and "The Paradise of Bachelors and the Tartarus of Maids." Melville himself did not have a name for these works of complementing episodes. Jay Leyda called them *diptychs*.[11] They are difficult to label because there is little precedent for them. Because the term *diptych* has something of an ecclesiastic flavor and because it may suggest a more pronounced separation than is actually there, I have chosen to call them *bipartite* stories. The two sections that make up a bipartite story are not mutually exclusive. A critic cannot accurately talk about "The Tartarus of Maids," for example, as if it were an independent story, for without "The Paradise of Bachelors" it loses a great deal of its meaning. The two parts create together a single effect. In a work like "Poor Man's Pudding and Rich Man's Crumbs" the second episode depends upon the first for much of its emotional impact. One builds upon the other; the effect is cumulative. The same character narrates both episodes and thus adds to this unity in doubleness. Melville's interest in the bipartite story can be seen in still other works, notably "The Encantadas" and "Jimmy Rose," where he creates two structural units but makes the division subtle enough so that it is scarcely noticed.

In addition to pairing episode with episode (or one section

---

11. Jay Leyda, ed., *The Complete Stories of Herman Melville* (New York: Random, 1949), p. xx.

with another) in a single work, as he did in the bipartite stories, Melville also paired one story with another. Customarily (though not always) he would compose two stories at about the same time with the same central complex idea but with contrasting emphases. Whether he sent these complementary stories to different magazines, as he did in the case of "Bartleby," which he submitted to *Putnam's,* and "Cock-A-Doodle-Doo!," which he sent to *Harper's,* or to the same magazine, as with "The Bell-Tower" and "Benito Cereno," which were both published in *Putnam's,* he apparently made no mention of their interrelatedness (another act of concealment, perhaps). Unlike the bipartite stories such works as those just mentioned and others, like "The Happy Failure" and "The Fiddler," are independent and can be analyzed effectively by themselves. Indeed they almost always are. But Melville's rich and complicated artistry unfolds to a greater extent when such works are juxtaposed and one viewed in the light of the other. "Bartleby" and "Cock-A-Doodle-Doo!" are both on the subject of the rebellious exceptional man in opposition to the ordinary world, but their narrators are diametrically opposite in nature, and thus two perspectives on the same theme result. "Benito Cereno" is seen to be much less concerned with the question of slavery in antebellum America than is often assumed and much more concerned with universal human slavery and the results of misanthropy when it is examined alongside "The Bell-Tower." Such works, separate and independent though they are, complement each other and contrast. Thus they are probably more nearly like diptychs, as the term is used in painting, than the bipartite stories, but to avoid confusion I have labeled them *counterstories.* Melville seemed so aware of the unusualness of his short stories that he was not sure what they were. He called them "articles." [12]

Not all of Melville's short fiction falls into these two cate-

---

12. *The Letters of Herman Melville,* ed. Merrell R. Davis and William H. Gilman (New Haven: Yale University Press, 1960), p. 177.

gories of bipartites and counterstories. "The Lightning-Rod Man" is similar in theme to several other stories, but it does not appear to have been written as a counterstory to any specific one. "The Piazza," the only one of the short works not submitted to a magazine for publication, was composed as an introductory story for the collection he put together called *Piazza Tales* (1856). Consequently "The Piazza" was written with five other stories in mind. The idea of collecting some of his stories into a single volume, incidentally, was an afterthought of Melville's. In examining the body of his short stories it is important to keep in mind that with the exception of "The Piazza" they were not originally written for a book, that is, as part of a collection, but as contributions to popular magazines. Nor does the *Piazza Tales* necessarily represent a gathering together between hard covers of all those stories Melville valued as his best. The volume was issued by the firm of Dix and Edwards, which had bought *Putnam's* and wanted only the stories that had been published in its own magazine. Consequently none of the works that had appeared in *Harper's* was included.

Melville's originality is strongly in evidence in his creation of unusual fictional forms, but structure was not an end in itself for him so much as it was a means toward a still higher aim. His first purpose throughout his short fiction was the delineation of character. More than anything else these short stories are a gallery of people, and it is through their characterization that Melville's two motives—concealment and artistic experimentation—fuse into his greatest achievement.

An effective author employs so many devices to characterize that it is difficult to generalize about the subject. Successful characterization has become known as the magic touch of fiction. Either a writer has it—whatever it is—or he does not. "Humanity is immense," Henry James reminds us. "The most one can affirm is that some of the flowers of fiction have the odour of it, and others have not; as for telling you in advance how your nosegay should be composed, that is another affair."[13] Nevertheless a few after-the-fact observations about Melville's particular mode of characterization can be made. Without exception it is impossible to understand these stories without coming to an understanding of the narrative voice. In all but "The Bell-Tower" and "Benito Cereno" this means comprehending to the fullest possible extent the narrator since these works are all written from a first-person point of view. Probably the most elemental error is that of immediately assuming that the author is the narrator. Some of the narrators are much like Melville; some are very different. But to a large extent what the narrator is *is* the story.

Typically, a short story of Melville is the depiction of a mind. It consists of an overt and a submerged plane of characterization. Overtly Melville characterizes in most of the traditional ways. The narrator tells about himself, his age, his occupation or way of life, his likes and dislikes. By describing his actions and feelings and his reactions to other people, he projects an impression of the kind of man he is. His wit, his strengths and weaknesses as a human being all become a part of his overt characterization. It is tempting to stop with this plane of delineation, to take the narrator as he seems and to turn our attention to other, broader matters—historical, social, political, economic issues—and to assume that these were Melville's primary interests. A major premise of this book is that they were not. Wherever they occur they are secondary to the unfolding of character, an unfolding that takes place on the second plane submerged beneath layers of inoffensive wit, congenial reminiscing, and Irvingesque worldly maturity. The narrator of "I and My Chimney" on the surface is a mild, lazy old country gentleman, henpecked into submission by his shrew of a wife. Readers of

13. Henry James, "The Art of Fiction," *Longman's Magazine* 4 (May–October 1884): 509.

Putnam's may have smiled and had a chuckle or two over his unwonted stubbornness—expressed in mock heroic terms—when his wife wants to tear down his dear old chimney. But he is no joke. He is of the breed of Ahab, though his obsessiveness is so camouflaged as to be recognizable only upon close and persistent scrutiny.

Such scrutiny—it may be too close and too persistent for some readers, though I hope not—is the method of the chapters that follow. They are directed chiefly at uncovering submerged characterizations. On this plane Melville subordinates all else to revealing character perception. If the story is the narrator, the narrator is his particular way of perceiving, and his mode of seeing is embodied in all the analyzable stuff of the work—its style, its structure, its imagery. It is not enough to listen to the narrator of "Bartleby," to take him at his word and accept his characterization of himself, for he is a deceiver—even of himself. One must examine closely not only his pattern of behavior but also the patterns that emerge from his use of words: his concern with age and death, his frequent references to eating and to money, his use of superficial and easy terms like *curious* and *strange* when he is confronted with unfathomable mystery. Only after all these patterns are discovered and fitted together is the figure in the carpet discernible. In some instances this is the same figure we detected on the surface, but greatly filled out and deepened. In more cases than not the submerged characterization stands in contrast to the overt one. A stunning, revelatory irony results.

Melville's ironic method of characterization is just as much in evidence in the two stories where he does not use a first-person point of view. In both "The Bell-Tower" and "Benito Cereno" he combines with the third-person point of view an authorial perspective with what may be called the world's view. The two have to be carefully identified and separated just as a narrator's words in the other stories have to be analyzed from the standpoint of both what they say and what they suggest about the speaker. Melville's own view is submerged in the image patterns, in allusions, and in dozens of subtle indirections. In "The Bell-Tower" the authorial view of Bannadonna is vastly different from that of the community for which he works, yet both opinions are blended into a single voice. Melville's most complicated and most sophisticated use of point of view is in "Benito Cereno," where the narrative presents four separate ways of seeing the same event. Three of these represent aspects of the vision of the common and ordinary world with which Melville was almost constantly at odds. The most important view is, as always, the submerged one, underlying and undercutting the others. If most readers of *Putnam's* did not find "Benito Cereno" a profoundly dark story, it is probably because most of them who read it read it only once, not enough for the irony that is so essential to both Melville's art and vision to swim into focus, not enough for the realization that one voice is expressing a variety of views.

What readers of *Harper's* and *Putnam's* did not miss, however, were the many references in Melville's stories to the contemporary scene. To grasp the extent that these works reflect interests and happenings of mid-nineteenth-century America, the modern reader needs almost to keep one eye on the stories and the other on contemporary newspapers and magazines. This aspect of Melville's work must have delighted the editors of *Harper's* and *Putnam's,* for both magazines made a concerted effort to keep up with the times. The "Publishers' Notice" that concludes the second volume (1853) of *Putnam's* expresses the intent of the magazine to "extend as widely as possible its field of view, passing over no genuine human interest, and especially no genuine national interest." [14] Much information to keep the reader up to date, particularly on books and music, was to be found in the "Editorial Notes" of each issue, and nonliterary articles on a wide range of current interests were commonplace.

14. *Putnam's* 2 (July–December 1853): iv.

Harper's included a section called the "Monthly Record of Current Events" that listed sensational happenings (such as murders) as well as important political news. The magazine soon added a section titled the "Editor's Easy Chair," devoted to a great variety of current goings-on and gossip, and another department called the "Editor's Table," where such broad issues as American education, religion, and women's rights were discussed.

With their wealth of allusions to what was going on, Melville's stories fit in well in these magazines. In "Bartleby" he referred to one of the most sensational murders of the nineteenth century involving the brother of Samuel Colt, the firearms inventor and manufacturer. In another place in the same story he has one of his characters mention Monroe Edwards, who was known as the Great Forger and who captured the imagination of the country with his ingenious and ambitious swindles. In "Cock-A-Doodle-Doo!" Melville compares the sound of a noble rooster to the singing of a popular opera star of the day named Beneventano. When the narrator of "I and My Chimney" says that the grass in his part of the country is "like Kossuth's rising of what he calls the peoples," he is alluding to a figure that every literate American of the time would recognize, the great and heroic advocate of freedom and democracy, the "Hungarian Patrick Henry," as he is called in the "Editor's Easy Chair" of *Harper's* for January 1852.[15] Kossuth's visit to America caused a great stir, and his speeches were voluminously reviewed in newspapers and magazines.

If Melville was a name-dropper he was also a fad-dropper. He mentions the spiritualism craze that was sweeping the country in the 1840s and 1850s in "I and My Chimney" and also in "The Apple-Tree Table," where he refers to the most famous of the spiritual mediums, those queens of table rapping, the Fox sisters. Child prodigies were in such demand in the great enter-

15. *Harper's* 4 (December 1851–May 1852): 265.

tainment halls of the period that they constantly packed the houses. There was little Paul Jullien, for example, with his magic violin, and little Joseph Burke, likewise a violinist, William Henry Marsh, who was called the "Little Drummer," Master William Saar, a child piano wonder, and numerous others. Melville's story "The Fiddler" is about one of these child prodigies, whom the narrator compares to the popular boy actor Master Betty. A character in another story, a comic old gentleman in "The Happy Failure," has become caught up in still another nineteenth-century craze, the invention mania. He spends ten futile years trying to develop a portable swamp-draining machine that will make him a millionaire. He calls it his "Great Hydraulic-Hydrostatic Apparatus." His idea was no sillier than hundreds of others of the times.

The numerous references to contemporary people (most of whom are now forgotten), to events, and to current interests gave Melville's stories an air of modernity that appealed to many readers of *Harper's* and *Putnam's*. To modern readers who will take the time to pursue them, these allusions furnish insights into the popular culture of mid-nineteenth-century America. Such references also function thematically: they are both a part of the pleasing surface that Melville realized that he had to maintain and frequently an important aspect of submerged characterization. For example, in "The Two Temples" the narrator seems highly interested in the contemporary stage. He dedicates his story to the actor and playwright Sheridan Knowles, mentions the great French actor Talma, and recounts a visit to a theater in London to see William Charles Macready—perhaps the most respected English actor of his time—in Bulwer-Lytton's popular play *Richelieu, or the Conspiracy*. On the surface the narrator seems to admire Macready for the same reason as the people around him in the theater. In actuality he views Macready in a far different light from the ordinary world. He sees a great actor playing his role as a metaphorical representation of sensitive man dealing with society. He likes actors because he is himself an actor, consciously playing a part but at the same time retaining his own innermost identity.

In his short fiction as in most of his other writings Melville revealed a good deal about himself. Some of it is on the surface; most of it is submerged. He includes so many details that are autobiographical that he seems at times to be merely recounting his own experiences. The setting for several of the stories is clearly Melville's own farm, Arrowhead. His house is described almost exactly in "I and My Chimney" and "The Piazza," and the surrounding countryside in "Cock-A-Doodle-Doo!" and other works. Sometimes, as in "The Apple-Tree Table," the narrator is surrounded by a household of women, as was Melville himself in these years. The visit from a salesman in "The Lightning-Rod Man" is based upon an actual incident. Melville probably had two of his own relatives in mind when he created Jimmy Rose and the old inventor in "The Happy Failure." The narrator of "The Encantadas" is an ex-seaman who, like Melville himself, had once visited the Galápagos Islands. Melville's visits to the Knights-Templars in London and a paper mill near Pittsfield became the basis for "The Paradise of Bachelors and the Tartarus of Maids." The list of such autobiographical material grows long, but it does not result in a revelation of what Melville was like at this period of his life any more than the overt characterizations of his stories give the best and deepest insights into his characters. Hawthorne's statement in "The Old Manse," an essay Melville once greatly admired, could well have been his own: "So far as I am a man of really individual attributes, I veil my face; nor am I, nor have I ever been, one of those supremely hospitable people, who serve up their own hearts delicately fried, with brain-sauce, as a tidbit for their beloved public." [16]

16. Nathaniel Hawthorne, "The Old Manse," in *Mosses from an Old Manse*, The Centenary Edition of the Works of Nathaniel Hawthorne, general eds. William Charvat, Roy H. Pearce, C. M. Simpson, vol. 10 (Columbus: Ohio State University Press, 1974): 33.

Yet there is much of the inner Melville in his stories as there was much of Hawthorne in his, not openly served up with brain sauce for the reader, but covered to keep the flies away. He created a gallery of characters, but in a sense he was always writing about himself, from the lower depths of his depression in "The Encantadas" to a more balanced view of life in "Jimmy Rose." These were not his happiest years for several reasons, some of which are shadowed forth in the stories. After *Pierre* his reputation seemed on the wane, and he was landlocked on a farm, rimmed in by hills, in a household of too many women and children. The only friendship that promised stimulation and warmth, that with Hawthorne, died prematurely on the vine, a victim of Hawthorne's diseased self-contemplation and Melville's over-fertilization. His expectations and his disappointments with regard to Hawthorne flicker in and out of the stories, especially "The Encantadas" and "The Piazza," and make for one of the most revealing instances of submerged autobiography in all his works. In his friendship with Hawthorne he had expected a great deal but received very little. Such introspective reminiscences, concealed as they are in the texture of these stories, do not result in glad tidings on the level that counts most, internally, as Emily Dickinson put it, "Where the Meanings, are." But neither are these works documents of bitterness and frustration. Taken as a whole they represent a deeply personal dialectic through which Melville is seen to be coping painfully—but coping nevertheless—with life.

UNCONSCIOUS DUPLICITY

"Bartleby, the Scrivener"

Chapter 1

The narrator of "Bartleby, the Scrivener" is a mild lawyer who admires aggressiveness in others. If he were alive today, he might be among that host of nonviolent men who spend their autumnal Sabbaths vicariously engulfed in the bold strategies and violent executions of professional football. He passes his days in the safety of a snug little office which he refers to as a "retreat." He does a quiet business tracing titles for deeds and performing unexciting and unchallenging work among rich men's bonds and mortgages. Yet he looks up to bold and noble men. Timid himself, he keeps a bust of the great lawyer Cicero in his office to remind him of the beauty of eloquence. As he modestly confirms, he never addresses a jury or strives for public applause. When he says that he is an "eminently *safe* man," he implies more than that he is merely discreet and trustworthy (p. 547).[1] He is "safe" because he takes no chances. Neverthe-

1. Quotations from "Bartleby, the Scrivener" are from the first print-

18

less he prizes in others a sense of adventure and a vision of greatness. He has heroes in each of three broad areas of life. In law, his own profession, Cicero is his idol. In the arts he admires the bold poet Byron; and in the world of business and high finance, his hero is John Jacob Astor, one of America's finest examples of the self-made man.

The narrator is understandably proud that he was once in the employ of John Jacob Astor, who generously complimented him for his abilities. He loves to say that great man's name, for to him it "rings like unto bullion" (p. 547). Astor represents to him not only material wealth, but the genuine article, the symbol of which is bullion, the pure, unadulterated form of precious metal.[2] Byron awes him for the same reason. Astor is "bullion"; Byron is "mettlesome." The pun on "metal," which serves to link Byron to Astor, is anything but accidental in the story, for it is the beginning of a subtle but carefully developed and recurrent contrast between authenticity and counterfeit, honesty and duplicity. In this distinction beats the heart of Melville's story of two men, Bartleby a tragically honest rebel, the lawyer a fraud who is not fully aware of his duplicity.

To see clearly Melville's development of these two types, it is helpful to consider "Bartleby, the Scrivener" alongside "Cock-

---

ing in *Putnam's Monthly Magazine* 2 (November–December 1853): 546–557, 609–615. The title of the lawyer's newly acquired position, Master in Chancery, suggests his timidity, his helplessness in embarrassing situations, for the phrase "in chancery" has (and did have in Melville's time) the slang meaning of being powerless in "an awkward fix or predicament" (*OED*).

2. "Precious metal in the mass"(*OED*). It is important to understand that the lawyer is not a greedy man. His interest in money is, as I shall later show, a symbolic gesture. To find "greed expressed in the bullion metaphor," as one critic does, is to misunderstand the function of money in the story: Liane Norman, "Bartleby and the Reader," *New England Quarterly* 44 (1971): 22–39. See David Shusterman's response to Norman's article: "The 'Reader Fallacy' and 'Bartleby the Scrivener,' " *New England Quarterly* 45 (1972): 118–124.

A-Doodle-Doo!" which was published about the same time.[3] These two works reflect Melville's interest in and experimentation with counterstories. They depict similar situations with opposite outcomes: a first-person narrator tells of a time of crisis in his life. The lawyer of "Bartleby" needs "help" because of a demanding new job he has undertaken, and he advertises for an extra scrivener. The narrator of "Cock-A-Doodle-Doo!" is dangerously depressed and needs another kind of help, inspiration and encouragement. Into the life of each man enters a strange character, who is like no one else he ever encountered before. These two characters, Bartleby and Merrymusk, have cut themselves off from the past, and they refuse to talk about it. In fact, in their extreme eccentricity, they both seem irrational and out of touch with the world.

The situation develops where both narrators find themselves in the middle, with the world of ordinary life on one side and the puzzling, unworldly, but compelling stranger on the other. Both men must choose one or the other alternative, the expediency of the world or defiant individualism. They choose oppositely. The lawyer of "Bartleby" stays in and of the world; the narrator of "Cock-A-Doodle-Doo!" rejects the world.[4] In the end Bartleby and Merrymusk both die, and the two narrators go opposite ways. Melville achieved in these counterstories the brilliant portrayal of two kinds of men. The contrast operates within each of the stories—the lawyer versus Bartleby and the bill collector versus the narrator of "Cock-A-Doodle-Doo!" But in each story one character is delineated more fully and thus occupies the spotlight: in "Bartleby" it is the lawyer, the undefiant man of the world; in the other work it is

3. "Cock-A-Doodle-Doo!" was published in the December issue of *Harper's*.

4. Sidney P. Moss makes the point that "Cock-A-Doodle-Doo!" and "Bartleby" are companion pieces, but he draws a far different conclusion from my own when he states that "Bartleby is defeated by life and withdraws even into death." See " 'Cock-A-Doodle-Doo!' and Some Legends in Melville Scholarship," *American Literature* 40 (1968): 210.

he and his employees play because it is beneficial to them all. Turkey is the marshal of this pseudoruler, and he speaks to the lawyer as if he were in a king's court. "With submission, sir," he begins most of his comments, "I consider myself your right-hand man. In the morning I but marshal and deploy my columns; but in the afternoon I put myself at their head, and gallantly charge the foe, thus," and with this he makes "a violent thrust with the ruler" (p. 548). As long as no one offers a full-scale challenge to his authority, the narrator can go on playing his role as authority figure, telling himself that Turkey and Nippers are indeed odd and often ineffectual but that they nevertheless are "useful" to him. In the first part of "Bartleby," then, the lawyer fills out his own image as a man motivated by fear: he is the proverbial man who is afraid of a shadow.

While he is unconsciously depicting the underlying terror of his existence in the first section of the story, he is also revealing his defense against it, his private confidence game. He is deeply fearful, but he tells himself that it is "prudence" that dictates his actions, not fear. He is incapable of genuine rage and violence, but he calls this lack of force "restraint," and he labels it a virtue: "I seldom lose my temper; much more seldom indulge in dangerous indignation at wrongs and outrages; but I must be permitted to be rash here and declare, that I consider the sudden and violent abrogation of the office of Master in Chancery, by the new Constitution, as a—premature act" (p. 547). The pause in his comment (as represented by the dash) is telling. Even in the privacy of his personal narrative and years after the events, he can be only so "rash" as to call the abolition of his job "a premature act"! He attributes his failure to deal sternly with Turkey to his being "a man of peace" (p. 548).

An indispensable tool of the lawyer's "method" is an ingratiating and often humorous form of self-derision. When he admits that "from his youth upwards, [he] has been filled with a profound conviction that the easiest way of life is the best" (p. 546), he appears to be not only mature and good-natured,

---

the defiant narrator. Viewed together, the stories depict two ways of confronting and dealing with fear, the archenemy of dignity and self-respect—unconscious duplicity and honest rebellion.

"Bartleby," then, is concerned chiefly (though not entirely) with the first of these alternatives, unconscious duplicity, as seen in the mild lawyer whose hero is John Jacob Astor. The compliment Astor paid him was in pronouncing his "first grand point to be prudence"; his next, "method" (p. 547). This remark, which the lawyer recalls near the beginning of the story, says much more than it seems to. What Astor told the lawyer, and what the lawyer is telling the reader, is that he is a wise and effective attorney, but as this self-portraiture fills out, "prudence" becomes synonymous with "fear" and "method" with "rationalization." In the lawyer's mind to be fearless is to be imprudent; a healthy respect for fear enables one to remain safe. But then one cannot allow himself to recognize freely the overwhelming role of fear in his existence and still retain his stability. Consequently he must play the mental game of protective rationalization by accounting for his emotions and his actions in terms other than what they really are, responses to fear. Rationalizing is the highest form of "method." Unconsciously the narrator is summing up in Astor's compliment to him both the chief motivating force in his life, fear, and his own private way of dealing with it, rationalization. In the analysis that follows, I have divided the story into five structural parts of about equal length, each of which will be examined in turn. Each section focuses on a different aspect of the narrator's life or his response to Bartleby, but all of them dramatize the omnipresence of his particular brand of "prudence" and his ingenious and expedient "method." [5]

5. For differing analyses of the story's structure, see the following: Leo Marx, "Melville's Parable of the Walls," *Sewanee Review* 61 (1953): 602–627; Marvin Felheim, "Meaning and Structure in 'Bartleby,'" *College English* 23 (1962): 369–376; and Richard Abcarian, "The World of Love and the Spheres of Fright: Melville's 'Bartleby the Scrivener,'" *Studies in Short Fiction* 1 (1964): 207–215.

In beginning the first section of his narration (which ends when Bartleby appears), the lawyer feels that "it is fit I make some mention of myself, my *employées*, my business, my chambers, and general surroundings; because some such description is indispensable to an adequate understanding of the chief character about to be presented" (p. 546). The "chief character" is the narrator himself, though he seems unaware of it. Nearly every word he utters carries two meanings: the one he intends and another he does not intend. The resultant irony is opposite from that in "Cock-A-Doodle-Doo!," where the narrator is consciously playing on words, understating, and sardonically laughing. Here, the narrator reveals himself while not meaning to, says more than he realizes rather than realizes more than he says. He reveals even before Bartleby appears in the story that age and death are fearfully on his mind much of the time, that he craves safety—physical, intellectual, and spiritual—and that this supreme need of security will make him go to great lengths to avoid the slightest anger or displeasure of other people. Never in literature has there been a greater advocate for not rocking the boat.

"I am a rather elderly man," he begins the story, and in the paragraphs that follow, he frequently shows concern with his own age as well as with other people's. He carefully estimates the age of each one of his clerks. The oldest scrivener, Turkey, knows the most effective way to appeal to him—to discuss their common concern with advancing age. "Behold these hairs," pleads Turkey after one of his afternoon blunders in copying. "I am getting old. Surely, sir, a blot or two of a warm afternoon is not to be severely urged against gray hairs. Old age—even if it blot the page—is honorable. With submission, sir, we *both* are getting old" (p. 548). The narrator is appeased, for Turkey, he confesses, has made an "appeal to my fellow-feeling" (p. 548). His anxieties about aging derive not from a desire to be eternally vigorous and productive but from a deep dread of approaching death. He shows his concern with death even in small

details of his narration. He cannot refer to his hero, Astor, for example, without calling him "the *late* John Jacob Astor," and he conjectures that the father of his office boy, Ginger Nut, desires "before he died" to see his son established as a lawyer.

Second only to his fear of death is his fear of life. "A Story of Wall-Street," the subtitle which Melville used for the version of the story in *Putnam's,* describes the kind of mind being revealed. The lawyer must have walls; they are necessary for his fragile security. Psychologically, his walls are made of "method." External, literal walls give him comfort because they seal off the threats of life. Consequently he selects a Wall Street office from which only walls can be seen. One end of his chambers overlooks "a lofty brick wall," the other end, the white wall of a sky-light shaft. "This view," he explains, "might have been considered rather tame than otherwise, deficient in what landscape painters call 'life' " (p. 547). Life—its risks and dangers—is what this eminently safe man wants to wall out, to retreat from. In his snug office behind the protective walls of his methodical life he can minimize the sound of the howling infinite.

But cracks in his protective walls occur now and then even prior to Bartleby's appearance. He deals carefully with his part-time eccentrics (but full-time employees), Turkey and Nippers, because he is afraid of them. When he remonstrates with Turkey, who is more destructive than helpful in the afternoons, he does so "very gently," for Turkey "was disposed, upon provocation, to be slightly rash with his tongue, in fact, insolent" (p. 547). He will not fire these odd and only partly effective scriveners, as a bolder employer would have done, nor will he correct or scold them in any but the mildest fashion, "unwilling," as he puts it, "by my admonitions to call forth unseemly retorts" (p. 548).

The lawyer is like an emasculated king who rules over his realm only at the pleasure of his subjects. The Master in Chancery—he had just been appointed to this position when the story opens—is no master, but they all pretend that he is. It is a game

but also remarkably insightful and frank about himself. Such confessions, however, are in reality substitutes for true self-knowledge. He tells himself that he is "one of those unambitious lawyers," that he likes the easy and quiet way of life, and that he will never be a great man. But he dares not probe consciously beyond to ask why he must live the quiet and safe life. By stopping where he does in his self-examination, he can give himself and others the illusion of honesty and not have to face squarely the terrible truth of his fear. His opening words, "I am a rather elderly man," immediately win approbation from the reader for his openness, his lack of vanity, and his calm acceptance of age. Yet what he is doing is essentially the same thing as many old people who talk endlessly about fatal illnesses, deaths, and funerals and who turn first in the evening newspaper to the obituaries. By confronting the idea of death constantly but superficially, they can keep the more profound and disturbing questions muffled.

The portrait painted of the lawyer in the first section of the story is not that of an average man in a strictly realistic sense. In fact, he is somewhat unusual in the extent of his timidity and isolation. He apparently has no family at all. The kind of life he lives seems intolerably dull by even the most unexciting standards. He seems cut off, "a bit of wreck in the mid-Atlantic," as he himself later calls Bartleby. His characteristics, however, are different in degree rather than in kind from those of the average person. Most people are "prudent" and "methodical," that is, they live under the shadow of fear and rationalize their actions, but in varying degrees. In the lawyer, Melville has presented the distillation, as he saw it, of the ordinary man. Now the stage is set for the kind of confrontation that interested Melville intensely: the distilled ordinary man meets what Melville called in *The Confidence-Man* an "original character." If the sometimes rebellious Turkey and Nippers cause cracks in the lawyer's wall of security, Bartleby is just the man to bring it down in thundering silence. Bartleby represents the most se-

25

vere test that the man of prudence and method has ever faced, for this seemingly harmless young man threatens to drag from behind the walls and into the open all the worst fears of the narrator. Bartleby, therefore, is the threat of a self-revelation that would force the lawyer to see himself honestly and clearly. The mental gymnastics that the lawyer goes through in order to avoid genuine (and extremely painful) self-examination is the primary substance of the story.

The second structural unit of "Bartleby" begins with the appearance of the scrivener and ends with the lawyer's reluctant acknowledgment that his new employee has made himself "permanently exempt from examining the work done by him" and is "never on any account to be dispatched on the most trivial errand of any sort" (pp. 552–553). This section deals chiefly with the lawyer's responses to Bartleby's refusal to be a normal worker. He hires the forlorn young man because he believes that such a neat, respectable, "singularly sedate" employee will be safe and pliable and might even "operate beneficially upon the flighty temper of Turkey, and the fiery one of Nippers" (p. 549). Bartleby is not in the office three days before he fills his employer with "consternation" by preferring not to read copy. The lawyer's reactions to this initial refusal of Bartleby establish a pattern of response that recurs several times in the story: he shows shock and fear ("I was turned into a pillar of salt"), questions Bartleby or tries to reason with him (*"Why* do you refuse?"), questions himself ("What had one best do?"), retreats from the scrivener, makes some excuse to himself ("But my business hurried me"), and rationalizes as he looks back by claiming that he wisely (but narrowly) averted violence, which in reality he is incapable of ("Had there been any thing ordinarily human about him, doubtless I should have violently dismissed him from the premises").

This, then, Melville is saying, is the way of the ordinary man, the man of prudence and method. A few days later, upon Bartleby's second refusal, he follows the same pattern of response.

26

"With any other man," he says, trying to convince not only the reader but himself that he is capable of direct, forceful action, "I should have flown outright into a dreadful passion, scorned all further words, and thrust him ignominiously from my presence" (p. 551). He adds one extra step in his predictable reaction, however. He turns to others—Turkey, Nippers, and Ginger Nut—for support. All agree that Bartleby should "come forth and do your *duty*" (p. 551, italics mine). Throughout this second section, Bartleby stubbornly refuses to carry out the ordinary duties of the worker, the public man, and the lawyer with pathetic ingenuity comes up with an infinite variety of reasons for not doing anything about it. Benevolence and self-interest are among his most frequent rationalizations:

Poor fellow! thought I, he means no mischief; it is plain he intends no insolence; his aspect sufficiently evinces that his eccentricities are involuntary. He is useful to me. I can get along with him. If I turn him away, the chances are . . . he will be rudely treated, and perhaps driven forth miserably to starve. Yes. Here I can cheaply purchase a delicious self-approval. To befriend Bartleby; to humor him in his strange wilfulness, will cost me little or nothing, while I lay up in my soul what will eventually prove a sweet morsel for my conscience. (p. 552)

In passages like the above, the lawyer frequently refers to various aspects of money and food and to the activities of buying ("I can cheaply purchase"; "will cost me little or nothing") and eating ("a delicious self-approval"; "a sweet morsel for my conscience"). Imagery associated with these two areas of life permeates the story. The narrator is highly impressed with John Jacob Astor's money. He says that he had counted "upon a life-lease of the profits" from his position as Master in Chancery. He tells us exactly how much he pays Ginger Nut. His references to food and to activities associated with eating are even more frequent. The lunch hour marks the sharp change in Turkey and Nippers. The narrator insists that Turkey go home every day and "rest himself till tea-time." He feels that Nippers is a victim of indigestion. Turkey's coat, he says, smells too much "of eating-houses," and when he gives him one of his own cast-offs and the old scrivener becomes arrogant, the lawyer's conclusion is that "too much oats are bad for horses" (p. 549). His office boy is nicknamed for a small ginger cake, and the narrator dwells on how the lad furnishes the other scriveners with these cakes and with apples. It was one of these delicacies that Turkey once clapped down on a document (instead of a seal). When Bartleby begins in the office, he pursues his copying of documents, says the narrator, "as if long famishing for something to copy," never pausing "for digestion" (p. 550). Such references as these, which I have cited from only the first two sections of the story, continue throughout, and, as we shall see, gradually take on an important symbolic import that reveals the narrator's unconscious duplicity and the nature of the great difference between him and Bartleby.

The armor of benevolence and self-interest does not prove permanently protective against Bartleby, who silently attacks the lawyer's shaky authority. Toward the end of part two, after several unsuccessful attempts to get Bartleby to run even the most trivial errand, the lawyer makes a final effort to exert his authority and asks the scrivener to fetch Nippers from the next room. Bartleby's "I prefer not to" evokes from the lawyer a mere "Very good, Bartleby," but in a tone "intimating . . . some terrible retribution." He "half intended" some such action, he unconvincingly claims, but "as it was drawing towards my dinner-hour," he puts on his hat and retreats from the office (p. 552). In almost every episode either food or money becomes entangled in the lawyer's attempt to deal with Bartleby. Soon after this, he talks himself into accepting Bartleby's extreme eccentricities as a worker.

The third section of the story begins as did the second, with the lawyer expressing his hope that Bartleby's "unalterableness of demeanor under all circumstances" would make him "a valuable acquisition" and with his feeling that papers would be "perfectly safe" in the hands of the scrivener. Despite Bartleby's strangeness, the narrator asserts, "I had a singular confidence in his honesty" (p. 553). He does not understand Bartleby, but his admiration, even yearning, for genuineness, which he earlier revealed in references to Astor and Byron, attracts him to the scrivener. Very shortly, however, his fragile peace is again shattered as he "inadvertently" asks Bartleby to perform some task. The lawyer's fear and insecurity continue to make it impossible for him to act positively. In fact, each time Bartleby prefers not to, the lawyer is that much more cowed: "How could a human creature with the common infirmities of our nature, refrain from bitterly exclaiming upon such perverseness—such unreasonableness. However, every added repulse of this sort which I received only tended to lessen the probability of my repeating the inadvertence" (p. 553).

Whereas the second section of "Bartleby" concentrates on the lawyer's discovery of and futile attempts to deal with the public side of his new scrivener, the third depicts the narrator's responses to the private Bartleby. Much of this section is taken up with the lawyer's discovery that Bartleby refuses to have a normal private life, that he eats and sleeps in the office. Describing the events of that Sunday morning when he finds Bartleby holed up in his chambers, the lawyer initiates a series of references to his religious life, which is, like all the other areas of his existence, not genuine but merely another aspect of his game of prudence and method. That particular Sunday he did not set out for church in order to worship, but, as he puts it, "to hear a celebrated preacher" (p. 553). The juxtaposition of his church-going and his discovery of Bartleby in his office is significant, for if Bartleby challenges the lawyer's authority, he also tests his religion and reveals it to be counterfeit. "I did not accomplish the purpose of going to Trinity Church that morning," the lawyer says. "Somehow, the things I had seen disqualified me for the time from church-going" (p. 555). He probably means here that his discovery of Bartleby living in his law office had frightened him (again he uses the word "consternation") and upset him to such a degree that he felt out of the mood—the usual Sunday mood of superficial piety—to attend church. A genuine worshiper in troubled times turns not away from but to God and the church. The lawyer's churchgoing is nothing more than the surface glitter of a fake coin.

When the narrator finds Bartleby in his chambers and is ordered to come back later, he retreats, "incontinently" slinking away from his own door. Once again the pattern occurs: first comes the challenge, then the fear and indecisiveness, then the retreat, and finally his rationalization for his behavior. In this incident his explanation has that deceptive confessional quality which is to be found in some of his early comments about himself. Like those early remarks, this is a false confession, a tool of his method to prevent painful self-awareness. He admits that his feelings of rebellion against the scrivener are mere "twinges" and are "impotent." Continuing to use references to emasculation, which is one of his deep-seated but systematically smothered fears, he confesses to being "unmanned": "For I consider that one, for the time, is a sort of unmanned when he tranquilly permits his hired clerk to dictate to him, and order him away from his own premises" (p. 553). This is subtle and effective self-deceit, for he hides the true picture in the deep inner vaults of his mind and substitutes for it one that is genuine in every detail but one—the words, "for the time." By rationalizing that he was "unmanned" only in that remarkable and unprecedented episode, he can push the terrible knowledge of permanent emasculation back out of his consciousness.

Ironically Bartleby's influence on the lawyer reaches its peak of intensity when the scrivener is not present. This climactic point occurs when the lawyer returns to his chambers, begins to think about Bartleby living there, and experiences a sense of loneliness. The most profound loneliness known to humanity is self-alienation. One may be at peace when physically isolated from others or abysmally alone whether in the company of others or not. If a man cannot keep honest company with himself, he is doomed to loneliness. The lawyer comes close to realizing this truth in part three of the story by dwelling on Bartleby's isolation. He is struck with the terrifying silence of Wall Street on Sunday: "Of a Sunday, Wall-street is deserted as Petra; and every night of every day it is an emptiness. This building too, which of week-days hums with industry and life, at nightfall echoes with sheer vacancy, and all through Sunday is forlorn. And here Bartleby makes his home; sole spectator of a solitude which he has seen all populous—a sort of innocent and transformed Marius brooding among the ruins of Carthage!" (p. 554).[6]

The lawyer's differentiation between busy and quiet Wall Street suggests a distinction between the outer and the inner man. He is horrified at the marked difference. His is the Wall Street of weekdays; he cannot and will not let himself dwell in the Wall Street of Sunday, that silent region of self-knowledge. Consequently in the story he seems to have no life apart from his law practice. He exists only in terms of the Wall Street of external (and largely meaningless) activity. Bartleby, however, at this time in the story lives day and night, weekdays and Sundays—always—on Wall Street. For the lawyer the external life is all. For Bartleby there is no difference between the two Wall Streets.

An "over-powering stinging melancholy" grips the lawyer as he thinks of Bartleby and of himself as both "sons of Adam," and in this climactic moment when self-confrontation lies just ahead, he sees in his imagination the scrivener—but in reality

6. In *Plutarch's Lives* the unwelcomed Marius is reported to have sent a message to his would-be host, Sextilius, in Africa: "Tell him, then, that thou hast seen Caius Marius a fugitive, seated amid the ruins of Carthage." Trans. Bernadotte Perrin (London: Heinemann, 1920), 9: 577. Another likely source for Melville's image of Marius is a steel engraving by A. L. Dick, taken from a painting called "The Ruins of Carthage" by William Linton. The engraving was published in the New York *Mirror*, 2 January 1841.

himself—"laid out, among uncaring strangers" in a burial sheet
(p. 554). "Presentiments of strange discoveries," he says, "hov-
ered round me" (p. 554). What he discovers, however, is not
his own deeper, inner self, but a savings bank in Bartleby's desk.
He then thinks of the scrivener's peculiar habits, especially
his failure to visit "any refectory or eating house," or to drink
beer, tea, or coffee. Again Melville associates money with food,
contrasting the lawyer, who frequently talks literally and figuratively of eating and who in many places speaks of money or of
trying to purchase something, with Bartleby, who has been
fasting more than eating, saving more than buying.

The food and money metaphors which recur in "Bartleby"
are directly associated with the central thematic contrast between
duplicity and honesty. Melville recognized that self-esteem is
the one indispensable possession of the truly noble man and a
much sought-after possession of nearly all men whether they
are conscious of the fact or not. The lawyer would like to act
in such a way as to create real self-approval, but his all encompassing fear prevents it. His use of the food metaphor illustrates poignantly his hunger for self-approval.[7] He feeds this
hunger, however, with the false food of prudence and method,
which does not really nourish his self-esteem, his rationalizations
to the contrary. Just as eating is an appropriate metaphor for the
lawyer's deep need to nourish his self-esteem, so "purchasing"
is an equally effective metaphor for the wrong way which he
goes about trying to feel good about himself. A person buys his
good opinion of himself by never fooling himself and by acting
truly. But the lawyer's actions do not ring true; he is trying to
purchase self-esteem with counterfeit money.

The lawyer's moment of profound loneliness and his thoughts

7. Allen F. Stein argues convincingly that the many references to food
in the story create "a sinister atmosphere of unrestrained voracity" and
that "Melville is using physical hunger as a manifestation of the consuming need for personal aggrandizement." "The Motif of Voracity in
'Bartleby,' " *ESQ* 21 (1975): 29–34.

of Bartleby's use of money and food in contrast to his own do not last long. The white doe of truth has run before him; he has looked but he has not seen. Soon, he says, "a prudential feeling began to steal over me," as his melancholy and pity "merge into fear" (p. 554). Here he has himself made that connection between prudence and fear which has been present in his narration from almost the beginning. From fear-prudence, his mind proceeds to rationalization-method as he concludes that "common sense" dictates that he not dwell any longer on the subject but "be rid of it." He then plans to try to convince Bartleby to be a normal private person even if he insists upon being an eccentric worker. He therefore asks the scrivener several personal questions but receives, as ever, Bartleby's "I would prefer not to" in answer. During this interview, Bartleby "kept his glance fixed upon my bust of Cicero, which as I then sat, was directly behind me, some six inches above my head" (p. 555). Bartleby keeps his eyes on the bust but in a sense he *is* looking at the lawyer, for the pale imitation of a man, the plaster-of-paris Cicero, is a stunning symbol for the lawyer.

Again cowed by Bartleby's quiet determination, the narrator turns to his other employees for help. The scene that follows could well be taken for a comedy of the absurd, for the lawyer, Turkey, and Nippers all find themselves unconsciously employing Bartleby's word *prefer*. When the lawyer realizes this, he "trembled" to think that Bartleby had perhaps "turned the tongues, if not the heads of myself and clerks" (p. 556). There is no danger of that, however, for their *prefer* like the bust of Cicero is a mere copy. Frightened, nevertheless, that Bartleby may have "seriously affected" him "in a mental way"—the irony is piercing—the lawyer determines to dismiss him, but "I thought it prudent not to break the dismission at once" (p. 556).

Throughout the story, the lawyer has been looking at Bartleby, who spends much of his time looking out the window. The narrator wonders at this because there is nothing to see from the window but a wall. While Bartleby looks at the plaster-of-

33

paris Cicero, the lawyer looks at him. The scrivener's eyes much of the time seem glazed or unseeing, but the lawyer's are clear. Yet it is the lawyer who cannot see. When toward the end of the third section Bartleby informs him that he will do no more copying (by which he means that he will not ape ordinary man but will be different), and the lawyer asks the reason, Bartleby replies: "Do you not *see* the reason for yourself?" (p. 556, italics mine). Characteristically the lawyer does not see the real reason because he cannot himself look inward honestly and act accordingly. Although he looks steadfastly at the scrivener, he sees only the glazed eyes and thus concludes that Bartleby has eyestrain and needs a rest. He is still blind to the reason for Bartleby's stubborn abnormalities as both a public and private man when this section ends with the scrivener's declaration: "I have given up copying" (p. 556).

It is not until the fourth section of the story that the lawyer can actually bring himself to ask Bartleby to leave. This section, which begins right after Bartleby's announcement that he will copy no more and ends with the lawyer himself moving to new chambers, is chiefly concerned with the narrator's mental processes as he again and again encounters Bartleby's determination to remain in the Wall Street chambers. In part two the lawyer found that his scrivener was a hopelessly eccentric worker. In part three he discovered that Bartleby was also highly abnormal in his private life. Now in part four the narrator attempts to limit Bartleby's extraordinary behavior to one sphere, the private, by trying to remove him from public view.

Part four opens on the familiar note of the lawyer's indecision. Bartleby has become "still more of a fixture than before," and the question remains: "What was to be done?" (p. 556). Early in this section the lawyer tells Bartleby that he must leave in six days. That period over, the narrator approaches the scrivener, offers him money, and tells him that he must go. At this point, the narrator again emphasizes a fact that he has mentioned at least twice before, that Bartleby is impeccably honest:

"Now I had an unbounded confidence in this man's common honesty. He had frequently restored to me sixpences and shillings carelessly dropped upon the floor" (p. 556). Then he, in effect, offers to *purchase* Bartleby's surrender, which would in turn buy the lawyer, as he vainly hopes, self-esteem. Bartleby refuses the money, leaving it where the lawyer places it on a table as if it were worthless. As usual, the narrator then retreats, leaving a parting order for Bartleby to be gone by the next morning. This time the lawyer's rationalization for his retreat is not eating or business, but his hollow doctrine of assumption.

As I walked home in a pensive mood, my *vanity* [italics mine] got the better of my pity. I could not but highly plume myself on my masterly management in getting rid of Bartleby. Masterly I call it, and such it must appear to any dispassionate thinker. The beauty of my procedure seemed to consist in its perfect quietness. There was no vulgar bullying, no bravado of any sort, no choleric hectoring, and striding to and fro across the apartment, jerking out vehement commands for Bartleby to bundle himself off with his beggarly traps. Nothing of the kind. Without loudly bidding Bartleby depart—as an inferior genius might have done—I *assumed* the ground that depart he must; and upon that assumption built all I had to say. (p. 557)

This passage is highly revealing for a number of reasons. It clearly shows the lawyer's "method" in action. Incapable of "bullying," "bravado," "choleric hectoring," and "vehement commands," he twists his inadequacy into the virtue of "perfect quietness." The irony is inescapable, for his "quietness" like his earlier inadvertent use of "prefer" recalls Bartleby. Bartleby's silence is strong and pregnant with meaning. The lawyer's comes from weakness. The passage above is also important for suggesting a distinction that is fundamental to an understanding of the narrator, the difference between vanity and self-esteem. It is a distinction which Melville implies in a great many characters throughout his works. Vanity is fake self-esteem; it feeds hungrily on the good opinions of others. Thus the narrator turns to Turkey and Nippers to hear them say that he is right in his demands of Bartleby, and in the passage above, he asks "any dispassionate thinker" to concur that his actions are "masterly." Vanity, therefore, is not genuine self-approval which comes from within and is independent of the approval of others, but a pitiful and sometimes desperate substitute. It suggests "that which is vain, futile, or worthless, that which is of no value or profit."[8] In an older sense, which Melville would have been keenly conscious of, a *vanity* was a tale without foundation, a kind of lie. Melville may even have been thinking of one of his favorite biblical verses: "Vanity of vanities; all is vanity."[9] In this sense, "Bartleby, the Scrivener" *is* a vanity, for it constitutes a great but unconscious lie that the narrator is perpetrating on the reader for the purpose of trying to win some measure of sympathy and approval. This, principally, is his motivation for telling the story.[10]

The doctrine of assumption, however, does not move Bartleby, who is still in the lawyer's chambers when morning comes.[11] Once again the pattern repeats itself. The narrator is

8. *OED*, s.v. "vanity."

9. Eccles. 1:2.

10. On this point I am in agreement with Norman Springer, who writes: "What the narrator wishes to demonstrate is clear: the charity of his own total attitude, as well as his final obeisance to the mystery of Bartleby. When he is done with Bartleby he can, despite some uneasiness, congratulate himself, at least on his handling of a situation that was in the main beyond him." The narrator reveals, according to Springer, "the limits of any decent man's charity." See "Bartleby and the Terror of Limitation," *PMLA* 80 (1965): 413. A similar point is made by Karl F. Knight, "Melville's Variations of the Theme of Failure: 'Bartleby' and *Billy Budd*," *Arlington Quarterly* 2 (1969): 44–58.

11. On his way to the office the lawyer symbolically tries to purchase self-approval when he offers to gamble that Bartleby will be gone when he arrives at his chambers. "Put up your money," he says to a stranger. This person, however, has been talking about an election, not Bartleby, and the narrator, embarrassed at his mistake, hurries away, failing as always to use his money, his purchasing power, for what he most deeply needs.

"thunderstruck" (he thinks continually in images of death), finds that he is incapable of anything like violent or summary action, and ponders the question: "What was to be done?" "Turn the man out by an actual thrusting I could not; to drive him away by calling him hard names would not do; calling in the police was an unpleasant idea" (p. 609). What he does do is again to ask Bartleby to leave, or if he does not want to do that to be a little more normal. When Bartleby simply goes into his "hermitage" without further reply, the lawyer feels it "prudent to check myself at present from further demonstrations" (p. 610). It occurs to him that he and Bartleby are alone in the office, and he becomes afraid as he remembers a famous murder:

I remembered the tragedy of the unfortunate Adams and the still more unfortunate Colt in the solitary office of the latter; and how poor Colt, being dreadfully incensed by Adams, and imprudently permitting himself to get wildly excited, was at unawares hurried into his fatal act—an act which certainly no man could possibly deplore more than the actor himself. Often it had occurred to me in my ponderings upon the subject, that had that altercation taken place in the public street, or at a private residence, it would not have terminated as it did. It was the circumstance of being alone in a solitary office, up stairs, of a building entirely unhallowed by humanizing domestic associations—an uncarpeted office, doubtless, of a dusty, haggard sort of appearance;—this it must have been, which greatly helped to enhance the irritable desperation of the hapless Colt. (p. 610)

The murder the narrator remembers occurred in New York City on 17 September 1841. John C. Colt, brother of the famous inventor of firearms, Samuel Colt, murdered a printer named Samuel Adams, who had come to Colt's office to collect a debt. The trial was covered in detail on the front pages of the New York newspapers.[12] Both men were well known, and the murder itself was highly sensational. Colt split the head of his

12. See, for example, the coverage of the trial in the New York *Daily Tribune*, 18–31 January 1842. The trial was so popular that on 27 January the *Tribune* issued an *Extra* on it.

victim with a hatchet and then stuffed the body into a packing crate with such violence that several bones in the corpse were broken. He then attempted to ship the crate to New Orleans but was caught by the police, tried, and convicted of first-degree murder. He was sentenced to be hanged in the yard of the Tombs on 18 November 1842. When the officials came to his cell to escort him to the gallows, he was found dead, stabbed in the heart. A coroner's jury concluded that he had killed himself with a dirk which some unknown person had smuggled to him.[13]

The lawyer says that he thought it "prudent" to "check himself" since he was alone with Bartleby, and he wants to give the impression that he identifies with poor Colt, who "imprudently" allowed himself to get so agitated that he committed a horrible murder. Here as elsewhere the narrator is playing his confidence game on the reader and on himself. It would be impossible for him to commit the rash and violent actions of a man like John Colt. He is, then, bragging in a sense when he claims to be

13. What actually happened in Colt's cell in the Tombs remains a compelling mystery. The newspaper account gives the following details. On the day set for his hanging, he asked that he be allowed to marry his mistress, Caroline Henshaw, who had previously borne his child. The marriage was performed in his cell, and he was left alone for a little while. When the guards came for him to escort him to the gallows, he was found stabbed, an apparent suicide. One newspaper, the *Herald,* wrote that the sheriff had been offered a bribe of one thousand dollars from Colt's family for allowing him to escape. There were those who claimed that the body found in the cell was not Colt's but a cadaver placed there to cover his escape. It has been argued that Caroline Henshaw was the wife of Samuel Colt, John's brother, and that the child belonged not to John but to Samuel, who was ashamed of Caroline and wanted her name linked with John's rather than with his. The entire fascinating controversy is told in William B. Edwards, *The Story of Colt's Revolver: The Biography of Col. Samuel Colt* (Harrisburg, Pa.: Stackpole, 1953). See also T. H. Giddings, "Melville, the Colt-Adams Murder, and 'Bartleby,' " *Studies in American Fiction* 2 (1974): 123–132. Giddings feels that "chronologically and geographically" Melville was accurate in his use of the Colt-Adams murder but that the "allusion seems rather carelessly applied to Bartleby's story" (p. 130).

worrying that he may become "imprudent." He is pitifully incapable of anything but prudence and method. What he is
really afraid of is not that he will be another John Colt, the
killer, but that he may be another Samuel Adams, the victim.

When a man who supposedly occupies a place of authority
fears that he is not strong enough to stifle or defeat a stubborn,
trouble-making subordinate, he can save face by loving him. A
weakness then looks to others and to himself—if he fakes well
enough—like a Christian virtue. So here again, the role of religion in the lawyer's method of protective rationalization is apparent. With unconscious irony, he relates how he arrived at
a temporary solution: "But when this old Adam of resentment
rose in me and tempted me concerning Bartleby, I grappled him
and threw him. How? Why, simply by recalling the divine in-
junction: 'A new commandment give I unto you, that ye love
one another.' Yes, this it was that saved me" (p. 610). The
quotation is from John 13:31–35, where Jesus is speaking to
his disciples during the Last Supper. In his development of the
theme of duplicity in "Bartleby," Melville could hardly have
chosen a more appropriate passage, for the genuine words of
Jesus on love have the ring of terrible hollowness when made
a part of the lawyer's confidence game with himself. Equally
meaningful is the inescapable context of falsity and treachery
surrounding Jesus' admonition, for Judas had just left him on
his errand of infamy. What "saved" the lawyer was, as he puts
it, this "vastly wise and *prudent* principle" (p. 610, italics
mine). He then talks himself into a state of counterfeit benevolence: "I strove to drown my exasperated feelings towards
the scrivener by benevolently construing his conduct. Poor fellow, poor fellow! thought I, he don't mean any thing; and besides, he has seen hard times, and ought to be indulged" (p.
610). From the "prudent" principle of Christian love, he moves
to the comforting rationalization of Christian determinism as he
reads "Edwards on the Will" and "Priestley on Necessity,"
books that "induced a salutary feeling" (p. 610) that "Bartleby

was billeted upon me for some mysterious purpose of an all-wise Providence" (p. 610).[14]

Counterfeit religion cannot withstand the angry stares of the outside world without withering, and so the lawyer once again finds himself in the fearful plight of having to take some action when his "professional friends" begin to make "unsolicited and uncharitable remarks" about his keeping the eccentric scrivener, who gives all of them the same "I prefer not to" when he is asked to do something. Now one of the greatest of the lawyer's fears, fear of the world's scorn, overcomes all his other anxieties, and after a period of not unusual indecision ("What shall I do? . . . What shall I do?") when he rejects all positive forms of action that would require him to remove Bartleby forcefully or have him driven out, he decides that he will himself move out. At the end of part four, he says goodbye to Bartleby and slips money into his hand. But this attempt to buy dignity and self-esteem fails, for Bartleby lets the money slip to the floor.

The fifth and concluding section of the story opens on the now familiar note of the lawyer's fear: "Established in my new quarters, for a day or two I kept the door locked, and started at every footfall in the passages. When I returned to my rooms after any little absence, I would pause at the threshold for an instant, and attentively listen, ere applying my key" (p. 611). Once rid of Bartleby, the lawyer would like to keep it that way— "a certain squeamishness" kept him from visiting the scrivener —but the world of which he is so much a part will not let him off easily. The new occupant of the Wall Street chambers appears and requests information about the extraordinary scrivener who will not scrive. Then a few days later a deputation consisting of the narrator's old landlord and several tenants of the Wall Street building arrive and demand that the narrator do some-

14. For a discussion of the role of necessity in the story, see Walton R. Patrick, "Melville's 'Bartleby' and the Doctrine of Necessity," *American Literature* 41 (1969): 39–54.

thing about Bartleby. Terrified, the lawyer would have retreated
if possible: "Aghast at this torrent, I fell back before it, and
would fain have locked myself in my new quarters" (p. 612).
His response to this group is very much like that of a confidence
man who is afraid that he is about to be publicly exposed. "Fearful then," he explains, "of being exposed in the papers (as one
person present obscurely threatened) I considered the matter,"
and decided to talk to Bartleby (p. 612).

This talk is their longest and perhaps the single most revealing in the story. For the lawyer, it is the most frustrating of all
their exchanges, for while Bartleby in his actions has previously
violated the narrator's sense of ordinary expectations, now he
baffles the narrator also with what appears to be a series of oral
contradictions as well. The lawyer begins by stating that Bartleby
must either do something or have something done to him. He
then puts before Bartleby five possibilities for employment. To
the lawyer's offer of a new job as scrivener, Bartleby says that
he "would prefer not to make any change." To the prospect of
a clerkship in a store, he says, "There is too much confinement
about that," yet he adds that he is not "particular." The narrator wonders how he could be any more confined than he is
at present, but he asks him to consider a bartender's job, which
Bartleby declines to do, adding again that he is not particular.
Contradictions appear rife. He does not want to change at all,
but he is not particular. He would not like a clerkship because
that is too confining, yet he *is* confined. To the last two possibilities, a traveling bill collector and an international traveling
companion, he simply remarks that he likes to be "stationary,"
to have something "definite," but he adds again that he is not
particular.

These five occupations mentioned by the narrator can be seen
as five concentric circles, each one representing a wider, more
sophisticated range of public contact. The smallest circle in the
center represents the occupation of scrivener, which is the most
confining and restrictive of the jobs. From that the lawyer moves

to the next and larger circle of store clerk, where one might at least experience a limited amount of variety and meet to some extent a segment of the public. The next circle, that representing bartending, is even larger, however, for in that occupation one meets a great variety of people and encounters a cross-section of life. But even bartending is sedentary work; so the lawyer moves on to the fourth and still larger circle of bill collector, which includes not only social intercourse but also the advantages of travel—which none of the previous possibilities had. The final and largest of the five circles is that of the international traveling companion, the most promising in terms of variety and social experience and the least demanding in terms of monotonous business routine.

The lawyer, then, presents Bartleby with a full range of possibilities from confinement to freedom, and yet each offer is met with a refusal. What the lawyer cannot see is that Bartleby is working his way through the circles of independence in the opposite direction. Thus their visions of independence are in direct opposition. Bartleby moves not outward to larger circles but to smaller and smaller circles. From the outer circles of physical freedom, jobs not so confining and monotonous as scrivener, to the lawyer's employment, he has now traveled further inward to an even smaller circle. He will go on shortly to the smallest circle of all, the world of the Tombs, and then to death. Freedom and independence for Bartleby are to be found inwardly, within the self. His fascination with walls derives from his determination to retain his inner freedom in the face of the greatest barricades to personal independence the universe can erect.[15] Walls have opposite meanings, then, to Bartleby and the lawyer, for whom walls are safety and security. Blind to Bartleby's concept of independence, the lawyer presents Bartleby with the prospect of increasing freedom in the shallow terms of oc-

15. Leo Marx states that walls to Bartleby "are abstract emblems of all the impediments to man's realization of his place in the universe" (p. 623).

42

cupations that offer merely the chance to move about physically and be with more people.

Bartleby's five reasons for refusing the five occupations seem contradictory to the lawyer, but actually they are not.[16] Bartleby insists upon being (1) unchanging, (2) unconfined, (3) unparticular, (4) definite, and (5) stationary. The paradox that pervades this conversation about jobs is that one can be a prisoner and still be independent; and, contrarily, one can be "free" and still be a prisoner. Bartleby, with his increasing physical confinement that ends in the Tombs, remains as independent as one can be. At the center of his being, he is unchanging, "definite," and "stationary." And if a man possesses that inner freedom, he is never truly confined. Bartleby's inner wholeness is underscored by his saying three times during the conversation that he is not "particular," which is to say that he is not particularized, not a part or fragment, but of one piece. The lawyer, on the other hand, is free to come and go as he likes, but he is a slave to fear.

The narrator falls back into the same pattern of fearful frustration, inaction, and retreat when confronted with Bartleby's latest stubbornness. "Stationary you shall be, then," he tells the scrivener, and then makes one of his comically ineffectual threats: "If you do not go away from these premises before night, I shall feel bound—indeed I *am* bound—to—to—to quit the premises myself!" (p. 612). With that, he asks Bartleby to go home with him, but Bartleby does not see that move as representing a smaller circle, so he merely answers: "I would prefer not to make any change at all." Bartleby knows that by not making any change away from the Wall Street office he ultimately will be jailed, and he *wants* to be, for he is preoccupied with the idea of independence and with the act of dramatizing the paradox of freedom by moving physically to-

16. In another context Jack B. Moore argues that "Bartleby is greatly the rational man." "Ahab and Bartleby: Energy and Indolence," *Studies in Short Fiction* 1 (1964): 293.

ward smaller and smaller circles of confinement while remaining unconfined and free within himself. Although he appears to be merely "a bit of wreck in mid-Atlantic," Bartleby willfully controls his fate, initiating the series of events in the story by first *applying* for the job of scrivener. In reality it is the lawyer, as I pointed out earlier, who is the "bit of wreck," for he is acted upon and controlled by his fear.

As the lawyer retreats from Bartleby he resembles a fugitive who is fearful of being apprehended: "effectively *dodging* everyone by the suddenness and rapidity of my *flight*, [I] rushed from the building, ran up Wall Street towards Broadway, and jumping into the first omnibus was soon removed from *pursuit*" (p. 613, italics mine). His fear, as always, is in the forefront as he hides out: "So fearful was I of being again *hunted out* by the incensed landlord and his exasperated tenants, that, *surrendering* my business to Nippers, for a few days I drove about the upper part of the town and through the suburbs, in my rockaway; crossed over to Jersey City and Hoboken, and paid *fugitive* visits to Manhattanville and Astoria. In fact I almost lived in my rockaway for the time" (p. 613, italics mine). The language strengthens the already distinct suggestion that the lawyer, in a sense more than the obvious and usual, is not an honest man. Bartleby *is* honest, as we are reminded several times. The lawyer is afraid of being *exposed* in the papers; he *dodges* and *flees*, and worries about being *pursued*. He is "fearful of being hunted out." He *surrenders* his business for *fugitive* visits.

The narrator's unconscious duplicity is poignantly projected when he complies with a summons to visit the Tombs to identify Bartleby. He does identify Bartleby, but more significantly, Bartleby identifies him, just as he did when he stared at the plaster-of-paris bust of Cicero. "I know you," Bartleby says, again refusing to look at him, "and I want nothing to say to you" (p. 613). The lawyer encounters the grub-man and pays him to prepare meals for Bartleby. The money which the lawyer gives the grub-man, and their ensuing talk about food and eat-

44

ing, function like the earlier references to suggest that the lawyer's coin is in a symbolic sense worthless, for it will not buy
genuine self-approval, nor does the food of the lawyer provide
real nourishment.

The conversation which the narrator has with the grub-man,
incidental and insignificant as it appears on the surface, is in
reality of signal importance in developing the theme of the
story:

> "How's this?" said the grub-man, addressing me with a stare of
> astonishment. "He's odd, aint he?"
> "I think he is a little deranged," said I, sadly.
> "Deranged? deranged is it? Well now, upon my word, I thought
> that friend of yourn was a gentleman forger; they are always pale and
> genteel-like, them forgers. I can't help pity 'em—can't help it, sir.
> Did you know Monroe Edwards?" he added touchingly, and paused.
> Then, laying his hand pityingly on my shoulder, sighed, "he died
> of consumption at Sing-Sing. So you weren't acquainted with Mon-
> roe?"
> "No, I was never socially acquainted with any forgers." (p. 614)

This passage crackles with irony. The lawyer says that he has
not been "socially acquainted with *any* forgers," gentlemen or
otherwise. But as we have seen, he is a forger, a self-swindler
without allowing himself to face that fact. His words are ironic
because he is telling far more of the truth than he intends. He is
not even "acquainted"—socially or intimately—with what he
himself really is. His prudence and method insure self-deceit.

The lawyer's final visit to the Tombs is depicted in terms of
a journey made to the innermost sanctum of existence by a man
who sees but does not comprehend. He makes his way into the
Tombs, down the corridors in search of Bartleby, and finally
into the center yard, "the heart of the eternal pyramids, it
seemed. . . ." Then in the center of the prison he finds "the
silent man," as a turnkey calls Bartleby, "strangely huddled at
the base of the wall, his knees drawn up, and lying on his side"
(p. 614).

45

Bartleby's death is the culmination of a movement to ever smaller concentric circles of physical confinement, as I discussed earlier, and also to diminishing circles of age. Just as the world foolishly equates freedom with physical nonconfinement in activities and occupations, so it believes that growing up and maturing bring ever greater circles of freedom: from fully dependent infancy to the cutting of the silver cord of parental confinement to the less restricted but somewhat insecure days of early youth to full maturity marked by greater security but also the burden of employment to, finally, the golden days of easy and secure employment or retirement, when wisdom and self-owned time combine to produce the freedom of age. People who cannot travel or enjoy themselves in other ways because of limiting responsibilities often dream of the days of retirement when they will be freer than they have ever been before. This way of thinking about the five ages of man that I outlined can be projected concretely just as previously was the lawyer's concept of freedom in his talk about occupations—five concentric circles, each larger circle representing a greater age and, in this illusory scheme, greater freedom.

The five characters in the lawyer's office represent five concentric circles of age.[17] The outer circle is the narrator, who at the telling of the story is as he says, "rather elderly," close to, if not in, retirement. Going back in time he tells in the first part of the story of his three employees, Turkey, Nippers, and Ginger Nut, who represent smaller and smaller circles in that order. Although Turkey is about the lawyer's own age, approximately sixty, the lawyer's voice is heard in the present, whereas Turkey is seen only in an earlier time when he was younger, a man of late maturity but not old age. Nippers is in the prime of youth, and Ginger Nut in the throes of puberty. If life were lived according to the normal illusion, the oldest would be the

17. Moore observes that the lawyer's three employees, Turkey, Nippers, and Ginger Nut, "represent a sort of cross-section of humanity" (p. 293).

freest from all those things that dictate to man and control him. At a glance this seems indeed to be true with these characters. The lawyer now has time to look back on his past and relate a segment of it; he has earned freedom from financial pressures and a measure of comfort and security. In the story he narrates, Turkey, the oldest of the scriveners, has aged beyond the stage of unsettling ambition and those other terrible overseers of troubled and insecure youth that ride poor Nippers. And yet, even Nippers seems freer than Ginger Nut, who is placed in the office by his father to follow the instructions of anyone there who cares to order him about. He is the smallest of the four circles.

Bartleby insists upon revealing that everything the world believes in, especially its fake concept of freedom, is vanity. In blatant opposition to what is "normal," he prefers to exist not in the largest circle, but always in the smallest. Just as he has worked his way from larger circles of freedom to smaller ones of confinement, ending at the "heart of the eternal pyramids," so he seems determined to reverse the process of normal growth. He is willfully moving from the circle of youth to the smaller circles of boyhood and infancy and then to prebirth. He comes more and more to resemble first a child who inexplicably will not mind and do what the adult world expects of him and then a fully dependent infant who is helplessly acted upon. He does not save his money in a bank account, as an adult would ordinarily do, but in a child's savings bank. He does not eat like an adult, but like a child, preferring apples and cakes to more substantial food. He eats less and less, and finally will not eat at all the solid food which the grub-man prepares for him. When he is found dead he is in a fetal position, "strangely huddled at the base of a wall, his knees drawn up, and lying on his side." [18] To the grub-man's question as to whether Bartleby is asleep, the

18. See Henry A. Murray, "Bartleby and I," in *A Symposium: Bartleby the Scrivener*, ed. Howard P. Vincent (Kent, Ohio: Kent State University Press, 1966), pp. 3–24.

lawyer answers, "with kings and counsellors." He means, of course, that Bartleby is dead, but the words carry an additional significance probably lost on the speaker. The lawyer's words are from the third chapter of the book of Job, in which Job wishes not for death that comes at the termination of life, but for the death that precedes life. He laments the night he was conceived and curses the day that he was born, and he wishes that he had died in the womb. If he had never seen the light of day, he says, "should I have lain still and been quiet, I should have slept: then had I been at rest, with kings and counsellors of the earth, which built desolate places for themselves; or with princes that had gold, who filled their houses with silver: or as an hidden untimely birth I had not been; as infants which never saw light" (3: 13–16).

Bartleby's willful regression seems to be a personal defiance of things as they are. He proclaims his independence in the most difficult and trying of all situations, namely that state where he is by necessity most dependent physically. Before his death he has moved to the smallest circle of dependency and thus exercised the highest degree of independence possible. This is his final affront to the normalcy of life. Besides illustrating Bartleby's rebellion and his preoccupation with independence, these images and references to birth suggest a paradox involving the scrivener's death. In works both earlier than "Bartleby" and later, Melville uses the imagery of birth, death, and rebirth (or even resurrection) to suggest that two kinds of death come to the hero who achieves the greatest possible degree of independence, death to his ordinary human characteristics as well as actual death. Throughout the story Bartleby is described in imagery that suggests that he is already dead. The lawyer says that there is nothing "ordinarily human about him," and when the scrivener appears at the door of the chambers on a Sunday morning, the narrator calls him "the apparition of Bartleby." He is constantly described as "pallid," or "pale." His eyes are "dull and glazed," his mouth "white." He possesses a "cadaverously gentlemanly nonchalance"; he makes a "mild cadaverous reply"; and he achieves a "cadaverous triumph" over the lawyer. At one time the narrator imagines Bartleby's "pale form . . . laid out . . . in its shivering winding sheet." Bartleby "died" when he achieved that extraordinary power to say "I prefer not to" to society and to the universe. He ceased to be an ordinary man, which means that he rose above that level where fear is man's ruler but which also means that he no longer feels what ordinary people experience—the joy, the petty worry, the hopes, the compassion, the small pleasures, and the humility that make up life.

Bartleby's portrait, then, is not unequivocally sympathetic. Like Melville's other great rebels, he has to pay the terrible price of his humanity for being stronger, greater, and more honest than an ordinary man. After his first "death," he cares for no one; he is indifferent to everything but his own determination to unbind himself. His isolation is by necessity extreme. His fetal position in actual death does not suggest new birth in the Christian sense but what Melville called in *Moby-Dick* "apotheosis," that state of the highest degree of independence obtainable by mortal man, noble in itself but always accompanied by the loss of ordinary feelings. Little wonder that readers find it difficult to understand him or identify with him. He is of that type Melville termed in *The Confidence-Man* "the Indian hater *par excellence*," which is to say, a man of exceptional will who feels so victimized by some force alien to himself that he comes to direct all his energies into striking back.[19] And his energies

---

19. Bartleby's identity and the cause of his actions are widely disputed among critics. Newton Arvin, *Herman Melville* (New York: Sloane, 1950), and Richard Chase, *Herman Melville: A Critical Study* (New York: MacMillan, 1949), both argue that Bartleby is suffering from schizophrenia. Nathalia Wright sees Bartleby as Melville's illustration of Burton's melancholy man: "Melville and 'Old Burton,' with 'Bartleby' as an Anatomy of Melancholy," *Tennessee Studies in Literature* 15 (1970): 1–13. Robert D. Spector writes that Bartleby is "the symbolic universe," indifferent to man: "Melville's 'Bartleby' and the

are all but supernatural. About such a man little can be known: "How evident that in strict speech there can be no biography of an Indian-hater *par excellence*, any more than one of a sword-fish, or other deep-sea denizen, which is still less imaginable,

Absurd," *Nineteenth-Century Fiction* 16 (1961): 175–177. A number of critics, including Leo Marx, interpret Bartleby as the artist in society or as Melville himself. See Alexander Eliot, "Melville and Bartleby," *Furioso* 3 (1947): 11–21; and Mario D'Avanzo, "Melville's 'Bartleby' and John Jacob Astor," *New England Quarterly* 41 (1968): 259–264. Daniel A. Wells, " 'Bartleby the Scrivener,' Poe, and the Duyckinck Circle," *ESQ* 21 (1975): 35–39, argues that Bartleby suggests Melville, that the lawyer is based on Evert Duyckinck, and that Turkey and Nippers represent Cornelius Mathews and Edgar Allan Poe. Richard H. Fogle argues against the position that Bartleby represents the artist or Melville and sees him as an "all-or-nothing man" afflicted with "absolutism": *Melville's Shorter Tales* (Norman: University of Oklahoma Press, 1960), pp. 14–27. Egbert S. Oliver agrees that Bartleby is not Melville; he offers the theory that the scrivener is meant to represent Henry David Thoreau withdrawing from society: "A Second Look at 'Bartleby,' " *College English* 6 (1945): 431–439. Martin L. Pops, in *The Melville Archetype* (Kent, Ohio: Kent State University Press, 1970), sees the narrator of the story as Washington Irving and Bartleby as "Pierre made passive" (p. 127). Several critics interpret Bartleby as Christ or as Christ-like. See particularly the following: H. Bruce Franklin, *The Wake of the Gods: Melville's Mythology* (Stanford: Stanford University Press, 1963), pp. 126–136; Donald M. Fiene, "Bartleby the Christ," in *Studies in the Minor and Later Works of Melville*, ed. Raymona E. Hull (Hartford: Transcendental Books, 1970), pp. 18–23; John Gardner, *"Bartleby*: Art and Social Commitment," *Philological Quarterly* 43 (1964): 87–98; and Wiliam Bysshe Stein, who sees Bartleby as "an emasculated Christ" (p. 111): "Bartleby: the Christian Conscience," in *A Symposium*, pp. 104–112. Marvin Fisher feels, with Bruce Franklin, that Bartleby may be representative of Christ but that he may also be suffering from a form of mental illness that makes him think he is Christ "reacting to the indifference, self-absorption, or ridicule of mid-nineteenth-century American society": " 'Bartleby,' Melville's Circumscribed Scrivener," *Southern Review* 10 (1974): 59–79. Otto Reinert, on the other hand, calls Bartleby "forever neuter": "Bartleby the Inscrutable: Notes on a Melville Motif," in *Americana Norwegica: Norwegian Contributions to American Studies*, vol. 1, ed. Sigmund Skard and Henry H. Wasser (Philadelphia: University of Pennsylvania Press, 1966), pp. 180–205. For Maurice Friedman, Bartleby is an example of the "modern exile" who dies because he does not know how to live: "Bartleby and the Modone of a dead man. The career of the Indian-hater *par ex-cellence* has the impenetrability of the fate of a lost steamer." [20] Melville marks Bartleby as the same type when he has the lawyer say: "While of other law-copyists I might write the complete life, of Bartleby nothing of that sort can be done. I believe that no materials exist for a full and satisfactory biography of this man" (p. 546). [21] He is, like the Indian-hater *par excellence*, "a soul . . . peeping out but once an age." [22]

Melville also refers to this rare type in *The Confidence-Man* as "an Original Character," and by implication places his great and mysterious swindler in the category. Bartleby is also associated with swindling. His role in what might be termed noble fraudulence is suggested by the grub-man's linking him with Monroe Edwards, a notorious genteel confidence man whose trial in 1842 in New York made headlines. Edwards, like Bartleby in the Tombs, was not one of "the common prisoners" (p. 614). As with the Adams-Colt affair, which occurred at approximately the same time as Monroe Edwards's great swindles and trial, Melville uses a contemporary event of notoriety to

---

ern Exile," in *A Symposium*, pp. 64–81. John Seelye, "The Contemporary 'Bartleby,' " in *Studies in the Minor and Later Works of Melville*, pp. 12–18, states that Bartleby is a practicing Emersonian who reveals the absurdity of Transcendentalism. Louise K. Barnett, "Bartleby as Alienated Worker," *Studies in Short Fiction* 11 (1974): 379–385, sees the story in Marxist terms and Bartleby as "victim of and protest against the numbing world of capitalistic profit and alienated labor" (p. 385). For Daniel Stempel and Bruce M. Stillians, Bartleby is Melville's conscious attempt to illustrate in fiction Schopenhauer's concept of the ideal man, the "saint" in a depraved world who denies the will to live: *"Bartleby the Scrivener: A Parable of Pessimism," Nineteenth-Century Fiction* 27 (1972): 268–282.

20. *The Confidence-Man*, ed. Hershel Parker (New York: Norton, 1971), p. 131.

21. Johannes Dietrich Bergmann suggests that the "satisfactory biography" referred to here was a popular novel by James A. Maitland which Melville may have known, at least in part. See " 'Bartleby' and *The Lawyer's Story*," *American Literature* 47 (1975): 432–436.

22. *The Confidence-Man*, p. 131.

underscore his theme. Without awareness of these events, the modern reader loses some of the richness of implication in the story.

An extremely shrewd and knowledgeable man, Colonel Monroe Edwards was a fraud with class. He once forged a letter of introduction to Lord Spencer in England and signed Daniel Webster's name to it. Completely taken in, Lord Spencer advanced Edwards 250 pounds on confidence. So unpredictable was Edwards that after swindling a Liverpool firm of about twenty thousand dollars, he paid Lord Spencer back his money.[23] During his trial (over forty-four thousand dollars had been found in the trunk in his room), the courtroom was packed with people curious to see the "Great Forger," as he was called. Aloof and somewhat contemptuous of the proceedings, the gentleman forger was sentenced to ten years in prison. Like Bartleby, he was taken to the Tombs. Later he was transferred to Sing Sing Prison, where he died of consumption in 1847.

When the grub-man mistakes Bartleby for a "gentleman forger" like Monroe Edwards and the lawyer answers that he has never known any forgers, a distinction is suggested which again differentiates by implication Bartleby from the lawyer. Monroe Edwards was not just any forger. He was the "Great Forger." The prosecuting attorney at his trial claimed that when Edwards was arrested, "the master spirit seemed to have left the stage, and the public ear was pained with no more announcements of the great forgeries. All that followed were the mere ordinary occurrences of every day." [24] He was the forger *par excellence*, an "original character," who is "like a revolving Drummond light," Melville explains in *The Confidence-Man*, "raying away from itself all round it—everything is lit by it." [25]

23. George Ticknor Curtis, *Life of Daniel Webster* (New York: Appleton, 1872), 2: 89–91.

24. New York *Daily Tribune*, 8 June 1842, p. 1, col. 4.

25. *The Confidence-Man*, p. 205.

Bartleby is himself an original character and in a sense a "Great Forger" because he cheats the world, and all that the world is an agent for, of its victory over him. The distinction between the Great Forger and just any forger is the distinction between Bartleby and the lawyer, and this, in turn, is precisely the distinction between *the* Confidence Man in Melville's later novel and those lesser, even petty confidence men who are the ordinary people of the world and who deceive and cheat mainly themselves because of their fear, their greed, or their corruption.

"Bartleby, the Scrivener" is the story of two men, one who will not communicate with the world and one who will not communicate with himself. In the end the lawyer reports a "rumor" that Bartleby had previously worked for the "Dead Letter Office at Washington, from which he had been suddenly removed by a change in the administration" (p. 614). That was not the last time he was "removed" by such a change. He is taken from the lawyer's office when tenants change, and finally he is taken from life. The point is that he will not communicate with a world or a cosmos that wants only to enslave him. He *is* a dead letter, for in the world he has no place to go.[26] He has erased the return address of his past and written his future in words that the world cannot understand. The lawyer is stirred by the rumor of the dead-letter office, but without having received any true communication from Bartleby. It is death which really troubles him: "Dead letters! does it not sound like dead men?" In his imagination he sees a dead letter with a ring—"the finger it was meant for, perhaps, moulders in the grave," a

---

26. See Peter E. Firchow, "Bartleby: Man and Metaphor," *Studies in Short Fiction* 5 (1968): 342–348. For possible sources of Melville's reference to the dead-letter office, see George Monteiro, "Melville, 'Timothy Quicksand,' and the Dead-Letter Office," *Studies in Short Fiction* 9 (1972): 198–201; John Middleton, "Source for 'Bartleby,'" *Extracts*, no. 15, September 1973, p. 9; and especially Hershel Parker, "Dead Letters and Melville's Bartleby," *Resources for American Literary Study* 4 (1974): 90–99.

banknote, now too late to help the one it was meant for who neither "eats nor hungers any more," a word of pardon "for those who died despairing," a word of hope "for those who died unhoping," and "good tidings for those who died stifled by unrelieved calamities." His final words seem to reveal his greatest compassion and understanding: "Ah Bartleby! Ah humanity!" (p. 615). In reality, they show him as the world, unreached by a dead letter. There is pity for Bartleby and for humanity in his final words, but it is born of fear and self-pity. We all die, he is saying, and it is terrible. In linking Bartleby with ordinary humanity, he has failed to see with what force and finality Bartleby rejected and transcended humanity.[27] "Bartleby" is more the portrayal of unconscious duplicity, however, than it is of noble fraudulence. The lawyer has the center stage.[28] In terms of contrasting metaphors of honesty and dis-

27. Some critics argue that the lawyer has learned or grown from his experience with Bartleby. See the following: Abcarian; Fisher; Patrick; Stempel and Stillians; James L. Colwell and Gary Spitzer, " 'Bartleby' and 'The Raven': Parallels of the Irrational," *Georgia Review* 23 (1969): 37–43; John Bernstein, *Pacifism and Rebellion in the Writings of Herman Melville* (Hague: Mouton, 1964), pp. 166–171; Marjorie Dew, "The Attorney and the Scrivener: Quoth the Raven, 'Nevermore,' " in *A Symposium*, pp. 94–103.

28. Indeed, it is possible, although somewhat limiting, to read the story in terms of a single mind—the narrator's. Several critics have argued convincingly that Bartleby is the lawyer's double, who has come forth to trouble, challenge, or save him. For treatments of "Bartleby" as a double story, see the following: Kingsley Widmer, "The Negative Affirmation: Melville's 'Bartleby,' " *Modern Fiction Studies* 8 (1962): 276–286, reprinted with minor revisions in *The Literary Rebel* (Carbondale: Southern Illinois University Press, 1965), pp. 48–59, and in revised form as "Melville's Radical Resistance: The Method and Meaning of 'Bartleby,' " *Studies in the Novel* 1 (1969): 444–458; Albert J. Guerard, "Concepts of the Double," in *Stories of the Double*, ed. Albert J. Guerard (Philadelphia: Lippincott, 1967), pp. 1–14; Mordecai Marcus, "Melville's Bartleby as a Psychological Double," *College English* 23 (1962): 365–368; Herbert F. Smith, "Melville's Master in Chancery and His Recalcitrant Clerk," *American Quarterly* 17 (1965): 734–741; and C. F. Keppler, *The Literature of the Second Self* (Tucson: University of Arizona Press, 1972), pp. 115–120.

honesty, noble fraudulence and petty forgery, Melville in "Bartleby" has written his most effective and detailed analysis before *The Confidence-Man* of the unconscious duplicity of ordinary man, using the brilliant Drummond light of an extraordinary scrivener as his tool.

HIGH-SPIRITED REVOLT

"Cock-a-Doodle-Doo!"

Chapter 2

"Cock-A-Doodle-Doo!" has been called everything from a masterpiece to a "painfully concocted and convictionless" tale,[1] one in which the author was "at his weakest."[2] It has been widely interpreted as a satire on Emerson, Thoreau, and New England Transcendentalism in general,[3] a parody of Wordsworth's poem "Resolution and Independence,"[4] and an attack on the Apostle Paul.[5] Recently Sidney P. Moss has offered a corrective by argu-

1. Newton Arvin, *Herman Melville* (New York: Sloane, 1950), p. 235.
2. Lewis Mumford, *Herman Melville* (New York: Harcourt, 1929), p. 236.
3. See particularly Egbert S. Oliver, " 'Cock-A-Doodle-Doo!' and Transcendental Hocus-Pocus," *New England Quarterly* 21 (1948): 204–216; and William Bysshe Stein, "Melville Roasts Thoreau's Cock," *Modern Language Notes* 74 (1959): 218–219.
4. Leon Howard, *Herman Melville* (Berkeley: University of California Press, 1951), p. 210.
5. William Bysshe Stein, "Melville's Cock and the Bell of Saint Paul," *Emerson Society Quarterly*, no. 27 (2nd quarter 1962), 5–10. Stein also believes the story to be "a savage caricature of Wordsworth's leech-gatherer and his genial faith."

ing that "Cock-A-Doodle-Doo!" is not satiric in nature.[6] The tendency to read the story as satire or parody is understandable. It arises from the attempt to see serious purpose and meaning behind a series of highly implausible events which the narrator of the story relates with a sardonic grin.

The story concerns a man who finds himself deeply depressed by personal problems as well as by the general world situation. One day he walks out and hears the fantastically loud and beautiful crowing of an unseen rooster. Taking heart, the man searches for the cock, and at length he finds that it belongs to an extraordinary woodcutter with a mortally ill wife and four sick children. He offers to buy it but is refused. Returning home, he continues to hear its crow night and day. After a while he makes his way back to the shanty of Merrymusk, the woodcutter. There he witnesses in quick succession the death of every member of the family as the cock crows on. When they are all dead, including Merrymusk, the cock fills the air with one final blast and expires. The narrator-hero buries them all, supplies a gravestone with a cock carved on it, and then proceeds to crow himself: "Cock-a-doodle-doo!—oo!—oo!—oo!—oo!" (p. 86).[7]

Obviously "Cock-A-Doodle-Doo!" cannot be treated as a realistic piece of writing. Like Hawthorne's "Young Goodman Brown" it relies heavily on the reader's willingness to suspend the usual demand for plausibility so that the nature of the protagonist's perception and state of mind can be projected. That is precisely the *raison d'être* of "Cock-A-Doodle-Doo!": the revelation of an unusual mind. It is a mind dominated in the first of the story by fear, particularly fear of emasculation, fear of

6. " 'Cock-A-Doodle-Doo!' and Some Legends in Melville Scholarship," *American Literature* 40 (1968): 192–210. Moss's own interpretation, however, seems wide of the mark in its implication that the story is as optimistic as Whitman's "Song of Myself."

7. All page references to "Cock-A-Doodle-Doo!, or, the Crowing of the Noble Cock Beneventano," are to *Harper's New Monthly Magazine* 8 (December 1853–May 1854): 77–86.

the world's disapproval and scorn, and fear of death. In tracing the protagonist's conquest of fear, I shall treat first, because it is least profound though almost always ignored, the comic level of the story which reveals the narrator's victory over sexual insecurity, then another and more significant level of the narrator's personality, his melancholia, and finally the wider implications of the theme of freedom from fear.

The narrator's description early in the story of a fatal train accident reveals the association then in his mind of sex with death: "And that crash on the railroad just over yon mountains there, where two infatuate trains ran pell-mell into each other, and climbed and clawed each other's backs; and one locomotive was found fairly shelled, like a chick, inside of a passenger car in the antagonist train; and near a score of noble hearts, a bride and her groom, and an innocent little infant, were all disembarked into the grim hulk of Charon" (p. 77). As his mood changes, however, he feels a new virility, and the subject of sexual self-confidence is treated as a kind of elaborate joke. Soon after first hearing the cock, he sits in his room reading Sterne's *Tristram Shandy* (a highly appropriate book for him to enjoy in his state of mind) and drinking stout when one of his impatient creditors enters. "Sit down," he says. "I'll finish this chapter, and then attend to you. Fine morning. Ha! ha!—this is a fine joke about my Uncle Toby and the Widow Wadman! Ha! ha! ha! let me read this to you" (p. 79). The creditor refuses, indicating that he is too busy. The narrator insists: "Let me read you this about the Widow Wadman. Said the Widow Wadman—" (p. 79). Interrupting him, the "dun" abruptly presents his bill. The narrator commands him to twist it up and light his cigar with it. The scene ends with the narrator seizing the outraged creditor by his coat and throwing him out of the house.

Tristram Shandy so abounds with hilarious passages involving my Uncle Toby and the Widow Wadman that it is difficult to determine the particular one that amused Melville's narrator. Just about all of them, however, are sexual in nature and revolve around the question of my Uncle Toby's possible emasculation. As the Widow Wadman pursues him with matrimony in mind, she becomes more and more curious and anxious about his old war wound in the groin. Much sparring conversation is given over to her attempts to learn whether he is or is not able to perform sexually. Innocent as he is, he never seems to understand why she is so solicitous about his wound. The joke intensifies when she finally comes out and asks him directly where he was wounded. To answer her he fetches a map of Namur, the site of the battle, and tenderly places her finger on the exact spot where he received his wound. Sterne's comic intention in ending *Tristram Shandy* with the thought that it was all a cock-and-bull story was not lost on Melville, who has himself written a tale in which the term *cock* is used to designate more than a rooster and in which the owner of this great bird is called *Merrymusk*, a name with its own set of comic overtones.[8]

To understand what Melville is about—not only in terms of the story's comedy but also the more serious purposes—it is essential to realize that Merrymusk functions as the narrator's alter ego. In seeking the great rooster and its owner, the narrator is searching for the source of his newly felt virility. The search is marked frequently by double entendre. When he asks the first old man he meets if he knows anything of the extraordinary cock he is seeking, the old man answers: "Well, well, . . . I don't know—the Widow Crowfoot has a cock—and Squire Squaretoes has a cock—and I have a cock, and they all crow. But I don't know of any on'em with 'strordinary crows" (p. 80). The other farmer he meets may be more perceptive, although he seems foolish to the narrator, for he refuses even

---

8. The *Oxford English Dictionary* traces the word *cock*, as it refers to the penis, to Nathan Bailey's *An Universal Etymological English Dictionary* (1730–36) and cites early English translations of Rabelais, a favorite of Melville's. William Bysshe Stein points out that etymologically *Merrymusk* means "sweet or pleasant testicle." "Melville's Cock and the Bell of Saint Paul," p. 5.

to answer such a question. More searching over a period of days does not bring results. Meanwhile, the narrator relates an incident described with comically sexual suggestiveness. Lunching in a tavern one day, he is startled to find that his "cigar" has been wrapped in a civil process notice. His creditors seem to be part of the conspiracy to emasculate him. Indignant that the notice was presented to him in this indelicate fashion, he complains: "It was ungenerous; it was cruel" (p. 82).

Finally his diligence brings results as he comes upon Merrymusk, whom he knew earlier as his woodcutter, and discovers his "noble cock." It was "more like a Field-Marshal than a cock. A cock, more like Lord Nelson with all his glittering arms on, standing on the *Vanguard's* quarter-deck going into battle, than a cock. A cock, more like the Emperor Charlemagne in his robes at Aix la Chapelle, than a cock. Such a cock! He was of a haughy size," and he crows like an opera baritone who seems "on the point of tumbling over backward with exceeding haughtiness" (pp. 83, 84).[9] When Merrymusk refuses to sell him the cock, the narrator says: "I stood awhile admiring the cock, and wondering at the man. At last I felt a redoubled admiration of the one, and a redoubled deference for the other" (p. 84). In prideful, defiant Merrymusk the narrator sees what it takes to ward off emasculation. He must fear nothing; he must be no one's pawn. When Merrymusk has served his function, he dies with his family and the cock, and the narrator is ready to do his own crowing.

That Merrymusk is intended to represent what the narrator wants to be and can be is suggested by the fact that no one

9. The narrator adds: "His pace was wonderful. . . . He looked like some Oriental king in some magnificent Italian Opera" (p. 83). The opera Melville had in mind may have been Donizetti's *La Favorita*. The Beneventano of the story's subtitle was a favorite opera singer of the day. His performance in *La Favorita* is reviewed as follows in the New York *Daily Tribune*, 25 January 1851, p. 5, col. 1: "The brave Beneventano expended energy enough for many potent and outraged monarchs upon his single scene."

else ever sees him or hears the crowing of the cock. Merrymusk and "Trumpet," as the cock is called, may be real only to the narrator, for he alone among his neighbors can hear the crow, and he alone knows the way to Merrymusk's shanty. Furthermore, their language points to their identification. Early in the story the narrator described the dun, who represents collectively his worldly woes, as "lean," and calls him a "lantern-jawed rascal" (p. 78). Later Merrymusk uses these precise words, "lean, lantern-jawed," to describe the world around him. The narrator's discovery of Merrymusk and the cock, then, is on one level a symbolic and comic account of the conquering of his fears of emasculation.

Comic though it may be, "Cock-A-Doodle-Doo!" cannot be dismissed as merely a sexual joke.[10] The quality of the narrator's humor and, indeed, the subject of his humor demand some explanation. If he enjoys a good laugh, he sometimes overdoes it. In his early mood he wants to be made "Dictator in North America" so that he can "string up" those who manage the affairs of the world. He would "hang, draw, and quarter; fry, roast, and boil; stew, grill, and devil them, like so many turkey-legs" (p. 78). He cannot understand why the creditor whom he threw out bodily will not consider the episode merely a joke and forget it. He "claps" mortgages on his property cavalierly, as if such transactions are of little importance. He offers five hundred dollars, which he does not have, for a rooster. He becomes obsessed with the cock, hearing its crow at all hours of the day and night, and he ends the story by literally crowing himself. His humor often has a peculiar quality, shrill, forced, even frantic at times. To understand the story, therefore, it is necessary to go deeper into the man who tells it and to understand him.

On the first day Merrymusk appears to the narrator, he is

10. Martin Green sees the sexual comedy of "Cock-A-Doodle-Doo!" but he refuses to think that the story offers anything more. *Re-Appraisals* (New York: Norton, 1965), pp. 108–112.

reading Burton's *The Anatomy of Melancholy*. Seeing the spartan woodcutter eating stale bread and salt beef outside in the snow, the narrator puts his book down, rushes out to him, and brings him into his home for a hot meal. From that moment on his admiration for Merrymusk increases. Like *Tristram Shandy*, *The Anatomy of Melancholy* furnishes some important clues about the nature and eccentricities of the narrator. Robert Burton's massive treatise on melancholy was of inestimable importance to Melville, who early in life read an abridged version of it in his father's library and then over twenty years later purchased that same copy from a bookseller in New York.[11] Burton's influence is to be seen both directly and indirectly in many of Melville's works, notably *Mardi*, *Moby-Dick*, *The Confidence-Man*, and "Bartleby."

The puzzling mixture of humor and desperation in the narrator of "Cock-A-Doodle-Doo!" can be accounted for by viewing him as a victim of what Burton called laughing or sanguine melancholy. This was considered the melancholy of geniuses, the divine sickness of poets, the penalty of perception. Melville must have found himself described in the long preface to *The Anatomy of Melancholy*, where Burton takes the pseudonym of "Democritus Junior" and confesses that he himself is so prone to melancholy that he must write in order to avoid its destructive depths. He has, he says, been a man of sorrows: "Something I can speak out of experience, painful experience hath taught me, and with her in the Poet: *Not unschool'd in woe, I have learned to succour the woeful*."[12] Democritus saw the corruption of mankind and the absurdity of life, yet like Melville he became neither passive nor bitter. He worked on, tolerating the tragedy of existence with humanistic amusement

---

11. See Nathalia Wright, "Melville and 'Old Burton,' with 'Bartleby' as an Anatomy of Melancholy," *Tennessee Studies in Literature* 15 (1970): 1–13.

12. Robert Burton, *The Anatomy of Melancholy*, ed. Floyd Dell and Paul Jordan-Smith (New York: Tudor, 1948), p. 17.

flavored with the instability of insight. In *Mardi* Babbalanja refers to a laughing sage called Demorkriti, and in his own wild outbursts of almost mad wit, Babbalanja himself seems to be suffering from the same malady. Ishmael, too, as I have pointed out elsewhere, is possessed by the need to laugh and to tell his story in order to avoid complete madness.[13]

Burton described those suffering from laughing melancholy as "humorous . . . beyond all measure, sometimes profusely laughing, extraordinary merry, and then again weeping without a cause."[14] It is the melancholy of great minds. In "Cock-A-Doodle-Doo!" Melville presents us with just such a character as Burton describes. The "divine inspiration," as Burton puts it, which the melancholic sometimes believes he experiences, comes to the narrator in the form of a cock, whose crow seems to say *"Glory be to God in the highest"* and *"Never say die!"* (p. 78). Before this inspiration he is low-spirited, out walking because he is "too full of hypoes [hypochondria] to sleep" (p. 77). As he broods the landscape seems starkly grim: "all the humped hills looked like brindled kine in the shivers. The woods were strewn with dry dead boughs, snapped off by the riotous winds of March" (p. 77). He sits on a rotting log and observes "a lagging, fever-and-agueish river, over which was a duplicate stream of dripping mist" (p. 77). In the distance he sees "a great flat canopy of haze, like a pall" (p. 77). The way these sights strike his eye reveals the state of his mind as he muses upon the "slight mark" which he has made "on this huge great earth" (p. 77).

During his moment of profoundest despair, when he feels betrayed and forgotten by the very heavens who "themselves ordain these things" (p. 78), there comes without reason or warning a note of inspiration. Typical of the melancholic, he is in the depths of depression one minute and elated the next.

13. "The Narrator of Moby-Dick," *English Studies* 49 (1968): 20–29.
14. Burton, p. 335.

With the trumpet sound of the cock, his perception of his surroundings changes drastically. He feels "in sorts again"; the
mist disappears; the sun begins to shine; his appetite returns;
the train, which had seemed nightmarish to him before, now
flashes like silver, the engine chirping pleasantly; and the landscape now appears idyllic. Through inspiration, symbolized in
the story by the crowing cock, the narrator now returns to his
studies, facing life with that half-mad laughter that accompanies
his ejection, a short time later, of the "lean rascal" who comes
to demand payment of a bill: "My soul fairly snorted in me.
Duns!—I could have fought an army of them! Plainly, Shanghai
[the cock] was of the opinion that duns only came into the
world to be kicked, hanged, bruised, battered, choked, wal-
loped, hammered, drowned, clubbed!" (p. 79).

His inspiration continues through the day; the cock's crow at
noontide is like the sound issuing from a golden-throated muse:
"It was the . . . most strangely-musical crow that ever amazed
mortal man . . . so smooth and flute-like in its very clamor—
so self-possessed in its very rapture of exultation—so vast,
mounting, swelling, soaring, as if spurted out from a golden
throat, thrown far back" (p. 80). It is louder and more trium-
phant than the sound of Keats's nightingale, but it serves a
similar function of symbolizing the creative insight and inspiration that furnishes escape from the cares of life. In the evening
the narrator again ascends a hill and hears the same miraculous
sound.

The strictly subjective nature of these experiences is made
clear when the narrator starts to search for the cock. As I
pointed out earlier, no one else has heard it, not even his closest
neighbors, and even the narrator cannot tell from what direction the sound comes. Significantly he cannot find the source of
his inspiration by seeking it directly. It is only through Merrymusk that the cock can be found. When the narrator and his
alter ego meet and look into each other's eyes, they seem to
recognize the kinship. "You seem a glorious independent fel-

low," says the narrator, to which Merrymusk responds: "And I don't think you a fool, and never did. Sir, you are a trump" (p. 85). Later he will in a sense be Trumpet, for he ends the story crowing.

The deaths of Merrymusk, his family, and the cock take place at practically the same time, a fact which illustrates again the illusory nature of the experience. Certainly the reader is not expected to believe that any of this could really happen except in the mind of the narrator. It is a cock-and-bull story in this, as well as the other (comically sexual) sense.[15] Burton writes often in *The Anatomy of Melancholy* of the phenomenon of hallucination among those suffering from various forms of the malady: "Melancholy men and sick men, conceive . . . absurd suppositions, as that they are Kings, Lords, cocks."[16] The narrator's tendency to "crow late and early with a continual crow" after Trumpet's death closely resembles some of the strange cases Burton describes: "One fears heaven will fall on his head; a second is a cock; and such a one Guianerius saith he saw at Padua, that would clap his hands together and crow. . . . Some laugh . . . some dejected. . . . Some have a corrupt ear, (they think they hear musick)."[17]

The portrait of the narrator of "Cock-A-Doodle-Doo!" as a laughing melancholic resembles in several other ways Burton's

15. The term "cock-and-bull story" probably originated from the "legendary sexual prowess of cocks and bulls," and has come to mean "a fabricated tale passed off as true, especially in self-glorification." *Webster's Third International Dictionary* (1966). Burton uses the term (see *OED*) in *The Anatomy of Melancholy*, and in the "Argument of the Frontispiece," he describes one scene as follows:

> Two fighting-Cocks you may discern;
> Two roaring Bulls each other hie,
> To assault concerning venery.
> Symbols are these; I say no more,
> Conceive the rest by that's afore.
> (p. 2)

16. Burton, p. 222.
17. Ibid., p. 343.

description. Among the exacerbating factors of melancholy, Burton finds that "loss and death of friends may challenge a first place."[18] At the beginning of "Cock-A-Doodle-Doo!" the narrator bemoans the loss of his good friend in a steamboat accident. Death is uppermost in his mind as he thinks of all kinds of "dreadful casualties" (p. 77). He is concerned, too, about being in debt, a condition which Burton saw as most conducive to melancholy.[19] Burton also considered diet an important contributing cause of melancholy, and he devoted a considerable amount of space to discussing the subject. The diet which Melville furnishes his narrator, who incidentally tells us that he suffers from dyspepsia, consists generally of foods that Burton says are dangerous, foods that feed the melancholy. On the day when he first hears the cock, the narrator decides to go home and have "brown stout and beefsteak" for breakfast. Burton warns his readers about the dangers of beef to melancholics, and dark and strong beer, he says, is condemned by many authorities as unwholesome.[20] The narrator is also fond of cheese, a food marked by Burton as unhealthy to a melancholic.[21]

Melville's reading of "Old Burton," as he called the author of *The Anatomy of Melancholy*, apparently left an indelible impression upon him, for echoes of that phenomenal work reverberate throughout several of his writings. Nowhere is Burton more in evidence than in "Cock-A-Doodle-Doo!" From the pages of Democritus Junior, Melville has taken the laughing melancholic and made him the narrator of his story, which he tells with a voice that combines laughter and tears.

The search for independence is also a primary theme of "Cock-A-Doodle-Doo!" but the terms of the search are different from those in such novels as *Mardi* and *Moby-Dick*. The drama is no longer enacted upon some cosmic stage, nor is the

18. Ibid., p. 305.
19. Ibid., p. 314.
20. Ibid., pp. 190, 195.
21. Ibid., p. 191.

protagonist a raver. The search for independence is still basic, but the sound and fury have quieted to the crow of a cock, which is Azzageddi's new voice proclaiming freedom to a protagonist who lives a life of quiet desperation amid the mild surroundings of hills and valleys. An old antagonist has changed, too. From *Pierre* onward, the "world" plays an increasingly important part as antagonist. The major conflict in "Cock-A-Doodle-Doo!" is between an unusual man, one who does not seem to be able to fit himself into any of the provided pigeonholes of life, and the world. This situation is revealed early in the story as the narrator describes his mood while walking among the hills near his home: "This toiling posture brought my head pretty well earthward, as if I were in the act of butting it against the world. I marked the fact, but only grinned at it with a ghastly grin" (p. 77). He blames the world for his depression—"A miserable world! Who would take the trouble to make a fortune in it, when he knows not how long he can keep it, for the thousand villains and asses who have the management of railroads and steamboats, and innumerable other vital things in the world" (p. 78).

The very personification of this world is the dun, who constantly presses the narrator to be normal, that is, to fulfill his responsibilities as a solid citizen. This man of the world offers him the path of ordinary existence, shows him by example the way he must live in order to fit the pattern which the world imposes. The dun cannot stop to drink with him because he must do his noon chores. His life is ordered and prearranged. He offers the narrator religion, but it is religion with conditions: "[He] comes and sits in the same pew with me, and pretending to be polite and hand me the prayer-book opened at the proper place, pokes his pesky bill under my nose in the very midst of my devotions, and so shoves himself between me and salvation: for how can one keep his temper on such occasions?" (p. 78). It is significant that this representative of the world is a bill collector, for that vocation symbolizes the nature of the world. One must pay its price or suffer its terrible wrath. The world-creditor offers the narrator one kind of salvation—material and shallow; Merrymusk offers him another kind.

What this salvation consists of is probably the most crucial concept in my interpretation of the story. In the ordinary sense in which the word *salvation* is used, it suggests deliverance from hell by divine intervention. This is one of a number of religious terms and references which Melville uses for his own special purpose, for "Cock-A-Doodle-Doo!" is clearly not a religious story. The hell of this tale is the world which the narrator finds himself already living in, and divine intervention does not come as God's grace manifested through religious conversion. The narrator's salvation comes through his self-glorification which raises him in his own mind above the world and enables him to defy it. He thinks of the crow of the cock as supernatural just as Ahab believes that his inspiration comes from above and lifts him far beyond the level of ordinary human existence. Taji also comes to think of himself as almost divine, a demigod. Equality to the gods is their ultimate goal. If the crowing cock seems to be saying "Glory be to God in the highest," it also suggests to the narrator the "Brother of the Sun! Cousin of great Jove!" (p. 80). The point is that the crowing of the cock is not a manifestation of some force external to the narrator but the externalization of his newly acquired "universal security," crowing "solely by himself, on his own account, in solitary scorn and independence" of the world and the things the world fears most (p. 80). In one of the narrator's most telling descriptions of the rooster's crow, he describes it as "the crow of a cock who crowed not without advice; the crow of a cock who knew a thing or two; the crow of a cock who had fought the world and got the better of it, and was now resolved to crow, though the earth should heave and the heavens should fall. It was a wise crow; an invincible crow; a philosophic crow; a crow of all crows" (p. 80). He no longer fears failure or the creditor who has been hounding him. As fear disappears the world begins to seem petty: "I heard the inspiring blast, again felt my blood bound in me, again felt superior to all the ills of life, again felt like turning my dun out of doors" (p. 81). The crow seems to say: "What's the world compared to you?" (p. 82).

Through self-glorification the narrator overcomes his fears of emasculation, of the consequences of worldly failure, and finally, of death. The threat of death hangs over him as the story opens. It is present in the heavy mist of the morning, in the river he describes, and in every detail of the terrain. He morbidly dwells on fatal accidents and bloody revolutions. With the crow of the cock he can scorn this most terrifying of life's sorry tricks, death: "I felt as though I could meet Death, and invite him to dinner, and toast the Catacombs with him, in pure overflow of self-reliance and a sense of universal security" (p. 80). He describes the second old farmer he encounters in his search for the cock as "this woeful mortal."

By this time he is ready to see the image of his deepest defiant self, Merrymusk. In terms of an anatomy of melancholy, this encounter reveals the peculiar state of the narrator's mind; in terms of the story's sexual comedy, the meaning is obvious. What is more important and less obvious is the serious purpose of the joke. Sexual matters in Melville's writing are almost always symbolic of larger and more comprehensive ideas. "Cock-A-Doodle-Doo!" is one of the best works in which to view this symbolic process in operation. The narrator's discovery of a magnificent cock suggests humorously the fulfillment of his wish to be more virile, but that in turn has a deeper implication: the narrator's comic-bitter desire for such supreme self-confident masculinity that he can, in the modern vernacular, screw the world. He wants his manhood, and for Melville that meant dignity through self-sufficiency. Merrymusk is what the narrator would like to be, what he already is, and what he will become. Merrymusk is his own destiny, independence carried to the extent of heroic but destructive obsession. Such is his mad defiance of the world and all the ills of human life that Merry-musk dies insisting that he is well.

The heart of the heroic concept which Merrymusk represents is expressed in the verse from First Corinthians which the narrator has chiseled on the gravestone:

Oh! death, where is thy sting?
Oh! grave, where is thy victory?

Above these words on the gravestone appears the figure of a "lusty cock in act of crowing" (p. 86). Frequently used as a religious symbol, the cock, together with the biblical quotation, might appear to suggest the narrator's belief in Christian resurrection. In fact, many details of the story parallel the Christian resurrectional tradition. It opens with a man seen amidst an atmosphere of death. It is the spring of the year, but the hill which the man toils to reach the top of is like Golgotha in its starkness. Misunderstood and even victimized by the world, the man at his lowest moment feels forsaken by the heavens. Then a cock, Trumpet, sounds "Glory be to God in the highest! . . . Never say die!" and the man instantly feels new and elated, his surroundings beautifully transformed. "In the twinkling of an eye," Paul wrote in I Corinthians 15:52, "the trumpet shall sound and the dead shall be raised incorruptible, and we shall be changed." Such parallels notwithstanding, what may seem to be almost a Christian allegory is, again, a cock-and-bull story. Utilizing the basic idea of Christian rebirth, Melville arrives at a far different concept. The narrator of "Cock-A-Doodle-Doo!" does not have Merrymusk's gravestone made in the spirit of Christianity but in the spirit of prideful defiance.

The victory which Merrymusk has won and which the narrator is moving toward when at the end he gives Trumpet's cry has a special meaning just as the term *salvation* which was used earlier. Neither the narrator nor Merrymusk has been converted to Christianity and made a candidate for the resurrection Paul is referring to in First Corinthians. What the gravestone means is that in the eyes of the narrator Merrymusk won a victory through the way he lived and perished by achieving absolute indifference toward the terrifying forces of human life. He tore himself loose from the body of ordinary human beings who are subject to all the petty fears and stupid aims that limit and degrade. It is while man is alive that death wins its victory, occupying his thoughts, filling him with the terrors of anticipated annihilation, intimidating and enslaving him. Only in life can the grave sting. Merrymusk like Bartleby refused death that victory by elevating himself to such heights of pride and independence as to feel untouchable by poverty, disease, and death. That death is inevitable is not important; what is important is that he remains inviolable to the end. In the act of perishing he reaches the apex of human dignity. This concept is given its fullest expression in *Moby-Dick*, not only in the character of Ahab but also in Bulkington, who is to Ishmael what Merrymusk is to the narrator of "Cock-A-Doodle-Doo!" [22] After describing the "sympathetic awe and fearfulness" with which he looked upon Bulkington, Ishmael expresses his notion of heroism: "Terrors of the terrible! is all this agony so vain? Take heart, O Bulkington! Bear thee grimly, demigod! Up from the spray of thy ocean-perishing—straight up, leaps thy apotheosis!" [23]

22. The Merrymusk-narrator and Bulkington-Ishmael relationships are only two of a number in Melville's works where one character seems to mirror the destiny of the other. In *An Artist in the Rigging* (Athens: University of Georgia Press, 1972), I have suggested that this is also the situation with Taji and Babbalanja in *Mardi*.

23. *Moby-Dick*, ed. Harrison Hayford and Hershel Parker (New York: Norton, 1967), p. 98. Compare with the final stanza of *Clarel* (1876):

> Then keep thy heart, though yet but ill-resigned—
> Clarel, thy heart, the issues there but mind;
> That like the crocus budding through the snow—
> That like a swimmer rising from the deep—

As we saw in the case of Bartleby, apotheosis carries a heavy penalty. Melville's attitude was always ambivalent toward the character who pushes his drive for independence to the ultimate. Emotionally he cheered them on—the Tajis and Ahabs who defy the highest powers of the universe—but he saw clearly the destruction that such an obsession causes, and perhaps he feared that he might himself undergo that metamorphosis from laughing philosopher to heroic but self-destroying madman. The concept of apotheosis is thus paradoxical.[24] The urge for independence is noble, but it is insatiable and proceeds through melancholy to madness; the desire to lift oneself above the level of ordinary man is admirable, but the closer one comes to being a demigod, the less human and consequently humane one becomes.

The negative aspects of this form of heroism can be seen in "Cock-A-Doodle-Doo!" As the narrator is increasingly inspired to break away from the world and live above it, he seems less and less human.[25] In the beginning he is greatly troubled by accidents and recent deaths, especially that of a friend. He has in his pocket a medicinal powder he was going to send to a sick baby at an Irishman's house. He mentions giving up his berth on a riverboat one night to an ill woman even though he had to stand all night in the rain. With the crowing of the cock he

---

That like a burning secret which doth go
Even from the bosom that would hoard and keep;
Emerge thou mayst from the last whelming sea,
And prove that death but routs life into victory.

24. Richard Harter Fogle considers the ambivalence of the story a flaw and believes that it results from a lack of artistic control: "Intended as a trumpet call of affirmation, it reveals in its dissonances the note of underlying despair." *Melville's Shorter Tales* (Norman: University of Oklahoma Press, 1960), p. 35.

25. Judith Slater, "The Domestic Adventurer in Melville's Tales," *American Literature* 37 (1965): 268–269, sees the narrator and Merrymusk as both sacrificing their humanity by indulging in "emotional extremes," but she fails to see any heroism in them. To her they are merely "grotesque."

begins to care less about others. Intense self-glorification is always accompanied by selfishness. He begins to see the pains of others in a new light: "I thought over my debts and other troubles, and over the unlucky risings of the poor oppressed *peoples* abroad, and over the railroad and steamboat accidents, and over even the loss of my dear friend, with a calm, good-natured rapture of defiance, which astounded myself" (p. 80). Later when some of his own relatives die, he seems strangely unfeeling, so wrapped up is he in his glorious mood. He does not even wear black but jokes about drinking dark stout for a while instead of the lighter porter. True to Merrymusk, his alter ego, the narrator will pay for his heroic defiance of life and the world by hardening his heart to the cry of humanity. Ahab could not stop to help find the lost children of the *Rachel* because of his selfish—if heroic—drive toward superhumanness.

The narrator of "Cock-A-Doodle-Doo!" has not yet reached that stage when the story ends. He is still the laughing melancholic, closely resembling Ishmael, who has to make his jokes in order to tolerate existence. His course is clearly charted, however. He cannot avoid financial ruin, but more importantly his growing thirst for independence and the pride that accompanies it will lead him to a solitary death. This flawed heroism, the defiance of Merrymusk, inspires in the reader both those emotions which Ishmael experienced when he looked at Bulkington: "sympathetic awe and fearfulness."

Three important aspects of "Cock-A-Doodle-Doo!," then, are suggested by three allusions in the story. The narrator's references to *Tristram Shandy* are provocative in seeing and understanding the story's sexual comedy. To fail to see this level of meaning, bawdy and somewhat distasteful as it may be, is to remain blind not only to a rather obvious aspect of this particular work but also to a recurrent technique in Melville's writings. Indeed, what is most remarkable about "Cock-A-Doodle-Doo!" is that it is at the same time one of the most comic and one of the most serious of Melville's works. Burton's great

73

work on melancholy suggests a second level of the story, for it is a miniature anatomy of melancholy. Peculiarities in the narrator's actions and in his general tone can be explained partly by the fact that he is suffering from the mental aberration Burton explored with such thoroughness and wit. Melville's quotation from First Corinthians is the most important of the three allusions, for it suggests the primary theme of the story—the narrator's need to insure his individuality, to gain independence from a world that intellectually stifles and emotionally enslaves. To be free of the fears that ordinarily dictate man's thoughts and actions and to defy openly the world with its threats of everything from civil suits to ostracism is to win a victory, even if that victory is fully realized only in death.[26] This was a favorite theme of Melville's, and in "Cock-A-Doodle-Doo!" he developed it with the help of three of his old favorites—*Tristram Shandy*, *The Anatomy of Melancholy*, and the Bible.

26. In using a cock as the symbol of victory, Melville was utilizing a long-standing tradition. In his *Universal Etymological English Dictionary* (1730–36), Nathan Baily wrote: "The cock, say others, is the Emblem of . . . Victory. Because he rather chooses to die than yield. . . . The cock crows when he is Conqueror, and gives notice of his Conquest."

AN HOURGLASS
RUN OUT

"The Encantadas"

Chapter 3

Shortly after "Bartleby" and "Cock-A-Doodle-Doo!" appeared in print, Melville received from Harper and Brothers on 7 December 1853 an advance of three hundred dollars for a new book on "Tortoises and Tortoise Hunting." Presumably he expected to complete the work in January or February. For some reason now unknown he did not deliver a full-length work to *Harper's* as he had agreed to do. Instead he submitted to *Putnam's Monthly Magazine* ten sketches about the Galápagos Islands entitled "The Encantadas, or Enchanted Isles." The work was published in three installments in the March, April, and May issues of 1854.

A month before the first installment of "The Encantadas" came out, the New York *Evening Post* announced its forthcoming appearance with obvious delight and put all lovers of *Typee* and *Omoo* on alert that the Herman Melville of old, the traveler and adventurer, had awakened from his "distempered dreams" and once again would entertain his readers with "refreshing fountains of pleasure and delight."[1] In certain ways "The Encantadas" is reminiscent of Melville's early novels. Like them it is based on Melville's observations as a seaman and rover. He visited the Galápagos Islands twice, first aboard the *Acushnet* in the fall and winter of 1841–42 and then aboard the *Charles and Henry* about a year later. The area was then a popular whaling ground, and, as Jay Leyda suggests, Melville's personal reactions to these desolate islands must have been intensified by the legends and stories he heard from other sailors.[2]

"The Encantadas" also resembles such books as *Typee* and *Omoo* in its travelogue-like description of an exotic, faraway place. The first-person narrator guides the reader about the Galápagos, pointing out their dismal features and recounting stories, both comic and tragic, about some of the former human inhabitants. Nothing that he wrote during this period of 1853–56 calls to mind so clearly as this work the artistic methods of Melville at the beginning of his writing career. Here, too, he relied sometimes upon the work of other writers to fill out his own sketches. As he himself notes at the end of the ninth sketch, he was heavily indebted to Captain David Porter's *Journal of a Cruise Made to the Pacific Ocean* (1815), a volume Melville greatly admired and one that he had lifted materials from for *Typee*. He may also have used (but to a lesser degree) such works as James Colnett's *A Voyage to the South Atlantic . . .* (1798), John M. Coulter's *Adventures in the Pacific* (1845), and James Burney's *Chronological History of the Discoveries in the South Sea or Pacific Ocean* (1803–17).[3]

But "The Encantadas" is also very different from Melville's

1. Quoted in Jay Leyda, *The Melville Log: A Documentary Life of Herman Melville, 1819–1891* (New York: Harcourt, Brace, 1951), 1: 484–485.
2. *The Complete Stories of Herman Melville* (New York: Random, 1949), p. 456.
3. For an extended treatment of Melville's sources, see Russell Thomas, "Melville's Use of Some Sources in *The Encantadas*," *American Literature* 3 (1932): 432–456.

early work. Its imaginative impact is of another kind, more closely related to what Poe called a "singleness of effect." The ten sketches do not develop a theme so much as they objectify a condition or state, that barren condition that results when a fire has burned out and left only ashes, when time has run out and left deserts of vast eternity, when passion, enthusiasm, and love of life have melted down to the stasis of despair. For all this—the waste products of the life process—"The Encantadas" is a metaphor.

Without a sustained plot, "The Encantadas" relies upon mood (and imagery to develop that mood) much as does Thomas Hardy's poem "The Darkling Thrush," with those memorable images of the landscape as "Winter's dregs." Melville's vision of barrenness, expressed in "The Encantadas" nearly a half-century before Hardy's poem was written, is of the same order. The "special curse" of the Enchanted Isles is that "to them change never comes; neither the change of seasons nor of sorrows. Cut by the Equator, they know not autumn and they know not spring; while already reduced to the lees of fire, ruin itself can work little more upon them" (p. 311).[4] The blackish burned-out covering of the land looks "like the dross of an iron-furnace" (p. 312). Here, then, is what is left from the furnace of life: "Nothing can better suggest the aspect of once living things malignly crumbled from ruddiness into ashes. Apples of Sodom, after touching, seem these isles" (p. 312). After establishing that the islands are the leavings of burned-out volcanos, Melville time and again returns to the idea and imagery of the waste products of fire. The islands appear to be the results of a "penal conflagration." Some vast, uncontrollable, fiery energy seems to have spent itself here.

The bleak and blasted islands are changeless because they are burned out, a "fallen world" in the sense that dregs fall and

4. "The Encantadas, Or Enchanted Isles," *Putnam's Monthly Magazine* 3 (March, April, May 1854), 311–319, 345–355, 460–466. All references to "The Encantadas" are to this first printing of the story.

sink to the bottom.[5] The perfect living counterparts to these "lees of fire" are the tortoises, for they are the dregs of the animate world: "They seemed newly crawled forth from beneath the foundations of the world" (p. 314). Their "crowning curse" is the same as that which hangs over the land they inhabit, changelessness. They seem to live forever, but they grow no wiser. No matter how belittered their path, they will not change their course. In one of the most effective passages in the work, the narrator writes that in his imagination he sees often in moments of merriment "the ghost of a gigantic tortoise with 'Memento * * * * *' burning in live letters upon his back" (p. 313). The tortoise is a reminder of death, a memento mori, in two senses. First, because the tortoise represents so aptly the Enchanted Isles, it suggests, as they do, the stark remains of exhausted life. Inevitably, life will burn out. All that remains of the energetic and boisterous buccaneers who once took refuge on these islands are ruined seats of stone and turf (that in turn recall the ruined coliseums Melville earlier connected with the tortoises),[6] ancient daggers and cutlasses "reduced to mere threads of rust," and "fragments of broken jars" (p. 347). On this same grim note of death, but with an added element of sardonic humor, Melville ends "The Encantadas" by depicting the isles as a literal burial ground, a "convenient Potter's Field." It is man's fate to be finally and eternally linked with the Enchanted Isles because he will inevitably be "tucked in with clinkers" (p. 466); indeed, he will become but a clinker himself.

5. My interpretation here of "fallen world" disagrees with those critics who feel that Melville was dealing with the subject of human evil or the theological concept of the fall of man. See, for example, Richard Harter Fogle, *Melville's Shorter Tales* (Norman: University of Oklahoma Press, 1960), pp. 92–115; I. Newberry, " 'The Encantadas': Melville's *Inferno*," *American Literature* 38 (1966): 49–68; and Robert C. Albrecht, "The Thematic Unity of Melville's 'The Encantadas,' " *Texas Studies in Language and Literature* 14 (1972): 463–477.

6. In the three tortoises, he says, "I seemed to see three Roman Coliseums in magnificent decay" (p. 314).

The tortoise also represents another kind of death, death in
life, which takes two principal forms: degradation to bestiality
and the changeless state of catatonic hopelessness. The tortoises
suggest the fall of that life force that informs the spirit and passion of man down to the most basic and mechanical form of
energy, life without life. Half humorously, the narrator tells of
a superstition of mariners that tortoises are really transformed
sea-officers, "more especially commodores and captains" (p.
312). The joke has a serious side, for it prepares for the characters Melville later introduces. As different as they are, they
have one essential feature in common—their transformation to
human tortoises. The Creole of the seventh sketch was once a
hero in the cause of Peru's independence. Ambitiously he sought
to become ruler of Charles Isle, but all who eat of the tortoise, as
he and his followers did, seem to become bewitched and finally
to merge with that hopeless crawler through the labyrinthine
wastes of life. The national hero becomes a mock king, who tries
and fails to rule a "Riotocracy" and who finally is degraded almost to the level of the dogs he depends on to keep his subjects in line.

The hermit Oberlus, who deserts his ship to live on Hood's
Isle off the tortoises and "degenerate potatoes and pumpkins,"
is also transformed when he comes to live on the islands. He
seems to be "the victim of some malignant sorceress" and to
have "drunk of Circe's cup" (p. 460). He is what is left when
all the best in human nature has been distilled away. Blistered
and humped, he has come to look like the humped isles and the
tortoises that inhabit them: "the sole superiority of Oberlus over
the tortoises was his possession of a larger capacity of degradation" (p. 461). The sailors that Oberlus captures and enslaves
undergo the same kind of reverse evolution to a lower form of
life.[7] They are "rotted down from manhood by their hopeless

7. At least two scholars believe that Melville had Darwin and *The
Voyage of the Beagle* (1839) in mind when he wrote "The Encantadas."
H. Bruce Franklin argues that Melville's prime purpose in "The En-

misery on the isle" (p. 463). The fall from a higher form of life to a lower through the witchery of the Enchanted Isles was not an idea Melville used only in "The Encantadas." Several years later he repeated the notion as he wrote about the tortoises of the Galápagos in *Clarel*:

> . . . the eyes are dull
> As in the bog the dead black pool:
> Penal his aspect: all is dragged,
> As he for more than years had lagged—
> A convict doomed to bide the place;
> A soul transformed—for earned disgrace
> Degraded, and from higher race.
>
> (IV. iii. 68–74)

If Oberlus resembles the tortoises in his mindless bestiality, the Chola widow of the eighth sketch, Hunilla, comes to be like them in another sense, her silent, hopeless endurance. With her husband, Felipe, and her brother, Truxill, she comes to Norfolk Isle to subsist off the tortoises and to bring back as much of their oil as possible. But it is Hunilla who is tried out. The metaphor is appropriate; it suggests the fate of those who come to this "arid archipelago" to hunt the tortoises for their meat and oil. They who try out the tortoises are in turn reduced themselves through a kind of fire of life and suffering to the dregs, and the higher form of life's energy is cooked from them. Hunilla watches as her husband and brother are drowned. She is victimized then by the treachery of a French sea captain, who does not return to pick up the party as he had promised. She also suffers some nameless indignity at the hands of men the narrator will not name, but perhaps the greatest suffering of

cantadas" was to refute elaborately Darwin's theory of upward evolution. "The Island Worlds of Darwin and Melville," *Centennial Review*, 11 (1967): 353–370. See also Benjamin Lease, "Two Sides to a Tortoise: Darwin and Melville in the Pacific," *The Personalist* 49 (1968): 531–539.

all comes from her having to be alone for months on the Enchanted Isles with little but tortoises for her larder.

The description of Hunilla as she leaves Norfolk Isle behind reveals her transformation from a vital young wife to a stoic, hopeless endurer: "Her face was set in a stern dusky calm. . . . She never looked behind her; but sat motionless. . . . She seemed as one, who having experienced the sharpest of mortal pangs, was henceforth content to have all lesser heartstrings riven, one by one. . . . A heart of earthly yearning, frozen by the frost which falleth from the sky" (p. 355). She is a "silent" woman, riding when last seen "upon a small gray ass" into Payta, eying before her "the jointed workings of the beast's armorial cross" (p. 355). There is no Christian hope here, as some readers would like to see.[8] There is only hopelessness intensified by the irony of the Christian image. She has been hurt so much that she has declined to that terrible and almost changeless condition of the tortoise, that "formal feeling" that Emily Dickinson wrote about. Riding slowly into Payta, she resembles the "tortoises creeping through the woods" (p. 352).

The shadow of the tortoise, then, is cast over "The Encantadas" as that of the whale is over *Moby-Dick*. That Melville originally spoke of this work—or what it was in an earlier stage—as "Tortoises and Tortoise Hunting" suggests the centrality in his imagination of this vast, lumbering, mysterious creature which like the whale is hunted, eaten, and tried out by those who in a cycle of metaphoric cannibalism are themselves subjected to the same fate. The poignancy of the tortoise as metaphor and symbol is enhanced when we realize its effect not only on the characters of the sketches, but on the narrator as

8. See for example Nicholas Canaday, Jr., "Melville's 'The Encantadas': The Deceptive Enchantment of the Absolute," *Papers on Language and Literature* 10 (1974): 66. What Melville actually wrote in the final sentence of this sketch is now impossible to say. At *Putnam's* Charles Briggs altered the final paragraph, apparently to make it more palatable to readers with strong religious convictions.

well. He, too, has light-heartedly eaten of their flesh and has to pay the price.

The narrator's first view of the giant tortoise came "some months" before he actually set foot on the Enchanted Isles. While his ship was cruising off the coast of Albemarle, the largest of the islands, the captain ordered a boat's crew to go ashore and bring back tortoises for food. The boat returned after sunset with "three huge antediluvian-looking tortoises" (p. 313). The narrator was profoundly affected by the sight of them. Lantern in hand, he inspected them minutely: "I seemed an antiquary of a geologist studying the bird-tracks and ciphers upon the exhumed slates trod by incredible creatures whose very ghosts are now defunct" (p. 314). He marveled at their apparent age and their capacity for endurance, but he was also struck by what seemed their stupid refusal to go around obstacles in their path: "That these tortoises are the victims of a penal, or malignant, or perhaps a down-right diabolical enchanter, seems in nothing more likely than in that strange infatuation of hopeless toil which so often possesses them" (p. 314). Through the night he listened to the slow draggings of the three tortoises on deck and imagined what the land they came from must be like: "With them I lost myself in volcanic mazes; brushed away endless boughs of rotting thickets; till finally in a dream I found myself sitting crosslegged upon the foremost, a Brahmin similarly mounted upon either side, forming a tripod of foreheads which upheld the universal cope" (p. 314). This, he says, was the "wild nightmare" brought on by his "first impression of the Encantadas tortoise" (p. 314).

The vision was nightmarish because he had dived so deep. He had, in effect, gone down to "wondrous depths" where he saw "strange shapes of the unwarped primal world," as Pip did in *Moby-Dick*. In his dreams he is among Brahmins because they are the chosen caste, the interpreters of truth as written in the sacred scriptures, and they are each riding upon a tortoise because it was sacred to the Hindus, who believed the tortoise to be one of the earliest avatars of Vishnu. As such the tortoise was not killed for food or oil. The narrator, therefore, did not remain a "Brahmin," for the very next evening after his dream he sat down with his shipmates and "made a merry repast from tortoise steaks and tortoise stews" (p. 314). If this act is considered within the framework of the dream and thus Hindu thought, he has committed sacrilege and will be eternally cursed.[9] But even in less theological and esoteric terms, his actions are strange if not incongruous. The tortoise had inspired in him serious thoughts disturbing in their cosmic implications. From this profound mood he abruptly changes and merrily eats the very creature that provoked such thoughts.

That he made a "merry" repast of the tortoise is especially telling. Whenever gaiety is mentioned in "The Encantadas," it raises questions and precedes disaster. The narrator asks if one may "be gay upon the Encantadas" (p. 313), and he answers, "Yes: that is, find one the gayety, and he will be gay" (p. 313). In other words, gaiety resides within one's self. It is a state of mind. Melville never had much regard for shallow jolliness, but in "The Encantadas" that quality of the mind is unusually destructive. The sea captain who fails to fulfill his agreement and deserts Hunilla is "a joyous man," and the narrator warns, "nought else abides on fickle earth but unkept promises of joy" (p. 350). Joy and elation of spirit also bring on the death of Hunilla's husband and brother. Happy with their success in killing and trying out tortoises, they hastily construct a raft and *"merrily* started on a fishing trip" (italics mine, pp. 350–351). Their drowning results from "natural negligence of joyfulness" (p. 351).

9. Traditionally his punishment would be threefold: he would become an outcast, he would be preoccupied with guilt, and he would be transformed in the next existence to a lower form of life. Arlene M. Jackson takes an opposite view. By eating the tortoise, she argues, the narrator gains knowledge and perspective and rids himself of the nightmare he earlier had. "Technique and Discovery in Melville's *Encantadas*," *Studies in American Fiction* 1 (1973): 135.

The narrator, then, has seen both sides of the tortoise in both literal and figurative senses. He examined the great hulk of its shell and then dreamed deep and frightening dreams. Then he viewed its bright side, became merry, ate of its flesh, and polished its "yellowish" calipee into a "gorgeous" salver. But his merriment does not last. From whatever cause, he has incurred a curse just as surely as would a Brahmin who committed sacrilege upon the tortoise. The narrator's curse is to be preoccupied with the tortoise and what it symbolizes. Some years have gone by since he was a sailor visiting the Enchanted Isles, but still he cannot get the tortoises out of his mind:

> Nor even at the risk of meriting the charge of absurdly believing in enchantments, can I restrain the admission that sometimes, even now, when leaving the crowded city to wander out July and August among the Adirondack Mountains, far from the influences of towns and proportionally nigh to the mysterious ones of nature; when at such times I sit me down in the mossy head of some deep-wooded gorge, surrounded by prostrate trunks of blasted pines . . . [I] recall, as in a dream, my other and far-distant rovings in the baked heart of the charmed isles; and remember the sudden glimpses of dusky shells and long languid necks protruded from the leafless thickets. (p. 313)

Despite his "firmest resolutions," he periodically beholds "the spectre-tortoise" as it emerges from "its shadowy recess" (p. 313). The spectre-tortoise appears to him often in "scenes of social merriment, and especially at revels" in old homes (p. 313). "I have drawn the attention of my comrades by my fixed gaze and sudden change of air, as I have seemed to see, slowly emerging from those imagined solitudes, and heavily crawling along the floor, the ghost of a gigantic tortoise . . ." (p. 313).

The narrator thus is cursed because he is incapable of sustaining any optimism, pleasure, or tranquility. When he escapes to the country to enjoy nature, he sees the spectre-tortoise. Whenever he tries to laugh with his friends at a party, he sees a giant tortoise creeping across the floor of a further room. This special curse of his is evidenced in his method of narration. He can

84

be darkly serious as he frequently is in the first two sketches; he can be mocking, as he is when describing the dog king of Charles Isle; he can be condescending and sardonic as he is when relating the escapades of Oberlus. There is no true joyousness, however, in the tone of any of the sketches. And when he attempts to be an optimistic humanist in the Hunilla story, he seems false. Figuratively, the dark shape of the tortoise creeps over his narration. Consequently the tone of this sketch fluctuates to such extremes of optimism and pessimism, piousness and blasphemy, sentimentality and dark dignity that it has puzzled and displeased some of Melville's most sympathetic critics.[10] The narrator seems to be straining to see goodness and nobility and to sustain his human sympathy. The ship he was on at the time is a "good ship," and the captain is a "good fellow." His shipmates are his "comrades," who are unselfish and sympathetic. He even argues that whiskey, bad as it is, sometimes "does a deal of good," parodying, as it seems, what he says earlier about there being two sides to the tortoise, light and dark, good and bad. He strenuously avoids the details of the dark side of humanity by refusing to go into the "two unnamed events which befell Hunilla on this isle" (p. 353). Through Hunilla he purports to depict the nobility of the human spirit: "Humanity, thou strong thing, I worship thee, not in the laurelled victor, but in this vanquished one" (p. 352). This may well be what he is trying to see and believe, but the underlying darkness of tragedy and the hopelessness of despair constitute the

10. Newton Arvin, for example, feels that the sketch is "written in a manner so forcedly and self-consciously pathetic that not even its substance redeems it from the lachrymose." *Herman Melville* (New York: Sloane, 1950), p. 241. Several critics see the problem as one involving point of view. See Howard D. Pearce, "The Narrator of 'Norfolk Isle and the Chola Widow,'" *Studies in Short Fiction* 3 (1965–66): 56–62; Diane L. Fay, "The Meaning of Herman Melville's 'The Encantadas'" (M.A. thesis, Emory University, 1972); and Bert C. Bach, "Melville's Theatrical Mask: The Role of Narrative Perspective in His Short Fiction," *Studies in the Literary Imagination* 2 (1969): 43–55.

basic stuff of the Hunilla sketch while the sentiment and humanism seem forced and insincere.[11]

He tries to see both sides of the tortoise, but it is the dark hump that dominates his imagination and, in fact, his perception of phenomena. Not only has his thinking been deeply influenced by what may be called the curse of the tortoise but also his way of seeing. A single image, in several variations, recurs over and over in his descriptions—the shape of the tortoise shell, the "unverdured heap." His very first words establish his preoccupation with this image of the mound or heap: "Take five-and-twenty heaps of cinders dumped here and there in an outside city lot; imagine some of them magnified into mountains, and the vacant lot the sea; and you will have a fit idea of the general aspect of the Encantadas, or Enchanted Isles" (p. 311). His vision is filled with the same basic image whether he is describing the islands as "extinct volcanoes," or as "split Syrian gourds left withering in the sun" (p. 311), or as "tumbled masses of blackish or greenish stuff" (p. 312). The hermit Oberlus is the unverdured heap personified. In appearance he resembles "a heaped drift of withered leaves" (p. 460). "Bowed over" as he works upon his potato mounds, he is both an illustration and a product of that pernicious barrenness of the Encantadas.

Rock Rodondo, which is discussed in three of the sketches, is a variation on the image of the unverdured heap and is of central importance. Not so much a rock as a huge mound, it rises from a broad base in graduated shelves to a "shaven summit." When the narrator indicates that he was once atop Rock Rodondo, he seems to be speaking as symbolically as he was when he described his dream of sitting atop a giant tortoise, for the rock is almost impossible to climb. "How we get there, we alone

11. A suggestive argument to the contrary is offered by John Bernstein, *Pacifism and Rebellion in the Writings of Herman Melville* (The Hague: Mouton, 1964), pp. 174–179. See also Ray B. Browne, *Melville's Drive to Humanism* (Lafayette: Purdue University Studies, 1971), pp. 280–301.

know. If we sought to tell others, what the wiser were they?"
(p. 317). Here as elsewhere, the subject of perception is uppermost. The narrator takes the reader to the summit of Rock Rodondo so that he can see, but as it turns out, there is actually
very little in sight from there, mostly blankness, "a boundless
watery Kentucky" (p. 317). The narrator describes the relative
positions of the other islands, but he admits "you see nothing"
(p. 317). For some, nothingness is always the terrible vision
from the unverdured heap. It is what Hunilla witnesses as she
watches the dumb show of her husband's and brother's drowning from her "blasted tower." It is also what she sees as she
rides atop the ass into Payta. But when those happy souls like
the buccaneers look out from atop the heap, as they do from
their seats built on the hills of Barrington Isle, they are filled
with joy and contentment. Only to those who seem to be under
the spell of the tortoise curse does the unverdured heap appear
and reappear in all its barren terror. The narrator sees it
wherever he looks: "while we know it to be a dead desert rock,
other voyagers are taking oaths it is a glad populous ship"
(p. 317).

A further manifestation of the unverdured heap, the grave
mound, calls to mind, of course, the ultimate in nothingness.
From the grave mound the narrator and those similarly cursed
see the same thing as from Rock Rodondo. In the final sketch,
which deals with the grave mounds on the Encantadas, the narrator sardonically describes happy mariners who come across
such graves: "They usually make a table of the mound, and
quaff a friendly can to the poor soul's repose" (p. 466). In contrast to these merry seamen, Hunilla throws herself in tragic
hopelessness upon the grave mound of her husband. The crucifix
she carries has been "worn featureless, like an ancient graven
knocker long plied in vain" (p. 354). All around her are images
of the unverdured heap—the volcanic islands themselves; the
live tortoises tied up to supply "Hunilla's lonely larder"; the
"skeleton backs of those great tortoises from which Felipe and

Truxill had made their precious oil" (p. 354); Hunilla's pathetic hut, which "seemed an abandoned hayrick" (p. 353); and that lonely grave mound upon which Hunilla lies prostrate. "The mound rose in the middle; a bare heap of finest sand, like that unverdured heap found at the bottom of an hourglass run out" (p. 354). The predominant imagery of "The Encantadas" is compacted in this passage. The Enchanted Isles are but a magnification of that unverdured heap found at the bottom of an hourglass. It is in this sense of the hourglass that the islands represent a "fallen world." They are the unchanging dregs of time, life, fire, passion, energy. They are cursed. The tortoises are cursed. All those who have had the unverdured heap forcefully planted in their vision—"fixed, cast, glued into the very body of cadaverous death" (p. 312)—they, too, are cursed. Shun the Enchanted Isles, the narrator warns as he quotes from Spenser for his first epigram:

> For they have oft drawne many a wandring wight
> Into most deadly daunger and distressed plight;
> For whosoever once hath fastened
> His foot thereon may never it secure
> But wandreth evermore uncertein and unsure.
>
> (p. 311)

So it is with the narrator himself, whose perception is filled "even now"—long after wandering from the Galápagos—with those terrible images of the unverdured heap.

Located at a central position on the globe where the meridian of 90° meets the equator, the group of Enchanted Isles is the very center of deceit and illusion, subjects that recur throughout the work and help tie the ten sketches together. The waters and the air around the islands are given to "perplexing calms," and yet at other times "there is a mysterious indraft, which irresistibly draws a passing vessel among the isles, though not bound to them" (p. 312). At one period navigators believed that "there existed two distinct clusters of isles in the parallel of the Encantadas" instead of only one (p. 312). This "strange delusion" was only one of several that "originated in that air of spell-bound desertness which so significantly invests the isles" (p. 312). Rock Rodondo participates fully "in that enchantment which pervades the group," appearing as it does from afar to be a sail (p. 315). The wild, fierce birds of the rock contribute significantly to the "dreary spell" of the islands, and the fish that swim around the rock are "fairy fish." Cowley's Enchanted Isle is a "spell within a spell," appearing "sometimes like a ruined fortification," sometimes "like a great city," and at other times offering still another deceptive illusion (p. 319). "No wonder though," the narrator comments, "that among the Encantadas all sorts of ocular deceptions and mirages should be met" (p. 319). He refers to the "enchantments of the neighborhood," an "enchanted ship" chased in vain by the *Essex*, and the "charmed vicinity of the enchanted group."

The ocular deceptions described in the first five sketches prefigure a pattern of human deception described in the last five sketches. The buccaneers of the sixth sketch betray and rob others, but they deceive mostly themselves by imagining that they have found a hiding place where they can be happy, free, and safe. The epigrams which Melville chose for this sketch are highly ironic. They praise freedom, condemn servitude, and promise ease and tranquility, all illusory.[12] The quotation Melville used from Spenser's *Mother Hubberd's Tale* to begin the seventh sketch serves much the same function:

12. D. Mathis Eddy, "Melville's Response to Beaumont and Fletcher: A New Source for *The Encantadas*," *American Literature* 40 (1968): 374–380, identifies for the first time the source of the third epigram of this sketch about the buccaneers, Beaumont and Fletcher's *Wit Without Money* (I. i). Eddy also points out that the passage in the play is ironic and that it performs the same function in "The Encantadas": "as adventurers, the buccaneers prey on the fortunes of others, but they are, in turn, subject to ruin among themselves and preyed upon by time" (p. 379). A differing view (one I disagree with) is offered by Buford Jones, who considers the sketch more idyllic than ironic. "Spenser and Shakespeare in *The Encantadas*, Sketch VI," *Emerson Society Quarterly* 35 (2nd Quarter, 1964): 68–73.

We will not be of any occupation,
Let such vile vassals, born to base vocation,
Drudge in the world, and for their living droyle,
Which have no wit to live withouten toyle.

(p. 347)

The speakers could be those members of the "Riotocracy" that follow the dog king to Charles Island to colonize it. Their illusions are overwhelming, for they see the "arid archipelago" as a "promised land." Illusion and deceit, suggested through the narrator's sardonic tone, are central in this sketch.

Deceit plays an important role also in Hunilla's story and in the sketch about Oberlus. Hunilla, her husband, and her brother are deceived by the French captain and she, by implication, by the very heavens that seem to desert her in her need. Oberlus is the archdeceiver. He betrays the seamen who visit his miserable hut and enslaves them, but like all who labor under the illusion of power and freedom, he ends up himself enslaved, "burrowing in all sorts of tragic squalor" (p. 464). The final sketch discusses the fatal error of those who, seeking illusory freedom, desert their ships for these labyrinthine isles. Some manage to survive, but most are "tucked in with clinkers."

These, then, were the subjects that occupied Melville's mind when he wrote "The Encantadas" during the final weeks of 1853 and the early part of 1854—the dregs of life, the curse of a bleak vision, and the power of deceitful illusion. Just three and a half years before, in the late summer of 1850, he was in the midst of his most intense period of creativity and intellectual discovery. Now, early in 1854, he felt burned out. To understand fully the biographical implications of "The Encantadas," it is necessary to realize that Melville was not writing merely about a place. He was also writing about a state of mind. As Lewis Mumford recognized, "the landscape of these islands corresponded to his inner state."[13] Melville strongly implies this

13. *Herman Melville: A Study of His Life and Vision*, rev. ed. (New York: Harcourt, Brace, 1962), p. 164. Richard Chase comments that

connection in his description of Cowley's Enchanted Isle: "That Cowley linked his name with this self-transforming and be-mocking isle, suggests the possibility that it conveyed to him some meditative image of himself. At least, as is not impossible, if he were any relative of the mildly thoughtful, and self-upbraiding poet Cowley, who lived about his time, the conceit might seem [not] unwarranted; for that sort of thing evinced in the naming of this isle runs in the blood, and may be seen in pirates as in poets" (p. 319). What that single isle was to Cowley—"some meditative image of himself"—the Galápagos were to Melville.[14] Even when he tried to be merry, with a house full of guests at Arrowhead, bleak images dominated his vision and mood.

"the idea that he was living in Tartarus during the years from 1853 to 1856 often occurred to Melville." *Herman Melville: A Critical Study* (New York: Macmillan, 1949), p. 210. Ronald Mason writes that "Melville was retreating from dilemmas that at least represented life, to solitudes which smacked pervasively of death." *The Spirit Above the Dust* (London: John Lehmann, 1951), p. 189. Louis Coxe feels that "The Encantadas" represents a "portrait of the artist . . . as a middle-aged failure." "Reconsideration: Melville's *The Encantadas*," *New Republic*, May 12, 1973, p. 33.

14. In certain places in "The Encantadas" Melville may be "self-upbraiding." His comically scornful treatment of the "Riotocracy" on Charles Isle in the seventh sketch could well be a sardonic comment on his own earlier pronouncements in favor of democracy. And Oberlus, the hermit of the ninth sketch, is clearly the earlier Melville hero made abominable. He has the key traits of the earlier heroes: he possesses a sense of "misanthropic independence," he nourishes in himself "a vast idea of his own importance," and he develops an intense "scorn for all the rest of the universe." Yet he is a mindless, bestial clown. He is a mock version of the Melville hero, not merely a "lesser Ahab" as John Seelye asserts (*Melville: The Ironic Diagram*, Evanston: Northwestern University Press, 1970, p. 102), but an Ahab without a trace of stature or nobility. Melville modeled Oberlus on a real person named Patrick Watkins, who is described in David Porter's *Journal of a Cruise Made to the Pacific Ocean* (Philadelphia: Bradford and Inskeep, 1815), 2: 141–144. But significantly Porter does not make Watkins a misanthropist. That was Melville's invention, one that relates Oberlus to Melville's heroes.

"The Encantadas" may have been written, among other reasons, in order to get these images of desolation out of his system. In that great period three years before when he felt his genius coming to fruition, he had composed an essay that bubbled with enthusiasm, energy, and even passion. That inspired essay was the result of his discovery of Nathaniel Hawthorne through his reading of *Mosses from an Old Manse*.[15] Whether intentional on Melville's part or not, "The Encantadas" is a devastatingly effective answer to his own earlier essay, "Hawthorne and His Mosses."[16] In both works the subject of enchantment is pervasive, but the forms of enchantment are diametrically opposed. In "Hawthorne and His Mosses" Melville is bewitched in the happiest possible sense. "A man of deep and noble nature has seized me," he writes. "His wild, witch-voice rings through me."[17] Melville's reading of Hawthorne's book in the summer of 1850 convinced him that at last he had found someone so like himself that he could communicate those profound and troublesome thoughts that haunted him. He could not but be "charmed," he wrote, that Hawthorne's view of life so closely paralleled his own, that there was "such a parity of ideas . . . between a man like Hawthorne and a man like me."[18] Time and again he returns to the notion of enchantment. He quotes Hawthorne's words from "The Old Manse": "What

15. When Melville wrote the essay, probably in July 1850, he had never met Hawthorne. Their first meeting was on a picnic excursion around Pittsfield on 5 August 1850. On 17 August, the first installment of the essay appeared, but Hawthorne did not know who wrote it for some time. Melville's letters to Hawthorne during 1851 make clear the importance he placed on this new friendship.

16. *The Literary World*, 17 August and 24 August 1850.

17. "Hawthorne and His Mosses," in *The Works of Herman Melville* (London: Constable, 1924), 13: 123.

18. Ibid., p. 142. In a provocative article Jerome M. Loving argues that Melville was so eager to find reflections of his own dark vision of life that when he read *Mosses* he misinterpreted Hawthorne to be like himself. "Melville's Pardonable Sin," *New England Quarterly* 47 (1974): 262–278.

better could be done for anybody who came within our magic circle, than to throw the spell of a magic spirit over him?" And he exclaims: "How magically stole over me this Mossy Man!" [19] Hawthorne, the "wizard," has woven about him a "web of dreams," a "spell." [20]

With "this Hawthorne's spell," he contrasted the opposite form of enchantment in "The Encantadas," that "spell-bound desertness" (p. 312) of the inner self. In "Hawthorne and His Mosses," he had referred to "the enchanting landscape in the soul of this Hawthorne." [21] A few years later the enchanting landscape was barren and baked. Perhaps one reason why Melville in his essay chose to refer continually to his personal response to Hawthorne's work in terms of enchantment and benign witchery was that the stories and sketches in *Mosses from an Old Manse* are themselves frequently concerned with some form of spell or illusion as, for example, "The Birth-Mark," "Young Goodman Brown," "Rappaccini's Daughter," and "The Celestial Railroad." In fact, Melville read in Hawthorne's introductory sketch, "The Old Manse," a phrase he later used in more than one place in "The Encantadas." "In one respect," Hawthorne wrote, "our precincts were like the Enchanted Ground." [22] Later Melville wrote that seamen call the

19. "Hawthorne," p. 125.
20. Illusion is also an important subject in the essay as it is in "The Encantadas." Throughout, Melville praises Hawthorne as a kind of literary confidence man who appears one way to most readers and another way to a select few. Hawthorne is thus not as he has generally been taken to be: "In one word, the world is mistaken in this Nathaniel Hawthorne" (ibid., p. 129). He finds him deeper and darker than people think. "The Truth seems to be," Melville continues, "that like many other geniuses, this Man of Mosses takes great delight in hoodwinking the world" (p. 139). Melville finds Hawthorne's titles especially deceptive: "it is certain that some of them are directly calculated to deceive" (p. 140).
21. Ibid., p. 124.
22. *Mosses from an Old Manse*, The Centenary Edition of the Works of Nathaniel Hawthorne, general eds. William Charvat, Roy H. Pearce,

area of the Galápagos "the Enchanted Ground," and when he describes his recurrent vision of the creeping tortoises, he says, "in my time I have indeed slept upon evilly enchanted ground" (p. 313).

The setting for both "Hawthorne and His Mosses" and "The Encantadas" is mountainous, but the unverdured heaps of the later work are in stark contrast to the lushly green hills of the earlier essay. The openings of the two works are vastly different, the one describing a "fine old farmhouse . . . dipped to the eaves in foliage"[23] and surrounded by verdant mountains, the other describing its setting as "five-and-twenty heaps of cinders." Whereas barrenness characterizes "The Encantadas," luxuriant growth is everywhere in "Hawthorne." Melville refers to the stories in Hawthorne's collection as being of "perennial green," describes the volume as "verdantly bound," plays upon the words *mosses* and *Hawthorne*, and claims that he read the stories while stretched out on "new mown clover." In the early work he was surrounded by verdure; in the later work he is amid ashy barrenness. In approval he had quoted Hawthorne: "Will the world ever be so decayed, that Spring may not renew its greenness?"[24] Three years later he answered the question by describing the Encantadas as a place where spring is unknown. In the essay he spoke of beautiful apples of "perfect ripeness," which symbolized Hawthorne's thoughts. Later he described the Galápagos as apples, but they are the "Apples of Sodom, after touching." The "bird voices" which he found "delicious" in "Hawthorne" become the cruel cries of the fierce seabirds on Rock Rodondo. The fire of the hearth which he praised in the essay becomes the tormenting flame of the Galápagos sun.

Significantly, in both works Melville used pseudonyms, a very rare practice for him. His choice of names suggests how different

C. M. Simpson, vol. 10 (Columbus: Ohio State University Press, 1974): 28.

23. "Hawthorne," p. 123.

24. Ibid., p. 126.

his moods were from one period to the other. The essay was signed "By a Virginian Spending July in Vermont." The sketches carried the name "Salvator R. Tarnmoor." The first suggests leisure, tranquility, and the beauty of domesticized nature. The second—*Tarnmoor*—has a certain wildness about it and a bleakness that fits the landscape described. Melville was familiar with those distorted and wild landscapes of the Italian painter Salvator Rosa and may well have had him in mind when he created the pseudonym.[25]

The number of paired opposites in the imagery of the two works is startling, but none is more telling than the contrast between the doe and the tortoise. In what has become one of Melville's most quoted statements, he commented in his essay upon "the great Art of Telling the Truth": "For in this world of lies, Truth is forced to fly like a scared white doe in the woodlands; and only by cunning glimpses will she reveal herself. . . ."[26] In a key passage in "The Encantadas" (earlier quoted), he speaks of going periodically into the forest, but now what he sees is the creeping spectre-tortoise: "and [I] remember the sudden glimpses of dusky shells, and long languid necks protruded from the leafless thickets" (p. 313). In his barren vision the woodland has become the "leafless thickets"; the white image of truth, "dusky"; the scared doe, a dull tortoise. And whereas truth was once brilliant and elusive and could be seen only partially and then through cunning, now its heavy and lumbering form intrudes itself oppressively upon all his reveries.

It is a long way from the green world of "Hawthorne and His Mosses" to the cinders of "The Encantadas." The route by which Melville arrived there is well known—the abysmal failure of *Pierre*, growing financial pressures, physical troubles, and so forth—but one fact has been largely neglected: in 1853 he

25. See Sharon Furrow, "The Terrible Made Visible: Melville, Salvator Rosa, and Piranesi," *ESQ* 19 (1973): 237–253.

26. "Hawthorne," p. 131.

tried, in a sense, with the help of family and friends to recapture his green world and failed. It may have been his family's idea that he seek a consulship abroad for his health, but the choice of location seems to have been his own—Honolulu, in what was then known as the Sandwich Islands. Although Leon Howard believes that the efforts of Melville's father-in-law, Judge Shaw, and uncle, Peter Gansevoort, both influential men, would have been greater "if either Herman or Elizabeth had been actively interested," [27] Maria Melville had written to Gansevoort that her son "earnestly wished" for the position. And on 16 June 1853, after the appointment to the Sandwich Islands had fallen through and Melville had refused to consider other possibilities such as Rome, Lemuel Shaw, Jr., wrote to his mother: "I am astonished Herman wants to go to the Sandwich Islands but I suppose he knows best." [28]

In retrospect it is not at all astonishing. He had come to associate his woes with Pittsfield. The mountains that had been so pleasing to him when he wrote "Hawthorne" now had become oppressive. The two short stories that he wrote just prior to "The Encantadas" show his growing emotional response to his physical surroundings. The Berkshires that rimmed him in become the walls of "Bartleby." The opening description of the hills in "Cock-A-Doodle-Doo!" presents a bleak and ugly mountainous world: "all the humped hills looked like brindled kine in the shivers. The woods were strewn with dry dead boughs," and at a distance runs "a lagging, fever-and-aguish river." [29] It is not as astonishing that Melville wanted to leave this landlocked setting for a green island in the sea as it is that he remained as long as he did in Pittsfield. In the Sandwich Islands he could go back to happier times; there the green days might return. In short, Melville's desire for the consulship at Honolulu was prob-

27. *Herman Melville: A Biography* (Berkeley: University of California Press, 1951), p. 205.
28. Quoted in *The Melville Log*, 1: 476.
29. *Harper's New Monthly Magazine* 8 (1853–54): 77.

ably far stronger and his disappointment in not getting it far keener than has been generally recognized.

The key figure in this episode was Nathaniel Hawthorne. He had known Franklin Pierce in college and had written his campaign biography. When Pierce was elected president, he appointed Hawthorne consul to Liverpool. It is not surprising, then, that the Melville family pinned their hopes on Hawthorne to get the consulate appointment for Herman. On 19 April 1853, when the efforts were just beginning, Maria Melville wrote to her brother Peter about Hawthorne's key role: "Mr. Hawthorne is the personel friend of President Peirce [sic], & the Consul for Liverpool. He has promised to receive those letters [recommending Melville] & speak to the President [.] [H]e will befriend Herman all in his power, and he has a good deal of influence."[30] Although Hawthorne, in his own quiet and conservative way, did try to get the position for Melville, Pierce appointed someone else.

Melville was a man of far greater stature and humanity than to blame Hawthorne openly for his failure to get the consulate position, but such episodes in the lives of even the closest of friends leave their mark. Melville could not have failed to note, either, that Hawthorne's fame had soared since "Hawthorne and His Mosses" (and that he had himself contributed to Hawthorne's fame with this essay), while his own reputation had gone steadily down.[31] Through no fault of either man, their friendship was a series of disappointments for Melville. After

30. Quoted in *The Melville Log*, 1: 469.

31. In writing about Hawthorne in his essay, Melville was also writing about himself, for he makes it clear that in this writer he has just discovered he sees "a man like me." Therefore, when he cries out for America to wake up to its new writers and to recognize that a Hawthorne can equal a Shakespeare, he is pleading for his own fame. He confesses that in praising Hawthorne "I have served and honored myself" (p. 137). During his lifetime, however, he was never to achieve the reputation that Hawthorne enjoyed. See Marvin Fisher, "Portrait of the Artist in America: 'Hawthorne and His Mosses,' " *Southern Review* 11 (1975): 156–166.

Hawthorne moved from Lenox in 1851, they saw little of one another, but Melville the next year heard a story about a long-suffering widow named Agatha Robertson that he felt Hawthorne could and should make into a great work of fiction. In fact, he seemed actually to want to collaborate in some way with Hawthorne on the work and through this means revitalize their waning friendship. Momentarily he recaptured that enthusiasm reflected in the Hawthorne essay. He wrote Hawthorne telling him his ideas about how this story of a woman deserted by her husband should be told and later visited his friend at Concord to talk it over. Their temperaments had always been vastly different, but this meeting brought out that difference sharply. Hawthorne backed away, showed only polite interest in the project, and ended by suggesting that Melville himself undertake it. As with the consulate episode in the following year, Melville took his disappointment silently. He simply wrote to Hawthorne asking him to return all the materials about Agatha which he had sent him.

Never again was Melville to think of Hawthorne with the same hopeful excitement, the same anticipation of a close rewarding friendship. When Melville visited Hawthorne in Liverpool in November of 1856, Hawthorne confessed in his journal that he "felt rather awkward at first; because this is the first time I have met him since my ineffectual attempt to get him a consular appointment from General Pierce." [32] Their last meeting, brief and uneventful, was on Melville's return from the Near East in May of 1857. Eight years later Hawthorne died, and Melville wrote his revealing elegy "Monady," the first stanza of which reads:

> To have known him, to have loved him
> After loneness long;
> And then to be estranged in life,
> And neither in the wrong;

32. *The English Notebooks*, ed. Randall Stewart (New York: Modern Language Association of America, 1941), p. 432.

And now for death to set his seal—
Ease me, a little ease, my song![33]

Later, in the character of Vine in *Clarel*, Melville brooded over this inexplicable man who always seemed to have some powerful secret, but who would never allow anyone to get close enough to learn it.[34]

In Melville's relationship with Hawthorne, then, the turning point was clearly in 1852–53 when Hawthorne showed little interest in the Agatha theme and then failed to secure for Melville the consular position. In the wake of these disappointments came "The Encantadas." Melville did not write "The Encantadas" merely because Hawthorne had disappointed him. On the other hand, that period of great change in Melville's spirits framed by his essay in 1850 and "The Encantadas" in 1854 was inextricably bound up with Hawthorne. In 1854 Melville could not have looked back on the inspiration and creative fire that he felt in 1850 without thinking of the man to whom he dedicated *Moby-Dick*, and to remember Hawthorne

33. Melville transcribed the poem on the title page of his copy of Hawthorne's *Our Old Home* (1863) and later published it in *Timoleon* (1891).

34. Even before they met, Melville seemed convinced that Hawthorne had undergone some form of intense suffering. In "Hawthorne" he wrote: "And we see that suffering, some time or other and in some shape or other,—this only can enable any man to depict it in others" (p. 127). When they became friends, Melville was even more convinced that Hawthorne had some great "secret," and he seemed to anticipate that some day Hawthorne would open his heart to him and reveal it. Part of his great disappointment was that that day never came. Years later when Hawthorne's son Julian visited Melville in New York to ask him questions about his father for a biography he was writing, Melville was at first "disinclined to talk." But he did finally say one thing that Julian Hawthorne found "remarkable": Melville said that "he was convinced Hawthorne had all his life concealed some great secret, which would, were it known, explain all the mysteries of his career." Quoted in *The Melville Log*, 2: 782. For an excellent treatment of Vine as Hawthorne in *Clarel*, see Walter E. Bezanson, ed., *Clarel* (New York: Hendricks House, 1960), xc–c.

and the essay he wrote about him was to be excruciatingly aware of the changes in his own life. Having lost the green world he had discovered when he wrote "Hawthorne," he tried to go to the Sandwich Islands, a move that he hoped would help him regain some of his old enthusiasm. But that was not to be; so what was left was not the bright green isles that he might have written from and about but the barren and baked Galápagos that were but the materialization of his mental state, an hourglass run out.

When "The Encantadas" is read as a contrasting companion piece to "Hawthorne and His Mosses," glimpses and suggestions of Hawthorne the man turn up in several places. In the first and second sketches, for example, the word *moss*, which Melville had played on frequently in his essay to describe Hawthorne, is used in crucial places. It is at the "mossy head of some deep-wooded gorge" that the narrator recalls the creeping tortoises and thinks that he has slept on evilly enchanted ground. He describes the dark "slimy" moss that grows on the shell of tortoises, and he says that in examining a tortoise, he scraped "among the moss." In his imagination he sees the "sooty moss [that] sprouted upon their backs" (p. 314). If he recalls the mosses, he also remembers the Old Manse, for the spectre-tortoise appears to him when he is present in "old-fashioned mansions" (p. 313). Although he would probably not have admitted it, Melville may well have felt a sense of betrayal when he reflected on Hawthorne. The French captain, who betrays Hunilla, is called "a blithe stranger" and his oath to return for Hunilla is "a blithesome promise" (p. 350). Coincidence is possible here, but when Melville wrote these words, he had not been long from his reading of Hawthorne's most recent novel, *The Blithedale Romance*. One wonders, too, if Hawthorne was not on his mind when he wrote in the same sketch, "But they cannot break faith who never plighted it" (p. 351).

The story of Agatha that Hawthorne refused to write may well have been the source, as many critics believe, for the

Hunilla sketch, but not in the way generally suggested.[35] Hunilla's is not a story of patience in the sense Agatha's was. The
Chola widow's tragedy is far greater, and she is transformed by
having been subjected to it. Agatha not only endured; she refused to let her husband's desertion destroy or permanently
disillusion her. Like all else in "The Encantadas," the story of
Agatha—warmly humane and basically optimistic in outlook—
was metamorphosed in the crucible of Melville's suffering into
dark and barren tragedy. And yet, as I mentioned earlier, the
narrator in that particular sketch seems to want to be optimistic
and humanistic. In fact, the narrator's stance is an effective
exaggeration, indeed, almost a parody, of Hawthorne's narrative
method in *The Blithedale Romance*. Despite the narrator's
protestations of fellowship with his shipmates and his avowed
sympathy for humanity, he is a lonely figure, one who would
like to fit into the magnetic chain of humanity but who obviously does not. Like Coverdale, the narrator of *The Blithedale Romance*, he has an indefatigable curiosity that he likes to think of
as sympathy. "It was not curiosity alone," he protests, "but it
seems to me, something different mingled with it, which
prompted me . . . once more [to] gaze slowly around" (p. 354).
He follows along unseen behind the grieving Hunilla as she
goes to her husband's grave, and he watches her as she throws
herself upon it. "She did not see me," he continues, "and I
made no noise, but slid aside, and left the spot" (p. 354). His
surface piousness which overlies skepticism and his particular
brand of ambiguousness—he will not say what the crew of
whalers did to Hunilla—are also more characteristic of Coverdale (and perhaps Hawthorne) than of Melville. Since Haw-

35. See Patricia Lacy, "The Agatha Theme in Melville's Short Stories,"
Texas Studies in English 35 (1956): 96–105; and Charles N. Watson,
Jr., "Melville's Agatha and Hunilla: A Literary Reincarnation," *English
Language Notes* 6 (1968): 114–118. It is particularly difficult to accept
Watson's argument that Melville took the Agatha story and "merely
shifted its setting to the Galápagos and transformed it in substantial
detail into the story of Hunilla" (p. 114).

thorne refused to write the Agatha story, Melville wrote his own dark version of it but in a narrative voice that sounds remarkably like Coverdale-Hawthorne.

Besides Hawthorne, the other two writers that Melville had discussed in his essay of 1850 were Spenser and Shakespeare. He compared the "sweetness" and "sublimity" of Spenser to Hawthorne. In "The Encantadas" he returned to Spenser, but for the qualities opposite to sweetness and sublimity. He chose as epigrams for all ten of the sketches quotations from Spenser that emphasized delusion and ugliness.[36] In "Hawthorne" Shakespeare is praised for his creation of characters like Hamlet, Timon, Lear, and Iago, through whom he "craftily says, or sometimes insinuates, the things we feel to be so terrifically true."[37] For "The Encantadas" Melville chose for a source a character the opposite of Hamlet and Lear, the base and ugly Caliban. The island setting of *The Tempest* becomes Hood's Island among the Galápagos, and the beast-man is now a man-beast called Oberlus. That Melville had Shakespeare in mind when he wrote this sketch is abundantly clear. Oberlus quotes Caliban exactly when he says to himself, "This island's mine by Sycorax my mother" (p. 461). When Prospero calls to Caliban in *The Tempest*, he says, "Come, thou tortoise" (I. ii. 316). Both *The Tempest* and Melville's sketch about Oberlus deal with enchantments, and a later version of *The Tempest*, collaborated on by Davenant and Dryden and printed in 1670, was called *The Tempest, or The Enchanted Island.*

In Melville's vision, then, the green world of 1850 had so

36. Leon Howard was the first to identify the quotations Melville used from Spenser (only a few scattered epigrams in "The Encantadas" come from other writers). "Melville and Spenser—A Note on Criticism," *Modern Language Notes* 46 (1931): 291–292. See also Russell Thomas and D. Mathis Eddy. Howard also discusses the quotations in *Herman Melville: A Biography*. His argument that all the passages that Melville used from Spenser reflect the theme of patience is in my opinion most tenuous.

37. "Hawthorne," p. 130.

completely disappeared by 1854 that it was the unverdured heap that stood out to him everywhere, even in the writers he had once taken the most pleasure in. To place "Hawthorne and His Mosses" side by side with "The Encantadas" is not only to see two sides of the metaphorical tortoise, but also to glimpse the brightest and darkest hours of a man's soul.

SOME SLY ENCHANTER'S SHOW

"The Two Temples"

Chapter 4

The connections between "Bartleby" and "Cock-A-Doodle-Doo!" and between "The Encantadas" and "Hawthorne and His Mosses" reveal a tendency in Melville's short fiction to deal in complementary or contrasting themes. It is even clearer in his work "The Two Temples," the first of three bipartite stories that present contrasting episodes or situations. Unlike the later "Poor Man's Pudding and Rich Man's Crumbs" and "The Paradise of Bachelors and the Tartarus of Maids," however, it was not published during Melville's lifetime. Submitted to *Putnam's* in May 1854, it was rejected because of its scathing portrayal of the congregation of the new and affluent Grace Church in New York City and its warden, Isaac Brown.[1] Both the editor of *Putnam's,* Charles F. Briggs, and the publisher, George Pal-

1. Beryl Rowland points out that many of the details in the story apply to another fashionable church in New York City, Trinity Church at the head of Wall Street. Melville's church is therefore based on not merely Grace Church but Trinity as well. "Grace Church and Melville's Story of 'The Two Temples,' " *Nineteenth-Century Fiction* 28 (1973): 339–346.

mer Putnam, wrote to Melville to explain that their rejection did not represent a negative evaluation of the work. On the contrary, both found it extremely effective. Putnam even offered to reconsider the story if its "point," as he put it, could be "avoided." Melville quietly put away the manuscript. It was found with the two letters after his death.

Briggs and Putnam were understandably hesitant to publish "The Two Temples" because it was a more open attack than Melville had made in his earlier stories upon America's wealthy, hypocritical, Christian churchgoers. Furthermore, it depicted the English lower classes as more charitable and democratic than Melville's own fellow countrymen. These matters constituted the "point" Putnam wanted changed. The affront is direct and brutal, but it is only the surface. The congregation of Grace Church is small game in Melville's cosmic hunting. "The Two Temples" may well be a criticism of America for its failure to live up to its own ideals.[2] But it is a great deal more than that. It is the story of a man who makes a discovery that is much more fundamental than the failure of the American dream.

This man is the narrator, and like Melville's other narrators he must be understood before the surface of the story can be penetrated. The trait most quickly recognizable in him is his unusualness. He does not act like an ordinary person. As the story opens he is exclaiming "too bad" because he has "tramped" three miles from the Battery on a Sunday morning and now cannot get into church. His appearance is shabby, his manner peculiar. Consequently, he is turned away as a suspicious character. This action might have been predicted, for he chose one of the richest, most exclusive churches in New York

2. See Marvin Fisher, "Focus on Herman Melville's 'The Two Temples': The Denegration of the American Dream," in *American Dreams, American Nightmares,* ed. David Madden (Carbondale: Southern Illinois University Press, 1970), 77–86; and Ray B. Browne, *Melville's Drive to Humanism* (Lafayette: Purdue University Studies, 1971), pp. 200–208.

City. If his aim were really to worship as most people do, why did he not select a church more in keeping with his situation, where he would have fitted in? At any rate, his second peculiar act is to try to witness the service by slipping up into the tower of the church and peeping at the congregation and the minister below. He cannot really see much from the little screened window high above, but his imagination supplies what he cannot clearly perceive. Then when he finds himself locked in the tower at the end of the service, he rings the church bell to attract attention. He is discovered and summarily arrested.

His actions in the second half of the story are equally puzzling. He has arrived in London by way of "the paternal, loving town of Philadelphia."[3] There he encountered two women (one of them ill) looking for a physician to accompany them on a tour of Europe. He does not anywhere say that he *is* a physician, but he does get the job. Soon after landing in England he is "very cavalierly dismissed" (p. 158). Although it was not unknown for physicians to take on positions like this and to be left stranded, the episode adds another dimension of mystery to the narrator, for this is the only time that he mentions anything definite about being a doctor.[4]

In fact, through much of the work he uses language that would suggest that he may be a sailor. He calls the lofty steps he ascends in "Temple First," a "Jacob's ladder." His vocabulary is spiced with terms like "streaming," "current," "cut adrift," and "drifted." He talks of "whirlpools," the "Norway Maelstrom," and he says that it is better to "perish mid myriad sharks in mid-Atlantic" than die penniless in London (p. 159). He describes the crowds on the streets of London as "those

3. "The Two Temples," in *The Complete Stories of Herman Melville*, ed. Jay Leyda (New York: Random, 1949), p. 158. All page references to "The Two Temples" are to this edition.

4. Jay Leyda conjectures that Melville based this misadventure of the narrator on a similar event in the life of Dr. Franklin Taylor, cousin of Bayard Taylor, whom Melville had met on the *Southampton* on his way to England in 1849. *Complete Stories*, p. 463.

turbulent tides against which, or borne on irresistibly by which, I had so long been swimming" (p. 160). As he stands in the theater, he is "at the very main-mast-head of all the interior edifice" (p. 164). He thinks of a mariner "drawing up the line, with his long-drawn musical accompaniment" (p. 163). The music from the orchestra below breaks in "showery spray and foam" against "our gallery rail" (p. 163), and when he leaves the theater, he moves as if "borne by that rolling billow" of the music (p. 165).

All that is certain about the narrator's past is that he is a wanderer. Images such as those above that involve the sea and ships underscore his role as drifter and help project his lonely situation. He is moved by the tides of life from one place to another, and is as alone among masses of people as a sailor in the midst of the sea. "Gloom and loneliness" almost overcome him in the church tower (p. 155). So great is his loneliness in London that he thinks of pawning his coat just to get into the theater. He is, in his own words, a "forlorn and fainting wanderer," a drifter with a past of "strange wanderings."

But loneliness has not only driven him over the world. He is afflicted with a "wandering mind" as well as with restless feet. As in the case of Ishmael, another lonely wanderer, he is not always perfectly normal and sane. He speaks of his "momentary lunacy" in the theater as Ishmael speaks of that "strange sort of insanity" that periodically comes over him.[5] Viewing the narrator in this light accounts for that quality in his voice that Newton Arvin somewhat uncertainly referred to as "a real grimness or anger or extremity of feeling."[6] As the lonely wanderer, an Ishmael figure prone to do strange things at times, he is a perennial outsider, and he seems constantly aware of that position. In the first paragraph he complains, "I can't get in." He is "excommunicated," "excluded." Even inside the

5. *Moby-Dick*, ed. Harrison Hayford and Hershel Parker (New York: Norton, 1967), p. 348.
6. *Herman Melville* (New York: Sloane, 1950), p. 236.

church tower, he says, "though an insider in one respect, yet am I but an outsider in another" (p. 151).

To emphasize the narrator's role as outsider, Melville has him portray himself as if he were a ragged child trying to take part in the world of respectable adults. His sneaking up into the church tower is more the act of a curious and deprived boy who has been rejected by the staid adult world than that of an educated adult. When he looks out into the street from the tiny hole he scrapes in the paint of the window, he sees the beadle-faced man "in the act of driving three ragged little boys" out of the church (p. 151). He trembles for his own safety, associating himself with the ragged boys. In the second part of the story a tattered little girl appears outside the theater passing out handbills. She approaches the narrator, but then she seems to recognize that he is much like herself, penniless, and she withdraws. Inside the theater still another ragged youth appears, a boy selling ale. He gives the narrator a cupful. The narrator is quick to notice children, especially poor ones. He comments on "an aproned urchin" here and there in the gallery of the theater. In the church his eye falls on a painting of Madonna and Child. In one of the most significant passages in the story he again seems to identify with an outcast child, for in the Child of the painting he sees "the true" Ishmael (p. 155).

Deeply affected by his situation as a perennial outsider, the narrator wanders from place to place seeking churches to attend. His reason is not so much to worship God as it is to try to find an answer to his terrible loneliness.[7] Since the church is the temple of brotherhood and charity on earth, he feels that an

7. Richard Harter Fogle makes a similar point here: "Melville makes the desire to go to church of a morning, or to while away a lonely evening in a foreign city, the mask of a deeper longing." *Melville's Shorter Tales* (Norman: University of Oklahoma Press, 1960), p. 38. For a reading of "The Two Temples" similar to that of Fogle, see Martin Leonard Pops, *The Melville Archetype* (Kent: Kent State University Press, 1970), pp. 50–51.

answer *ought* to be found there. In "Temple First" he speaks of "these splendid, new-fashioned Gothic Temples" as if he has been in them before and knows his way around. He has also experienced rejection in them before, even in England, because of the "scruples of those fastidious gentry with red gowns and long gilded staves, who guard the portals of the first-class London tabernacles from all profanation of a poor forlorn and fainting wanderer like me. Not inns, but ecclesiastical hotels, where the pews are the rented chambers" (p. 160).

The reason he persists in trying to get into rich churches rather than small humble ones becomes clear as the story progresses, for Melville develops an elaborate tension between poverty and riches as symbolic states. In the mind of the narrator, riches have come to represent the mainstream of life, the world of respectability, the controlling and ruling segment of society. In a modest way the narrator of "Bartleby" belongs to this realm, and he admires those with greater riches than his own. In "The Two Temples" the narrator has been trying to break into that world, to be accepted by it, when the story opens. He bitterly complains that he would have gotten into the fine church if he had been dressed properly and if he could have "tickled the fat-paunched, beadle-faced man's palm with a banknote" (p. 149). Therefore he seems envious of those who are rich because they have perhaps found what he is searching for. He comments on the "sinners" in the church who confess "to such misery as *that*"—their having great possessions—and he himself confesses that he dodges about as if he wanted to get into the "aristocratic circle" of the richly dressed carriage drivers (p. 150).

The narrator thus has been trying to find his answers in the wrong place, in the world's highest temples of respectability. That he will never find them there is suggested by the fact that he is poor, which symbolically means that he perceives life in a way so basically different from those in the church that he can never become a part of the congregation. He is cursed with "poverty," which is really a richness of insight. It causes him to view always from afar, and this distance causes a veil to be cast over all that he sees so that he does not perceive as do the rich.[8] In this symbolic scheme, the richer one is, the more closely he is aligned with the values that society proclaims and the closer he sits to the altar of the temple. The poorer one is, the further removed is he from the altar and therefore from those values so cherished by the world. Ironically, however, the closer one is to the altar, seemingly viewing the service with great clarity, the blinder is he to its meaning (or lack of it), and the farther he is removed from it, as the narrator high up in the tower where in actuality he sees very little, the more aware is he of the nature of the service.

In contrasting riches with poverty, the fat beadle-faced man with the hungry narrator, a pharisaical society with a man reproached and cast out from it as evil, Melville almost certainly had in mind the Beatitudes. In the margin of his own Bible, he marked three vertical lines of emphasis beside the final verse of the following passage from Luke:

Blessed be ye poor: for yours is the kingdom of God.

Blessed are ye that hunger now: for ye shall be filled. Blessed are ye that weep now: for ye shall laugh.

Blessed are ye, when men shall hate you, and when they shall separate you from their company, and shall reproach you, and cast out your name as evil, for the Son of man's sake.

Rejoice ye in that day, and leap for joy: for, behold, your reward is great in heaven: for in the like manner did their fathers unto the prophets.

But woe unto you that are rich! for ye have received your consolation.

---

8. Melville seems almost certainly to have had Hawthorne's story "The Minister's Black Veil" in mind when he has his narrator describe the vision from a small screened window in the church tower: "That wire-woven screen had the effect of casting crape upon all I saw. Only by making allowances for the crape, could I gain a right idea of the scene disclosed" (p. 153).

Woe unto you that are full! for ye shall hunger. Woe unto you that laugh now! for ye shall mourn and weep.

Woe unto you, when all men shall speak well of you! for so did their fathers to the false prophets. (Luke 6:21–26)

Even by the beginning of "Temple Second" the narrator has not learned the truth of the Beatitudes, for he is still yearning for just such a rich temple as the one he was recently thrown out of. In dreary London on a Saturday evening, he wishes that it were Sunday morning so that he might "conciliate some kind female pew-opener, and rest me in some inn-like chapel, upon some stranger's outside bench" (p. 159). When he sees the lights of a theater, he hurries toward the spot, "thinking that it might prove some moral or religious meeting" (p. 159). He exposes his continuing and false idealism with regard to the church and what he hopes to find there when outside the theater he says: "What I wanted was not merely rest, but cheer; the making one of many pleased and pleasing human faces; the getting into a genial humane assembly of my kind; such as, at its best and highest, is to be found in the unified multitude of a devout congregation" (p. 160). But "no such assemblies were accessible that night," and recalling what must have been bitter experiences with churches in the past, he doubts that he could get in even if they were open.

Such is the narrator's state of mind—scarred by being rejected by the world of the church but still seeking fellowship there—when he comes upon the theater in London, which becomes for him the true church: "it was like emerging upon the green enclosure surrounding some Cathedral church" (p. 159). In what should have been the Promised Land for him, his native America and the temple of God, he found but hell. The imagery of "Temple First" strongly supports this point. Suggestions of gold, the heavenly hue, are frequent; even the carriage drivers have gold hatbands. On the ceiling of the church among the frescoes are "gilded clouds." At the end of the service the congregation, "like the general rising at the Resurrection," pour down the "gilded aisles" like "gilded brooks" (p. 154). The keeper of the keys, the beadle-faced man, seems a parody of Saint Peter, who turns the narrator away from the gates of this "heaven," then makes sure that he is tried and punished in a comic Judgment Day episode where the narrator is arrested, jailed, and fined. The rich congregation may have found in their "sumptuous sanctuary" a heaven on earth, but the narrator finds only hell. The air that comes up from the main floor of the church is like that from a furnace. The minister first seems holy in white, but he soon changes his garb to black. The narrator is impressed with the richness of the sanctuary, but on a second look, after the congregation leaves, he is struck with its "desertness." It suddenly changes in his vision from a "Canaan" to a "wilderness" (p. 155).

If the paradise of "Temple First" is but tartarus for the narrator, the tartarus of "Temple Second" proves to be a kind of paradise. The imagery of the two sections is reversed. Sunday becomes Saturday. Morning becomes evening. The Promised Land of America becomes the "monstrous rabblement" of London streets. The opulence of a wealthy congregation becomes the poverty of the English lower classes. Suggestions of hell pervade the setting of "Temple Second," this "Babylonian London." The "fiendish gas-lights" shoot their "Tartarean rays across the muddy, sticky streets," and light up "the pitiless and pitiable scene" (p. 159). Even the Thames, a "muddy Phlegethon," is part of this hellish picture. It is through "Pandemonian lanes" that the narrator makes his way to the second temple. What was gold in the first section of the story now becomes redness and fire. Ironically it is here, in the most hellish and depressing of places and in his most extreme poverty—he is "without a solitary shilling"—that he finds a way to cope with the loneliness and frustration that result from rejection.

The irony mounts as the narrator moves toward that answer in "Temple Second." He undergoes a series of epiphanies that may first appear to support the truth of the Beatitudes and thus to end in a Christian rebirth. What the narrator finds by being poor and hungry, however, what he discovers by being reproached, hated, and rejected by the world, is not the kingdom of God but that of the theater. He finds that the theater is a profoundly meaningful symbol. It is a discovery of such magnitude as to constitute the initial stage of a kind of rebirth that is described in Christian terms but is not Christian in nature. The concept of rebirth held a continuing fascination for Melville, as we saw in "Cock-A-Doodle-Doo!" In every case where a character seemingly is transformed through some deep revelation or experience, however, the rebirth is not so sudden as it may first appear. Rather, it is the culmination of a process slowly taking place for some time in the character and brought to a head through an intense experience which he undergoes. Ahab did not change from a sweet-natured old man into a raving monomaniac at the precise moment when the white whale severed his leg. He had long been a frustrated and rebellious man who had suffered greatly. He had been mysteriously stricken off Cape Horn on an earlier voyage and "lay like dead for three days and nights." He had been involved in some strange but "deadly scrimmage with the Spaniard afore the altar in Santa." He had blasphemously spat into "the silver calabash."[9] He was, in short, ripe for his first encounter with Moby Dick, ready, that is, to find a tangible object to hate when he had psychologically reached the point where he could no longer go on hating merely the abstraction of evil.

Similarly, the narrator of "The Two Temples" is ready to find his revelation in the London theater. Even in the first part of the story, while seeking to be accepted by the world of a rich church congregation, he seems to see and to think in theatrical terms. The beadle-faced man tells him, apparently in answer to his own question or request, that the church has no "galleries." That the narrator is familiar with the famous actors of the day is

9. *Moby-Dick*, p. 87.

apparent when he says that the minister had "a form like the incomparable Talma's" (p. 153). Francois-Joseph Talma (1763–1826) was perhaps the most celebrated French actor of his time. More and more, the religious service seems to the narrator a kind of stage production, "some sly enchanter's show" (p. 153). Without recognizing it, he already sees life through a veil that causes all to appear as a vast play.

He is therefore emotionally and psychologically primed for the events of "Temple Second" that end with his asking himself two fundamental questions (which I shall discuss later) and with a sleepless night. Running through his experiences of this section of the story are slight but significant suggestions of Christian belief and ritual and biblical echoes. For example, the narrator tells of his great longing to get into this "special theater" and of his temptation to do something drastic to gain entry. He adds that he was "providentially" withheld from such action by "a voice unmistakably benevolent" (p. 161). This stranger out of nowhere seems to be able to read his mind and to detect his deep desire to enter the theater, and he offers the narrator the means to enter what turns out to be the place of his discovery. With a hint of Christ's blood sacrifice, the stranger offers him a "plain red ticket," tells him to use it to enter, and explains that he himself is "suddenly called home." With this, the narrator has a debate with himself about the subject of charity. Still trying to follow many of the values of the church congregation, he hesitates to accept charity, but he finally comes around to the position expressed in another passage that Melville had marked in his Bible, I Corinthians 13:4: "Charity suffereth long, and is kind; charity envieth not; charity vaunteth not itself, is not puffed up." Melville's interest in this verse and in those that follow it is indicated by the fact that he has the deaf-mute in *The Confidence-Man* write excerpts from them on his slate. Realizing with somewhat biting irony that it is to charity that he owes everything, even his very life, the narrator enters the theater, where he is reminded of the church he attended in New York. The ticket-taker appears like "some saint in a shrine" despite his surroundings that are more like tartarus than paradise. These Christian references in the story offer valuable clues as to the nature and meaning of the narrator's progress toward a new view of life, but they are not meant to suggest that the narrator becomes a Christian. Indeed, they function ironically to show how the teachings of Christianity can lead to a position far removed from it.

Almost every experience or observation of the narrator inside the theater has overtones of renewal, revelation, or rebirth. As if entering a new way of life, he speaks of his ticket as "my diploma." Some of the sea imagery suggests a revelatory experience. As he describes his progress far up into the "dizzy altitude" of the theater, he uses language that once again suggests a ship at sea: "the rail was low. I thought of deep-sea-leads, and the mariner in the vessel's chains" (p. 163). The language is richly suggestive if considered in the light of Melville's earlier works. As the first chapter of *Moby-Dick* makes clear, Melville perceived a correspondence between water and the murky and treacherous substance of life that hides from us the truth of the universe. "Yes," Ishmael says, "meditation and water are wedded for ever." Man gazes into the water for answers, hoping to see "the ungraspable phantom of life."[10] Figuratively and metaphysically, some of Melville's characters do more than gaze into the sea; they "dive." Through some experience or some revelation, they are carried deep into the ocean that covers all and afterward they are greatly changed.

The experience of the narrator in "The Two Temples" is one of "diving" in this sense. It is related in some ways, though much less intense and disturbing, to that of Pip, the cabin boy in *Moby-Dick*. After Pip jumps from a whale boat, Stubb, who is in command, orders him left in the sea. Although later picked up, Pip is transformed by the experience: "The sea had jeeringly

10. Ibid., pp. 13, 14.

kept his finite body up, but drowned the infinite of his soul. Not drowned entirely, though. Rather carried down alive to wondrous depths where strange shapes of the unwarped primal world glided to and fro before his passive eyes; and . . . Pip saw the multitudinous, God-omnipresent, coral insects, that out of the firmament of waters heaved the colossal orbs . . . and therefore his shipmates called him mad. So man's insanity is heaven's sense." [11] Melville marked still another verse in I Corinthians (3:18) that expresses this paradox of wisdom, which is the essence of the narrator's discovery in "The Two Temples": "Let no man deceive himself. If any man among you seemeth to be wise in this world, let him become a fool, that he may be wise." The narrator of "The Two Temples" is in a figurative sense likewise carried down deep into the sea that covers all. He looks down from his place high in the theater through the "fine-spun, vapory crapey air" and sees the "human firmament below": "And, like beds of glittering coral, through the deep sea of azure smoke, there, far down, I saw the jewelled necks and white sparkling arms of crowds of ladies in the semicirque" (p. 163). Unlike Pip he does not emerge from this sea experience an idiot, but in the end the truth seems to be dawning upon him: cope with the world not by deceiving one-self but by being wise through being a clown or actor, in short, a fool.

After viewing the "beds of glittering coral" below, he checks his "momentary lunacy" and is approached by a youth who in the best tradition of Christian charity invites him to take part in a kind of symbolic communion.[12] It makes no difference to the youth that the narrator is penniless. He offers the narrator a cup of ale in the name of his father who has gone on to the Promised Land of America "a-seekin' of his fortin" (p. 163).

11. Ibid., p. 347.
12. Frederick Asals sees this scene as a parody of the communion. "Satire and Skepticism in *The Two Temples*," *Books at Brown* 24 (1971): 7–18.

The narrator partakes of the ale, and at this point the truth of the Beatitudes (but not their religious significance) unfolds to him: "'Tis not always poverty to be poor, mused I; one may fare well without a penny. A ragged boy may be a prince-like benefactor" (p. 164). The most drastic change in him seems to occur when he takes part in this strange form of communion. His spirits are lifted as if by magic: "Stuff was in that barley malt; a most sweet bitterness in those blessed hops. God bless the glorious boy!" (p. 164). Now he looks about him in the topmost gallery of the theater with delight and an "unhurt eye." From drinking the ale the narrator has become intoxicated with a new vision, and his mood has become one of "sweet bitterness," a term significantly like "genial misanthrope" used in *The Confidence-Man* as a possible description of the great fraud of that novel. The narrator's new pleasure increases when he remembers that the actor on stage is the noted William Charles Macready (1793–1873) about whom he apparently knows much already as he did about Talma. Earlier a minister had reminded the narrator of an actor. Now an actor reminds him of a priest. With the end of the play and the loud and sincere applause of the audience, he is ready to ask the crucial questions: "And hath mere mimicry done this? What is it then to act a part?" (p. 165). Though the story ends before the narrator articulates the answer for himself, it is inherent in the story and clear—the way to deal with the world, the way to gain sincere applause, is through mere mimicry. Earlier, in the first of the story, the narrator had believed the best way to cope with the world was to lay one's heart bare, to present oneself openly and honestly. Locked in the church tower, he says: "in a position of affairs like this, it is generally best, I think, to anticipate discovery, and by magnanimously announcing yourself, forestall an inglorious detection" (p. 156). He announces himself loudly and clearly through ringing the church bell. Biographical implications here—as in several other places in the story—are strong enough to be almost inescapable. Melville may well have been thinking of his own earlier writing, especially *Pierre*, where he "announced" himself—where he wrote too personally and openly for the taste of critics. When he bared his heart it was like the abrasive clang of a huge bell, discordant din to the ear of the public. When they heard, they handled him as the narrator in the story is treated, as if he were a "disturber of the Sunday peace" (p. 157). The world's answer to his openness and honesty in revealing himself was bigoted rejection.

The theater shows the narrator a new way, acting. His admiration for the great actors of the time grows, and he dedicates the story to Sheridan Knowles (1774–1862), a well known Irish-born actor and playwright who was trained as a physician but who gave up healing the sick for playing roles before them. The great actors have become the narrator's heroes because the better the actor the more inscrutable the man and consequently the less able is the world to get to him and destroy him. Melville divided people into those who act and do not realize it, the larger category by far, and those who consciously play roles in their relationship with others but do not deceive themselves, a small and distinctive group who practice the art of noble fraudulence. "The Two Temples" has added significance because it is a meaningful link between two of Melville's greatest novels, *Moby-Dick* and *The Confidence-Man*. In the former, Melville was concerned in great measure with the "covers" of life—the sea, colors, masks. So is he also in "The Two Temples." But beyond *Moby-Dick* he came to shift his concept of the hero from the Titan who tries to strike through the mask to the actor *par excellence* who knowingly puts on new masks. The ultimate actor in his fiction is thus the Confidence Man. In "The Two Temples" we can see with unusual clarity this shift taking place, for a character is portrayed in the very act of making the discovery that acting, not harpooning, is the best revenge.

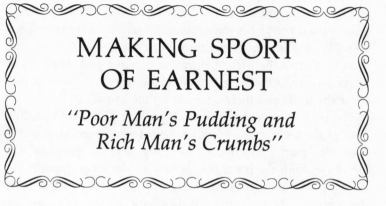

MAKING SPORT
OF EARNEST
"Poor Man's Pudding and Rich Man's Crumbs"

Chapter 5

On the surface "Poor Man's Pudding and Rich Man's Crumbs" is a bland story with nothing specific there to offend as did the sting of "The Two Temples." In the first section of the work, entitled "Picture First," Melville has his narrator visit a pathetic American family caught in the grip of poverty. In "Picture Second" the same narrator recalls a visit to England where he observed how the British feed their poor on the crumbs left over from noblemen's banquets. The subject of poverty is rife with opportunities for outcries against social injustices, but Melville's narrator seems more saddened than outraged in the first section, more fearful than sympathetic in the second.

The contrast implied in the title between poverty and riches never quite comes off in the work. Poverty is depicted in both parts of the story, but the rich are never really seen. The narrator, not a rich man himself, makes a point of questioning his host in the country, a poet named Blandmour, about his finances and finds him only modestly well off: "You are not what might rightly be called a rich man; you have a fair competence; no more" (p. 98).[1] In "Picture Second" the narrator's guide is a simple working man, a minor official of some sort who wears a uniform and knows his way around the various charities of London. Nothing is seen of the royal personages who dined in the great Guildhall the night before the narrator visits the hungry beggars there. All that remains behind are their banners that cover the walls and their scraps from the banquet.

The rich are mere shadows in "Poor Man's Pudding and Rich Man's Crumbs" because Melville did not wish to set class against class. His quarrel was not with the rich, and his sympathy was not always with the poor. But there is a clear set of opposites in the work: real poverty versus false views of it. On a deeper level the contrast is between the human condition, as represented by poverty, and the way the world deals with that condition through the use of labels. Thus the contrast Melville establishes is not so much between the poor and the rich as between poverty of the soul and glibness of the mouth.

"Poor Man's Pudding and Rich Man's Crumbs," then, is very much a story about language. Appropriately, the first voice heard is that of one who ought to use language in its truest form, a poet. But it is soon evident that *poet* when applied to Blandmour is a meaningless label, as are countless others in the work. He is an expert, however, in the use of language as the world uses it. In the opening dialogue between Blandmour and the narrator, such words as *said, say, tell, replied, hear, talking, speak,* and *narrate* are repeatedly used to drive home the extent to which empty words are the province of this poet of the world. He has a label of bright optimism to paste over and thus obscure every black night of life. Although the cold snow falls upon

1. "Poor Man's Pudding and Rich Man's Crumbs" was probably written about the same time as Melville's previous bipartite story, "The Two Temples," but he had better luck placing it. It appeared in *Harper's New Monthly Magazine* 9 (June 1854): 95–101. All references to the story are to this edition.

man, Blandmour labels nature "the blessed almoner" and the snow "Poor Man's Manure." When the labels are questioned, he distorts reality in order to make them fit. His twisting of words even extends to the Bible from which he quotes Psalm 147 to prove that God sends snow "like wool" to keep the ground warm in the winter. This enables him to apply the label "beneficent" to both nature and God. In reality the verse Blandmour quotes is used by the Psalmist not to illustrate God's charity but to prove His power: "He giveth snow like wool; he scattereth the hoarfrost like ashes."

Blandmour's labels are used in order to convince the narrator that a poor man named William Coulter does not have it so bad after all. Coulter, he explains, has not only "Poor Man's Manure," but also "Poor Man's Egg," and "Poor Man's Plaster," all free gifts from nature. As long as such tags can be applied Blandmour can remain blind to what underlies them. As in most of Melville's stories, references to seeing or not seeing are numerous here. Blandmour keeps on hand "Poor Man's Eye-Water" for "weak eyes," which means, ironically, that his labels will enable him to see as does the world and mercifully blind him to the truth. Whenever he might be in danger of seeing deeply, he can apply one of his optimistic labels, such as "Poor Man's Pudding," and it becomes his "eye-water" that transfigures harsh reality.

Blandmour's counterpart in the second part of the work is an Englishman, "some sort of a civic subordinate," who guides the narrator around London. Labels like "charity," "philanthropy," and "kindness," which recur in the first episode of the story, sound their empty chords also in this section. Blandmour and the Englishman are both characterized by their interest in these tags and by their talkativeness. The narrator has several "conversations" with Blandmour, and his guide in England entertains him with his chatty "discourse" on the "noble charities of London." That the civic official wears a uniform is significant, for dress in the story is the visual equivalent of labels. By his dress the narrator himself is tagged a "gentleman," and in the first section of the work the Coulters offer him all the respect due that label by the poor. They refer to him repeatedly as "the gentleman," and they eye his clothing as if it were some sort of official uniform. In "Picture Second" when the narrator's hat becomes crushed and his coat fouled and torn in the Guildhall, his label is destroyed, and a red-gowned official mistakes him for one of the mob of hungry poor. His guide has to *tell* the carriage driver outside the Guildhall that he is a "gentleman" so that he will receive the proper treatment.

The names of "gentlemen and kings" abound in "Picture Second": the Prince Regent, the Czar of Russia, the King of Prussia, the Duke of Wellington, the Lord Mayor of London. Their titles are dear to the uniformed guide, and their labels deck the great Guildhall in the form of flags. If Blandmour is an apologist for nature and a poet of the world justifying God's ways to man, the guide is an apologist for the state. Blandmour sees the poor as recipients of divine and natural charities; the guide sees the poor as equally fortunate because they receive the charity of those highest representatives of the state, the titled nobility. Like Blandmour, the guide cannot or will not see beneath the labels he so cherishes. The world which Melville has created here is saturated with words. Names, titles, and tags continually flow from the loquacious lips of optimists. Words are their tools for making all seem right in heaven, in nature, and in the state. Blandmour and the guide appear overanxious to show how well off the poor are because it is on the question of charity that God, nature, and the state are most vulnerable. If the apologists of the world can say often enough that the Coulters and the hungry rabble are fortunate and if they can supply enough labels to support their view, they will soon believe it themselves. Such is the power of talk.

The narrator not only recognizes the language of labels for what it is, but he also finds a way to cope with its users. That he sees through the hollow designations of Blandmour and his guide in London is clear from his every response to them. Like the narrator of "The Lightning-Rod Man," he toys with the world's spokesmen and leads them on with his questions. He gently probes beneath the labels Blandmour supplies, seemingly learning from the poet but actually uncovering absurdities. He urges Blandmour on, knowing that the more the poet speaks the more he reveals unwittingly his true self. He accepts none of Blandmour's theories about the poor, but his disagreements are good-natured. His method is indirection. He knows that the best way to deal with the Blandmours of the world, the purveyors of talk without truth, is through irony. He calls his host "dear Blandmour," tells him that he likes to hear him talk, begs him to speak on because he wishes to be guided by his "benevolent heart," and at every turn makes fun of him. When Blandmour explains that Coulter's land has had enough snow ("Poor Man's Manure") and that "enough is good as a feast," the narrator replies, "Yes . . . of this damp fare." When Blandmour claims that in addition to being good manure the snow is also good for the eyes and thus serves two distinct ends, the narrator seizes the opportunity to make a joke, playing upon the word *ends* anatomically as he answers, "Very distinct indeed."

He is a confirmed ironist in a world largely incapable of irony. To create irony one must first have the ability to see the difference between appearance and reality. Blandmour makes sure that the one passes for the other. To people like the poet and the English guide the narrator is merely a wit. "Ah! that is your way," Blandmour tells him, "making sport of earnest" (p. 96). The guide simply calls him "merry." What they fail to see is that his merriment, his making sport of earnest, is actually a form of sardonic commentary. He is a man of vision in more areas than the plight of the poor. In fact, he has adopted the way of Herman Melville himself, the arch ironist.

When Melville visited Hawthorne in Liverpool in November of 1856, he made the startling confession that he had "pretty much made up his mind to be annihilated." [2] Through the years most readers, I suspect, have assumed that he meant he no longer hoped for immortality, either as a man or as a writer. But *annihilated* has another meaning which he might well have had in mind, namely "to be silenced." He knew by this time that the language of the world was hollow. That being the case, he saw three courses of action. The first was to join in the chorus of label-makers and become oblivious to the dreadfulness of the human plight. But he knew that for the sensitive and seeing man, the unusual man, this was not a real possibility. That left two alternatives, the first of which was to retain his vision, painful as it might be, and at the same time continue to live in the world and keep intact his sanity. To do that he could not act upon his vision directly. Irony was the one solution. Through irony he could see and have his say but still survive. The other alternative was rebellion and alienation through refusing to participate in any degree in the world of labels. To be annihilated, then, was to become a silent man, a Bartleby, to use language not at all. In his darkest moments, like that with Hawthorne in Liverpool, Melville feared that he would progress from irony to silence knowing that that particular route ended in obsessiveness, bitterness, and destruction. Fortunately he managed to keep himself in the healthier middle way of irony where he could still live in the world but not be a part of its sham.

The struggle to retain the middle ground between the Blandmours and the Bartlebys is the real subject of "Poor Man's Pudding and Rich Man's Crumbs." Perhaps no other narrator comes closer to being Melville himself than the one in this story. One key to the narrator's struggle is in his many references to health. It is a subject always uppermost in his mind, and when-

2. Nathaniel Hawthorne, *The English Notebooks*, ed. Randall Stewart (New York: Modern Language Association of America, 1941), p. 432. Since Hawthorne quotes these words in his notebook, it is likely that the word *annihilated* was Melville's rather than his.

ever it comes up it means mental health, although the narrator makes that clear only indirectly. Who or what the narrator is we never know. All we know is that he seems determined to see as much as he can (and yet be as agreeable as he can in spite of what he sees) and that in the two episodes he recounts he was traveling for his health. He has come to visit Blandmour in the country, he says, "for the benefit of my health" (p. 96). The following summer he visits England because " a sea-voyage was recommended to me by my physician" (p. 98). What he encounters in the country and later in London does not do much for his health; he is so shaken by what he sees that his chief weapon against life, irony, becomes useless for a time, and he is in danger of being consumed first by bitterness and then by fear.

In a general sense the word *health* implies wholesomeness and oneness, the proper cooperating of all parts; it means that all is right in the cyclic functionings of the body whatever that body may be. For Blandmour this definition applies also to all of nature, which he sees as a single body cyclically functioning with a resultant health that on a large scale is like that of his two ruddy children. "Picture First" is pervaded with references to the cycle of life, first as Blandmour sees it and then as the narrator sees it under the influence of his visit to the Coulters. The time of year is March, the end of winter and the beginning of spring. Blandmour speaks of renewal in nature, describing the fertilization of the soil by moisture in terms that unite heaven and earth in a kind of divine intercourse: "Distilling from kind heaven upon the soil, by a gentle penetration it nourishes every clod, ridge, and furrow" (p. 95). Other suggestions of fertility and reproduction emerge as Blandmour talks on of "Poor Man's Manure" and "Poor Man's Egg." Blandmour's is an optimistic synecdochical cosmology. To him the universe is one vast body in which God, nature, and man function as one and in which even an insignificant part, a poor man, gains health and benefits from the perfect health of the whole.

This was, of course, a view Melville encountered many times, not just in such romantic optimists as Emerson and Thoreau,[3] but also in the orthodox Christian teachings upon which he had been raised. Melville, like the narrator of this work, did not believe such a view, but at the same time he knew that it did not pay to dwell on just how false it was. Sometimes, however, he could not help but dwell upon it, for certain experiences laid bare the pathos of the human condition. When this happened, when, for example, he witnessed the human agony in a Liverpool slum, he found himself on the brink of such a disturbing vision of emptiness that it threatened his health.

Such is precisely the case of the narrator when he goes to visit the Coulters. His trip to the Coulters' house and later to the Guildhall are not only literal journeys but also symbolic ones, deep dives to truth, epiphanies. He can deal with Blandmour by telling him that his conversation is "agreeable" and by getting in his ironic digs without the poet's fully realizing what he is doing, but the Coulters represent to him a terrible truth against which even irony is an inadequate weapon. Underlying Blandmour's label of health is the reality of disease, rot, and death. Unhealthiness is everywhere suggested to the narrator as he visits the Coulters. Martha Coulter has "a quiet, fathomless heart-trouble" (p. 96). She washes clothes while she stands upon "a half-rotten, soaked board" placed on the "penetrating damp of the bare ground" (p. 96). She is "pale and chill," and her health is in double jeopardy because she is pregnant. The references early in the story to fertility and reproduction are matched by those here, but now fertility is that of a disease-infested bog and reproduction is that kind which merely perpetuates the disease. Even the furniture of the Coulters seems

---

3. At least two critics believe the story to be an attack on Thoreau and *Walden*. See Ray B. Browne, *Melville's Drive to Humanism* (Lafayette: Purdue University Studies, 1971), pp. 209–210; and Martin Leonard Pops, *The Melville Archetype* (Kent: Kent State University Press, 1970), p. 151.

"enfeebled," and dampness is all pervading—on the window sills, on the walls, and in the rotten wood that burns with the sound of "hissing, and vain sputtering" (p. 96).

What all of this represents to the narrator is clearly more than just how the poor have to live. He sees in them the basic situation of the human race. As in other stories Melville uses poverty here metaphorically to represent man's place in the universe, a pitiful, dominated, maltreated, and enslaved creature caught in the cyclic processes of nature as a victim. What the narrator gets a glimpse of through the Coulters' plight is what drove Bartleby to silence. And it threatens to do the same to the narrator of this story. To visit the poor, as we have seen in other works, is often to "dive," to penetrate beneath labels to the nature of things. To do so, to see the unhealthy rot at the core, is an extremely dangerous experience.

As the narrator looks about in the Coulter cottage he is increasingly disturbed, not only by the dampness and barrenness but also by a book he sees, the only one in the house, "an old volume of Doddridge" (p. 97). Melville probably had in mind *The Rise and Progress of Religion in the Soul* (1745), an extremely popular work of Philip Doddridge (1702–1751), an English minister and hymn writer. A copy of the book was owned by Melville's grandmother. Translated into French, Dutch, German, and other languages and published in several editions in the United States, it was a common sight in homes of the rich and poor alike, passed down from generation to generation. It offered not only spiritual guidance but easy answers to hard questions. Melville would have considered Doddridge, no less than Blandmour, a label-maker who put Christian tags on the afflictions suffered by his readers. Consider such afflictions "blessings," he admonishes his readers, and tells them to praise God for sending troubles, which are "chastisements of love." [4] As the narrator stares at the book and thinks

4. Philip Doddridge, *The Rise and Progress of Religion in the Soul* (Northampton: William Butler, 1804), p. 273.

of Doddridge, he produces a deep sigh, which signals his disturbance of mind and which moves Martha Coulter to say: "You must have walked a long way, sir; you sigh so with weariness" (p. 97). Her remark suggests the depth of the revelation he is experiencing, for it is indeed a long way from the language Blandmour uses to describe the human condition to the reality of that condition. And that distance is made to seem even greater to the narrator because the very words of Doddridge, the world's label-maker, are there in the innermost heart of woe, as if a dark design were made to seem even darker by placing it on a background of light.

Doddridge seems to remind the narrator of Blandmour and his labels, for soon after seeing the book he refers to the poet: "Now if Blandmour were here . . . he would call those green shavings 'Poor Man's Matches,' or 'Poor Man's Tinder,' or some pleasant name of that sort" (p. 97). The Coulters would not use those labels, would not call their humble meal "Poor Man's Pudding," as Martha makes plain to the narrator. But it is important to realize that Melville is not saying that to be poor is to be free of the language of labels. If the Coulters would reject Blandmour's labels, they accept or try to accept those of Doddridge and those supplied by Squire Teamster, who pays William Coulter to chop his wood. All the way up and down the line, from the poorest to the richest, mankind as a general rule finds its opiates, its labels, in order to protect itself from the realization that man is a pitiable and deserted creature in the universe.

The climactic moment in the narrator's first of his two visions, at the Coulters' house, comes when he joins them in eating a meal. Along with references to seeing and to health, images connected with eating function to unite the work artistically and to project the theme. As in "Bartleby," eating is a highly symbolic act in "Poor Man's Pudding and Rich Man's Crumbs." Traditionally, joining together in a meal represents the highest form of community. In Christianity, Jesus's last meal with his disciples has come to be the symbol of communion, the source for one of the most important rituals of the Christian church. The wafer and wine of the communion ritual are understood (literally by some, symbolically by others) to be the body and blood of Christ. His interest in cannibalism ever keen, Melville was fascinated by this concept, and scenes of meals in his fiction are frequently informed with overtones that suggest the communion ceremony without being precisely symbolic of it.[5]

So it is in "Poor Man's Pudding and Rich Man's Crumbs." The word *pudding* means, among other things, the entrails of an animal. When the narrator partakes of the Coulters' "pudding," he is symbolically partaking of them, that is, he is experiencing a form of transubstantiation wherein he tastes the desolation and hopelessness of the life lived by them and realizes his kinship to them. After William Coulter has left to return to his wood cutting, the narrator remains at the table with Martha, and it is at this point that his vision penetrates deepest. Martha tells him first of the death of her two children, and then she confesses that even with the help of Doddridge's words she cannot always believe in the beneficent cycle of life. Death seems terribly final to her; new children would not replace the dead ones. Reproduction seems cruel and meaningless. Her grief is overpowering, and she is intolerably lonely: "Strive how I may to cheer me with thinking of little William and Martha [her dead children] in heaven, and with reading Dr. Doddridge there—still, still does dark grief leak in, just like the rain through our roof. I am left so lonesome now; day after day, all the day long, dear William is gone; and all the damp day long grief drizzles and drizzles down on my soul. But I pray to God to forgive me for this; and for the rest, manage it as well as I may" (p. 98).

5. Overtones of cannibalism occur in *Moby-Dick* when Ishmael describes his eating of that part of the whale called "plum pudding," which tasted, he says, "something as I should conceive a royal cutlet from the thigh of Louis le Gros might have tasted." *Moby-Dick*, ed. Harrison Hayford and Hershel Parker (New York, Norton, 1967), p. 349.

Labels are more absurd than ever at such a moment, and even the narrator's irony, as he painfully realizes, is impotent. Consequently, he becomes for that moment the silent man, plunging his spoon into the pudding and forcing it into his mouth "to stop it." In describing the pudding he is also describing his revelation: "The mouthful of pudding now touched my palate, and touched it with a mouldy, briny taste" (p. 98). The food is unhealthy because the vision is; if the narrator ate more than a mouthful of Poor Man's Pudding, dwelt, that is, upon the poverty of man, he could become as bitter as the pudding: "Bitter and mouldy is the 'Poor Man's Pudding,' groaned I to myself, half choked with but one little mouthful of it, which would hardly go down" (p. 98).

When the narrator leaves Martha Coulter abruptly, realizing the uselessness of words, any words, he is escaping for the sake of his "health." "I could stay no longer," he says, "to hear of sorrows." He takes one final look around him: "Cheerless as it was, and damp, damp, damp—the heavy atmosphere charged with all sorts of incipiences" (p. 98). Once outside he is even more acutely aware of the unhealthiness of the house, "laden down with that peculiar deleterious quality, the height of which —insufferable to some visitants—will be found in a poor-house ward" (p. 98). The unhealthiness of the poor cannot be avoided, but he can avoid remaining there. His return to Blandmour is as symbolic as his visit to the Coulters. He had originally come to Blandmour, the world with all of its blindness and all of its labels, for his health, and now he returns to Blandmour for the same reason. The final lines of "Picture First" constitute a scene of healthfulness, the narrator sitting on Blandmour's comfortable sofa before a blazing fire with one of the poet's ruddy children on his knee. He has rejoined the world, but not as one of the Blandmours, for he will remain the skeptic, and he will avoid labels: "If ever a Rich Man speaks prosperously to me of a Poor Man, I shall set it down as—*I won't mention the word*" (p. 98, italics mine). To do so would be to label. The narrator's hasty retreat from Martha Coulter and his return to the comfort of Blandmour's sheltering arms should not be interpreted, as some critics have claimed, as a "cop-out"[6] any more than Melville's own necessary compromise with the world was treasonous or hypocritical. It was merely a matter of health, of self-preservation, and it was a compromise made on Melville's terms, not the world's.

The view of man's plight which Melville presents in "Picture First" through the Coulters is essentially the same as that depicted in "Bartleby." The vision of "Picture Second" is that of "Benito Cereno." In the first part of the work the narrator sees man as victim. It is a profoundly saddening experience, one which, if repeated, could lead to a rebellious withdrawal like that of Melville's scrivener. In the second section the narrator sees man as savage and bestial, a vision which is not saddening but terrifying. Like Benito Cereno, who is faced repeatedly with the same view of man's basic savagery, the narrator faints. Fortunately, his exposure is much briefer than that of Cereno's, and his "health" is saved. In the first half of this bipartite story, then, the narrator escapes the bitterness and rebellion that makes Bartleby a man of silence; in the second half he escapes the all-pervading and everlasting fear that drives Cereno to silence.

Visiting London in November of 1849, Melville made a point to attend what he called the "Lord Mayor's Show," the procession for the annual dinner given by the Lord Mayor of London. "A most bloated pomp, to be sure," he marked in his journal. From Cheapside, where he observed the procession, he walked down to the Thames and was impressed by the contrast between the "Lord Mayor's Show" and the hellish things he saw around the river: "While on one of the Bridges, the thought struck me

6. See, for example, Marvin Fisher, " 'Poor Man's Pudding': Melville's Meditation on Grace," *American Transcendental Quarterly* 13 (1972): 36—"Whether Melville intended it or not, his narrator would strike a good many alert students of literature as something of a cop-out. He has recognized the inadequacy of charity in each instance and really done nothing about it."

again that a fine thing might be written about a Blue Monday in November London—a city of Dis (Dante's)—clouds of smoke—the damned, etc. . . . Its marks are left upon you." [7]

He waited five years to write that "fine thing" about the "city of Dis," a kind of hell, but that is what he did with "Picture Second." [8] It begins in very much the same fashion as "Picture First" with the narrator (after a few preliminary comments) recounting a conversation about charity which he had with one of the world's label-makers. As before, the narrator is a skeptic and an ironist; he questions his uniformed guide and at times makes sardonic jokes. When they witness on the table of scraps a pheasant with the two breasts gouged out, the guide remarks: "Look! The Prince Regent might have dined off that." "I don't doubt it," replies the narrator. "He is said to be uncommonly fond of the breast" (p. 100.). It is obviously a sexual joke, and there may be others in the work. [9] More significantly, however, it is one of a number of references to cannibalism, which gives this "Pit" seething with "the Lost" much of its horror. What they are observing is, in the narrator's eye, a symbolic cannibalistic feast at which the defeated armies of Napoleon are being consumed. "But where is Napoleon's head in a charger?" the narrator asks. "I should fancy *that* ought to have been the principal dish" (p. 100). As he is squeezed in by the crowd of

7. *Journal of a Visit to London and the Continent by Herman Melville, 1849–1850,* ed. Eleanor Melville Metcalf (Cambridge: Harvard University Press, 1948), p. 25.

8. Newton Arvin found "Picture Second" to have "a startling ferocity of effect that suggests an essay of Elia suddenly turning Zolaesque before one's eyes." *Herman Melville* (New York: Sloane, 1950), p. 236.

9. For an extensive discussion of such possible jokes, see Beryl Rowland, "Sitting Up with a Corpse: Malthus According to Melville in 'Poor Man's Pudding and Rich Man's Crumbs,' " *Journal of American Studies* 6 (1972): 69–83. To date, this is the most ambitious analysis of the story. Rowland's thesis is that various sexual jokes contribute to Melville's treatment of the "pointless role of charity in a Malthusian world" (p. 74). Rowland feels that Melville set his story in 1814 because that was the year Malthus published *Observations on the Effects of the Corn Laws.*

hungry poor, "it was just the same as if I were pressed by a mob of cannibals" (p. 99).

What seems to have gone completely unnoticed is that this grotesque feast in "Picture Second" is a version of what has come to be known as the "Lord's sacrifice" which is mentioned in several places in the biblical Old Testament [10] but given fullest treatment in the thirty-ninth chapter of Ezekiel, one of the strangest and most repulsive passages in the Bible. In Ezekiel's prophecy, Gog, leader of the savage hordes to the north and a personification of cosmic evil, is defeated by God's chosen people of Israel. Afterward, the Lord commands that His victorious people call together all the ravenous beasts of the fields and birds of the air to eat what is left of the slain enemy and to drink their blood: "And, thou, son of man, thus saith the Lord God: Speak unto every feathered fowl, and to every beast of the field, Assemble yourselves, and come; gather yourselves on every side to my sacrifice that I do sacrifice for you, even a great sacrifice upon the mountains of Israel, that ye may eat flesh, and drink blood. Ye shall eat the flesh of the mighty, and drink the blood of the princes of the earth. . . . And ye shall eat fat till ye be full, and drink blood till ye be drunk, of my sacrifice which I have sacrificed for you" (Ezekiel 39: 17–19).

In Melville's story, Napoleon and his forces represent Gog and Magog (which is the land ruled over by Gog). The war that the narrator speaks of in the opening lines is meant to suggest the war in Ezekiel, in which the invading armies of evil are smashed by God's righteous people. But in Ezekiel, the feast

---

10. The feast is described as follows in the book of Revelation: "And I saw an angel standing in the sun; and he cried with a loud voice, saying to all the fowls that fly in the midst of heaven, Come and gather yourselves together unto the supper of the great God, that ye may eat the flesh of kings, and the flesh of captains, and the flesh of mighty men, and the flesh of horses, and of them that sit on them, and the flesh of all men, both free and enslaved, both small and great" (19: 17–18). The Lord's sacrifice is also mentioned in Isa. 34:6ff, Jer. 46:10, and Zeph. 1:7–9.

that follows is not for human beings but for beasts. The Guildhall charity, on the other hand, is not for beasts but for people.
Since they are human beings, their participation in the sacrifice
is cannibalistic (in a symbolic way, although, of course, not
literally). But Melville has not deviated very far from his
biblical model after all. His references to cannibalism suggest
that the frenzied poor in the Guildhall have atavistically re-
gressed so far that they are more animal than human. They are
described as "a mass of lean, famished, ferocious creatures," a
"yelping crowd," a roaring "murderous pack," and howling
"creatures." They are, therefore, frighteningly like the beasts
who are called together to eat the slain enemy. But the implications of the analogy become even more terrifying with the realization that they are simply eating leftovers, that the feast was
originally called for the nobles and the rich. By extension, therefore, the two classes are linked, the poor with the rich. They
have all eaten in the Guildhall in the Lord's sacrifice, and thus
they are *all* beastly and cannibalistic, violent and savage, though
the poor are the ones who show it because they are the ones
who have been driven to it through desperate hunger. What the
narrator sees to his horror is man's natural propensity for violence and savagery under certain conditions. It is what the
Spaniard Cereno sees in Babo and his followers.

Ezekiel prophesied about the defeat of Gog and Magog and
the great sacrificial feast that was to follow in order to show that
"behind everything in the universe (and especially as it relates
to God's people) there is the controlling hand of God, who
orders all things with a view to the ultimate vindication of His
honour among the nations." [11] If Melville used, as I believe he
did, the Lord's sacrifice as a kind of model for the Guildhall
charity, his purpose was far different from Ezekiel's. The scene
is one of grotesque horror, and it results not in praise of God
for His rightness and mercy but in an uncovering of man's basic

11. John B. Taylor, *Ezekiel: An Introduction and Commentary* (London: Tyndale Press, 1969), p. 246.

nature as cannibalistic and savage. Overlooking the scene are the two gigantic effigies, which have stood in the Guildhall in London for centuries, representing Gog and Magog.[12] The guide remarks: "A noble charity, upon the whole, for all that. See, even Gog and Magog yonder, at the other end of the hall, fairly laugh out their delight at the scene" (p. 100). To Melville's narrator Gog and Magog are not laughing because all is right in God's world; they are, in a sense, having the last laugh because they have won. The actions of the hungry mob prove to the narrator that there is more of Gog than God in mankind. The smile on the face of the effigies, therefore, is a smirk of victory. "But don't you think," replies the narrator to his guide, "that the sculptor, whoever he was, carved the laugh too much into a grin—a sort of sardonical grin?" (p. 100).

Disturbed though he is by witnessing this exhibition of human degradation, the narrator manages to remain personally aloof, just as he does in "Picture First" until he is forced to taste the pudding and hear of Martha Coulter's grief. Such a climactic moment also occurs in "Picture Second," and precisely as in the other part of the work, the narrator is defenseless when it comes. Again, an offer of food becomes the symbol whereby the narrator is imaginatively swept into his vision of mankind and becomes a part of what he sees. This macabre form of communion is more violent in the second episode, and his revelation is more terrifying. One of the red-gowned officials takes him to be a member of the hungry mob instead of a "gentleman." "Here, take this pastry, and be thankful that you taste of the same dish with her Grace the Duchess of Devonshire. Graceless ragamuffin, do you hear?" (p. 100). For a terrifying moment he senses that the official is right, that basically they all "taste of the same dish," the Duchess of Devonshire, himself, and the ravenous mob around him. His horror is exemplified in his

12. Statues of Gog and Magog have existed in the Guildhall of London since the time of Henry V. Various legends are attached to them, but in all of them they are alien giants representing savagery and evil.

response: " 'Surely he does not mean *me*,' said I to my guide; 'he has not confounded *me* with the rest' " (p. 100). The guide's answer is more telling than he realizes: "One is known by the company he keeps" (p. 100). The narrator decides to visit no more poor families and no more charities. The company there reminds him too much of his place in the universe.

If the poor in the Guildhall are mere beasts in their ferocious efforts to obtain food, holding up their blue tickets as if to be admitted into this company of the "Lost," they become a raving mob when the food is gone. What little sympathy the narrator had for them now disappears as they swarm over the Guildhall destroying anything in their way: "The yet unglutted mob raised a fierce yell, which wafted the banners like a strong gust, and filled the air with a reek as from sewers. They surged against the tables, broke through all barriers, and billowed over the hall—their bare tossed arms like the dashed ribs of a wreck. It seemed to me as if a sudden impotent fury of fell envy possessed them" (p. 100). Melville had an instinctive disgust for a mob because it represented to him all the evil man is capable of. What the narrator of this work sees in the mob of violent poor is what Melville saw in the mob that made up the draft riots of 1863 in New York City. Melville expressed this view in a poem called "The House-top." The poem comes close to recreating the situation and the vision of the Guildhall scene:

No sleep. The sultriness pervades the air
And binds the brain—a dense oppression, such
As tawny tigers feel in matted shades,
Vexing their blood and making apt for ravage.
Beneath the stars the roofy desert spreads
Vacant as Libya. All is hushed near by.
Yet fitfully from far breaks a mixed surf
Of muffled sound, the Atheist roar of riot.
Yonder, where parching Sirius set in drought,
Balefully glares red Arson—there—and there.
The Town is taken by its rats—ship-rats
And rats of the wharves. All civil charms

And priestly spells which late held hearts in awe—
Fear-bound, subjected to a better sway
Than sway of self; these like a dream dissolve,
And man rebounds whole aeons back in nature.
Hail to the low dull rumble, dull and dead,
And ponderous drag that shakes the wall.
Wise Draco comes, deep in the midnight roll
Of black artillery; he comes, though late;
In code corroborating Calvin's creed
And cynic tyrannies of honest kings;
He comes, nor parlies; and the Town, redeemed,
Gives thanks devout; nor, being thankful, heeds
The grimy slur on the Republic's faith implied,
Which holds that Man is naturally good,
And—more—is Nature's Roman, never to be scourged.[13]

In both works sea imagery is utilized to suggest the force of the mob's surge. In both, the members of the mob are compared to animals. The facade of civilization has crumbled as man's violent and evil nature emerges. Draco, like Gog, has won, and Calvin, who preached the innate depravity of mankind, has by the actions of the mob been proved correct. In the story, London is proud of the red-gowned officials who supervise the Guildhall charity and who are able to cope with the mob,[14]

13. *The Battle-Pieces of Herman Melville*, ed. Hennig Cohen (New York: Yoseloff, 1963), pp. 89–90.

14. The officials of the state in the Guildhall do not share the narrator's consternation. To them this is a regular and expected performance in which the mob is treated a certain way and in turn reacts always predictably. The entire episode strongly resembles the ancient ritual involving a scapegoat. According to Theodor H. Gaster, a scapegoat is "an animal or human being used in public ceremonies to remove the taint or impairment consequent upon sin which, for one reason or other, cannot be saddled upon a particular individual. Such a scapegoat is a means of 'cleansing' a community of collective stain which cannot be wiped out by the normal procedure of individual penitence, restitution, and reform. . . . Its purpose is not, as in the case of surrogates, to transfer punishment or discomfort, but to remove from the body politic any pollution or disaster responsibility for which cannot be precised." *The New Golden Bough by Sir James George Frazer*, ed. Theodor H. Gaster (New York: Criterion, 1959), p. 554. Such is an almost perfect de-

just as America was proud of its soldiers who put down the draft rioters. Few in either country could see the dark implications about mankind hidden in the fact that mobs exist in the first place. The world continues to make its labels, to say that man is naturally good. The narrator of "Poor Man's Pudding and Rich Man's Crumbs" has learned differently. As he comes from the Guildhall, caught up in the mob he abhors, he faints and has to be supported by his guide, who explains to the carriage driver: "He is just from the Guildhall Charity, which accounts for his appearance" (p. 101). His "appearance" is that of a man who has just glimpsed the heart of human darkness.

Since one of the episodes in this work takes place in America and the other in England, and since the narrator himself makes a comparison between the way poverty affects people in the two countries,[15] some readers with good reason have assumed this subject of relative poverty to be Melville's fundamental concern.[16] It is not, but it is nevertheless important in the work for what it contributes to the major theme. Melville set the time back in the story (to 1814)[17] for two reasons, one of which

scription of the situation in this story, where the state, in this case England, feeds the poor, calls it charity, and eases the collective guilt. Plutarch, whom Melville read, describes "a traditional rite of sacrifice" called the "driving out of bulimy [hunger]": a poor man or servant is struck repeatedly and driven out of doors while others shout "Out with Bulimy, in with Wealth and Health." *Plutarch's Moralia*, trans. Paul A. Clement (Cambridge: Harvard University Press, 1969), 8: 495–497.

15. At the end of "Picture First," the narrator states: "The native American poor never lose their delicacy or pride; hence, though unreduced to the physical degradation of the European pauper, they yet suffer more in mind than the poor of any people in the world" (p. 98).

16. According to Richard Harter Fogle, "the general point is that, whatever the differences of time and place, the misery of poverty is, has always been, and will continue to be, the same everywhere." *Melville's Shorter Tales* (Norman: University of Oklahoma Press, 1960), p. 40.

17. Beryl Rowland has pointed out that the banquet Melville describes was actually held on 18 June 1814, but that contrary to what Melville says in the story, Waterloo did not take place until *after* the banquet, in 1815. "Melville's Waterloo in 'Rich Man's Crumbs,'" *Nineteenth-Century Fiction* 25 (1970): 216–221.

(I shall give the second one later) was to place the events in a period in which a debate between the Old and New Worlds was raging about the poor. By the time "Poor Man's Pudding and Rich Man's Crumbs" was actually being written, this controversy had waned, but toward the end of the eighteenth century and in the early years of the nineteenth patriots on both sides of the Atlantic were acting very much as Blandmour and the English guide, as apologists for the way poor people in their respective countries were treated.

One of the main aspects of this debate centered on the question of America's climate. In books, newspapers, and magazines Americans defended the climate as beneficent; both Benjamin Franklin and Thomas Jefferson joined in the chorus. On the other hand, many Europeans seemed to believe that Americans were doomed to a kind of degeneracy because of "the European supposition of America's excessive humidity." [18] Benjamin Franklin energetically attacked this theory, but it persisted. Indeed, it was "supported by the trend in medicine, from 1750 to 1850, which repudiated the contagion theory and was in 'favor of . . . the classical concept of poisons emanating from decaying animal and vegetable materials, transmitted by impure airs and waters.' This seemed to support arguments that America's heavy forests, rank vegetation, improperly cultivated soil, excessive humidity, noxious vapors, and generally unsatisfactory climate must lower animal vitality." Naturally, attention focused on the poor, who would suffer most from such conditions. Their "excessive use of salt pork," for example, was cited as a contributing cause of their problems.[19]

In "Picture First," Melville presents first the view of American apologists. Blandmour states that nature works for, not against, man in America and that the poor man's diet of "pudding" and

18. Edwin T. Martin, *Thomas Jefferson: Scientist* (New York: Collier, 1961), p. 174. Chapter 8, "The New World vs. the Old," in Martin's book is an excellent general treatment of the entire debate.

19. Ibid., p. 170.

salt pork is as delicious and as healthy as any in the world. Then Melville proceeds to show how the European view of American poverty is closer to the truth. He emphasizes dampness throughout, has Mrs. Coulter speak of her two children who have died, apparently, from the impossible conditions they were born into, and stresses the rottenness of their meal of pork and pudding. Every charge made by Europeans against America's "health" seems justified by the picture of the Coulters' way of life.

Melville turns the table in "Picture Second" and introduces now an apologist for the English way of dealing with the poor. Americans were defending themselves by attacking the situation of the poor in Europe. Melville himself had indulged in a scathing criticism of Old World cruelty toward the poor in a chapter in *Redburn*. Numerous other travelers abroad sent back descriptions that made America sound like a paradise in comparison. Madame Octavia Walton LeVert wrote in her *Souvenirs of Travel* (1857) of the incredible splendor of London mansions in juxtaposition to starving beggars:

The ball-room and the dining-room are superb in size and in decorations. Around the house are gardens, with green bowers, radiant flower-beds, and tall trees. The balcony has a fine view of Hyde Park, and its brilliant equipages and dashing horsemen. While I was looking out upon the animated scene, my eyes fell upon a miserable woman in the side-street, just under the wall. Scanty rags hung about her withered form, and two children, as wretched as herself in appearance, clung to her. Their eyes, with that fearful look of starvation in them, were fixed upon the balcony, and their hands clasped in supplication. It was indeed the beggar at the rich man's door. I felt I could read the starving mother's thoughts, as she gazed upon the grandeur before her, and was famished for one crust of bread. It must be more terrible to endure poverty, when plenty is around us, and yet never within the grasp.[20]

The narrator's guide in London tries to make the Guildhall charity sound like a great boon for the poor, but the spectacle of

20. Madame Octavia Walton LeVert, *Souvenirs of Travel* (New York: Carleton, 1871), p. 57.

the hungry mob speaks eloquently for the American view that in England the poor are cruelly neglected and driven to madness partly because of the opulent splendor about them. There is no such separation in the United States between the rich and poor, the democratic American argued with pride.

If "Picture First" supports the English claim that in spite of what Americans say their poor exist in the unhealthiest of situations, eat gross foods, and often die young, "Picture Second" supports the American claim that in spite of what Englishmen say, their poor are so brutally treated that they descend to the levels of beasts and grovel for a crust of bread in the very lap of royal luxury. Who, then, is right? The thrust of Melville's story sweeps us to the inescapable conclusion that both views are right, but not for the reasons each apologist would give. These horrible glimpses of poverty are accurate not merely because they faithfully depict actual conditions in America and England but because they reveal a deeper truth. They show two fundamental aspects of the universal human condition—man as victim in the cosmos and man as animal when circumstances are right to bring out that aspect of his nature.

From the destructiveness of this truth the narrator is saved because he runs away from it, first out of the Coulter cottage and then out of the Guildhall. As he lies "bruised and battered" in his bed in London he asks to be saved from the "noble charities of London" and "equally from the 'Poor Man's Pudding' and the 'Rich Man's Crumbs' " (p. 101). What he is praying for is that he never again be required to partake of the terrible visions that emanated from these two experiences. If one reason for setting the story in the early part of the nineteenth century was to get it closer to the debate about poverty, especially in regard to America's humidity, the other reason was to suggest that these two seemingly insignificant events in the life of the narrator were not insignificant after all because they left an indelible impression upon his mind. He still recalls them and feels compelled to write about them after many years. He came close to seeing too much for his own good: those living metaphors of life that unleash the scorching light of truth and burn out the tongue. He, like Melville himself, escaped to tell about it and to retain the middle way of irony, to continue to cope with labels and label-makers in his own way—by making sport of earnest.

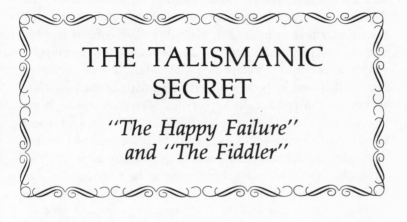

THE TALISMANIC SECRET

"The Happy Failure" and "The Fiddler"

Chapter 6

"The Happy Failure" and "The Fiddler" are so closely related in subject matter that critics have with good reason frequently linked them as companion pieces.[1] They contain both similar and contrasting ingredients that all work together to project a single coherent (but complex) point.[2] The fundamental concern

1. See, for example, Leon Howard, *Herman Melville: A Biography* (Berkeley: University of California Press, 1951), p. 215, and Marvin Fisher, "Melville's 'The Fiddler': Succumbing to the Drummer," *Studies in Short Fiction* 11 (1974): 153.

2. In the second printing of his biography of Melville (1958), Leon Howard added a footnote which indicated his belief that "The Fiddler" should no longer be considered in the Melville canon (p. 216). Francis Wolle had earlier revealed in his biography of Fitz-James O'Brien (1944) that the index to *Harper's* attributed the authorship of "The Fiddler" to O'Brien in the editions of 1875, 1880, and 1885 rather than to Melville. Like most of the stories in *Harper's*, "The Fiddler" did not carry the author's name except in the indexes. Therefore, this seemed valid evidence, and Howard was ready to agree with Wolle. Other scholars of Melville have not been so ready to give up "The Fiddler," however. The Melville Collection of the Houghton Library at Harvard contains two items which seem to prove that the *Harper's* index was in

of these counterstories is what Melville called in *Pierre* "the Talismanic Secret," the principle of happiness, and the role that failure may play in finding it. Melville's basic point is that for one kind of person the talisman can be found; for the other, it simply does not exist except as a momentary illusion. Weighty though this idea is, both stories are essentially comic in nature, and unless this fact is fully appreciated Melville's central theme is easily obscured. In developing his point about happiness and the kind of person who can find it, Melville created protagonists who are diametrical opposites, an ordinary man who discovers happiness when he stops trying to be extraordinary and an extraordinary man who temporarily deceives himself into thinking that he can find the talismanic secret by being merely ordinary.

An air of secrecy prevails in both stories. The narrator's elderly uncle in "The Happy Failure" has worked for ten years on an "apparatus" that no one knows anything about except his black servant, Yorpy. "As yet," the narrator says in the beginning, "the nature of the wonderful experiment remained a mystery to all but the projector" (p. 196).[3] The box containing the apparatus has a "sphinx-like blankness" that "quadrupled the mystery" (p. 196). Secrecy surrounds the meeting at the riverside which the old man sets up with his young nephew, and while they are together the uncle is constantly suspicious that some spy is lurking about. He insists upon rowing ten miles

---

error and that "The Fiddler" is indeed Melville's. The first is a copy of the *Harper's* text of the story which Melville's wife included in a binder collection she kept of his magazine stories. The second is a list of titles in Mrs. Melville's handwriting of Melville's magazine contributions. "The Fiddler" is included. The forthcoming volume of *The Piazza Tales and Other Prose Pieces, 1839–1860*, edited by Merton M. Sealts, Jr., in the Northwestern-Newberry Edition of Melville's works will include "The Fiddler."

3. Page references to both "The Happy Failure" and "The Fiddler" are to the original printings in *Harper's New Monthly Magazine* 9 (July and September 1854): 196–199; 536–539.

upstream so that the apparatus can be tested in secrecy. Even when the narrator discovers the object of the experiment and the nature of the apparatus, the principle of its operation remains a great mystery. How the old man has made the contrivance, how it is supposed to work, why it does not work, why it has taken him so many years to put it together—all this is unknown; the entire story is shot through with references to secrecy, mystery, and stealth. Just as the oblong box that holds the apparatus is "hermetically sealed" and the narrator "padlocked" in his inability to speak out, as he says in one place, so is the talismanic secret of happiness hidden from the uncle until his apparatus fails to operate as planned. At that moment all references to mystery and secrecy disappear. He awakes as if he had been in a dream, a Rip Van Winkle asleep for many years, and he becomes happier than he has ever been before.[4]

The old man's science, which he has practiced for ten years, bears many of the marks of a kind of alchemy, a subject that Melville showed considerable interest in in other places.[5] One of the tales in Hawthorne's *Mosses from an Old Manse* that impressed Melville most, "The Birth-Mark," was about an alchemist.[6] Hawthorne's Aylmer and the old uncle are both in-

4. Melville may have had Irving's story in mind when he wrote "The Happy Failure," whose subtitle is "A Story of the River Hudson." The Hudson River also plays a prominent part in "Rip Van Winkle," and the protagonists of both stories become contented failures after a long sleep (the uncle's, of course, is figurative).

5. For example, Melville mentions one of the prominent alchemists, Paracelsus, a sixteenth-century Swiss, in *Moby-Dick*: "And likewise call to mind that saying of Paracelsus about what it is that maketh the best musk." *Moby-Dick*, ed. Harrison Hayford and Hershel Parker (New York: Norton), p. 343.

6. Aylmer is not called an alchemist in the story, and he is said to have lived in the seventeenth century, somewhat late for the flourishing of alchemy. Nevertheless, his textbooks are those written by such alchemists as Paracelsus, and he is said to be able to accomplish what the alchemists set out to do. That he is less a "man of science" in the modern sense than an alchemist is apparent from his search for perfection and spirituality.

volved in a pursuit beyond their abilities and thus are doomed to failure. One of several passages in "The Birth-Mark" that Melville marked in his copy deals with the subject of failure as reflected in Aylmer's journal. Aylmer has a dark helper-servant, Aminadab, and so does the uncle in Melville's story. Furthermore, Aylmer's laboratory contains an "apparatus" for the purpose of distilling the elixir he gives Georgiana. With the "retorts, tubes, cylinders" and other "apparatus," Aylmer's inner chamber looks like an expanded version of the old uncle's oblong box.[7] But the uncle is no Aylmer. He has none of Aylmer's extraordinary ability. Hawthorne's protagonist is a kind of genius. Melville's is not; he is merely trying—with comedy and a flavoring of pathos—to be one. The nature of his dream and his attitude in pursuing it follow the broad outlines of alchemy because Melville probably wanted to emphasize two things in the uncle's characterization: that he is indulging in an activity that is related more to the secrecy and the hocus-pocus of magic than to actuality and that he stands in comic contrast to the real alchemists, some of whom were men of genius although they could not accomplish their primary aim. That aim was generally to find the means of converting such base matter as lead to a higher form, gold. Similarly, the uncle of Melville's story has put together an apparatus for converting worthless swamps and marshes "into fields more fertile than those of the Genessee" (p. 196).

By discovering the secret of converting matter, the alchemists felt that they would themselves be converted into a higher form of life and would experience wealth, fame, and immortality. Their guiding principles were the thirteen precepts of Hermes Trismegistos, who was revered as the founder of their science,

7. "The Birth-Mark," in *Mosses from an Old Manse*, The Centenary Edition of the Works of Nathaniel Hawthorne, general eds. William Charvat, Roy H. Pearce, C. M. Simpson, vol. 10 (Columbus: Ohio State University Press, 1974): 50.

often called Hermetic Art.[8] The eighth precept reads as follows: "Ascend with the greatest sagacity from the earth to heaven, and then again descend to earth, and unite together the powers of things superior and inferior. Thus you will obtain the glory of the whole world, and obscurity will fly away from you."[9] Such is the goal of the uncle. He talks much of the "glory" of his undertaking and his coming "immortal renown." Before he tries the apparatus out, he turns his eyes toward heaven and speaks of his ten long years of obscurity: "Fame will be the sweeter," he says, "because it comes at the last" (p. 198).

The old man's religiosity, his prayer before the experiment when he says "Sustainer! I glorify Thee," recalls the deep religious convictions of the alchemists. One very necessary condition for the alchemist in all of his experiments was that he be "prayerful and pure of heart."[10] To the alchemists, their esoteric doctrines and practices led to higher religious truths and experiences. For example, they thought of the central act of converting matter as a parallel to the Resurrection.[11] Their aim in finding the talisman, which they called the "Philosopher's Stone" (the young narrator in Melville's story accuses his uncle of having stones in the big box), was a high and noble one, and they termed their attempts "the Great Work." So is the uncle's apparatus "great," as he himself says. His contrivance is the "Great Hydraulic-Hydrostatic Apparatus," and the nephew pleases his uncle by referring to his "great experiment." The box containing the apparatus, like the vessel of the alchemist, is, as I mentioned earlier, "hermetically sealed."

8. For a good general treatment of the history of alchemy, see John Read, *Through Alchemy to Chemistry: A Procession of Ideas and Personalities* (London: G. Bell, 1957).

9. Ibid., p. 23.

10. Ibid., p. 39.

11. According to Read, "There was, indeed, a close connection between alchemical tenets and certain religious doctrines, including the Redemption and the Resurrection" (p. 59).

The central symbol of alchemy was the Ouroboras, a tail-eating serpent, which stood for regeneration. Of all the signs and symbols connected with alchemy, the snake, or serpent, was the commonest. Inside the uncle's box, the narrator sees a coiling mass of pipes and syringes that he describes in terms of a "huge nest of anacondas and adders" (p. 197). Other suggestions of alchemy appear in much of the story. The alchemist, for example, nearly always hired a lowly servant to do his dirty work. In engravings and paintings on the subject of alchemy, such a figure is usually depicted as dark, either from his race or from constant exposure to the smoke of the laboratory. The Negro Yorpy is a comic version of the alchemist's assistant. In "The Birth-Mark" Aylmer is extremely careful to maintain secrecy in his experiments because Hawthorne wanted to follow closely an attitude of the real alchemists. They "regarded their esoteric doctrines as a sacred trust to be maintained as a closed body of knowledge from [the] uninformed." [12] In this way, too, is the old uncle of Melville's story linked with the alchemists. He may have in reality nothing that anyone would want to steal, but he acts as if he has probed deeply into the hidden mysteries of the universe and learned the most profound secrets.

If the uncle finally awakes from a dream world where he has been futilely searching for the talismanic secret through methods described in terms that suggest alchemy, the protagonist (and narrator) of "The Fiddler," Helmstone, moves in the opposite direction during the events of the story, from reality *into* a dream world. As in "The Happy Failure," an atmosphere of secrecy and mystery prevails. Angrily rushing out into a crowded street after reading an unfavorable review of his poetry, Helmstone encounters an acquaintance named Standard who introduces him to a mysterious and puzzling stranger known as Hautboy. The stranger's identity, his background, his occupation, all remain a secret through much of the story. Even his real name

12. Ibid., p. 22.

is kept from Helmstone until the end, when Standard whispers it into his ear. For the reader it remains a mystery, although Standard suggests that his fame at one time was comparable to that of a young English prodigy of the stage, Master Betty.[13]

13. Master Betty's name was William Henry West Betty (1791–1874). He made his first appearance as an actor when he was eleven. He became immediately successful, packing houses wherever he played—Belfast, Edinburgh, or London. He made a great deal of money in the theater and lived well off this fortune. He was adored by royalty and commoner alike. Although he acted until he was thirty-three, public adulation cooled quickly. "He lived for fifty years afterwards in the quiet enjoyment of the large fortune he had so early amassed, and he frankly acknowledged that the enthusiastic admirers of his boyhood had been mistaken." *Dictionary of National Biography.* For an excellent survey of Betty's career and his incredible popularity, see William L. Slout and Sue Rudisill, "The Enigma of the Master Betty Mania," *Journal of Popular Culture* 8 (1974): 81–90. Jay Leyda (*The Complete Stories of Herman Melville,* New York: Random, 1949), pp. 467–468, and William H. Gilman (*Melville's Early Life and Redburn,* New York: New York University Press, 1951), p. 316, both feel that Melville modeled Hautboy on Joseph Burke (1815–1902), another child prodigy who played his violin in England and Ireland, came to America in 1830, performed in New York and other cities, and settled for some years in Albany, New York. Although Leyda and Gilman may have found the source for Hautboy, there is no conclusive evidence to support their guess. Indeed, it may be a mistake to try to pin down a single source, for the truth is that child prodigies were quite numerous and extremely popular during Melville's lifetime. Another likely candidate, one which has not been offered before to my knowledge, is Little Paul Jullien, a boy violinist who performed for great crowds in New York during the fall of 1852. A commentary in the "Editor's Easy Chair" of *Harper's* for November 1852 could have furnished Melville a key thought in his conception of Hautboy: "Little Paul Jullien—a wonder-working boy upon the violin—has carried off, from even the Countess [Countess Rossi], a great many of our autumn bouquets; and it would be curious to anticipate the probable phases of a life which has caught public attention so early, and in so dangerously charming way as his. A violin, at the best, seems an insecure thing to promote manliness; but when, as in this case, it makes a man of a boy, all the manliness it can give is already won" (p. 843). Another possible source for Hautboy is William Henry Marsh, a child musician known as "the Little Drummer." He was the rage of New York City when he performed there in February of 1851, just a few years before Melville wrote "The Fiddler." Coverage of

Helmstone has failed as a young writer to achieve glory and wealth. The conflict that then rages within him is between a militant inclination to blame the world for its insensibility and the temptation to succumb to the hypnotic state that Hautboy offers, one that seems to bring calm acceptance of the world. From the moment when Helmstone first looks at Hautboy, he is aware of some strange appeal: "I was instantly soothed as I gazed on the face of the new acquaintance" (p. 537). Hautboy acts upon him "like magic," and he watches the stranger's every move as they are entertained by a circus clown. The conflict continues, however, one mood reflecting Helmstone's depth and skepticism, the other revealing the influence of Hautboy's appealing optimism: "But much as I gazed upon Hautboy, and much as I admired his air, yet that desperate mood in which I had first rushed from the house had not so entirely departed as not to molest me with momentary returns" (p. 537). He lapses into a sardonic consideration of the world's stupidity, but his eye again falls on the "ruddy radiance of the countenance of Hautboy," and "its clear honest cheeriness disdained my disdain. My intolerant pride was rebuked" with Hautboy's "magic reproof" (p. 537).

In Hautboy, Melville has personified the temptation that sensitive and unusual people feel in moments of severe disappointment, the temptation to play the game of self-deception, to pretend that they can live the quiet and simple life and by accepting things as they are find happiness. Sometimes their disappointment is so keen that the desire for escape is overwhelm-

---

his remarkable performance on the drums and comments on the unusually large crowds that jammed Tripler Hall to see him are to be found in the New York *Daily Tribune* for 19, 21, 22, 25, 26, 28 February and 5 March 1851. If still another child prodigy is needed as a possible source, Master William Saar could be named. He was a pianist who captivated large audiences in New York and elsewhere with his youthful talent. There seems no more reason to accept Burke, then, for Melville's source than others in a large group of popular nineteenth-century prodigies. More than likely Melville did not have a single source in mind.

ing, and they become hypnotized, spellbound, by the call to be just an average person. There is much mystery surrounding Hautboy's characterization in the story because what he represents is a kind of magic spell calling Helmstone out from himself. Still he holds back for a while, the "dark mood" reviving in him, his "spleen" strong.

The climactic point in this conflict between Hautboy's compelling magic and Helmstone's deeper self occurs when they visit Hautboy's apartment and the host performs for his guests. Helmstone has reached the nadir of his bitterness when the fiddler starts his music. Then "miraculously" Helmstone is "transfixed." Symbolic death and resurrection seem to occur as in the case of the uncle in "The Happy Failure," for Helmstone apparently becomes a new man: "All my moody discontent, every vestige of peevishness fled. My whole splenetic soul capitulated to the magical fiddle" (p. 538). Melville heightens the intensity and the magic of Hautboy's spell by suggesting comparison with the myth of Orpheus. As Hautboy "plied the bow of an enchanter," Standard comments, "Something of an Orpheus, ah?" Helmstone's answer indicates the degree of his involvement in this spell: "And I, the charmed Bruin" (p. 538). The enchantment seems complete. Helmstone now believes that he has found the talismanic secret of happiness. Consequently, he tears up all his manuscripts, gives up writing, and becomes a disciple of this spellbinding Orpheus.

In both these stories the main characters seem to find happiness through a right relationship with the ordinary world. When the old uncle in "The Happy Failure" says "All depends on a proper adjustment," he is referring to the testing of his invention (p. 197). But that statement applies also to the secret he appears finally to learn—to get himself into the mainstream of life and to stop trying to row against its currents.[14] The same

14. Both "The Happy Failure" and "The Fiddler" contain water imagery. The uncle speaks first of going against the current of life but later is carried by the river current downstream. Although "The Fid-

thing could be said of what Helmstone learns. A number of critics who have commented on these works feel that this is what Melville wanted to convey—the importance of happiness and the necessity of "proper adjustment" to the world. William Charvat wrote that "The Fiddler" in particular reveals that Melville "had finally come to terms with himself as a writer, in his time, and in America." [15] Richard Harter Fogle appears to agree that in "The Fiddler," as well as in "The Happy Failure," Melville has created a standard of behavior which the "mature man" should work for.[16] Several other critics accept fundamentally this same idea that the uncle and Helmstone (in their final stance) and that Hautboy are all meant to represent an ideal that Melville had come to believe in and to cherish: tranquil acceptance.[17]

Whatever didacticism and optimism there may be in the two stories, however, are severely qualified by the element of comedy. It is difficult to take seriously the lessons offered by characters as ridiculous as the elderly uncle and the fiddling Hautboy. The uncle is a crackpot inventor who has worked ten years on an idiotic machine without once having tested it to see if it will function. Although he is an old man, he acts very much like a petulant child. When the apparatus fails to work, he tears into it in a fit of temper, kicking it like an angry brat. The narrator,

---

dler" is not set near water, Helmstone rushes out of his house and is swept up in the crowd on the street as if he had been caught in an ocean current.

15. "Melville and the Common Reader," *Studies in Bibliography* 12 (1959): 56.

16. *Melville's Shorter Tales* (Norman: University of Oklahoma Press, 1960), p. 60.

17. See Merlin Bowen, *The Long Encounter: Self and Experience in the Writings of Herman Melville* (Chicago: University of Chicago Press, 1960), pp. 236–237; Edward H. Rosenberry, *Melville and the Comic Spirit* (Cambridge: Harvard University Press, 1955), p. 145: James E. Miller, Jr., *A Reader's Guide to Herman Melville* (New York: Noonday, 1962), pp. 167–168; and Ray B. Browne, *Melville's Drive to Humanism* (Lafayette: Purdue University Studies, 1971), pp. 237–242.

his nephew, was at the time only a boy, but as he tells of his reactions to the uncle, he seems more mature. The old man is both sympathetic and comic in his eyes. The boy baits him sometimes; sometimes he pacifies him.[18]

The uncle's role as a comic figure is enhanced by several indirect comparisons in the story between him and extraordinary, and in some cases heroic, people such as the alchemists referred to earlier. For example, he is working on the same kind of invention as that of the archeologist and adventurer, Giovanni Battista Belzoni (1778–1823), a giant of a man who, among other things, discovered the entrance to one of the largest of the Egyptian pyramids. Melville was well acquainted with Belzoni's widely publicized activities as evidenced by the fact that he refers to Belzoni in several different works.[19] Although he is not mentioned by name in "The Happy Failure," Belzoni had invented a hydraulic machine for use on the Nile, an apparatus which was never utilized. Dorothee Finkelstein has observed that Melville's story "had something to do with Belzoni." [20] What it has to do with Belzoni is to suggest a comparison between this extraordinary man and the bumbling, childish uncle. The result is a comic or even farcical effect.

18. Youthfulness in both stories is associated with enchantment. As long as the uncle is pursuing his dream he acts like a child. When he wants someone to meet him at the river to help him, he picks a boy, his nephew. When he thinks he sees someone in a tree, it is a boy. Then he reacts as a child when the apparatus fails. At that point the enchantment is lifted and he then is, as he puts it, an "old man," or, to Yorpy, "old massa." Hautboy's enchantment is also represented in terms of youth. The fiddler seems strangely young. Only his hair indicates that he is not, as his name suggests, a boy. He plays youthful songs like "Yankee Doodle" and enjoys a clown in a circus as a boy would.

19. See Dorothee M. Finkelstein's treatment of Belzoni in Melville's works. *Melville's Orienda* (New Haven: Yale University Press, 1961), pp. 121–144.

20. Ibid., p. 142. See also Richard D. Lynde, "Melville's Success in 'The Happy Failure: A Story of the River Hudson,'" *CLA Journal* 13 (1969): 124.

The uncle is no more a Belzoni than he is a Roman emperor, though the narrator suggests such a comparison. "I am glad, dear uncle," he says, "you have revealed to me at last the nature and end of your great experiment. It is the effectual draining of swamps; an attempt, dear uncle, in which if you do but succeed (as I know you will), you will earn the glory denied to a Roman emperor. He tried to drain the Pontine marsh, but failed" (p. 197). The narrator may have Trajan (A.D. c. 53–117) in mind, who attempted unsuccessfully to drain the Pontine Marshes, but he is merely playing upon the old man's vanity to mention him in the same breath with a Roman emperor. Judging from the narrator's tone, he fully realizes the absurdity of the comparison. The uncle is more like a Prufrock than a Prince Hamlet.

Other such heroic comparisons occur in the story, and they all serve the same comic function as foils.[21] At least two biblical heroes find their way into the work, Samson and Christ. When the narrator first sees the uncle and his servant, they are advancing toward him under the trees, the uncle wiping his brow and Yorpy staggering behind him "with what seemed one of the gates of Gaza on his back" (p. 196). Presently the narrator sees that the "great gate of Gaza" is but an oblong box. Here is a Samson who lets his servant carry his load, or better still, simply a fake giant who would like to be a Samson but does not have the strength for it.[22] The uncle may even have messianic delusions, as suggested by the fact that he associates what he thinks he sees with what Christ once saw: "Ain't that a boy,

21. Lynde makes essentially the same point as I do here and in a few other places, but his conclusions about the story are far different from my own. Lynde feels that the work is "an attack upon commercialism and an indictment of scientific materialism" (p. 119).

22. In Judges 16:1–2, the story is told of Samson spending a night in Gaza and sleeping with a harlot. When the Gazites were informed of Samson's presence in the town, they locked the gates and waited until morning when they intended to kill him. Samson, however, arose at midnight and "took the doors of the gate of the city, and the two posts, and went away with them, bar and all, and put them upon his shoulders, and carried them up to the top of an hill that is before Hebron."

sitting like Zaccheus in yonder tree of the orchard on the other bank?" (p. 197). In Luke 19:1–10, Jesus is described as passing through Jericho when he spotted Zacchaeus, a tax collector, sitting in a sycamore tree. The incident is one of the more humorous events in the life of Christ. Zacchaeus was very short in stature like a boy and consequently unable to see over the heads of all the spectators waiting to see Jesus. So he scampered up into a sycamore tree to get a better look. Jesus saw him, told him to get down, and honored him by taking supper at his house. Though the uncle may have visions of saving the world (from swamps), he can work no miracles, and the Zacchaeuses he sees are not followers waiting to glorify and obey him but mere illusions. There may be a suggestion of still another biblical hero in the story, for the uncle does resemble a farcical John the Baptist, baptizing the world-saving apparatus (which has "entrails" like a human being) in the river. He wades into the river, looks up at the heavens, says a prayer glorifying God, and then gives commands to tip the apparatus into the water, lower and lower ("a *leetle* more! . . . Just a *leetle* more") until it rests "square on its bottom" (p. 198). When they raise it from the water, however, it has not come alive to redeem the world as Christ rising from the Jordan. The old man's fate is not to be that of a martyred hero; his head, alas, will never be brought in upon a platter.

Much of the quiet humor of "The Happy Failure" comes from the difference between what the elderly uncle thinks he is doing and what he is actually doing. He believes that when he opens that hermetically sealed box and turns those anacondas and adders loose upon the world, he will be responsible for a fundamental change in its future. He conceives of himself as a kind of male Pandora operating for good instead of evil.[23] But

23. On 7 November 1851 Hawthorne sent a copy of his new work, *A Wonder Book*, to Melville's young son Malcolm. One of the myths which Hawthorne retold in that book was that of Pandora. Unlike some of the other versions of the myth, Hawthorne's depicts the box, like

he discovers at last that he is no Pandora any more than he is a
Belzoni, a Trajan, a Samson, or a Christ. He has tried to be like
them all, and if the reader has not smiled at his attempts, he
has missed Melville's wry wit. The uncle's characterization is a
minor triumph of comedy. He is Melville's version of an Ahab
who, failing in his pursuit of the great white whale, pitches a
childish fit, has a fainting spell, and then suddenly decides to
turn back from his search and be normal and happy.[24] To do
that, of course, he could not have possessed in the beginning
those heroic and extraordinary qualities of an Ahab.

Hautboy, who some readers feel acts as Melville's spokesman,
is a kind of fiddling Plinlimmon. Just as "The Happy Failure"
is an attenuated and farcical shadow of *Moby-Dick*, so is "The
Fiddler" a brief and comic reflection of *Pierre*. Hautboy, says the
narrator, "assumed a sort of divine and immortal air, like that
of some forever youthful god of Greece" (p. 537). Melville
probably was thinking of a statue he lectured on a few years
later, the Belvedere Apollo in the Vatican. Of Plinlimmon, Melville wrote in *Pierre*: "Though the brow and the beard . . . indicated mature age, yet the blue, bright, but still quiescent eye
offered a very striking contrast. In that eye, the gay immortal
youth Apollo, seemed enshrined." [25] Besides this parallel, Haut-

---

the box in "The Happy Failure," as a very big one. In a comic repetition of the word "box," the uncle says: "Jump in, Yorpy, and hold on
to the box like grim death while I shove off. . . . Mind t'other side of
the box, I say! Do you mean to destroy the box?" (p. 196). Hawthorne
writes of Pandora: "So perseveringly as she did babble about this one
thing! The box; the box; and nothing but the box! It seemed as if the
box were bewitched." "The Paradise of Children," in *A Wonder Book*,
The Centenary Edition of the Works of Nathaniel Hawthorne, general
eds. William Charvat, Roy H. Pearce, C. M. Simpson, vol. 7 (Columbus: Ohio State University Press, 1972): 68.

24. Lynde has also made the point that the uncle resembles Ahab in
a comic sense.

25. *Pierre*, ed. Harrison Hayford, Hershel Parker, and G. Thomas
Tanselle (Evanston and Chicago: Northwestern University Press and
the Newberry Library, 1971): 290.

boy has much in common with Plinlimmon, but as R. K. Gupta has pointed out, it is the similarity in their philosophies which is especially striking.[26] Both are advocates of the "proper adjustment" to the world. That Melville had little sympathy with such a view is everywhere apparent in his works, even his later writings. It is surprising then that numerous critics would mistake Hautboy for an authorial mouthpiece. The name he is given, his jolliness, and his youthful appearance, if nothing else, ought to put the reader on alert that he is not among the figures of depth or heroism in Melville's work. He is a shallow, comic character, playing not a violin but a "fiddle," performing "Yankee Doodle" while sitting on a stool and wearing a bunged hat cocked absurdly on his insipidly virginal head. There is simply no way that Melville could have admired such a character or selected him to convey the burden of authorial message.

Helmstone, in this comedy, plays roughly the part of a Pierre. Both he and Pierre are stormy young men and aspiring writers; both receive adverse responses to their works. Both rush out into the street looking wild and suffering bitter resentment. But there the resemblance ends, for *Pierre* is a tragic novel while "The Fiddler" is a comic short story. Instead of killing his enemies, Helmstone finds Hautboy, whose voice has the high reedy pitch of happiness, and he seems there to discover the talismanic secret.

But there is every indication that he has found only a magic illusion, not permanent happiness. He has escaped from the harshness of the real world into the realm of Hautboy's enchantment. Such a spell cannot last, however, any more than can the uncle's dream of greatness. The uncle finally has to wake up from the alchemy he has indulged in for ten years. In both these stories Melville has created imagery of secrecy, magic, and enchantment. It would seem highly unlikely that in one story, "The Happy Failure," enchantment would stand for self-deception,

26. "Hautboy and Plinlimmon: A Reinterpretation of Melville's 'The Fiddler,'" *American Literature* 43 (1971–72): 437–442.

and in the other work, "The Fiddler," it would suggest the very opposite, truth and fulfillment. Actually enchantment has the same symbolic associations in both stories. It represents in them the same thing as it did in "The Encantadas," foolish illusion. The old uncle is foolish when he dreams he can be a great inventor, and Helmstone is foolish when he thinks that under Hautboy's hynotic spell he can become perfectly adjusted to the ordinary world and gladly accept its ways as Hautboy has done.[27]

A fundamental fact to grasp in reading these two stories, then, is that Melville has given us two very different kinds of men as protagonists. For one, being ordinary is natural. For the other, it is unnatural. Melville's reference to one of Aesop's fables gives the clue for this difference. After his failure and transformation, the uncle in "The Happy Failure" insists that they go back and pick up the box and remaining scraps of the apparatus so that Yorpy can sell them for tobacco money. "Dear massa! dear old massa!" replies the grateful Yorpy, "dat be very fust time in de ten long 'ear yoo hab mention kindly old Yorpy. I tank yoo, dear old massa; I tank yoo so kindly. Yoo is yourself agin in de ten long 'ear" (p. 198). The uncle replies, "Ay, long ears enough . . . . Esopian ears." He means simply that he has made a complete ass of himself but that now he is sensible again. Melville's meaning cuts deeper. In the Aesopian fable of the ass and the lion's skin, an ass is walking down a road when he sees lying there a lion's skin. He is fascinated and de-

27. In *Billy Budd* Captain Vere's dilemma is brought on largely because he, like Helmstone, has been enchanted by the "forms" of the world; thus he is "Starry Vere." As in "The Fiddler" so too in *Billy Budd* the myth of Orpheus is used as a metaphor for this compelling influence of the world. Vere comes to feel that "forms, measured forms, are everything; and that is the import couched in the story of Orpheus with his lyre spellbinding the wild denizens of the wood." *Billy Budd*, ed. Harrison Hayford and Merton M. Sealts, Jr. (Chicago: University of Chicago Press, 1962), p. 128. That the representative of forms ("proper adjustment") in "The Fiddler" should be a musician is therefore highly appropriate since music, such as the tune Hautboy plays, "Yankee Doodle," is form objectified.

cides to see what it feels like to be such a strong and fearful creature. He puts the skin on and continues down the road. Many small animals are frightened but a fox notices that even though he looks like a lion, his two long ass's ears are sticking out. So he tells the would-be king of beasts that he may be dressed up like a lion but that he is still nothing but an ass after all. The moral, of course, is not to try to put on a greatness that is not really in you.[28] In "The Happy Failure" Melville depicts an ass trying to be a lion; in "The Fiddler" he shows a lion trying to be an ass.

In Melville's terms, the old uncle has been trying unsuccessfully to "dive." The apparatus he has created, references to death and suggestions of resurrection, even his servant Yorpy, all function to show that the alchemy he has tried to practice is a gesture toward searching and probing for answers, the kind of pursuit Melville's extraordinary heroes engage in. All fail ultimately in such a search, but his failure is different from theirs. He never really begins because he is not the diving kind; he simply does not have the stature to be a tragic hero. Melville's heroes undergo, it will be remembered, a change to "apotheosis." As they transcend ordinary man they are in a sense reborn. Thus imagery associated with death and resurrection frequently occurs in Melville's works. At the same time that they achieve newness through stature, they die to humanity and become isolated from ordinary life. The uncle would like to achieve apotheosis. His attempt to baptize the box, a symbolic extension of himself, is his grand try for apotheosis.[29] It fails because he is an ass trying to be a lion. Instead of being reborn as a towering hero, great but isolated, he is abruptly thrown back into ordinary life where he belongs. He seems to die physically as

28. *Aesop's Fables*, ed. Frederick Burr Opper (Philadelphia: Lippincott, 1916), p. 193.
29. In chapter 23 of *Moby-Dick*, "The Lee Shore," apotheosis is associated with immersion in water: "Up from the spray of thy ocean-perishing—straight up, leaps thy apotheosis!" (p. 98).

the apparatus fails, and his nephew is alarmed. But he is simply coming back to himself, not becoming a demigod: "Glancing into my uncle's face, I started aghast. It seemed pinched, shriveled into mouldy whiteness, like a mildewed grape" (p. 198). Immediately afterwards he revives, a happy failure and a compassionately humane old man. His change was the direct opposite of apotheosis.

Melville's abilities as a psychological writer are evident here as they were a short time later in "Benito Cereno," where the dark Babo was created as a shadow or double figure to the Spanish captain. Cereno is an ordinary man who is destroyed by a kind of disintegration of personality, the splitting off of his primitive side and then the domination by that aspect of his personality over the rest of him. A similar situation threatens the old uncle, except that the shadow figure, Yorpy, is not savage as in "Benito Cereno." Nevertheless, what his shadow figure represents—cloddish, ordinary humanity—is unacceptable to the uncle.[30] Melville is dealing in psychology as well as in other areas when he shows the old man accepting Yorpy and looking out for his servant's welfare at the end of the story. In order to be happy the uncle must bring his shadow, from which he has been alienated, back into his psyche.[31]

The apparatus which the uncle has created is a tangible mani-

---

30. Just as Babo is approximately the same age as Benito Cereno, so is Yorpy about as old as the old uncle. At one point the uncle asks his nephew, "Am I Yorpy, boy?" (p. 197). In a symbolic sense, he is.

31. "*Shadow* is the term used by Jung to designate the repressed part of the personality." It "often figures in dreams as a rather shadowy other of the same sex as the dreamer that accompanies him in all his dream activity." Also, it "represents the unacceptable part of the personality." M. Esther Harding, *Psychic Energy: Its Source and Goal* (Washington, D.C.: Pantheon Books, 1947), pp. 304–305. Robert A. Clark points out that the shadow figure is often represented by a member of a minority group. "How We Know the Unconscious: The Shadow," in *Six Talks on Jung's Psychology* (Pittsburgh: Boxwood, 1953), p. 34. The definitive treatment of this subject is C. G. Jung's *The Integration of Personality*.

festation of his attempt (feeble though it proves to be) to probe into the secrets of his own existence. As James Baird recognized in his study of primitivistic symbolism, Melville used the anaconda in several places and associated it with the depths of the inner life, the life that underlies all else.[32] The box of anaconda-like pipes, then, suggests some attempt on the part of the uncle to probe the inner resources of his being for answers, some desire to achieve what the alchemist termed the "Great Work," which, if Jung was right, was generally representative of the collective unconscious.[33]

The uncle's failure to probe deeply is, of course, his success. Melville has used such serious means as the suggestive box and the double figure for a comic end. In this way "The Happy Failure" is unique among Melville's works. He has brought to bear the heavy equipment of tragedy and depth psychology for use on a character who has about as much potential for tragic heroism as Uncle Remus. Melville has the old man find peace not because in the author's view it is wrong to search in the howling infinite. What the uncle has to say about achieving fame, wealth, and glory indicates that his search never really left the lee shore, for his aims were shallow from the beginning. The fact of his final happiness is not a comment on the futility of heroic questing; it is a comment on him, the kind of man he is. That he gives up his dream so quickly and reverts to being a "good old man" suggests that he was never anything else but an ass in a lion's skin. "Happiness" is the reward for asses who discover in time that they can never be lions. Melville does not castigate him in the story or even sneer at him. He merely

32. James Baird, *Ishmael* (Baltimore: Johns Hopkins University Press, 1956), pp. 374–377. Although Martin Leonard Pops feels that both "The Happy Failure" and "The Fiddler" are "pathetically unfortunate" stories, his discussion of the former in Jungian terms is most suggestive. *The Melville Archetype* (Kent: Kent State University Press, 1970), pp. 142–144.

33. C. G. Jung, *Psychology and Alchemy*, 2nd ed., trans. R. F. C. Hull (Princeton: Princeton University Press, 1968).

treats him (through the story's narrator) with the bemused tone of an adult describing a child who tried to walk in his father's shoes.

The ass in "The Fiddler" is Hautboy (whose name, incidentally, sounds like a farmer's command to his mule or donkey). With his bunged hat and cheerful disposition he fits the part well. He has long since learned that he should not try to row against the world's current. He has found happiness through proper adjustment. Standard, a perfect representative of the ordinary man of the world, thinks him a genius, but Hautboy knows differently.[34] The fact that he once had fame and fortune does not necessarily mean that he also had true genius. Although several critics have seen Hautboy as a kind of ideal figure, others have rightly questioned this view and pointed out his shallowness.[35] The theme of the story, however, rests not so much with what Melville thought of Hautboy as with what he thought of Helmstone, who is the protagonist. On this issue I must say that I have not seen a single interpretation of "The Fiddler" that places Helmstone in the right perspective. By those critics who feel that Melville admired Hautboy, Helmstone is seen as a character who finds peace through the right values. By those who condemn Hautboy for one reason or another, Helmstone is seen as a shallow writer who gives up the good fight for the good life. In reality he is neither. He has the qualities of a young Melville hero; he is not of the type rep-

34. In his admiration of Hautboy, Standard is reminiscent of Charlie Millthorpe, that amiable average man of *Pierre* who so greatly admires Plinlimmon. Standard addresses Helmstone with the same words as Millthorpe characteristically uses in speaking to Pierre: "my boy."

35. See particularly the following: W. R. Thompson, "Melville's 'The Fiddler': A Study in Dissolution," *Texas Studies in Literature and Language* 2 (1961): 492–500; Maria A. Campbell, "A Quiet Crusade: Melville's Tales of the Fifties," in *Studies in the Minor and Later Works of Melville*, ed. Raymona E. Hull (Hartford: Transcendental Books, 1970), pp. 8–12; R. K. Gupta; Jesse Bier, "Melville's 'The Fiddler' Reconsidered," *American Transcendental Quarterly* 14 (1972): 2–4; and Marvin Fisher.

resented by the uncle in "The Happy Failure" or by Hautboy. He falls under the spell of Hautboy, but Melville suggests through subtle means that that enchantment was temporary.[36]

The proof for this theory resides in three areas: the nature and depth of Helmstone's dark mood and his adverse comments on Hautboy, the nature of his new-found happiness, and the implications of his role as narrator of the story. Helmstone is a young and ambitious poet who places too much emphasis upon public acclaim. The poem he has written about "Cleothemes the Argive" does not please reviewers. Indeed, it sounds like a rather immature performance, and Helmstone seems immature in his response to the adverse criticism of his work. Yet some critics of the story have confused Helmstone's immaturity with shallowness. Marvin Fisher sees Helmstone as "something of a buffoon, a literary clown, ridiculous at best . . . the lowest common denominator of the writer in America."[37] It may well be, as Hershel Parker states, that "Helmstone's poem is no great loss to posterity," but neither would be the poetry of, say, Hawthorne nor for that matter the juvenile efforts of almost any great writer.[38] To dismiss Helmstone as a fraud because he has

36. Indirectly Melville had commented on Hawthorne's enchantment in "The Encantadas." There is some reason to believe that in "The Fiddler" Melville again had Hawthorne in mind when he created Hautboy. The difference in age between the characters in the story is about that between Hawthorne and Melville. Melville, of course, had for a time fallen heavily under Hawthorne's spell. In addition, Hautboy's philosophy of life in terms of accepting both the light and the dark sounds much like a take-off on Hawthorne. Finally, Melville would have read in "The Custom-House" sketch of *The Scarlet Letter* a passage that could have influenced his creation of Hautboy as a fiddler. In taking the point of view of his Puritan ancestors, Hawthorne wrote about himself: "Why, the degenerate fellow might as well have been a fiddler!" *The Scarlet Letter*, The Centenary Edition of the Works of Nathaniel Hawthorne, general eds. William Charvat, Roy H. Pearce, C. M. Simpson, vol. 1 (Columbus: Ohio State University Press, 1962): 10. In Melville's story he may well have become one.

37. Fisher, p. 154.

38. *American Literary Scholarship, 1972,* ed. J. Albert Robbins (Durham: Duke University Press, 1974), p. 52.

written an inferior poem—and I believe there is less evidence
that it is inferior than some critics claim—is to argue by analogy
that Pierre has no depth because he once wrote worthless verse
which he was deceived about.

That Helmstone does have potentiality is suggested by his
dark mood that vies with Hautboy's magic. While in this frame
of mind, Helmstone's thoughts are those that often fill the
minds of characters whom Melville admires. Helmstone begins
to see in his bitterness a truth which Melville was thoroughly
convinced of: when applauded in the forum, one probably has
said something foolish. Helmstone's first appraisal of Hautboy is
astutely correct: "His great good sense is apparent; but great
good sense may exist without sublime endowments. Nay, I take
it, in certain cases, that good sense is simply owing to the absence
of those" (pp. 537–538). These are essentially the words of the
"honest scholar" of *Billy Budd* who wisely observes that people
who have good sense or "knowledge of the world" are not
usually those who have profound insight: "Nay, in an average
man of the world, his constant rubbing with it blunts that finer
spiritual insight indispensable to the understanding of the essential in certain exceptional characters." [39] When Standard suggests that perhaps Hautboy at one time had those sublime
endowments of genius, Helmstone again voices an attitude
characteristic of Melville: "For a genius to get rid of his genius
is as impossible as for a man in the galloping consumption to
get rid of that" (p. 538). This is the Aesopian moral over again,
but now slightly altered: a lion cannot be an ass no matter how
hard he tries. When his "dark mood" and "the spleen"—terms
that are not used in Melville to describe the mental states of
clowns and buffoons—are strongly with him, Helmstone de-
clares that Hautboy is "no pattern" for a person of his magnitude. If this seems like inflated ego, one must remember that

39. *Billy Budd*, p. 75.

none of Melville's rebels are without it. In fact, the hero's keen sense of his own greatness is indispensable to his heroism.

The greatest obstacle to accepting Helmstone as a young man of potential depth and substance is obviously his surrender to Hautboy's spell. But just as inferior juvenilia is no gauge of an author's real genius, so is an embracing of the world's way in a single instance no indication of any permanent alignment. Besides "The Birth-Mark," Melville admired another of Hawthorne's tales in *Mosses from an Old Manse*, "The Artist of the Beautiful." In that story Owen Warland works his way to being a mature artist through a series of failures. When he is in his most profound dejection during this process, he turns to the world with open arms, leaving behind his art and immersing himself in the attitudes and activities of ordinary existence. But he always comes back to his work because of what he is, because a genius cannot get rid of his genius. In the end he finds a way to be an artist and still live in the world, a way of preventing the common world from destroying him without surrendering to it. In "The Fiddler" Melville has in effect recreated a single early episode from the artistic career of an Owen Warland. It should be remembered, too, that the influence of Hautboy is described in the story as a kind of enchantment, an Orpheus spell. Thus by implication it is unreal and transitory just as the uncle's dream was.

It is certainly true that Helmstone is the target of irony in "The Fiddler," but it is his *own* irony.[40] He, after all, is the narrator of the story. The effect is something like that of Redburn speaking in retrospect of his early foolishness. Helmstone subtly indicates the difference between his present position at

---

40. Gupta argues (pp. 440–441) that since Helmstone is a target of irony, he is an unreliable narrator and thus discredited by Melville. Such a view confuses the mode of first-person narration with that of third-person.

the telling of the story and his attitude at the time the events happened when he says about Hautboy: "It was plain, then— *so it seemed at that moment, at least*—that his extraordinary cheerfulness did not arise either from deficiency of feeling or thought" (p. 537, italics mine). When he compares himself at the end to Cicero traveling in the East, he says more than he seems to. According to Plutarch's *Lives,* a source Melville dipped into many times, young Cicero, "full of expectation," felt destined for greatness in the area of political affairs, but when he visited "the god of Delphi," he was told that he should put his talents aside and not pursue that which he felt an affinity for. His silence was temporary, however, for he soon broke loose and proved himself the extraordinary man he was.[41] The god of Delphi was Apollo, with whom Hautboy is associated in "The Fiddler." Just as Cicero is told by Apollo (or his priestess) to stifle his genius, so is Helmstone influenced by Hautboy to tear up his manuscripts and abandon art. But Cicero did not remain under the spell of Apollo and neither does Helmstone.

The telling proof of this point is the story itself. If Hautboy's influence had lasted, if Helmstone had remained a fiddler, he would never have created the story of which he is the narrator. While relating an episode in his life when he was greatly tempted to create no more, he is revealing that once again he has become an artistic creator. This is not to say that he bounces back to his former self. The narrator Helmstone is not the angry young poet Helmstone who read an unfavorable review of his work, dashed it down, and rushed into the street in a state of wildness and desperation. From his stance as narrator of the story it is clear that he has learned the lesson of many another Melville protagonist—and, indeed, a lesson Melville himself learned: if one is endowed with extraordinary insight, he will be

41. Plutarch, *The Lives of the Noble Grecians and Romans,* trans. John Dryden, rev. Arthur Hugh Clough (Chicago: Encyclopaedia Britannica, 1952), pp. 705–706.

embittered if he sets out to please the public and work for fame and glory. He will then be destroyed if in his bitterness he pits himself in open conflict against the world. But neither can he give up his genius and become one of the mass. A lion cannot be an ass, but neither can he be a wild, rampaging lion. He must seem to be tame but nevertheless attack, scarcely detected except by those with unusually keen sight, in the obscurity of darkness. The answer, then—what answer there can be—lies not with the fanged growl but the sardonic grin. The person who narrates "The Fiddler" is a mature artist who knows this though once he did not. The narrator of "The Happy Failure," a kind of observing Ishmael to a comic Ahab, also learns a lesson. Early in his life he saw through his uncle the foolishness of an ordinary man trying to dive. "If the event," he says, "made my uncle a good old man, as he called it, it made me a wise young one. Example did for me the work of experience" (p. 199). This ambiguous statement is one of the few things the narrator of "The Happy Failure" says about himself. His role in the story is subordinate to that of the uncle. Yet his wry wit and skepticism are evident throughout, and it seems likely that he meant two things by his remark: first, that he has learned from the uncle the truth of Aesop's fable, that an ass cannot be a lion by donning the trappings of a lion, and secondly, that he has learned this truth by example rather than by experience because he is not himself an ass. Consequently, he will never be the kind of fool that his uncle has been, but neither will he ever find the talismanic secret of happiness. Both stories, then, define happiness in negative terms. There is no talismanic secret except for the old uncles and the Hautboys of the world. They are fortunate in a way because failure is often the means through which they find that they are just asses and can be contented only by not trying to be anything else. For others there is no talisman, there is no happiness, and if they think for a while that they have found it, they are trying to get a voice out of silence and they are deceived in their innocence.

GRAND IRREGULAR
THUNDER

"The Lightning-Rod Man"

Chapter 7

"The Lightning-Rod Man," published in *Putnam's* for August 1854, is one of Melville's shortest tales and at the same time one of his most deceptive. It consists mainly of a single conversation between a cottage dweller in the mountains (the narrator) and a peddler who visits him during a storm and tries unsuccessfully to sell him a lightning rod. The conversation ends abruptly when the narrator angrily calls the salesman a number of uncomplimentary names and after a brief struggle throws him out. During the time the story was written the area around Pittsfield, Massachusetts, where Melville was living, was subjected to an intensive sales campaign on the part of lightning-rod salesmen. Family tradition has it that Melville was visited by one of these high-pressure Yankee peddlers, whom he ejected with considerable heat.[1] The situation is not without its humor, and the story itself has a light side which is often ignored. Hershel Parker argues convincingly that it belongs to the genre of the

1. Jay Leyda, ed., *The Complete Stories of Herman Melville* (New York, Random, 1949), pp. xxvi–xxvii.

humorous salesman story and points out that it was reprinted in William E. Burton's *Cyclopedia of Wit and Humor* (1858).[2]

Despite its apparent basis in fact and the element of humor, "The Lightning-Rod Man" remains a peculiar and elusive story. The source of its strangeness is not so much the storm that rages in it or even the characterization of the salesman (though admittedly he is not your everyday Fuller Brush Man), but the narrator, who from the first paragraph is a highly unusual person. "What grand irregular thunder," he begins. He glories in grandness and in irregularity. He describes the setting of his cottage as "the Acroceraunian hills" (in ancient Greece near the seat of Jupiter), and he then speaks of the lightning and rain in hyperbolic imagery of war: "the scattered bolts boomed overhead and crashed down among the valleys, every bolt followed by zig-zag irradiations, and swift slants of sharp rain, which audibly rang, like a charge of spear-points, on my low shingled roof" (p. 131).[3] Apparently without the slightest fear of the lightning, he finds his elevation in the mountains during the storm invigorating. "It is far more glorious here than on the plain," he says, and his words seem to vibrate with some hidden meaning (p. 131).

Almost every word he utters seems to have a personal significance to him that underlies the surface. When he hears the salesman's knock at the door, he says: "Who is this that chooses a time of thunder for making calls?" (p. 131). Even this early in the story it is clear that there is thunder within him as well as without. His greeting to the salesman sets the tone of their entire conversation. With odd mock-hospitality he says to a perfect stranger: "Good day, sir. . . . Pray be seated," and he pronounces the raging storm outside "a fine thunder-storm" (p.

2. "Melville's Salesman Story," *Studies in Short Fiction* 1 (1964): 154–158.

3. All page references to "The Lightning-Rod Man" are to *Putnam's Monthly Magazine* 4 (July–December 1854), where the story first appeared, pp. 131–134.

131). If the salesman appears "singular," it should be remembered that *we see him only through the eyes of the narrator,* and his attitude toward the lightning-rod man from the first is condescending or even contemptuous. He insists upon calling the stranger "Jupiter Tonans" (the "thunderer," one of the Roman names for Zeus) because the sample rod that the salesman brings reminds him of a lightning bolt. Although there is an element of playfulness in his approach to the salesman, his humor, like that of the narrator in "Cock-A-Doodle-Doo!," seems born of something other than a joyful disposition: "Sir," he says, bowing with exaggerated courtesy, "have I the honor of a visit from that illustrious god, Jupiter Tonans? So stood he in the Greek statue of old, grasping the lightning bolt. If you be he, or his viceroy, I have to thank you for this noble storm you have brewed among our mountains. Listen: That was a glorious peal. Ah, to a lover of the majestic, it is a good thing to have the Thunderer himself in one's cottage. The thunder grows finer for that. But pray be seated. This old rush-bottomed armchair, I grant, is a poor substitute for your evergreen throne on old Greylock; but, condescend to be seated" (p. 131).

Surprisingly, critics have frequently dealt with this eccentric prospective customer as if he were the very essence of level-headedness and rationality.[4] The peculiarity of his exaggerated greeting to the salesman cannot successfully be explained away as simply good fun or as the ordinary language of a man accustomed to classical allusions.[5] Nor is his language a flaw in style,[6] for the sarcastic and often sardonic tone of the

4. Eric W. Stockton states that "the host shows the inherent human capacities for rationality and intelligence." "A Commentary on Melville's 'The Lightning-Rod Man,' " *Papers of the Michigan Academy of Science, Arts, and Letters* 40 (1955): 323. Hershel Parker asserts that the narrator "retains a quiet reasonableness" (p. 157). To Alan Shusterman the narrator is a "genial" person who is "a standard of humanity" and brotherhood. "Melville's 'The Lightning-Rod Man': A Reading," *Studies in Short Fiction* 9 (1972): 165–174.

5. Parker, p. 157.

6. Stockton, p. 328.

narrator is one of the most essential ingredients in the story. He is playing a cat-and-mouse game with his visitor reminiscent of the situation in Poe's "The Cask of Amontillado." He secretly mocks him and laughs at him, baits him, speaks to him words with private meanings and relishes the salesman's anxieties. When the moment is right, he drops the mask of humble courtesy and attacks with fierceness that can be explained only as the manifestation of some deepseated animosity which he has felt toward the salesman from the beginning but which he has held in check until the salespitch is completed. His outburst is sudden and to the salesman's mind unprovoked: "You pretended envoy extraordinary and minister plenipotentiary to and from Jupiter Tonans, . . . you mere man who come here to put you and your pipestem between clay and sky, do you think that because you can strike a bit of green light from the Leyden jar, that you can thoroughly avert the supernal bolt? Your rod rusts, or breaks, and where are you? Who has empowered you, you Tetzel, to peddle round your indulgences from divine ordinations?" (p. 134).

The narrator of "The Lightning-Rod Man" is not, as some critics have argued, an average man who keeps his head about him while others are losing theirs, but another of Melville's defiant heroes who clearly belongs in the company of Bartleby, Merrymusk, the narrator of "Cock-A-Doodle-Doo!," and Bannadonna in "The Bell-Tower." The conversation between the salesman and the narrator in "The Lightning-Rod Man" resembles that one in "Cock-A-Doodle-Doo!" involving the narrator and the dun. In both instances the hosts insist (but without success) that their "lean" visitors be seated. Both surprise their callers with their abnormal sense of humor. Both refuse to pay money asked of them, and both end the conversation by forcefully ejecting the infuriated visitors.

The salesman's role is, in fact, identical to that of the dun in "Cock-A-Doodle-Doo!" The narrator sees in him the world personified. He comes spreading fear, teaching inflexible rules, and claiming to have all the answers: "*mine* is the only true rod" (p. 132). He has been designated as Melville's satiric portrayal of a particular Calvinistic preacher[7] and more generally as the representative of Christian dogma.[8] He has been called the devil[9] and the personification of fear.[10] It seems to me unlikely that Melville had a single person in mind when he characterized the salesman, and it is unprofitable to limit his meaning to Christian dogma, Satan, or Fear. He can only be seen through the eyes of the narrator, and to him the salesman is all these things because of the way the narrator views the world. Like the creditor in "Cock-A-Doodle-Doo!" the salesman "shoves himself" between the narrator and "salvation." Like the dun in church he makes his appeals in God's name—"For Heaven's sake" and "merciful Heaven," he cries—but he requires a price too great for the narrator to pay: conformity to the ways of the average man.

But if he suggests the narrowness of organized religion, he also stands for all else in the world which repels the narrator. His is the voice of science, proclaiming with bland and false assurance a new day for man in his struggle with nature. His is also the voice of cringing mankind which has established a civilization based largely upon fear of the horrid specter of death, for self-preservation is the strongest human urge. If this man of the world is also depicted in Satanic terms, it is because the narrator has come to think of the mass of people and the way they think in this negative sense. His concept of the world, however, involves an emasculated Satan, not a strong and vigorous one, a Satan that lives by the rules of fear, not by the fire

7. Egbert S. Oliver in his notes to the *Piazza Tales* (New York: Hendricks House, 1948) identifies him as the Reverend John Todd, pastor of the First Church (Congregational) of Pittsfield.

8. Ben D. Kimpel, "Melville's 'The Lightning-Rod Man,'" *American Literature* 16 (1944): 30–32.

9. Stockton, p. 322.

10. Richard Harter Fogle, *Melville's Shorter Tales* (Norman: University of Oklahoma Press, 1960), pp. 57–58.

of rebellion. Thus when the narrator first describes his caller, he depicts him as lean and weak, almost diseased in appearance, his eyes surrounded "by indigo halos" and reflecting an *"innocuous sort of lightning: the gleam without the bolt"* (p. 131, italics mine). The narrator delights in calling him Jupiter Tonans because he envisions him as Jupiter Tonans's opposite: an ineffectual weakling who makes no lightning except that from a Leyden jar and who spends his life religiously following rules of conduct that supposedly protect him against real lightning.

The basic conflict in "The Lightning-Rod Man" is that of a solitary and rebellious man opposing the world of sanity and order. The hero feels affinity not with reason but with willfulness, not with regularity but with uniqueness. His realm is that of grand irregular thunder. In Bartleby's terms, the narrator of "The Lightning-Rod Man" prefers "not to be a little reasonable." In this encounter the salesman is clearly the more reasonable of the two. Although he is afraid of the lightning, he is not, as one critic asserts, hysterical.[11] If each of his statements about lightning rods and lightning is examined closely and measured against scientific fact, it will be seen that he is not dealing in superstitious nonsense; he is a spokesman for accepted scientific views on lightning and the proper functioning of rods. The most dangerous place in a house to stand during a severe thunder-storm is indeed the hearth; theoretically the safest place would be the center of the room. Copper rods are actually better conductors than iron ones, and they should be forked and pointed, as he says. The phenomenon of the returning-stroke, the theory about wet clothing, and the rest are factual or reasonable. His personal precautions against being struck may seem excessive, but they too have a sound grounding in fact.

It is important to understand this in order to grasp the situation which the story presents, the narrator's open and fearless defiance of the world and all its reasonableness. When he re-

11. Parker, p. 157.

fuses to leave his hearth and stand with the salesman in the middle of the room, he is not being calm and sane in the face of contagious fear or baseless superstitions. He is instead showing his independence of the world's governing laws of reason based upon empirical knowledge. Several times the world calls to him from the place of safety, conjures, even commands him to give up his dangerous independent course and take on its ways. But he prefers to remain apart, in the mountains rather than with ordinary mankind on the plain, on the hearth rather than on the lee shore. The salesman is a Plotinus Plinlimmon appealing to the hero to live horologically, by "virtuous expediency," to which the narrator says "No" in thunder.

But the narrator is defying more than the rules by which ordinary humanity lives. Like the other obsessed rebels in Melville's work, he is in open rebellion against all forces threatening his independence, even nature and supernature. His position on the hearth symbolizes more than his rejection of the ways of the average man: it represents his self-imposed exposure to any other force which would dare attempt to violate what he considers his invulnerability. His sudden and violent rebuke of the salesman at the end follows the latter's explaining that he will need only one rod. He tells him what size and price it would be, and then he increases his sales pressure: "Think of being a heap of charred offal," he warns, "like a haltered horse burnt in his stall;—and all in one flash!" (p. 134). The insult is intolerable for two reasons. The first is that the salesman thinks only finitely, in terms of dollars and cents and feet and inches. A rod costing twenty dollars and rising five feet above the roof will "protect twenty feet radius about the rod" (p. 134). He tries to force this formula of pettiness upon the narrator who thinks on a scale too grand for the caller to comprehend. The second and more significant reason is that the salesman has blindly touched the most sensitive nerve in the narrator's makeup. His entire being rebels at the thought of being a plaything of the gods, a haltered horse struck in the stalls. He will not entertain that possibility but will strike back by being free and fearless.

The most telling part of the conversation between the two men is that which deals with the returning-stroke of lightning. Explaining why the main floor of a house is safest in a storm, the salesman says: "Your house is a one-storied house, with an attic and a cellar; this room is between. Hence its comparative safety. Because lightning sometimes passes from the clouds to the earth, and sometimes from the earth to the clouds. Do you comprehend?" (p. 133). The narrator comprehends a great deal more than the other meant, for when the salesman then goes on to describe other safety measures, the narrator returns to the subject: "Something you just said, instead of alarming me, has strangely inspired confidence. . . . You said that sometimes lightning flashes from the earth to the clouds" (p. 133). Without recognizing the appeal in this phenomenon to a man who also strikes back, the salesman answers: "Aye, the returning-stroke, as it is called; when the earth, being overcharged with the fiuid, flashes its supplies upward" (p. 133). Unconsciously, he is describing the rebellious process, the heroic defiance of the narrator, who communicates his enjoyment of the idea of the returning-stroke but not his reasons for enjoying it. "The returning-stroke," he says, "that is, from earth to sky. Better and better" (p. 133). He then makes an appeal—which by this time he knows to be futile—for the caller to join him on the hearth. By echoing the narrator's own words, the salesman ironically illustrates the great difference between the two men: "I am *better* here, and *better* wet" (p. 133, italics mine).

The narrator's fiery anger at the end results, therefore, from a combination of his feeling immense superiority over the frightened salesman and his keen sensitivity to what he considers the visitor's presumption. Trying to sell him a lightning rod, a mere five feet of copper, is in his mind like trying to sell Shakespeare an enrollment in the Famous Writers School or Beethoven beginning lessons on the piano. Here we come to the significance

of the title and to the heart of the story. The title refers obviously to the salesman, but in a deeper and more meaningful sense,
which to my knowledge has not been pointed out, it describes
the narrator. The salesman peddles a protective copper rod
which he carries with him from house to house. But in the narrator's mind he is no *man*. He is less than a man, a representative figure, as I said earlier, of an emasculated world. He
substitutes a symbol of the world's reason and fear for his
manhood. Here again we see Melville using sexual symbolism
for the purpose of conveying the meaning of manhood which
as a concept has the same implications in this story as in "Cock-
A-Doodle-Doo!" The narrator's initial response to the salesman's
knock at the door sets the stage for the development of this
theme: "Why don't he, man-fashion, use the knocker, instead
of making that doleful undertaker's clatter with his fist against
the hollow panel?" (p. 131).

In opposition to the salesman the narrator is a human lightning-rod who exposes himself—as represented by his position on
the hearth—to all the perils of the howling infinite. He will be
truly a man, which is to say in Melville's paradoxical concept
more than an average man (or, as he calls the salesman, a
"mere man") in the ordinary world. He will not rely upon some
trifle produced through the world's degrading ingenuity to protect him from nature and the powers above nature, but he will
daringly expose himself to all the fury of the heavens. If he be
struck, so be it, but in that moment he will have reached the
pinnacle of dignity; he will have achieved apotheosis.[12]

In portraying the narrator as the true lightning-rod man of the
story and in suggesting the nature of the everyday world
through the salesman, Melville again employs a frame of Christian reference as ironic medium in developing a non-Christian
theme. The narrator's allusion at the beginning to the Acroceraunian hills as well as the general concern of the story with

12. In this respect he closely resembles Ahab, who has a scar on his
face and neck that looks as if it is the result of lightning.

thunder and lightning suggests that Melville may have had in mind Chapter 3, Book 6, of Cotton Mather's *Magnalia Christi Americana*, entitled "Ceraunius; Relating Remarkables Done by Thunder." [13] "The Lightning-Rod Man" may appear at first to follow closely certain ideas of "Ceraunius," which consists chiefly of a sermon Mather reprints. Supposedly delivered on 12 September 1694 (Melville has his story take place "early in the month of September"), by a preacher whose name is not given, it is entitled "Brontologia Sacra," the Sacred Lessons of the Thunder.

Mather explains that the preacher had intended to speak on another subject, but when a thunderstorm outside diverted the attention of his congregation, he put aside his prepared text and extemporized upon "the voice of the glorious God in the thunder." Much of what he says parallels on the surface certain aspects of "The Lightning-Rod Man." For example, like Melville's salesman, he talks in "scientific" terms about lightning, but like the narrator he also points toward the glories in it and its supernatural implications. He preaches calmness and, for believers, fearlessness in the face of lightning: "But, I pray, why then should we be *slavishly afraid* of the thunder?" [14] The narrator in Melville's story is saying the same thing. But Mather's preacher also depicts the terrible power of the lightning. "There is nothing able to stand before those lightnings. . . . Castles fall, metals melt; all flies, when 'hot thunder-bolts' are scattered upon them. The very mountains are torn to pieces." [15] Melville's lightning-rod salesman comments that "by nature, there are no castles in thunder-storms" (p. 132), and he later comments on how "all the granite Taconics and Hoosics," mountain ranges of Massachusetts, seem "dashed together like pebbles" (p. 134).

13. Mather's *Magnalia* also plays a prominent part in "The Apple-Tree Table" (1856), where the narrator sits up late in the evening reading it.

14. *Magnalia Christi Americana* (New York: Russell and Russell, 1967), a reprinting of the edition of 1852, 2: 366.

15. Ibid., 367.

Thus Mather's preacher sometimes resembles the narrator with his fearlessness and sometimes the salesman who spreads fear and says he offers the one true salvation. Again the preacher sounds like the narrator when he admonishes his people to watch out for evidences of evil traveling about in storms and ends by saying that the petty contrivances and symbols of mankind will not help against the supernal bolt. A simple faith and "serious thankfulness," he explains, answer man's need in the storm far better than "the crowns of laurels, or the tents of *seal*-leather, whereby some old Emperours counted themselves protected; or than all the amulets of superstition." [16] Yet ironically, the preacher's own house is struck during his sermon. Similarly, the salesman's rod could not protect a church at Criggan which was hit a week before he visits the narrator.

It matters little which way one takes if the sermon in *Magnalia* is to be used for a basis in interpreting "The Lightning-Rod Man." The one leads to the conclusion that Melville is using the salesman as a means of showing the narrowness of Calvinistic dogma as seen in the sermon. The other leads to the opposite conclusion that the narrator exemplifies the truth of Mather's preacher. Both routes lead to a dead end, to another instance of Melville's cock-and-bull technique.[17] For Melville's true concern in utilizing Christian sources and ideas is to show that the obsessed hero has raised self-glorification to the level of a religion. Like Stephen Crane after him Melville realized that

16. Ibid., 372.

17. Leyda, p. xxvii, was probably the first to point to Mather as a possible inspiration for Melville's story. He states that Melville is satirizing the sermon and the rigid Puritan creed through the salesman. Leon Howard takes a similar stand in *Herman Melville: A Biography* (Berkeley, University of California Press, 1951), p. 216. On the other hand, Judith Slater feels that "if Melville used 'Ceraunius,' it was as a basis for the characterization of the narrator." "The Domestic Adventurer in Melville's Tales," *American Literature* 37 (1965): 271. This disagreement thus illustrates how it is possible to use the sermon either way, but unfortunately both are off target.

a "devotee of a mad religion" (to use Crane's words) need not be a Christian, though one of the best ways to depict his fanaticism is through Christian allusions and symbols.[18]

The structure of "The Lightning-Rod Man" suggests still another use of Christian tradition, for it resembles the morality play—or perhaps more accurately, the briefer and simpler moralistic interlude. One character (the narrator) might stand for Everyman, the other (the salesman) Satan, and during the ensuing conversation a symbolic struggle for Everyman's very soul rages. Time and again the devil tempts him to join him, away from the hearth of home and family. Once the good man almost falters, but steps back on the hearth and finally, as if to say, "Get thee behind me, Satan," throws the "false negotiator," the "worm," from his home and proclaims his own staunch faith in a benevolent God.

"The Lightning-Rod Man," however, is no more a Christian temptation scene than it is an exemplification (or even refutation) of the sermon in Mather. What, then, is the meaning of the narrator's avowed faith in God? He seems to make an unequivocal statement of belief: "The hairs of our heads are numbered, and the days of our lives. In thunder as in sunshine, I stand at ease in the hands of my God. False negotiator, away! See, the scroll of the storm is rolled back; the house is unharmed; and in the blue heavens I read in the rainbow, that the Deity will not, of purpose, make war on man's earth" (p. 134). If this is a proclamation of piety it is not consistent with the narrator's characterization to this point. Therefore, Melville either changed the nature of his narrator at the last moment (it is almost as if Ahab had given up the chase and gone to Sunday School), or the words have a deeper and different meaning from that implied on the surface. Although the former is a possibility that cannot definitely be ruled out, the latter is more in keeping

18. Crane's use of the Christian tradition for non-Christian purposes can be seen throughout his works, but *The Red Badge of Courage* offers probably the best example.

with the narrator's general tendency to speak words with private meanings and, further, consistent with Melville's usual practice.

Within this context of Christian piety, the narrator is actually pronouncing his fervor for another kind of religion, the religion of self-glorification. His real meaning might be paraphrased as follows: "There are just so many days to live. Therefore, I will live fully and proudly, free of all shackles and fears, relying upon the god that is within *me*, my own defiant and independent self. Reason and the laws of man are meaningless in a universe where the 'Diety'—whatever that might be— makes thunder as well as sunshine, the shark as well as the lamb. My house had no lightning-rod, but it was not struck. Yet a church had a rod, an innocent servant girl had a rosary, and both were hit. War is made on mankind but it is made with no discernible purpose." [19] It is questionable that the salesman actually understands the implications, but his response is revealing. Instead of calling the narrator a religious fanatic who feels nothing can hurt him because God is his protector, he significantly pronounces him an "impious wretch," and he threatens to "publish" his "infidel notions" (p. 134). Although probably for the wrong reasons, the salesman has correctly labeled the narrator's statement; it is blasphemy in the guise of Christian conviction.

After the narrator ejects the salesman from his house, he goes among his neighbors warning them of the peddler, but apparently he does not communicate his feelings effectively, for "the lightning-rod man still dwells in the land; still travels in storm-time, and drives a brave trade with the fears of man" (p. 134). They do not view the salesman as he does. His is a different vision of everything; he cannot make himself understood by the world, and the world is below his own level of vision, "an entire stranger," as he says of the salesman at the beginning. Consequently, the conversation which he has with the world's representative is a masterpiece of noncommunication. In none of

19. It should be remembered that the narrator early in the story describes the storm in war imagery.

Melville's other stories is there a stronger sense of the separation between the world and the defiant, self-glorifying hero. This effect is intensified by making the encounter take place in conversation, the most common form of communication, but from the first it is clear that there is no meeting of the minds, no congeniality or mutual sense of common humanity; to each, the other's words are hollow or, in the case of the narrator, meaningful in a sense other than that intended. They converse throughout, but their attitudes and emotions are so different that the reader senses a profound gap between them.

Melville has created a conversation which serves as a metaphor for his theme of the obsessed rebel against the world. In the course of some eight pages, he includes no less than forty questions, some of them posed by the salesman, some by the narrator. Most of them are answered in one fashion or the other, but despite the great number of questions and answers exchanged between the two men, there is no real communion. Probably the greatest single impression with which the reader finishes this story is that of the insurmountable differences between the two characters. As always, Melville is deeply concerned with the phenomenon of perception. Each of the two characters sees himself as righteous and the other as Satanic. The narrator's view of the salesman is that of an ineffectual sniveling Satan and of himself as the equal of any gods. Ironically the salesman may likewise see his host as the devil, for he objects to being called by the "pagan" name, Jupiter Tonans, and accuses the narrator of being "profane in this time of terror" (p. 132). He charges him with impiety and with having "infidel notions." Furthermore, he apparently believes that the narrator is trying to tempt him to his destruction by inviting him to the hearth. Recalling Satan's temptation of Christ, he answers the narrator, "Not for worlds" (p. 131). Later he suggests Christ's crucifixion when he remarks, "The skies blacken—it is dusk at noon" (p. 133). Melville's purpose is not to present one character as good and the other as evil but to show through the ironic use of a Christian frame of reference how each views the other. The world cannot understand a lightning-rod *man*. On the other hand, he cannot clearly and understandingly perceive the ordinary world, for he has placed himself proud and erect upon such heights that he no longer dwells upon the plain of common humanity.

TRAVELERS
IN LAPLAND
"The Paradise of Bachelors and the
Tartarus of Maids"

Chapter 8

Melville's depiction of a kind of heaven and hell in "The Paradise of Bachelors and the Tartarus of Maids," which he published in *Harper's* in April 1855, owes a great deal to Boccaccio's *Decameron* and Dante's *Inferno*. The "paradise" described in the first section of this bipartite story is of that kind seen in the *Decameron*, and the "tartarus" of the second section resembles Dante's ninth circle of the *Inferno*, a frozen hell. Ten people in Boccaccio's work escape the plague raging in Florence in 1348 by sequestering themselves in villas with lovely grounds and gardens. There they live an elegant life, enjoying fine dining and the entertaining stories that they relate to each other. They experience a pleasant variety in their activities so as not to become bored, but it is variety within a highly ordered arrangement, to which the structure of the work itself attests. Each day, for example, is devoted to some special type of story, and each day ends with a song. In the midst of suffering and ugliness, theirs is an Eden where they eat well, stroll about in their gardens, engage in dances and songs, and listen with good humor to the charming stories of their companions.

The bachelors of the Temple in London live a similar existence. Their buildings are hidden away from the street and surrounded by walks and gardens. Going there, the narrator of the story says, "is like stealing from a heated plain into some cool, deep glen, shady among harboring hills" (p. 670).[1] The outside world is sick and careworn, like plague-ridden Florence, but here the bachelors find good health and warm companionship. Melville thus stresses, at least on the surface, the same points as Boccaccio, the gaiety of this group escaping the pain of the world, the pleasantness of their surroundings as opposed to the ugliness outside, their good health as opposed to pain and sickness without, and finally their envelopment in an orderly system which allows them variety while protecting them from chaos. That Melville had Boccaccio's great work in mind is made clear when after the bachelors have finished their meal the narrator comments that some of them were "going to their neighboring chambers to turn over the Decameron ere retiring for the night" (p. 673).

The Devil's Dungeon, setting for a paper mill that the narrator visits in the second part of the work, bears a striking resemblance to Dante's inferno, which is hopper shaped. At the bottom of the inferno, the very floor of hell, is the frozen lake Cocytus. The cold, white tartarus of Melville is entered from

1. "The Paradise of Bachelors and the Tartarus of Maids," *Harper's New Monthly Magazine* 10 (April 1855): 670–678. All page references to the story are to this, the first printing. The two episodes that comprise the work are both derived from Melville's experience. While in London in December 1849, he dined as the guest of Robert Francis Cooke (the R. F. C. of the story) in Elm Court, Temple, and recorded this pleasant event in his journal. During the winter of 1851, he took a sleigh ride to the Carson paper mill about five miles from Pittsfield near Dalton, Mass. He commented on this errand to buy paper in a letter of 12 February 1851 to Evert Duyckinck. See E. H. Eby, "Herman Melville's 'Tartarus of Maids,'" *Modern Language Quarterly* 1 (1940): 95–100.

what is called in the story "a Dantean gateway," and the paper mill, which represents a hell-on-earth for all of the silent, blank girls who work there like zombies, is within a "hopper-shaped hollow, far sunk among many Plutonian, shaggy-wooded mountains" (p. 673). The narrator visits this hell like Dante visiting the inferno, and like Dante he faints—or nearly faints—because of what he sees. He, too, has a guide, not Virgil, to be sure, but a lad named Cupid.

The relationship that the first section of this bipartite story, the "Paradise," bears to the second, the "Tartarus," is basically the same as that which Boccaccio's work bears to Dante's. John Addington Symonds articulated this relationship eloquently in 1895: "The great poem and the great prose fiction of the fourteenth century are opposed to each other as Masque and Antimasque. The world of the 'Decameron' is not an inverted world, like that of Aristophanes. *It does not antithesise Dante's world* by turning it upside down. *It is simply the same world surveyed from another side*, unaltered, uninverted, but viewed in the superficies, presented in the concrete. Dante . . . attempted a revelation of what underlies appearances. . . . Boccaccio deals with appearances, and does not seek to penetrate below experience. He paints the world as world, the flesh as flesh, nature as nature . . ." (italics mine).[2]

Almost every critic who has written about "The Paradise of Bachelors and the Tartarus of Maids" has apparently seen it as a study in contrast: the old world as opposed to the new, riches versus poverty, happiness versus suffering, the life of men as opposed to that of women, and so forth. Despite obvious differences in the two worlds represented, Melville's point was essentially the one Symonds makes about Boccaccio and Dante— the white world of the blank maidens is *not* a different realm from that of the merry bachelors; it is the same world seen from

2. *Giovanni Boccaccio as Man and Author* (London: John C. Ninno, 1895), pp. 85–86.

another angle. It is the vision of a Dante that goes below the surface of appearances.

"The Paradise of Bachelors and the Tartarus of Maids," then, echoes to a large extent Melville's insistence in "Poor Man's Pudding and Rich Man's Crumbs" that bleakness underlies the rosy labels of the world. To understand more fully what Melville is doing in the story, it will be helpful to recall the final paragraph of the chapter on "The Whiteness of the Whale" in *Moby-Dick*:

Is it that by its indefiniteness it shadows forth the heartless voids and immensities of the universe, and thus stabs us from behind with the thought of annihilation, when beholding the white depths of the milky way? Or is it, that as in essence whiteness is not so much a color as the visible absence of color, and at the same time the concrete of all colors; is it for these reasons that there is such a dumb blankness, full of meaning, in a wide landscape of snows—a colorless, all-color of atheism from which we shrink? And when we consider that other theory of the natural philosophers, that all other earthly hues—every stately or lovely emblazoning—the sweet tinges of sunset skies and woods; yea, and the gilded velvets of butterflies, and the butterfly cheeks of young girls; all these are but subtile deceits, not actually inherent in substances, but only laid on from without; so that all deified Nature absolutely paints like the harlot, whose allurements cover nothing but the charnel-house within; and when we proceed further, and consider that the mystical cosmetic which produces every one of her hues, the great principle of light, for ever remains white or colorless in itself, and if operating without medium upon matter, would touch all objects, even tulips and roses, with its own blank tinge—pondering all this, the palsied universe lies before us a leper; and like wilful travellers in Lapland, who refuse to wear colored and coloring glasses upon their eyes, so the wretched infidel gazes himself blind at the monumental white shroud that wraps all the prospect around him.[3]

"The Paradise of Bachelors and the Tartarus of Maids" is an

3. *Moby-Dick*, ed. Harrison Hayford and Hershel Parker (New York: Norton, 1967), pp. 169–170.

impressive elaboration of Ishmael's statement on whiteness. The first part of the story depicts travelers in Lapland who *do* wear colored and coloring glasses upon their eyes. They see color and variety, and they enjoy their lives to the fullest. The other section of the story presents the same world as a Lapland wrapped in a monumental white shroud. The narrator of "The Paradise of Bachelors and the Tartarus of Maids," then, presents the world in both ways, with colored glasses and without. Like the narrator of "Poor Man's Pudding and Rich Man's Crumbs," whom he resembles closely enough to suggest that they are perhaps the same man, he is aware of the implications of his experience in whiteness, and he narrowly escapes being the wretched infidel who stares himself blind.

The illusory world, which Ishmael calls that of "lovely emblazoning," is represented in the story through Melville's delineation of bachelorhood. That which underlies the illusory world, the palsied universe, is embodied in his concept of maidenhood. Therefore to understand the bachelor and the maid is to perceive much of what Melville is getting at in the story.

When Melville had unsmiling Ahab encounter in *Moby-Dick* a happy ship called the *Bachelor*, he set up a contrast between two types of men, types that recur in many of his works. Ahab is a monomaniacal rebel struggling to break free from human limitations. The ship he meets represents all those cheerful travelers in Lapland who never worry their heads about such things. The *Bachelor* is decked out in "glad holiday apparel," gaily sailing around among other ships. Flags of all colors fly from her rigging. Like the type of man represented, the ship has "met with the most surprising success" while cruising in the same grounds with other ships that have not had any luck at all. Indeed, those on board the *Bachelor* are so smug in their success that they refuse to believe in the existence of anything so frightening as the white whale. "No; only heard of him; but don't believe in him at all," says the good-humored captain.

When last seen the *Bachelor* was going off "cheerily before the breeze" while the *Pequod* fought stubbornly against that same breeze.[4]

The bachelors in "The Paradise of Bachelors and the Tartarus of Maids" are lawyers, not whalemen, but their view of life, their "luck," their insistence upon the pleasure principle, and their rejection of anything unpleasant make them indistinguishable from the men aboard the *Bachelor*. Like their sailor counterparts, the lawyers of the Temple are frequent travelers: "Almost all of them were travelers, too; for bachelors alone can travel freely" (p. 673). And like the captain of the *Bachelor* they do not believe in such unpleasantries as trouble and pain: "The thing called pain, the bugbear styled trouble—those two legends seemed preposterous to their bachelor imaginations. . . . How could they suffer themselves to be imposed upon by such monkish fables? Pain! Trouble! As well talk of Catholic miracles. No such thing" (p. 673).

In using the term *bachelor* to designate such people as these, with their smiling view of life, Melville was not speaking solely in a literal sense, for not all unmarried men in his works are "bachelors," Ishmael being an obvious case in point. Those who are bachelors in a metaphorical sense have not married themselves to an idea. The monomaniacal heroes take vows, commit themselves for life to some single purpose, and it is in this sense that they are "wedded." Bachelors cannot or will not commit themselves to any but the shallowest of pursuits.[5] But just as not all unmarried men in this metaphorical system are bachelors, so not all married men are heroic rebels. Some are *bene-*

4. Ibid., pp. 407, 408.
5. See Richard Harter Fogle's excellent discussion of bachelorhood in *Melville's Shorter Tales* (Norman: University of Oklahoma Press, 1960), pp. 46–48, 132–135. Fogle states that "Bachelors are men who have mastered life by learning the secret of living with impunity. More crudely, they know how to beat the game" (p. 46). It is more accurate to say that bachelors *think* they live with impunity, but in Melville's works no one beats the game.

dicts, Melville's term for oppressed men. They are married in the literal but not in the metaphorical sense. The benedict has neither the comfort and happiness of the bachelor nor the insight of the deep diver. He is simply a victim of life. His plight is suggested through the crew of another ship in *Moby-Dick*. The *Delight* has met the white whale and has been totally demoralized and defeated. There is no resentment or rebellion, only the pathetic melancholy and perplexity of weak souls victimized by the unfathomable workings of life. The bachelor is the happiest of men; the benedict is the most downtrodden. While the joyous bachelors amuse themselves in the Temple, "The Benedick tradesmen are hurrying by, with ledger-lines ruled along their brows, thinking upon rise of bread and fall of babies" (p. 670). William Coulter, the woodcutter in "Poor Man's Pudding and Rich Man's Crumbs," is a clear example of the benedict.

Different though they are on the surface, bachelors and benedicts are alike in being pawns of scientific law that operates throughout the universe. Even though the bachelor is hidden away from painful sights like Boccaccio's revellers escaping the plague of Florence, he is no freer from the enslaving and destructive forces of life than the benedict. He, like all puny victims of the unalterable laws that operate in nature, is at heart but a pale, frightened maid. Just as the white realm of the paper mill is really the same world as that of the Temple, so the white maids and the jolly bachelors are one and the same. This is the fundamental theme of the story. How Melville develops it through imagery is the high expression of his art.

The basic pattern of imagery in the story is that of envelopment, physical and psychological. But envelopment in the second part of the work does not suggest what it does in the first section. In "The Paradise of Bachelors" almost every detail of setting emphasizes the security which the smug bachelors think they possess. In "The Tartarus of Maids" envelopment suggests not security but enslavement.

In Melville's characterization of bachelors, physical envelopment symbolizes the fortification of their minds. The Temple is "quite sequestered from the old city's surrounding din" (p. 671), and the room in which they dine has a very low ceiling: "Who wants to dine under the dome of St. Peter's? High ceilings! If that is your demand, and the higher the better, and you are so very tall, then go dine out with the topping giraffe in the open air" (p. 672). Their predecessors, who are now enveloped for eternity in the "wondrous tombs in the Temple Church" (p. 670), were enclosed in armor while they were alive and thereby protected from their heathen foes. The narrator returns frequently to imagery of physical envelopment whether he is speaking of the ancient "defender of the sarcophagus" who was "cased in Birmingham hardware" or the modern Templar who enjoys life in his sequestered quarters.

Just as both the Knights Templars of old and the modern Templars physically enclose and protect themselves from the outside world, so have they also created mental insulation. For the ancient warriors it was the dogma of religion and the code of knighthood. For the modern lawyers it is the dogma of their profession and the code of gentlemanly decorum. Melville's method in this first part of the story, as well as in the second, is to undercut explicit contrast with implicit similarity. Early in the story the original Knights Templars are superficially contrasted with their later counterparts. But in a deeper sense they are alike. The narrator's irony is highly effective in a passage where he seems to be showing the deterioration of a noble order into baseness but where he is actually saying that the order has not fundamentally changed at all: "Though no sworded foe might outskill them in the fence, yet the worm of luxury crawled beneath their guard, gnawing the core of knightly troth, nibbling the monastic vow, till at last the monk's austerity relaxed to wassailing, and the sworn knights-bachelors grew to be but hypocrites and rakes" (p. 670). Hyperbole in both praise and condemnation here acts as an equalizer. The knights were but bachelors to begin with. Is it any surprise, then, that their oaths and allegiances turned out to be hollow? And the modern bachelors, as the narrator goes on in the story to show, are not really hypocrites and rakes but merely shallow men to whom forms, measured forms, as Melville said of Captain Vere, are everything. The knights were not so noble as the narrator pretends and the lawyers not so ignoble. They meet in the middle and fade into each other, bachelors all.[6] Through hyperbole and irony the narrator turns ostensible contrast into a telling common denominator and sets the stage for the most revealing scene of bachelorhood in the story, their elaborate dinner.

Through the device of the dinner the narrator is able to show clearly the extent to which the bachelors have enveloped themselves in a system of rules by which they think and act. The meal is a metaphor for their orderly existence. Although the narrator claims that the meal was casual and at times something of a "pell-mell affair," he describes it as if it were governed by the most definite rules of procedure. In fact, he describes it in terms of a well-planned battle campaign. After the "light skirmishers" of soup and fish, "the heavy artillery of the feast marched in, led by that well-known English generalissimo, roast beef" (p. 672). Other dishes and drinks he calls "aids-de-camp" and "avant-couriers." Then comes "a picked brigade of game-fowl encamped upon the board" with campfires lit by wine. The extended military metaphor continues, suggesting not only the rigid structure they follow in dining, but also again reminding the reader of the basic similarity between the peaceful lawyers and the warring crusaders whose quarters they now occupy.

The narrator calls the meal a feast, but the food is mostly plain English fare—ox-tail soup, turbot, roast beef, fat turkey, chicken pie, game fowl, tarts, pudding, cheese and crackers—

6. The narrator suggests that their difference is only an illusion, an enchantment: "Struck by Time's enchanter's wand, the Templar is to-day a Lawyer" (p. 670).

not exactly a menu to excite the gourmet. That is as it should be, for despite his emphasis upon the quantity and variety of foods, the narrator is primarily interested in focusing the reader's attention, little by little, on what the bachelors *drink*. The various courses described suggest the high degree of structure in their lives, but the abundance of food also provides an opportunity for abundant drinking. The act of drinking is made to seem almost incidental in the early stages of the meal. After the soup, the narrator says that they "drank a little claret," and he puts the comment in parentheses. After describing the fish, he states, again parenthetically, "at this point we refreshed ourselves with a glass of sherry" (p. 672). Humming ale is served in flagons, he mentions casually, after describing the roast beef and other "heavy artillery." Then with almost a note of apology he says: "By way of ceremony, simply, only to keep up good old fashions, we here each drank a glass of good old port" (p. 672). If the reader has not already seen that the bachelors are consuming a good deal of alcohol, this fact becomes inescapable when the tablecloth is removed and "in marched a fresh detachment of bottles" (p. 672). They seem drowning in a sea of wine; the narrator now indicates that his earlier references to their "taking a glass of claret, and a glass of sherry, and a glass of port, and a mug of ale" did not give a full picture, that in between "the periods of those grand imposing" drinks mentioned, which were "merely the state bumpers," they drained "innumerable impromptu glasses" (p. 672).

Never have so few drunk so much in such a short work of literature. The bachelors seem to get more thirsty as the evening wears on. The table becomes a "sort of Epsom Heath; a regular ring, where the decanters galloped round. For fear one decanter should not with sufficient speed reach his destination, another was sent express after him to hurry him; and then a third to hurry the second; and so on with a fourth and fifth" (p. 672). It is a credit to Melville's subtle artistry that this monumental imbibing does not become obtrusive or the purpose of it obvious. He has saturated this part of the story with wine, yet the nine bachelors appear merely to be having a dignified and pleasant evening after being duly lubricated with the grape.

Wine functions in the story as a measuring instrument. The narrator himself suggests this when he speaks of their telling time by how much wine is consumed: "And so the evening slipped along, the hours told, not by a water-clock, like King Alfred's, but a wine-chronometer" (p. 672).[7] Wine measures more than time, however. It determines the extent of the bachelors' entrenchment in their patterned way of thinking and acting. Even when they drink great quantities, they do not break out of this pattern as less devoted disciples of form might do. If anything, they develop an even greater awareness of decorum, the code of good form which they live by. The narrator marvels that they observe every single law of decorum: "Throughout all this nothing loud, nothing unmannerly, nothing turbulent." There was "aught of indecorum" (p. 672). The stories they tell are in the best taste. They follow a definite code in drinking—a bachelor will not imbibe unless some other joins him. Then they toast each other's health as good form demands. It is "a remarkable decorum . . . a decorum unassailable by any degree of mirthfulness" (p. 673). Since no quantity of wine, Melville's measuring device, can break down their devotion to order, they are true bachelors, fortified by the walls of form they carefully maintain.

The narrator indulges in perhaps his most poignant bit of satire about their walls of form when he describes the large convolved horn, from which the bachelors take snuff toward the end of the evening, as "a regular Jericho horn." The host lifts the horn from the table "as if he were about to blow an inspiring blast" (p. 673), but instead he takes a pinch of snuff from it.

7. Melville here seems to have confused the ancient water clock of the Egyptians, later used by the Greeks and Romans, with King Alfred's method of measuring time with candles of twelve inches in length that burned four hours.

Although this snuff horn has stimulated critics a great deal to speculate about sexual implications,[8] Melville seems more concerned with having the reader recall the biblical reference in Joshua 6:5: "And it shall come to pass that, when they make a long blast with the ram's horn, and when ye hear the sound of the trumpet, all the people shall shout with a great shout, and the wall of the city shall fall down flat. ...." The bachelors have a ram's horn (or at least one with goats' heads on it), and it looks like the kind that might have been sounded at Jericho. But no horns will be blown here, and no walls will come tumbling down. The bachelors are bachelors because they *have* walls. So they merely take snuff from the horn and with such firm allegiance to decorum that not one of them even sneezes: "Not a man so far violated the proprieties, or so far molested the invalid bachelor in the adjoining room as to indulge himself in a sneeze. The snuff was snuffed silently, as if it had been some fine innoxious powder brushed off the wings of butterflies" (p. 673).

The snuff is taken *as if* it were innoxious, but by implication the narrator suggests that it may be in fact noxious. The same could be said about the bachelors' lives in general. Robustness appears to permeate their existence. The world outside the Temple is sick, but inside the bachelors are "sunny-faced" and cheerful as they toast each other's health. Yet such excessive eating and drinking cannot be but noxious to their health. Through their revelry and their ostensible good health and their disciplined disbelief in suffering can be seen the faint outline of a grinning skull. While they enjoy themselves obliviously, a personification of disease and approaching death is but one room

8. Martin Leonard Pops believes that the horn is a phallic symbol and that the bachelors' holding of it represents "stimulation without consummation." *The Melville Archetype* (Kent: Kent State University Press, 1970), p. 148. According to Ray B. Browne, "the snuff in the horn becomes then an unequivocal condemnation of the lack of virile masculinity of the bachelors." *Melville's Drive to Humanism* (Lafayette: Purdue University Studies, 1971), p. 224.

away: an invalid insomniac who has finally gotten to sleep occupies an adjoining chamber. The bachelors are careful not to
"wake" this shadowy figure, for they are determined to keep
what he represents out of their minds. Theirs is a world where
noxiousness is disguised as "some fine innoxious powder
brushed off the wings of butterflies."

Ishmael had said, however, that the "gilded velvets of butterflies, and the butterfly cheeks of young girls . . . are but subtle
deceits, not actually inherent in substances, but laid on from
without." This theme, which is an undercurrent in "The Paradise of Bachelors," surfaces in "The Tartarus of Maids," where
the narrator has a terrifying experience similar to déjà vu. From
the moment he leaves the main road and begins to approach the
paper mill, everything seems familiar and he is reminded of his
earlier visit to the paradise of bachelors: "When, I say, turning
from that bustling mainroad, I by degrees wound into the Mad
Maid's Bellows'-pipe, and saw the grim Black Notch beyond,
then something latent, as well as something obvious in the time
and scene, strangely brought back to my mind my first sight of
dark and grimy Temple-Bar" (p. 674). Because the narrator
feels almost constantly that somehow he has visited this place
before, "The Tartarus of Maids" resembles a dream or vision.
Déjà vu is always characterized by this quality of strangeness
that is perhaps more real than the reality of everyday perception.[9]

9. Without designating the narrator's experience as déjà vu, several
critics have commented on the dream-like aspect of "The Tartarus of
Maids." Newton Arvin, *Herman Melville* (New York: Sloane, 1950),
comments that in its unreality the episode foreshadows "The Penal
Colony." William Bysshe Stein feels that in its "scenic complexity, it has
only one analogue—the dream." "Melville's Eros," *Texas Studies in
Literature and Language* 3 (1961): 303. One of Richard Chase's strongest objections to "The Tartarus of Maids" is that "the paper mill symbols do not rise freely or with integrity from that which they are
supposed to symbolize. . . . In short, they are the symbols of dreams
rather than of art." *Herman Melville: A Critical Study* (New York:
Macmillan, 1949), p. 162.

But for the narrator it is also a dangerous experience. The physical danger he is exposed to when his horse uncontrollably plunges into the Devil's Dungeon is merely an outward manifestation of his psychological peril. His tendency to see similarity instead of difference, his instinctive bent for linking the essence of a past experience with that of a present one despite obvious differences, prove him to be potentially that "wretched infidel" Ishmael speaks of who will stare himself blind in the whiteness of Lapland unless he puts on colored glasses. Dissimilarities in scenes or experiences serve in his mind but to highlight a core of sameness. Nothing seems to him to be completely new, not even his sensations when his horse wildly runs through the Black Notch and down into the Devil's Dungeon, for that experience fuses with an earlier one, when he was in a runaway London omnibus that rushed through the archway known as Temple Bar: [10] "Though the two objects did by no means completely correspond, yet this partial inadequacy but served to tinge the similitude not less with the vividness than the disorder of a dream" (p. 674).

Memory alone is not responsible for the narrator's perception of similitude. That "something latent," as he calls it, in the white scene before him is linked in his mind to the bachelors' paradise by the functioning of an imagination of the kind that cuts through variety to find unity. It is the opposite of what he earlier terms the "bachelor imagination." In the rude tower of the paper mill standing amid other buildings, he sees "the Temple Church amidst the surrounding offices and dormitories." The "marvelous retirement of this mysterious mountain nook" is the same to him as the sequestration of the Temple. He is "fastened" upon by a "spell." "Then, what memory lacked, all tributary imagination furnished, and I said to myself, 'This is

10. Melville does not call it the Temple Bar by name but clearly identifies it as such when he describes it as "the ancient arch of Wren" (p. 674). When Melville wrote the story the Temple was just a short distance from the Temple Bar.

the very counterpart of the Paradise of Bachelors, but snowed upon and frost-painted to a sepulchre' " (pp. 674–675). What he is now witnessing is in a sense the negative of a mental photograph he took in London. The outlines are there, but the color, the life, have gone out of it. Yet like a photographic negative, this is the basis for the picture. The narrator's description of this bleak setting is pervaded with images of death. The landscape somehow seems enfolded in death, its blood (the only bit of color in the scene) rapidly flowing out of its body to form a red, demonic river. As he views the square near the main building of the mill and Blood River that boils beside it, "the inverted similitude recurred—'The sweet, tranquil Temple garden, with the Thames bordering its green beds,' strangely meditated I" (p. 675).

The narrator's strange meditation has brought him to the disturbing intuition that there are no fundamental differences between the pleasant setting of the Temple in London and this bleak one he sees before him in New England. What he saw in London was basically this scene, but there it was "painted like the harlot" to appear attractive. Now he wonders if he is also to see the counterparts of the bachelors themselves: "But where are the gay bachelors?" (p. 675). His question is quickly answered as a pale girl runs into the main building. His initial view of the maids seems to disturb him, but it is not, as some critics have claimed, because he is afraid of women.[11] His role in the story and the context of his fearfulness demand another interpretation: that he recognizes in a revelatory flash of vision that the answer to the question he has just asked himself is before him. Here in the person of this pitiful creature is the gay bachelor as seen *without* colored and coloring glasses. The masculinity of the bachelors is "laid on from the outside" no less

11. See for example Stein, pp. 303–307, and Beryl Rowland, "Melville's Bachelors and Maids: Interpretation Through Symbol and Metaphor," *American Literature* 41 (1969): 389–405. Both these critics hold that the narrator harbors a deep-seated fear of women.

than is color upon whiteness. The masses of men are not men at all. True masculinity in Melville's stories is reserved for the exceptional man, the rebel, as we saw in "Cock-A-Doodle-Doo!" Ordinary man, and that includes the bachelor, is but a fearful and emasculated slave to the natural forces that control life.[12]

As the narrator is shown through the paper mill, his mind continues to dwell on the bachelors he had dined with in London. Even the rags from which paper is made recalls them: " ' 'Tis not unlikely, then,' murmured I, 'that among these heaps of rags there may be some old shirts, gathered from the dormitories of the Paradise of Bachelors. But the buttons are all dropped off' " (p. 676). The garments have no buttons because here, through the image of the silent maid, the heart of bachelorhood is laid bare. The boy Cupid, who acts as the narrator's guide, confuses the buttons at first with flowers when asked about them: "None grow in this part of the country. The Devil's Dungeon is no place for flowers" (p. 676). Melville is using flowers here to represent all that color stands for in Ishmael's statement about whiteness.

The occupation of the narrator and his reason for coming to the Devil's Dungeon suggest a good deal about his penetrating vision of sameness. He is, as he explains early in the second part of the work, a "seedsman" in search of "envelopes." Literally he means that he sells various kinds of seeds and that he goes to the paper mill to purchase envelopes to put them into for distribution. Other senses in which he is a seedsman have been the subject for much speculation among critics, one going so far as to suggest that the narrator is seeking contraceptives to contain his sperm.[13] The narrator's description of himself as a seedsman, however, is not simply a sexual joke. More importantly it is a

12. When the narrator asks one of the silent maids if there is not a "man about," he spots a male, but ironically he is not truly masculine in the sense of the exceptional man but merely another bachelor, the proprietor of the paper mill.

13. Stein, p. 304.

reference to his way of seeing and his need to restrict or contain that vision insofar as possible. The metaphors and images through which he describes his experiences form a consistent pattern and reveal his preoccupation with inwardness as opposed to the outwardness of surfaces and appearances. Even in the first part of the story, he repeatedly uses expressions like "stony heart," "sweet kernel," and "at the core." He is far from the heart of things in the Temple, but these and other like expressions reveal a prepossession on his part, and they foreshadow his being a seedsman in "The Tartarus of Maids," where he does indeed get to the core of existence. The narrator thus feels the urge to penetrate to the seed, to first principles. Instinctively he recognizes, however, that such penetration is extremely hazardous.

The narrator's physical location in the two settings of the story indicates how he perceives. In "The Paradise of Bachelors," he climbs from a lower place to a higher one, an "apartment well up toward heaven" (p. 671). In "The Tartarus of Maids," he descends from a high place into the Devil's Dungeon, where he finds the paper mill. What Melville is suggesting here is that the narrator first views bachelorhood from the top, from the outside. Its pleasantries, which constitute its outside, are stressed, but the narrator as he looks from the outside inward also glimpses the unhealthiness at the core. Then in the second section of the story he views bachelorhood from deeply within, where blankness is emphasized. From this interior perspective, however, he can glimpse the outside of bachelorhood, the surface characteristics that previously appeared so pleasant. The same basic pattern of imagery—that of envelopment—prevails in both sections. The maids are as enveloped, physically and mentally, as the bachelors. Deep cloven passages lead to the mill, which is described as a sepulchre and is enclosed by mountains. The snow (which suggests sterility) seems to cover everything. From his first vantage point the narrator perceives the degree to which the bachelors are encapsulated and the extent to which the envelope of form *seems* to protect them. From his second vantage point he sees that they are not actually protected at all, that they are emasculated and enslaved by the laws of existence that are much more fundamental than the laws and customs they practice and hide behind.

The bachelors have built themselves a fortification behind which they try to hide from the relentless processes and laws of nature. They do not marry and therefore do not take part in the natural act of reproduction. Thoughts of suffering, awareness of aging, and knowledge of the inescapability of death are pushed outside the walls for a time. Thus one kind of law is used to give them a sense of security against another kind; man-made law (they are all literally lawyers) and an elaborate system of decorum form their walls against nature's laws to which all things are subject. They appear to control the law themselves, since they are its high priests in society, but in actuality they are engulfed by the inscrutable laws of the universe, which make them a part of nature's inexorable processes. In other words, the true situation of bachelorhood is represented by the maids' relationship to the papermaking process: "Machinery—that vaunted slave of humanity—here stood menially served by human beings, who served mutely and cringingly as the slave serves the Sultan. The girls did not so much seem accessory wheels to the general machinery as mere cogs to the wheels" (p. 675).

The narrator's central experience in the story is his viewing of the "great machine." This machine, which produces blank sheets of paper from liquid poured into it, has determined in large measure the nature of critical commentary on the story. Whatever a critic makes of the paper machine is likely to dictate his interpretation of the work as a whole. If one sees it merely as a piece of machinery, he tends to read the story as Melville's attack on the evils of industrialism.[14] If one sees it as a repre-

14. A. R. Humphreys sees no symbolism of gestation in the work. It is, he says, "what it purports to be, Melville's reaction to industrial misery." *Melville* (Edinburgh: Oliver and Boyd, 1962), p. 98. Other

sentation of the human womb, he is likely to interpret the story largely in sexual terms, as, for example, Melville's expression of his disgust with childbearing.[15] No doubt both of these broad areas of interpretation contain elements of validity. It is obvious that Melville felt keenly the destructiveness inherent in a machine age and that on a superficial level "The Paradise of Bachelors and the Tartarus of Maids" carries this message of social protest. It is also obvious, though it seems not to have been to Melville's early readers, that the description of the paper machine is pervaded with allusions to conception, gestation, and childbirth. "Two great round vats" pour "white, wet, woolly-looking stuff" into "one common channel" that leads to the great machine which is in a room "stifling with a strange, blood-like, abdominal heat" (p. 676). It takes exactly nine mintues for the white liquid to be made into the finished product, which comes out of the machine accompanied by "a scissory sound . . . as of some cord being snapped" (p. 677). An old woman tending the paper as it comes out is a former nurse. Finally, the narrator compares the blank paper that comes from the machine with the blank minds of newly born babies, thinking of "that celebrated comparison of John Locke" (p. 677). When one remembers that "The Paradise of Bachelors and the Tartarus of Maids" was written about the time Elizabeth Melville was expecting her fourth child in six years, it is not difficult to suspect

---

critics do not deny that there is sexual symbolism in the work, but nevertheless feel that the main theme concerns the destructiveness of industrialism. See W. R. Thompson, " 'The Paradise of Bachelors and the Tartarus of Maids': A Reinterpretation," *American Quarterly* 9 (1957): 34–45; Bert C. Bach, "Melville's Theatrical Mask: The Role of Narrative Perspective in His Short Fiction," *Studies in the Literary Imagination* 2 (1969):43–55; Browne, pp. 219–229; and Marvin Fisher, "Melville's 'Tartarus': The Deflowering of New England," *American Quarterly* 23 (1971): 79–100.

15. See Arvin, p. 238; Eby, p. 97; Pops, pp. 147–150; Stein, pp. 303–308; and Egbert S. Oliver, "Melville's Tartarus," *Emerson Society Quarterly*, no. 28 (1962), 23–25.

that her husband had begun to regret his own fertility and to have much on his mind the machine-like aspect of human reproduction.

Nevertheless, if the critic stops after seeing Melville's note of social protest about America's factory system or even after discerning what may be the author's mockery of the so-called "sacred" things of life, as Leon Howard puts it,[16] he has failed to plumb the depths of the story. These two themes, if they exist at all, are merely manifestations of a broader theme, namely, the pitiful plight of ordinary man, who tries to escape a self-perpetuating, unfathomable nature but who is caught up in its grinding, steady, relentless process.

The great machine in the innermost room of the mill is Melville's symbol of universal nature. The predictable movements of the machine suggest the regular, unchanging laws of the universe. Yet there is a profound mystery about the machine just as there is about nature. The narrator stands in awe of it, knowing that it operates with "unvarying punctuality and precision" but not knowing how or why. Melville stressed the act of reproduction in his description of the machine because it is that aspect of nature with which man is familiar but about which man actually knows very little. All of the "unvarying punctuality and precision" of nature's operation in general is embodied in the one act of reproduction, as is all the unfathomable mystery. Melville has thus made the great machine a symbol of the womb, but he has in turn made the womb a symbol of the great machine we know as nature.[17] The narrator himself makes the con-

16. Howard states that Melville "slipped into his account of paper making a little natural allegory which amounted to a genuine mockery of what Evert Duyckinck considered the 'sacred' aspects of life. Taking his ease, with an active mind, he found himself disposed to violate deliberately some of the conventions he had inadvertently given the impression of violating in his earlier writings." *Herman Melville: A Biography* (Berkeley: University of California Press, 1951), p. 218.

17. On still another level, the paper mill suggests the reproductive processes of nature through a number of references and images that call

nection between the machine and nature when he leaves the mill, goes through the pass, and is in the midst of what he calls "inscrutable nature." Just previously he had used the same word, *inscrutable*, to describe the machine. "Your great machine," he tells the proprietor of the paper mill, "is a miracle of inscrutable intricacy" (p. 678).

Nature grinds on with precision and iron necessity, reproducing blankness. Human beings, weak and pathetic creatures that they are, are but handmaidens to its laws. This is the terrible truth at which the narrator finally arrives. Step by step, and with increasing emotional intensity, he works his way toward it. His progress in ever-deepening insight is suggested by his physical movements and by his emotional responses to what he sees. First he comes from the outside into the Devil's Dungeon. He is shaken by fear because his horse comes close to causing his death, but he is also struck by the bleakness of the setting and the strangeness of the first pale maidens he sees. Then he enters

---

to mind a bee hive. Before the narrator sees the mill, he hears it: "Where stands the mill? Suddenly a whirling, humming sound broke upon my ear" (p. 674). Inside the mill nothing can be heard but this hum: "Not a syllable was breathed. Nothing was heard but the low, steady, overruling hum of the iron animals. The human voice was banished from the spot" (p. 675). In the hot room where the great machine is kept, the narrator is again struck with this hum (p. 677). If Melville does intend to suggest a bee hive, the metaphor works well, for the great machine is much like a giant queen bee, the only fertile creature in the hive. As it goes about its job of producing mechanically, the queen bee is groomed and fed by sterile female attendant bees just as the great machine is attended to by the maids. The danger that this bee hive holds for the narrator may be suggested by recalling a passage in *Moby-Dick*, in the chapter called "Cistern and Buckets," where Ishmael tells of Tashtego's fall into the head of a sperm whale. He is rescued by Queequeg's "agile obstetrics" after being nearly entombed in the white "secret inner chamber and sanctum sanctorum of the whale." If he had perished, Ishmael adds, his fate would have resembled that of an Ohio honey-hunter "who seeking honey in the crotch of a hollow tree, found such exceeding store of it, that leaning too far over, it sucked him in, so that he died embalmed" (p. 290). The white world that nearly took Tashtego's life and the honeyed world are therefore alike.

the main building of the mill. He sees first the big room where the maids sit in rows folding blank paper. While he is viewing this scene, he has to be dragged out into the open air because his cheeks seem to be freezing.[18] For the second time he is in physical danger—both experiences symbolizing his psychological danger that results from his seeing too deeply. The process of moving toward some central truth nevertheless continues. From the outer folding room the narrator proceeds to the water wheel and the rag room, where girls are ripping old garments almost to lint. The omnipresence of death now overwhelms the narrator. But that is only a part of his deepening vision. His guide makes a joke of the maids' deathlike pallor, and he understands with something like sad horror a new dimension to the plight of man. The name of his guide is Cupid, but instead of manifesting love, the precocious boy embodies all the blindness and indifference of which man is capable. Cupid feels no sympathy for the maidens who serve the machine before his eyes because despite his "roguish twinkle" he is blind to everything except the magnificence of the great machine. He is Melville's version of a disciple of nature, one who appreciates its power and the beauty of its unalterable laws of operation, but who is totally oblivious to the fact that mankind is its victim: "More tragical and more inscrutably mysterious than any mystic sight, human or machine, throughout the factory, was the strange innocence of cruel-heartedness in this usage-hardened boy" (p. 676).

In the heat of the room where the narrator witnesses the operation of the great machine, he comes close to passing out. It is

18. The pain from his cheeks induces the narrator to say, "I seemed Actaeon" (p. 675). In Greek mythology Actaeon happened upon the goddess Artemis while she and her nymphs were bathing. To see a deity uninvited was to court destruction. Consequently, Actaeon, because he had seen too much, was turned into a stag and destroyed by his own hounds. Through this classical allusion, the narrator reveals that he is aware of the disastrous consequences of seeing too deeply into the heart of things.

not from the heat, however, but from the chilling vision he has while watching the machine:

But what made the thing I saw so specially terrible to me was the metallic necessity, the unbudging fatality which governed it. . . . I stood spell-bound and wandering in my soul. Before my eyes—there, passing in slow procession along the wheeling cylinders, I seemed to see, glued to the pallid incipience of the pulp, the yet more pallid faces of all the pallid girls I had eyed that heavy day. Slowly, mournfully, beseechingly, yet unresistingly, they gleamed along, their agony dimly outlined on the imperfect paper, like the print of the tormented face on the handkerchief of Saint Veronica. (p. 678)

The vision affects the narrator profoundly because the maids, who at first reminded the narrator only of the jolly bachelors, have come to suggest mankind in general caught in the iron grip of universal laws. When he questions the proprietor about whether all the women in the mill are maids, the answer, "All maids," seems to have a special and disturbing meaning for him. A "strange emotion" fills him, and the proprietor comments that his "cheeks look whitish" (p. 678). What the narrator hears in the proprietor's answer is that *all* are helpless maids, even himself, for he is taking on the chill and pallor characteristic of those he has been watching. But he manages to escape the mill and the vision without becoming embittered or losing his mental balance. He goes back to a world where he must at least partially make use of the forms that envelop the bachelors. Symbolically, he wraps himself as he leaves the mill in tippet, mittens, coat, and laprobe. As he leaves behind the mill and shoots through the pass, his last words reveal for the final time his vision of similitude and connect the two experiences he has had: "Oh! Paradise of Bachelors! and oh! Tartarus of Maids." The two, he is saying, are one.[19]

---

19. A contrasting view is that of John Seelye, who concludes that the narrator's final words are mere sounds "signifying nothing." *Melville: The Ironic Diagram* (Evanston: Northwestern University Press, 1970), p. 100.

The narrator's experience in the paper mill is characterized by a pattern of confrontation and escape, of seeing and turning away, of chill and returning warmth, of faintishness and revival. Such vacillation is the result of his being a "seedsman" who knows that he must have "envelopes." He represents that fourth alternative in Melville's classification, a type encountered with some frequency in the short stories—the ironist. He is neither bachelor, benedict, nor wedded man. He sees far deeper than either the bachelor or the benedict, and he shares neither the shallow optimism of the one nor the pathetic defeatism of the other. Nor does he join the heroic rebel in wedding himself to a gallant but futile assault on the laws of universal nature. His imagination conveys to him the meaning of the paper factory with its awesome machine, but he does not back away on his horse, lance in hand, and run full force against it. He enjoys his dinner with the bachelors, but he knows even then that it cannot last, and his treatment of its glories is permeated with irony.[20] His experience in the paper mill is his hangover from revelling with the bachelors. Just as surely as a hangover follows an evening of celebrating with strong drink the joys of life, so to a man of the narrator's depth and disposition a terrible vision of whiteness follows a view of the "gilded velvets of butterflies." Thus the nature of the narrator lends an inevitability, an artistic rightness, to the structure of the work. Given this narrator, "The Paradise of Bachelors" *had* to be followed by "The Tartarus of Maids." Even so, the narrator does not allow himself to gaze indefinitely at blankness. He is that traveler in Lapland who alternately removes his colored glasses

20. Several critics have commented on the undercurrent of disapproval in the narrator's praise of the bachelors. Edward H. Rosenberry, for example, says that the jovial description of the dinner is "overlaid with an ambiguous sincerity." *Melville and the Comic Spirit* (Cambridge: Harvard University Press, 1955), p. 143. Fogle makes the point that the "very exaggeration of his praise implies a criticism" (p. 47). See also Browne, p. 220.

long enough to perceive the terrible whiteness around him and then puts them back on to accompany at least for a while those travelers who never truly see the bleak landscape of life. Only in that oscillation is both insight and sanity.

CYNIC SOLITAIRE

"The Bell-Tower"

Chapter 9

What Melville set out to accomplish in his next two stories, "The Bell-Tower" and "Benito Cereno," resembles in a general way his achievement in "Bartleby" and "Cock-A-Doodle-Doo!" "The Bell-Tower" focuses on a rebellious extraordinary person, like the narrator of "Cock-A-Doodle-Doo!," with ordinary men in the background. In "Benito Cereno" he puts his ordinary man, Captain Delano, in the spotlight, as he did with the lawyer of "Bartleby," and the rebel, Babo, in the background (as is Bartleby himself). These counterstories were both completed during the early months of 1855 and submitted to *Putnam's Monthly Magazine* a few weeks apart.[1] Dissimilar in time and place they both deal with the frightening oneness of all. They depict a cynic solitaire in rebellion against a blind world, and

---

1. Melville sent the manuscript of "Benito Cereno" to *Putnam's* about early April 1855, and he submitted "The Bell-Tower" a month or so later. They appeared in reverse order, however, "The Bell-Tower" in the August 1855 issue and "Benito Cereno" in the October, November, and December issues.

they project an ultimate vision of futility in which all ambition and all endeavor are but part of the circle of necessity. Both stories are about freedom and slavery. Finally, these two works are linked together by the fact that they, unlike all the other stories, are not narrated in the first person.

Through the years "The Bell-Tower" has acquired a reputation as Melville's most uncharacteristic work. Lewis Mumford expressed the view of numerous critics when he wrote that the story "might be slipped into one of Hawthorne's volumes, without apology, as a minor work of his youth."[2] The similarities to Hawthorne are immediately very striking: the setting is Italy; the protagonist is a creative architect-artist-mechanician of the Renaissance who tries to outdo God and consequently isolates himself psychologically from the people around him and dies a grotesque death with Melville's epitaph of excessive pride hanging over him. The peculiar quality of ambiguity in the story also reminds one of Hawthorne. Though the temptation is great to interpret "The Bell-Tower" in Hawthornian terms, it ought to be resisted, for the similarities are more apparent than real. The story has some of Hawthorne's trappings, but below the surface it is unmistakably Melville.[3]

Whether because of the superficial similarity to Hawthorne or some other reason, "The Bell-Tower" is one of the most con-

2. *Herman Melville* (New York: Harcourt, Brace, 1929), p. 236. Robert E. Morsberger states: "The Bell-Tower" is a "somewhat uncharacteristic piece . . . resembling some of Hawthorne's moral allegories in both mood and meaning." "Melville's 'The Bell-Tower' and Benvenuto Cellini," *American Literature* 44 (1972): 459.

3. Indeed, it is—as Wayne R. Kine has shown in " 'The Bell-Tower': Melville's Reply to a Review," *ESQ* 22 (1976): 28–38—willfully Melvillean, for Melville appears to exaggerate in this story several of his basic characteristics as a writer. Kine believes he did this as a covert answer to a condescending review of his works by Fitz-James O'Brien. See, however, Gerard M. Sweeney, who argues that Melville was heavily indebted to Hawthorne's "The Minotaur." "Melville's Hawthornian Bell-Tower: A Fairy-Tale Source," *American Literature* 45 (1973): 279–285. Sweeney's article was later incorporated in his book *Melville's Use of Classical Mythology* (Amsterdam: Rodopi, 1975).

sistently misunderstood of Melville's short stories. Seldom analyzed at any length before some twenty-five years ago,[4] it
received at that time a great boost in reputation with Charles A.
Fenton's analysis in *American Literature*.[5] Unfortunately, his
article also had the effect of derailing a whole generation of
Melville critics. Fenton's contention that the story is a negative
response to nineteenth-century technology has much to recom-
mend it. Melville's antimachine bias is well attested to in several
places, notably in "The Paradise of Bachelors and the Tartarus
of Maids," and his dislike of science and scientists is reflected in
Clarel (1876) and other works. But just as those writings are
secondarily rather than primarily concerned with the evils of a
machine age, so the focus of "The Bell-Tower" is elsewhere.
Nevertheless since Fenton's article appeared, dozens of critics
have repeated his interpretation with only slight variation. They
see as the heart of the story "the dangers implicit in the scientific and mechanical progress of the nineteenth century—a
movement just then entering its heyday."[6]

4. During Melville's lifetime "The Bell-Tower" was reprinted in *Little
Classics: Tragedy,* ed. Rossiter Johnson (Boston: James R. Osgood,
1874), and in *A Library of American Literature from the Earliest Set-
tlement to the Present Time,* ed. E. C. Stedman and E. M. Hutchinson
(New York: Charles L. Webster, 1889). It therefore reached a wider
audience than most of his other stories.

5. " 'The Bell-Tower': Melville and Technology," *American Literature* 23 (1951): 219–232.

6. Tyrus Hillway, *Herman Melville* (New York: Twayne, 1963), p.
51. Bert C. Bach, "Melville's Theatrical Mask: The Role of Narrative
Perspective in His Short Fiction," *Studies in the Literary Imagination* 2
(1969), states that the theme is "the dangers of mechanism," and that
"attempting to rule nature for utilitarian purposes, man may forsake the
spiritual in favor of the practical" (p. 50). James E. Miller, Jr., follows
a similar approach, for he accepts the popular idea that "the architect is
a 'practical materialist.' " *A Reader's Guide to Herman Melville* (New
York: Farrar, Straus and Cudahy, 1962), p. 165. Merlin Bowen, *The
Long Encounter* (Chicago: University of Chicago Press, 1960), interprets
the story similarly, as does Marvin Fisher, who feels, however, that "The
Bell-Tower" is "not only a rejection of technological progress but also
a fearful response to that other contemporary phenomenon—the institu-

Probably the chief factor in such a misunderstanding of "The Bell-Tower" is the point of view. Although the story is told throughout in the third person, it is absolutely essential to realize that in some important places, this view reflects only the opinion of the community, not that of Melville or the protagonist, Bannadonna. By missing this fundamental point, the reader is almost certain to be misled into assuming, first, that Bannadonna shares the desire of the populace for materialistic success through technology, and, second, that their account of Bannadonna's nature, aims, actions, and death is the true one. Both of these two widely held assumptions are mistaken; Bannadonna does not have the same motivations as those around him, and the explanations given for his actions toward the end of the story represent another instance of a favorite theme of Melville's—the impossibility of the world's understanding an exceptional man.

One of the earliest, and certainly most striking, facts given about Bannadonna is that he is an "unblest foundling" (p. 123).[7] Melville furnishes so little information about his background that this detail stands out sharply. Six times he is referred to as "the foundling," and puns on the word are heard

tion of Negro slavery." "Melville's 'Bell-Tower': A Double Thrust," *American Quarterly* 18 (1966): 200–207. A few of my own conclusions agree with those of Richard Harter Fogle, *Melville's Shorter Tales* (Norman: University of Oklahoma Press, 1960), pp. 63–71, but the basis of my interpretation is fundamentally different from that of Fogle, who argues that the artist in the story is using reason to make a machine that will glorify mankind. Richard Chase's Freudian interpretation has the virtue of a different and suggestive approach, but it is flawed by mistakes and confusion in plot details. After mistakenly stating that "the bell is secretly dragged to the beach and sunk at sea" (it is Talus, not the bell), he then has the bell falling from the belfry at Bannadonna's funeral. Furthermore, whereas in the story the bell is melted down after Bannadonna's funeral and another one made, Chase writes that the bell "is hoisted back in place." *Herman Melville* (New York, Macmillan, 1949), pp. 123–125.

7. All page references to "The Bell-Tower" are to *Putnam's Monthly Magazine* 6 (July–December 1855): 123–130.

elsewhere, as when he insists that the earthen cup discovered in the belfry is "used in his founder's business" (p. 124). He is "unblest" in one sense because his great project is star-crossed from the beginning. In another sense he is unblest in the world because he is a foundling, a cast-off. Melville repeats the words often in order to drive home the world's view of Bannadonna. He is highly respected for certain achievements, and the common people hold him in awe, but officials of the government and the nobility seem never to forget that he is a foundling.

His status as an "unblest foundling" apparently affects in some measure his esthetic reputation. He is an architect, craftsman, builder, artisan, or—to repeat the term Melville uses most often to describe him—"mechanician," but in the world's eye he is not an artist.[8] He may be the greatest mechanician in all of Italy, but such a reputation carries with it the same stigma as the term *journalist* when applied in our day to an accomplished novelist. How the nobility views Bannadonna and his art is clearly shown in an early incident where the two elderly magistrates of the town conceal their awe (and uneasiness) when they view the covered figure of Talus, Bannadonna's manlike creation: "However, on their part, the visitors forbore further allusion to it, unwilling, perhaps, to let *the foundling* see how

8. Morsberger argues that Bannadonna is based on Benvenuto Cellini. A more likely source is perhaps Juanelo Torriano, who was the mechanician of Emperor Charles V. Melville had an abiding interest in Charles V, and mentioned him in such works as *Mardi*, *White-Jacket*, "Benito Cereno," and "I and My Chimney." According to Sir William Stirling-Maxwell, *The Cloister Life of Emperor Charles V,* 4th ed. (London: John C. Minno, 1891), "sometimes the workshop of Torriano was the resource of the Emperor's spare time. He was very fond of clocks and watches, and curious in reckoning to a fraction the hours of his retired leisure. The Lombard had long been at work upon an elaborate astronomical timepiece, which was to perform not only the ordinary duties of a clock, but to tell the days of the month and year, and to denote the movements of the planets" (p. 179). This masterpiece took years to complete. It had a "tapering top, which ended in a tower containing the bell and hammer" (p. 180). Despite his obvious genius Torriano was thought of not as an artist but as a mechanician.

easily it lay within *his plebeian art* to stir the placid dignity of nobles" (p. 125, italics mine). The masses think of him as one of them, a highly successful commoner; to them "mechanician" is no stigma. The nobility condescendingly recognize some of his ability, but they maintain always the gap between themselves and him.

Their choice of Bannadonna to build the tower is highly logical. If he is to commoners and nobles alike the personification of skill, ingenuity, and progress (he has, after all, come a long way from his ignoble beginnings even though his origin could not be forgotten), the tower is to them the monument to these secular gods. They want the tower as a reminder of their own enlightened progress as a community. It is to be the Empire State Building of Renaissance Italy, a symbol of wealth acquired through diligence and enterprise, a monument to materialistic progress. But it is more than their expression of community pride and their tithe to the god of progress. For the first time a clock-tower and a bell-tower will be combined in one grand structure. The idea is immensely appealing to them because of their acknowledged fealty to the forces of time and the supernatural as symbolized by the clock and bells. Traditionally bells have been associated with religious rites, and for hundreds of years in various parts of Europe ceremonial bells were rung as a means of breaking the "power of advancing thunderstorms, which were believed to be the work of evil spirits of the air."[9] The bell-tower is not only the people's monument to themselves; it is their lightning-rod sent up in recognition of the powers over them, temporal and spiritual.

The genius creator of this unique bell-tower, the private—as opposed to public—Bannadonna, is seen through glimpses, like the white doe of truth Melville wrote of in his famous review of Hawthorne. The first of these glimpses reveals that "the found-

9. Theresa C. Brakeley, "Bell," in *Dictionary of Folklore, Mythology, and Legend,* ed. Maria Leach (New York: Funk & Wagnalls, 1949), p. 133.

ling," "the mechanician" is profoundly resentful of his niche in life and those whose station by birthright is higher. The contempt in his words is unmistakable when with "ostentatious deference" he tells two of the city magistrates who visit the tower to return the next day at one o'clock: "To-morrow, then, . . . the poor mechanic will be most happy once more to give you liege audience, in this his littered shop. Farewell till then, illustrious magnificoes, and hark ye for your vassal's stroke" (p. 125). His exaggerated description of himself as a "poor mechanic" and as their "vassal" and his references to them as "illustrious magnificoes" as well as his general manner trouble one of the magistrates. He detects "a certain sardonical disdain, lurking beneath the foundling's humble mien," and he wonders "what might be the final fate of such a cynic solitaire" (p. 125). Solitary he certainly is, living and working alone, insisting upon doing all the important work with his own hands. Without friend or confidant, he exists totally apart.

All the holidays in his honor and all the fame which the world affords him merely increase his rebellion and contempt, for his true genius as an artist goes unrecognized. When he is asked to devise a seal for the state, he finds that he must engrave a hundred of them for use in customs. As he explains to the chief magistrate years later: "Now, though, indeed, my object was to have those hundred heads identical, and though, I dare say, people think them so, yet, upon closely scanning an uncut impression from the plate, no two of those five-score faces, side by side, will be found alike" (p. 126). The artistry that went into these hundred subtle differences is totally unappreciated. In fact, as he suggests, the public views all the faces on the seals as identical. It is also *artistry*, not science or technology, which produces the intricate figures on his great bell, each of the garlanded maidens—embodiments of the twelve hours— different in their expressions.

Through the tower, the bell, and Talus, Bannadonna's artistry has become the tool of his rebellion. To him the tower represents a far different thing from what it means to others. Commissioned to construct a monument to man, his own purpose is to rise above those who have marked him forever as "the foundling" and "the mechanician." They pay him to celebrate man while he busily goes about his task of belittling mankind. During the tower's construction he stands each evening alone "upon its ever-ascending summit, proud that his work increasingly overtops walls and trees," and inspired to self-esteem through the homage of petty humanity. The extent of his elevation, in his own mind, over ordinary humanity is indicated when the structure is completed: "Then mounting it, he stood erect, alone, with folded arms; gazing upon the white summits of blue inland Alps, and whiter crests of bluer Alps off-shore— sights invisible from the plain. Invisible, too, from thence was that eye he turned below, when, like the cannon booms, came up to him the people's combustions of applause" (p. 123). The crowd is excited by his daring in standing "three hundred feet in air, upon an unrailed perch." They are in awe of his physical daring but ironically are blind to the far more significant daring which the finished tower will represent, a daring of mind and spirit. "This none but he durst do. But his periodic standing upon the pile, in each stage of its growth—such discipline had its last result" (p. 123). Melville is speaking of more than just the tower here, for Bannadonna has stood upon the peak of life in each stage of his growth until he has now reached the summit of his achievement. He stands there contemptuous of those on the plain below who cheer him for the wrong reasons, and he sees what they can never see.

The bell-tower represents to Bannadonna the means to titanic self-glorification. To suggest Bannadonna's aim of achieving superhumanness, Melville makes allusion to such biblical giants as Anak. He is indirectly associated with such mythological gods as Titan and Vulcan.[10] He is called "fearless as Shadrach" in the

10. Melville compares the fallen tower to fallen Titan and calls Bannadonna's face "Vulcanic." The early Vulcan, an ancient god noted

fiery furnace, not because he has faith in God but because he has such faith in himself. Both the biblical and mythological references point up Bannadonna's psychological severance from humanity; he is as far removed from them as the tower's belfry from the plain. His building the tower is both self-glorification and rebellion against the world, a sweet (because secret) betrayal, a fatal "stroke" by their own "vassal." Another set of allusions suggests this theme of betrayal. Bannadonna first calls his creation Haman, whose story in the book of Esther deals with his betrayal of the Jews.[11] His plot overturned, Haman is himself hanged upon the gallows he had prepared for the Jew Mordecai. In another place one of the magistrates who visits the belfrey of the bell-tower compares the face of Una, who represents the first hour of the day on the great bell, to that of the prophetess Deborah in a painting by a Florentine artist. The analogy is deepened when the same magistrate compares Bannadonna with Sisera, "God's vain foe," to which the chief magistrate answers: "Deborah?—Where's Jael, pray?" (p. 126). And again, Talus standing over the dead Bannadonna is "like Jael over nailed Sisera in the tent" (p. 127). Finally, the "metallic stranger" in killing Bannadonna "drove but that one nail" (p. 129). The biblical story of betrayal which Melville repeatedly refers to here is found in the fourth chapter of Judges. Prophetess and judge of the Israelites, Deborah foresees the fall of mighty Sisera, and she instructs her people to attack him. He

---

for uncontrolled fire, such as in volcanoes, is an appropriate figure to compare Bannadonna with. The later Vulcan became confused with the Greek god Hephaestus, who used his fire and force for the good of mankind.

11. The mechanical man thus has two names, the one (Haman) suggesting Bannadonna's private motives—as well as his terrible fate—and the other (Talus) revealing the public's view. The mythological Talus (or Talos) was a bronze robot created by Hephaestus to serve the king and people of Crete by guarding the island from attack. Melville would also have been familiar with the iron man of Spenser's *The Faerie Queene*.

alone escapes the battle. Coming to the tent of the woman Jael, whom he considers friendly, he falls asleep of exhaustion. She then drives a nail through his temples and delivers him to the Israelites. The web that Melville weaves in this complex story is tangled, for if Bannadonna is betraying the trust of the people through his motives, he is himself betrayed by his own creation, Talus.

In addition to these two motives—self-glorification and the manifestation of contempt for the world—Bannadonna constructs the tower as an act of rebellion against those universal forces that control men. With Ahab he will have nothing "over" him. He will not offer sacrifices and build monuments to any gods, temporal or eternal, but he will rival their power through his own art. His defiance is made clear through his ignoring laws of every kind. He defies both civil and moral laws by murdering a workman who because of his fear threatens the successful casting of the great bell. Through the height of the tower and the weight of the bell, he defies the physical laws of the universe. The only law he obeys is what he calls the "law in art, which bars the possibility of duplicates" (p. 126). He has overcome fear, the great master of humanity. He sneers at death by standing on the unrailed tower, and he shakes his fist at the heavens through his creation of the bell and Talus. They signify to him the breaking of time's dominance, and they mock man and whatever powers created him.

Melville's language in describing Talus is carefully chosen to suggest that the creature is more than merely a robot. Strange sounds, like "half-suppressed screams and plainings," seem to issue from him (p. 127). When the chief magistrate admires the bell as Bannadonna's masterpiece, a sound is heard from Talus, as if he is jealously objecting. When a cup is found in the belfry, the reader is confronted with the possibility that the creature takes nourishment. In another place the suggestion is made that Talus has altered his sitting position and again that he is breathing. The spaniel that finds its way into the belfry after

Bannadonna's death shivers and then disappears as if to impart the notion that it has seen a sight too remarkable and too unnatural for such a simple creature to live with. Melville calls Talus "the magic and metallic stranger" (p. 129). The two magistrates who discover the dead Bannadonna will never reveal anything of what happened, perhaps because it would be too fantastic for the people to believe. Even the ostensible method of destroying Talus—by shooting him—seems more appropriate for the destruction of a man than for a statue or a machine.

The implication is that Bannadonna's art has resulted in a far more exalted and terrible achievement than anyone could have expected of a "mechanician." The old blacksmith who watches Talus being lifted by a crane to the bell-tower speaks truer than he realizes when he says the creature is "but a living man" (p. 124). When uncovered, Talus is not like a man to other men, but he very nearly represents Bannadonna's view of man: a crude Caliban kind of monster controlled by a routine of slavish fixity, a creature without a soul. When a noise from the direction of Talus is heard, one of the disturbed magistrates asks if they had not heard a soul there. "No soul, Excellenza," answers Bannadonna, and then with emphasis, "rest assured, no *soul*.— Again the mortar" (p. 126). To Bannadonna, man is but mortar, and to prove it, he has created what to his mind is a man.

As in so many other places in the story, the public's opinion of how Bannadonna conceived the idea of Talus is highly ironic; it provides another glimpse of the white doe of truth amid a world of lies. "It was from observing these exposed bells, with their [human] watchmen, that the foundling, as was opined, derived the first suggestion of his scheme. Perched on a great mast or spire, the human figure, viewed from below, undergoes such a reduction in its apparent size, as to obliterate its intelligent features. It evinces no personality," and it seems to have no will of its own (p. 128). They thus conclude that Bannadonna looking up at this sight devised his plan of a robot which could strike a bell "with even greater precision" than a human

and therefore be a helpful slave to man. To the young foundling setting out without name or fortune his station in life was
such that others did seem perched aloof upon some spire, and
his increasing bitterness wrought the image of man as petty,
stupid, even mechanical. Through his genius he gradually exchanged places, putting himself upon the perch and man upon
the plain. But even more important to him, he rivals the very
creator by duplicating what he conceives to be a man.

Bannadonna's purpose in having Talus strike the bell at the
precise spot where the figure of Una clasps the hand of Dua is
to celebrate symbolically his own breaking of the clasp of time.[12]
"The stroke of one," he says, "shall sever that loved clasp" (p.
125). It will represent his own complete break with the world
and the universe as he stands magnificently unique. The magnitude of his aim and its futility are both implied through the per-
vasiveness in the story of the idea of oneness. The bell-tower
upon the plain forms a huge figure one to symbolize the triumph
of this cynic solitaire, a giant without duplicate among men and
gods.[13] His is the first tower to combine bells and clock. Its

12. John Vernon makes the point that "the theme of time is most
important in 'The Bell-Tower,' for in Bannadonna's attempt to burst
through human limitations, the limitation of time becomes a chief obstacle." "Melville's 'The Bell-Tower,'" *Studies in Short Fiction* 7
(1970): 268.

13. The tower is also a rather obvious phallic symbol. As in "Cock-A-
Doodle-Doo!" the image of extraordinary sexual vitality is used metaphorically to suggest the hero's concept of his superiority over ordinary
men. Chase, Fenton, and Vernon all discuss the sexual symbolism of the
story. Chase argues that the theme of castration is primary; Fenton, on
the other hand, states that "the sexuality of the tower, with its connotations of energy here directed by reason, is Melville's conception of Man
—American Man in particular, one would guess—attempting through
science and mechanics to re-establish himself after the dislocations of
the Copernican and scientific revelations" (p. 224). Vernon argues that
"in sexual terms, his [the domino's] endless ringing of the bell in the
top of the Tower could be called a projection of Bannadonna's wish for
a constant, self-enclosed orgasm" (p. 276). Jacqueline A. Costello and
Robert J. Kloss see the story as "a tale of crime and punishment," the
crime being Bannadonna's attempt to "supplant his father as his

completion is to be celebrated at one o'clock. It is the face of Una, the first hour on the bell, that alarms the magistrates. And in death Bannadonna lies at the feet of Una. For one year after Bannadonna's death the bell-tower stands, and then on the first anniversary collapses in an earthquake, when "one loud crash was heard" (p. 130).

Bannadonna's concept of one involves his own glorified independence of all forces of enslavement, both temporal and supernatural. But his death and the destruction of his bell-tower argue for the ultimate reality of one in another sense—the unbreakable oneness of all. The betrayer is betrayed because final independence is an impossibility. Caught between rudimentary man, as he conceives him, and the bell of eternity, Bannadonna is shattered as the image of oneness sneers at his defeat.[14] The circle of time cannot be broken. The great figure one on the plain has through time's ravages become a mere gravestone. Like Anak and Titan, it too has been leveled and gathered back into the pernicious circle of oneness in which all things are inexplicably tied together. This setting which begins the story has been described aptly as "more like the familiar 'modern' desert of Surrealist painting than any locus from the poetry or fiction" of Melville's contemporaries.[15] It emphasizes the futility of human and even superhuman endeavor. What was "a once

---

mother's lover" in his fantasy and then to "eliminate his mother in his quest to create 'life' on his own." His punishment for this is castration. "The Psychological Depths of Melville's 'The Bell-Tower,'" *ESQ* 19 (1973): 254–261.

14. It may or may not be that Bannadonna was busy trying to change the expression on the face of Una when Talus struck him. But if he was, it would be logical to assume that he saw in this image of time a portent which he wanted to alter. Fogle offers the unlikely theory that Bannadonna "was trying to change Una's expression into uniformity" with the other figures (p. 66). Since Bannadonna explained earlier that on the bell "no two faces entirely correspond" (p. 214), this would be impossible.

15. James Baird, *Ishmael* (Baltimore: Johns Hopkins University Press, 1956), p. 397.

frescoed capital" is no more, and only the stump of the great
tower now stands, "with dank mold cankering its bloom" (p.
123). The idea of man's fall is prominent in this picture of
time's ravages and nature's creeping vengeance on human ambition. It is a powerfully evocative opening for a story which
deals with the inevitable failure of both titanic and ordinary
men to master the universal encompassing powers. That Melville had this idea uppermost in his mind seems clear from the
three epigrams with which he began the story. Omitted when
"The Bell-Tower" was reprinted in the *Piazza Tales*, they were
a part of the story when it appeared first in *Putnam's Magazine*
(August 1855). Quoted, as Melville put it, "From a Private
MS," they read as follows:

Like negroes, these powers own man sullenly; mindful of their
higher master; while serving, plot revenge.
The world is apoplectic with high-living of ambition; and apoplexy has its fall.
Seeking to conquer a larger liberty, man but extends the empire
of necessity. (p. 123)

The three words which end these three sentences—*revenge, fall,*
and *necessity*—furnish the keynote for the description of the
ruined tower on the plain. All is oneness. With one important
difference in meaning, Emerson's poem "Brahma" (1857) expresses Melville's concept perfectly:

> If the red slayer think he slays,
>   Or if the slain think he is slain,
> They know not well the subtle ways
>   I keep, and pass, and turn again.
>
> Far or forgot to me is near;
>   Shadow and sunlight are the same;
> The vanished gods to me appear;
>   And one to me are shame and fame.
>
> They reckon ill who leave me out;
>   When me they fly, I am the wings;
> I am the doubter and the doubt,
>   And I the hymn the Brahmin sings.

The strong gods pine for my abode,
    And pine in vain the sacred Seven;
But thou, meek lover of the good!
    Find me, and turn thy back on heaven.[16]

For Emerson, "me" in the final line is the harmonious principle of the universe, the oversoul; for Melville it is the unfathomable, interconnectedness of universal necessity. The man who enslaves is himself enslaved; he is ultimately overcome by the forces he thought he had mastered. He breathes to live, but each breath contributes to his death. The servants of mankind are but themselves part of a larger scheme of awesome unity which engulfs man. Yet the world in its "Shinar aspirations" has from the time of Noah's sons indulged in feverish and doomed activity, over and over building Towers of Babel. Common man seeks to be free of the more obvious forms of enslavement, illiteracy, poverty, and political and social discriminations ("All men are created equal"); extraordinary man aims higher and through superhuman endeavor attempts to shake himself loose from both worldly and cosmic shackles. But they are all caught up in the circle of necessity. In *Mardi* Melville dealt extensively with the same subject. Taji travels beyond the outer reef of the world only to "extend the empire of necessity," for he finds himself on an eternal cosmic merry-go-round, which he can never stop or escape from.

And yet Bannadonna like Taji commands respect for the magnitude of his aim and the fearlessness of his arrogance. Despite his obsessive rebellion against man and heaven which twists his mind and distorts his vision, he exemplifies that paradoxical heroism common to Melville's rebels. He proves, in a sense, what a man is capable of and therefore in his self-glorification gives a glimpse of human potentiality amid forces that ultimately are undefeatable. As in all instances of such heroism in Melville's works, the rise of Bannadonna to heights

16. Centenary Edition of *The Complete Works of Ralph Waldo Emerson* (Boston: Houghton Mifflin, 1918), 9: 195.

of psychological self-sufficiency and rebellion is paralleled by a corresponding decrease in his concern for humanity. Melville will never let us have it both ways: human compassion and unselfishness are admirable, but they are traits shared only by mere men, who are to the gods "As flies to wanton boys," killed for sport. To be more than a fly, a man cannot be a man, and to be more than a man is to lose the most priceless of human traits. The blemish in Bannadonna's bell is shed human blood.

If Melville had written "The Bell-Tower" earlier in his career, Bannadonna's characterization might have been more direct. Like Ahab, he might have been allowed to speak (or rave) for himself, and this battle with temporal and eternal forces might have been given spotlight and center stage. The method of "The Bell-Tower," however, reveals Melville's troubled belief during this period of his life in the world's failure of perception. Bannadonna's titanic endeavor is less important in the story for its own sake than for the world's interpretation of it, which Melville develops at such lengths and with such subtlety that many critics have accepted it erroneously as his own.

Most of the information about Bannadonna's motives in building the bell-tower as well as the occurrences immediately after his death is confined to a section which comes after the description of Talus standing over his dead creator. Beginning with "Uncertainty falls on what now followed" (p. 127), Melville mixes a few facts with long passages of questionable accuracy. Here Melville shifts his point of view from the more objective angle from which the earlier part of the story is told. After reaching the point at which Bannadonna is killed, he drops the curtain, and reflecting back upon Bannadonna and his aims, he acts as spokesman for the people who interpret in accordance with their own views and values. The earliest details reflect the conjectural quality of the entire section: "It were but natural *to suppose* that the magistrates would at first shrink from immediate personal contact with what they saw. At the least, for a time, they *would* stand in involuntary doubt; *it may be*, in more or less of horrified alarm" (p. 127, italics mine). All that is certain is that which is seen directly by the people below. They know, for example, that an arquebuss is sent above, and they hear its discharge, but they have to guess again about the target: "Some averred that it was the spaniel, gone mad by fear, which was shot. This, others denied." They know for sure only that the spaniel is seen no more (p. 127). A brief exception to the dominant point of view in this section then occurs as Melville shifts back to his authorial omniscience to recount the removal and secret burial of Talus, about which the two magistrates thereafter refuse to talk, "even in free convivial hours" (p. 128).

The passage that follows the explanation of Talus's burial and continues until the description of Bannadonna's funeral should be understood as the interpretation of those rational people of the world, who through common sense pretend not only to find the "solution of the foundling's fate" but also to "penetrate as well into his soul" (p. 128). Immediately the reader should be alerted to the dangers of accepting this account. One of the great ironies of *Billy Budd* derives from the report of the whole incident as flagrantly misinterpreted in the newspapers. And we remember the advice of the man of wisdom who tells the narrator: "Yes, X—— is a nut not to be cracked by the tap of a lady's fan. You are aware that I am the adherent of no organized religion much less of any philosophy built into a system. Well, for all that, I think that to try and get into X——, enter his labyrinth and get out again, without a clue derived from some source other than what is known as *knowledge of the world*—that were hardly possible."[17] And yet that is what the "less unscientific" populace of "The Bell-Tower" attempts to do—to get into and out of the labyrinth of Bannadonna by utilizing only "knowledge of the world."

The public account of Bannadonna's career is prefaced with

17. *Billy Budd, Sailor*, ed. Harrison Hayford and Merton M. Sealts, Jr. (Chicago: University of Chicago Press, 1962), p. 74.

these remarks: "In the chain of circumstantial inferences drawn, there may, or may not, have been some absent or defective links. But, as the explanation in question is the only one which tradition has explicitly preserved, in dearth of better, it will here be given" (p. 128). It is the world's "supposition" that Bannadonna got the idea of a mechanical man from looking up at human bell-ringers: it "was opined" that his creation was intended to be the ultimate in mechanical precision; it was their "conjecture" that Bannadonna was an enterprising spirit. They "intimate" and "project" that Talus is meant to be "a sort of elephantine Helot, adapted to further, in a degree scarcely to be imagined, the universal conveniences and glories of humanity," a slave to man (p. 128). If these "conjectures" are correct, Melville states, then Bannadonna must have been a crazy dreamer, but the world "averred" that he was instead "a practical materialist." Furthermore his means "were alleged to have been" the product of "sober reason."

Men attribute to him their own motives and values and then refuse to interpret him in any other way. Just as Bannadonna, in his rebellion and bitterness, creates what is in his distorted view a man, so men invent a Bannadonna who is equally distorted, for he is created in their own image. Even when he kills a workman, they retain this image intact. Their highest representatives of law, the judge and the priest, forgive him as an adult might a favorite and petted mischievous child. He is their darling because as they see it he uses all the right tools, reason, science, technology, to monumentalize them. It is *their* view, therefore, that he is "a practical materialist," that to him "common sense was theurgy," and "machinery, miracle" because these are their own values. Concluding his treatment of Bannadonna's nature and aims, Melville again makes his point of view clear: "Such, then, were the *suppositions* as to the present scheme, and the reserved intent" (p. 129, italics mine). The popular view of the circumstances surrounding Bannadonna's death is equally conjectural: "How, at the very threshold, so unlooked for a catastrophe overturned all, or, rather, what was the conjecture here, is now to be set forth" (p. 129). "It was thought that" Banna-donna spent the evening adjusting and oiling the mechanism. "It was surmised that" he forgot the time in putting final touches on the bell and was struck by the mechanical man. As always the whole truth is mysteriously hidden. After presenting this recapitulation of the public view of Bannadonna and how he died, Melville then shifts again to the earlier objective point of view and narrates the facts of the funeral, the fall of the bell, and finally the destruction of the tower itself by an earthquake a year later.

The effect of "The Bell-Tower," therefore, derives largely from the enormous difference between Bannadonna as he really is and as the world sees him. An obsessed artist of profound genius who is bent upon the degradation of mankind, he is popularly regarded as a kind of eccentric Ben Franklin who is struck by lightning while nobly trying to harness electricity for man. Through this vehicle of irony, as poignant as he ever created, Melville probes two areas incomparably more significant than the subject of nineteenth-century American technology, the strange and intricate contradictions in the mind and heart of a cynic solitaire of extraordinary stature and the nature of a fog-bound world in which those who want to be recognized clearly must stand no higher than the height of an ordinary man.

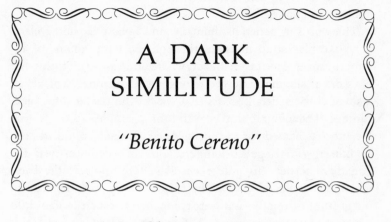

A DARK
SIMILITUDE

"Benito Cereno"

Chapter 10

When Melville opened the book that was to be his source for "Benito Cereno," Amasa Delano's six-hundred-page *A Narrative of Voyages and Travels* (1817), he saw looking back at him a portrait of the stout, moon-faced author. The face is kindly and cheerful; the eyes are its outstanding feature but not because they penetrate. They are blank and a bit sleepy in spite of their being wide open. It could well be that Melville's interest in Amasa Delano began with this frontispiece. By the time he had finished Delano's work and a "Biographical Sketch" appended to the volume, he must have had a well-formulated image of the plain New England sea captain. The sketch, composed by "a friend," tells of Delano's family background, his compassion, and his personal integrity. To illustrate his finer qualities, it cites an incident where Delano lost everything he owned in a shipwreck off Cape Cod. His crew were left destitute, but he could not help them. "He was greatly distressed

227

and mortified at his situation—for he was ever generous, humane and honest."[1]

The words of generous, humane, and honest Captain Delano flow like blackstrap molasses through the long volume of his reminiscences. He traveled everywhere and saw everything, but his work is singularly devoid of insight. Occasionally, however, a situation or a detail occurs that shocks the reader into wakefulness. The biographical sketch, for example, recounts that Delano was named for his uncle, Amasa Delano, who had been an officer with Rogers's Rangers. On an expedition near the Canadian border, his guides deceived him and left the band under his command lost in the forest. "They were reduced to the greatest extremity; and were compelled to eat an Indian child which they met in the woods."[2] Casually the writer conveys this startling instance of cannibalism as if civilized white people ate savages whenever the need arose. Such an episode would not have failed to impress Melville, who was deeply fascinated and horrified by the thought of cannibalism, and it was perhaps partly responsible for a strong suggestion of cannibalism in "Benito Cereno."

Chapter eighteen gave Melville the dramatic situation for his story. Delano tells of his experience off the coast of Chile in 1805, when his ship, the *Perseverance*, encountered a South American slave ship, the *Tryal*, which had been taken over by the slaves. The *Tryal*'s captain, Benito Cereno, was forced to deceive Captain Delano as to the true situation on board. When the American was about to leave the *Tryal*, Captain Cereno jumped into his departing boat and explained the facts to him. Although Melville used the basic situation, he changed the date of the event and the names of the ships; added a number of incidents not mentioned by the real Delano, such as the shaving scene and the meal; changed the traits of some characters;

1. Amasa Delano, *A Narrative of Voyages and Travels* (Boston: E. G. House, 1817), p. 592.
2. Ibid., p. 580.

altered the names and the fates of others; and swept into the episode those powerful currents of meaning that make "Benito Cereno" one of his true masterpieces.[3]

The lines that Melville affixed to "The Bell-Tower" (quoted in the previous chapter) apply equally to its counterstory, "Benito Cereno."[4]

Like negroes, these powers own man sullenly; mindful of their higher master; while serving, plot revenge.

The world is apoplectic with high-living of ambition; and apoplexy has its fall.

Seeking to conquer a larger liberty, man but extends the empire of necessity.

The theme of ultimate futility, which these lines emphasize, is stressed in "Benito Cereno" through the constant play upon appearance and reality. On the literal level of action, the ap-

3. The primary source for "Benito Cereno" was first pointed out by Harold H. Scudder, who reprinted as part of his article chapter 18 of Delano's *Voyages*. See "Melville's *Benito Cereno* and Captain Delano's Voyages," *PMLA* 43 (1928): 502–532. Scudder overestimated the extent of Melville's reliance on his source, however, and was corrected by Rosalie Feltenstein, "Melville's 'Benito Cereno,'" *American Literature* 19 (1947): 245–255. Among commentaries offering possible additional sources for the story, H. Bruce Franklin's " 'Apparent Symbol of Despotic Command': Melville's *Benito Cereno*," *New England Quarterly* 34 (1961): 462–477, has received the most attention. Franklin's argument is that William Stirling-Maxwell's *Cloister Life of the Emperor Charles V* (London, 1853) is "of more ultimate significance than Delano's *Voyages*" as a source for "Benito Cereno" (p. 462). The validity of Franklin's argument, which was repeated in his *The Wake of the Gods: Melville's Mythology* (Stanford: Stanford University Press, 1963), was effectively questioned by Hershel Parker, " 'Benito Cereno' and *Cloister-Life*: A Re-Scrutiny of A 'Source,' " *Studies in Short Fiction* 9 (1972): 221–232.

4. Similarities in the two stories have not generally been recognized, though a few critics have suggested connections. See, for example, David D. Galloway, "Herman Melville's *Benito Cereno*: An Anatomy," *Texas Studies in Language and Literature* 9 (1967): 239–252, and Charles Nicol, "The Iconography of Evil and Ideal in 'Benito Cereno,' " in *Studies in the Minor and Later Works of Melville*, ed. Raymona E. Hull (Hartford: Transcendental Books, 1970), pp. 23–25.

parent situation is not the real one. That simple dichotomy is misleading, however, for despite the insistence of numerous critics that "Benito Cereno" *contrasts* appearance with reality, the underlying conclusion reached in the story is that both appearance and what passes for reality are false and thus in a sense not opposites but similitudes. Whenever one layer of false perception has been cut away in order for bare reality to be seen below, that reality proves to be only another layer of appearance. This effect is like the result of Ishmael's running commentary and description of whales in *Moby-Dick*: he describes in detail the outer aspects—size, color, blubber—and then moves in other chapters inward toward the whale's brain and sense perception. But the inward progress does not end at a center; no revelation of the hidden essence of Whale is possible, for if there is such a reality, it remains unknown forever. The lesson of "Benito Cereno" is the same as that which Pierre had to learn: "because Pierre began to see through the first superficiality of the world, he fondly weens he has come to the unlayered substance. But, far as any geologist has yet gone down into the world, it is found to consist of nothing but surface stratified on surface. To its axis, the world being nothing but superinduced superficies." [5]

In "Benito Cereno" one layer is basically like another—only superficially different—although the characters in the story cannot understand this. This chapter will deal with how the authorial vision of "Benito Cereno," that of the underlying sameness of things, is developed (and this will involve an examination of the story's point of view); with how each of the three main characters sees life; and with how they cope with life by acting out a role as if they were in a play. These three aspects are manifested in the story in three broad patterns of images that relate to the circle, the eye, and the stage.

5. *Pierre*, ed. Harrison Hayford, Hershel Parker, and G. Thomas Tanselle (Evanston and Chicago: Northwestern University Press and the Newberry Library, 1971), p. 285.

In projecting an authorial vision of life as—to borrow a phrase from John Bunyan—"a dark similitude," Melville concentrates on four major areas of human existence: physical environment, personal freedom, experience, and religion. In all of these areas he rejects the idea of clear opposites, which is but illusory, in favor of a terrible sameness.

Most of the action in "Benito Cereno" takes place on the sea aboard the *San Dominick*, but almost from the very beginning Melville creates linking images, correspondences between things of the sea and the land. The "troubled gray fowl" of the ocean are like "swallows over meadows before storms."[6] The *San Dominick* is like a "superannuated Italian" palace with "tenant-less balconies" hanging over the "Venetian Canal" of the sea (p. 354). A little later the *San Dominick* is compared to a man lost in the forest, doubling back on himself (p. 359). The old upturned boat on the deck creates a "subterraneous sort of den" or "cave" (p. 465), and Benito Cereno's quarters, the "cuddy," resemble a "cluttered hall of some eccentric bachelor-squire in the country" (p. 466). During one of his moments of anxiety, Delano feels like one "alone on the prairie" rather than on the sea. The ocean swells are "terraces," and the balustrade of the ship "seemed the charred ruin of some summer-house" (p. 461). He feels landlocked in some "far inland country" in a château. Meanwhile a sailor seen behind some rigging vanishes "into the recesses of the hempen forest, like a poacher" (p. 461). Sailors and slaves on the ships are compared to people of the land: the hatchet polishers are like "tailors," an elderly Negro has the air of an "attorney," and Delano's men who board the *San Dominick* to battle the blacks are like "troopers in the saddle." In "Benito Cereno" Melville has dropped his metaphor of *Moby-Dick*, where the sea is the "howling infinite" and diametrically opposed to the "lee shore." Here "the country

6. All page references to "Benito Cereno" are to *Putnam's Monthly Magazine* 6 (October, November, and December, 1855).

and the ocean seem cousins-german" (p. 466); a pervasive sameness marks all physical environment.

Within this gray setting of life, ostensible freedom and slavery are never clear-cut and separate states. The slave and the enslaver share the same fate. Melville's interest in this idea was of long standing. Ishmael says in *Moby-Dick*: "Who aint a slave? Tell me that. Well, then, however the old sea-captain may order me about—however they may thump and punch me about, I have the satisfaction of knowing that it is all right; that everybody else is one way or other served in much the same way—either in a physical or metaphysical point of view, that is."[7] In "Benito Cereno" Melville deals with both these forms of slavery, physical and metaphysical, to show that all are, indeed, "served in much the same way."

With regard to freedom and slavery, the human condition is symbolized by the sternpiece of the *San Dominick*: "But the principal relic of faded grandeur was the ample oval of the shield-like stern-piece, intricately carved with the arms of Castile and Leon, medallioned about by groups of mythological or symbolical devices; uppermost and central of which was a dark satyr in a mask, holding his foot on the prostrate neck of a writhing figure, likewise masked" (p. 354). The figures here bear a resemblance to those in Raphael's painting of the archangel Michael slaying the dragon. The subject was treated by a number of artists, but Raphael depicted the dragon as a very dark

7. *Moby-Dick*, ed. Harrison Hayford and Hershel Parker (New York: Norton, 1967), p. 15. Margaret M. Vanderhaar, "A Re-Examination of 'Benito Cereno,' " *American Literature* 40 (1968), points out that in Melville's poem "The Swamp Angel," his metaphor for the Parrott gun which bombarded Charleston is a Negro slave: "A coal-black Angel / With a thick Afric lip." Thus Melville suggests that "the South (Charleston) is now victim of that which it once victimized" (p. 184). Howard Welsh argues that Melville is showing what can happen if those who impose slavery on others do not "keep up the repression requisite to the nature of the system." Thus the story is a prophecy of things to come after abolition. "The Politics of Race in 'Benito Cereno,' " *American Literature* 46 (1975): 556–566.

Satanic-looking creature. Mrs. Jameson, whose book *Sacred and Legendary Art* was popular when Melville wrote "Benito Cereno," described Raphael's "fiend" as "human," but, she continues, "the head has the god-like ugliness and malignity of a satyr."[8] This dark, semihuman fiend is, of course, a perfect representation of the way the whites come to view Babo. But if Melville did model his sternpiece on Raphael's painting, he made two important changes: he shifted the positions of the two figures and masked both of them. The first change suggests that the fiend (Babo) is master. Melville's addition of the masks, however, undercuts that simplistic conclusion: neither figure has true and final identity as free victor or defeated slave, as representative of the light or of the darkness, because there is no fundamental difference between the two positions. The masks suggest that they are merely involved in role playing.

The *San Dominick* then is a microcosm where freedom and slavery revolve like a dog chasing its tail. A sea captain is ordinarily an all-powerful master, but even so he is "chained to one dull round of command" (p. 356). Babo was a slave in his own land among his own people, but now aboard the *San Dominick* he is the master. Yet he must still play the slave to fool Delano. In the shaving scene he overuses with mock humility the word *master* while at the same time shaving Cereno with "the hand of a master" (p. 469). Circularity always prevails. In the end he is again the slave, caught and punished. Benito Cereno loses his command to a slave, but he is in a sense the enslaver even at that time, for Babo must have his white victim or his existence ceases to be meaningful. Cereno thus has Babo enslaved at the precise time that Babo enslaves Cereno. Layer underlies layer of almost maddening reversals that reveal only the futility of men "arranging," as they imagine

8. Anna Brownell Jameson, *Sacred and Legendary Art*, 2nd ed. (London: Longman, 1850), p. 64. Bernard Rosenthal surmises that Melville had in mind another version of the same subject, a painting by Guido Reni. "Melville's Island," *Studies in Short Fiction* 11 (1974): 7.

they are doing, each other's "fate" (p. 367): "Seeking to conquer a larger liberty, man but extends the empire of necessity."[9]

In the dark vision that takes form in "Benito Cereno," the empire of necessity is represented, as it is in "The Bell-Tower," by nature's indifferent rule over man. Melville begins "The Bell-Tower" with a startling image of nature's engulfment of man. The "once frescoed capital" has been leveled, and the great bell-tower is now but a stump with moss slowly creeping over it. "Benito Cereno" begins on a similar note of man caught in the grip of nature, fixed in its gray sameness: "Everything was mute and calm; everything gray. The sea, though undulated into long roods of swells, seemed fixed, and was sleeked at the surface like waved lead that has cooled and set in the smelter's mold" (p. 353).

Alternating with this stasis is the movement of nature, buffeting man about in winds and currents over which he has no control. Benito Cereno's story to Delano is full of this alternation of calms and gales. But the extent to which man is subject to nature's whimsical shifts is made clearest through the constant reminders in the story that all the characters are waiting for enough wind to bring the *San Dominick* to anchor. Even nature, however, is not the final, ultimate necessity. Nature is also subject to a higher but inexplicable force; nature is but a metaphor for what Ishmael referred to as "metaphysical" necessity.[10]

9. Whites and blacks alike are described as "pawns" and "chess-men opposed" (p. 460). A similar view of slavery in the story and of reversal of roles is offered by Ruth B. Mandel in an excellent treatment of "Benito Cereno" as an expression of unsolvable mystery. "The Two Mystery Stories in *Benito Cereno*," *Texas Studies in Literature and Language* 14 (1973): 631–642, and by Kermit Vanderbilt in an insightful article, " 'Benito Cereno': Melville's Fable of Black Complicity," *Southern Review* 12 (1976): 311–322.

10. Robert J. Brophy, "Benito Cereno, Oakum, and Hatchets," *American Transcendental Quarterly* 2 (1969): 89–90, suggests that the four oakum pickers and six hatchet polishers represent "the stance and function of the Fates, the Parcae of classical lore" (p. 89). The oakum pickers would be "Clotho who spun the thread of life from a distaff" and

Besides emphasis upon similitude in the areas of physical environment and human freedom, Melville extends the idea to define the nature of experience. Here also circularity proves to be the essence of his vision. In human experience the point of departure is the ultimate destination, and the first point of destination becomes in turn a starting place. Melville was in a sense rewriting *Mardi* with its ceaseless and meaningless repetitions and alternations. The great circle of the sun that rises over the entire scene as Delano first sees the *San Dominick* is the circle of necessity that presides over man and gives its shape to his experience. Melville must have been struck with the final "o's" that appear in the names of the real people mentioned in *Voyages*—Delano, Benito Cereno, Don Alexandro, Francisco, Hermenegildo, and so on. Perhaps because he wanted to emphasize those "o's" (as circles or zeroes), he changed the name of the black who stays at Benito Cereno's side in the original narrative, Muri, to Babo, who was in reality Muri's son. Circles and circular actions appear frequently in the story. For example, the blacks sit in a circle on deck (p. 460), and the other characters, especially Delano, perform acts that bring them back to something they did earlier. Delano alternately goes below deck and returns above; alternately he is suspicious and trustful, comfortable and uncomfortable. The point is not that experience is made up of alternating opposites but that there is no truly new experience under the sun. As Babbalanja says in *Mardi*, we go round and round and get nowhere we have not already been.

To make tangible the idea that similitude rather than difference is the essence of experience, Melville ingeniously built into his story a number of echoes. Situations with variations repeat themselves; the same words and phrases turn up in different contexts. For example, toward the beginning a bird is described in the tops, "a white noddy, a strange fowl, so called from its

---

"Lachesis who measured it out." The hatchet polishers would be "Atropos who, armed with a shears, remorselessly snipped it off" (p. 89).

lethargic somnambulistic character, being frequently caught by
hand at sea" (p. 354). A few pages later Benito Cereno is depicted in the act of faltering and then staring "like some som-
nambulist" (p. 358). He is like the white noddy, for he too is
caught at sea while sleeping. In another place an elderly Negro
approaches Delano and asks for the strange knot a sailor has
given him in an attempt to convey hints. After looking at the
knot casually, the Negro tosses it overboard with a "pshaw" (p.
463). As the story progresses it becomes clear that what the old
Negro does with the knot is what Delano is doing with the
mystery before him that he cannot solve. He looks at it, puzzles
over it, and always ends by tossing it out of his mind with a
"pshaw." When Delano puts his foot on Babo, who is "snakish-
ly writhing up from the boat's bottom," the description of the
sternpiece is recalled. Now, however, the black satyr-slave is no
longer the master as on the sternpiece, and the circularity of
freedom and of experience is again expressed. Benito Cereno
first asks Delano if his ship is armed; then many pages later
after the slaves' rebellion is uncovered, Delano asks Benito
Cereno the very same question about the *San Dominick.*

Nowhere is Melville's echo technique more effective than in
the deposition section. Ostensibly the means for unraveling all
aspects of the mystery, it gives no final answers; it brings the
reader back full circle with almost every detail echoing some
earlier one in the story.[11] Introducing the deposition, Melville
hints that the testimony of Benito Cereno is no more the final
truth than the account he was earlier forced to give Delano

---

11. The reliability of the deposition has been called into question
by several critics including the following: Allen Guttmann, "The Enduring Innocence of Captain Amasa Delano," *Boston University Studies in
English* 5 (1961): 35–45; Edgar A. Dryden, *Melville's Thematics of
Form: The Great Art of Telling the Truth* (Baltimore: Johns Hopkins
University Press, 1968), pp. 207–209; Kingsley Widmer, "The Perplexity of Melville: *Benito Cereno,*" *Studies in Short Fiction* 5 (1968):
225–238; John Seelye, *Melville: The Ironic Diagram* (Evanston: Northwestern University Press, 1970), pp. 104, 110; Jean Fagan Yellin, "Black

aboard the *San Dominick*. At that time Delano doubted some parts of the story about the ship's hardships and admitted to Cereno: "Why, Don Benito, had almost any other gentleman told me such a story, I should have been half disposed to a little incredulity" (p. 468). All the blacks, however, corroborate the details, and Delano finally accepts the story. The deposition is another version, incredible in parts, but backed up by all the whites and thus similarly accepted: "Some disclosures therein were, at the time, held dubious for both learned and natural reasons. The tribunal inclined to the opinion that the deponent, not undisturbed in his mind by recent events, raved of some things which could never have happened" (p. 637). The whites confirmed his charges, and the tribunal believed them just as Delano accepted the earlier story.

The deposition is a testament of similitude; the acts of the Negroes are echoed by the acts of the whites. When the blacks rebelled they killed eighteen whites (p. 638); when the whites attack them, they kill "nearly a score" (p. 637). After Babo jumps into Delano's departing boat, the American takes a dagger from him that he is about to use on Cereno; in the deposition we learn that after the whites recapture the *San Dominick*, Delano "wrenched from the hand" of a white sailor "a dagger secreted" and about to be used on a black. The white sailor's name is Barlo! And so it goes with action mirroring earlier actions. Just as the Negroes killed several whites in cold blood after their initial rebellion, so the whites slaughter several of the blacks: "besides the negroes killed in the action, some were killed after the capture and re-anchoring at night, when shackled to the ring-bolts on deck. . . . These deaths were committed by

---

Masks: Melville's 'Benito Cereno,' " *American Quarterly* 22 (1970): 688; and Mandel, pp. 634–635. The opposite (and somewhat shortsighted) view is expressed by Geoffrey Stone, who feels that the deposition "does away with the fascinating mystery." *Melville* (New York: Sheed and Ward, 1949), p. 220.

the sailors ere they could be prevented" (p. 642). After the deposition, Melville ironically writes that it possibly has "served as the key to fit into the lock of the complications which preceded it" (p. 642). But the reader grows suspicious when he remembers that the "key" Benito Cereno earlier possessed to unlock Atufal was an ineffectual key in an unreal situation.

The last of the four areas of man's existence which together form Melville's vision of similitude is religion. Christian allusions abound in "Benito Cereno," but they are linked to references to barbarism and savagery. Suggestions of Christian eternity are matched by symbols of finality and decay. Commonly viewed as a story contrasting the old world of Europe, with its sophistication, to the new world of America, with all its innocence, "Benito Cereno" is instead a story in which Christian civilization and godless savagery are basically the same.[12] Melville makes this point through imagery involving the ship, bones, and food.

Concurrently, the *San Dominick* is described as both a monastery and as a hearse, that is, as both a symbol of Christian devotion and as an emblem of darkness and death. It appears first like a "white-washed monastery after a thunder-storm," a "shipload of monks," with "Black Friars pacing the cloisters" (p. 354). In this monastery Benito Cereno is the "abbot" (p. 356), who appoints "shepherds" to oversee the "flock" (p. 361). Babo is a "begging friar of St. Francis" (p. 360).[13] The cuddy seems some monk's cell with crucifix and with rigging under a

12. Richard Harter Fogle writes that "the *San Dominick* is the old order of Western civilization." *Melville's Shorter Tales* (Norman: University of Oklahoma Press, 1960), p. 130. Stanley T. Williams feels that the story in part is concerned with "the disintegration of the Spanish grandeur of the past." "'Follow Your Leader': Melville's 'Benito Cereno,'" *Virginia Quarterly Review* 23 (1947): 70. For Richard Chase, *Herman Melville: A Critical Study* (New York: Macmillan, 1949), Delano as the New World does not have the spiritual depth of Benito Cereno, who represents the Old World.

13. Melville alludes to several saints in the story: Saint Mary, Saint Nicholas, Saint Dominic, Saint Francis, and Saint Bartholomew. See

table like "a heap of poor friar's girdles" (p. 466). Interspersed with this imagery are references to the ship as a vehicle of death: "Like mourning weeds, dark festoons of sea-grass slimily swept to and fro over the name, with every hearse-like roll" (p. 355). The chant of the oakum pickers is described as "a funeral march" (p. 355), and the ship's bell rings a "grave-yard toll" (p. 362). The dead-lights of the *San Dominick* are "all closed like coppered eyes of the coffined," and the door of the state-cabin is "calked fast like a sarcophagus lid" (p. 461). The sea partakes of the same terrible finality; it "seemed laid out and leaded up, its course finished, soul gone, defunct" (p. 463).

The presence of death is represented by Aranda's skeleton nailed to the bow of the *San Dominick*, but here again death and life are but part of the same circle. The skeleton replaces the figure of Christopher Columbus, a symbol of newness and re-newal, which in turn replaces the skeleton after the blacks are defeated. But even in the single image of the bones both life and death are symbolized. When Delano first sees the canvas covering the skeleton, he cannot tell whether it hides "re-furbishing" or "decay" (p. 355). It hides both, or neither, for neither is a separate reality. Traditionally bones have symbolized death but also Christian resurrection. Melville uses this tradition for his own purpose, which is not to suggest that resurrection follows death but merely to develop further his theme of similitude, to fuse apparent opposites. The *San Dominick* seemed launched "from Ezekiel's Valley of Dry Bones" (p. 354). In the Bible Ezekiel has a vision that he is in a valley full of bones. Suddenly the Lord breathes life into them and they come together, take on sinews and flesh, and men are reborn (chapter 37). Underlying sameness is the deeper import of Babo's frightening question posed to Benito Cereno and then to each of the white sailors about Aranda's skeleton, "whether, from its whiteness, he should

Charles R. Metzger, "Melville's Saints: Allusion in *Benito Cereno*," *ESQ* 58 (1970): 88–90.

not think it a white's" (p. 639). Whites and blacks seem very different, but beneath the canvas of the skin is that all pervading similitude represented by the bones.

Christian symbolism, linked with decay, is seen not only in the ship and bone imagery but also in allusions to food, especially fish and wine. Delano, who sends out fishing parties and then supplies those hungering aboard the *San Dominick* with the catch, is a mock Christ figure generously and impartially feeding the multitude. Indeed, he thinks of himself as a kind of savior when he requests particulars of the Spanish captain about his misfortunes so that he would be "better able in the end to relieve them" (p. 358). Benito Cereno later begs Delano, who has "saved" him, not to go with the boarding party to fight the blacks. The roles of savior and saved, however, are ultimately as meaningless in the story as free man and slave. Later Delano admits: "You saved my life, Don Benito, more than I yours" (p. 643).[14] Delano feeds the multitude and then takes part in a highly ritualized meal, suggestive of the Last Supper, but where the servant seems both "Christian and Chesterfieldan," and where the host is the suspected betrayer. Shortly after the meal Delano wonders if Benito Cereno is like Judas, "who refrained not from supping at the board of him whom the same night he meant to betray" (p. 633). But here again betrayer and betrayed are the same.

If eating in "Benito Cereno" is tied both to Christian tradition and to the manners of civilized behavior, it is also linked with the most frightening aspect of stark savagery in the story—cannibalism, the eating of the host not figuratively but literally. The episode in Delano's *Voyages* involving the white man's eat-

14. The relativity of "salvation" in "Benito Cereno" is attested to by the variety of Christ figures seen by critics. Galloway, for example, sees Babo as a "black Christ," a "savior" directing his people to the "Promised Land" (p 250). William Bysshe Stein nominates Don Alexandro Aranda as "the true Christ." "The Moral Axis of 'Benito Cereno,' " *Accent* 15 (1955): 226.

ing of the savage has its counterpart in the story where the savages eat the white man. In the deposition, Benito Cereno testifies that the fierce Ashantees under Babo's command "prepared the skeleton of Don Alexandro, in a way the negroes afterwards told the deponent, but which he, so long as reason is left him, can never divulge" (p. 641). That cannibalism is involved in the "preparation" of Aranda's skeleton is strongly suggested when near the beginning of the story Delano questions Benito Cereno about Aranda's death, and Cereno seems unhinged.[15] Trying to be sympathetic, Delano recalls the death and burial at sea of his own brother on a previous voyage with him. He explains that he could have borne well his death if it had not been necessary to bury him at sea. The thought of his flesh being eaten by sharks was terrifying: "all, all—like scraps to the dogs —to throw all to the sharks" (p. 362). When Delano ends his comment by saying that Cereno would feel much better if Aranda's "remains" were still somewhere on the ship, the Spaniard collapses "with horrified gestures, as directed against some specter" (p. 362). The fate that Babo has promised Benito Cereno and his crew is not merely death if they fail to comply with his wishes, but the fate of Aranda, to be eaten, to be thrown like scraps to the "dogs." Dog imagery in the story is often associated with the blacks. Delano thinks of them as "Newfoundland dogs," and Babo looking up at Cereno is com-

---

15. Only three critics have to my knowledge noticed the suggestions of cannibalism in the story. Sidney Kaplan mentions the possibility in a single sentence in "Herman Melville and the American National Sin: The Meaning of Benito Cereno," *Journal of Negro History* 42 (1957): 22. Janice Edens Mobley states that "although we are not told exactly what happens to the body, the deposition hints at some atrocity. . . . Considering Melville's abiding interest in cannibalism, it is quite possible that this is the horrifying method of disposal used." "Eating, Drinking, and Smoking in Melville's Fiction" (Ph.D. diss., University of Tennessee, 1974), p. 103. John Harmon McElroy discusses the subject at greater length, but he reaches conclusions different from those stated in this chapter. "Cannibalism in Melville's *Benito Cereno*," *Essays in Literature* 1 (1974): 206–218.

pared to "a shepherd's dog" (p. 356). It is this specter, the specter of cannibalism, that destroys Benito Cereno.

The purpose that seems to underly the references and images pertaining to religion in the story is to yoke violently the ideals of Christian civilization to its opposite. The rule of love is linked to the rule of hate. Brotherhood is fused with misanthropy, eternal life with eternal death, Christian ritual with savage ritual. And in the end Benito Cereno, so fearful of being the victim of cannibals, is self-cannibalized. Even when Delano first meets him he is biting his lip. Fear has so eaten away at him that he is "almost worn to a skeleton," a skeleton identical to the one that is nailed to his ship.

The vision of dark similitude which I have examined in four areas—physical setting, freedom, experience, and religion—is not the vision of any one character in "Benito Cereno." It is the authorial norm, the standard by which all other visions in the story are measured. It may be obscured, confused with the over-views of certain characters, or, indeed, missed completely if the complicated nature of the story's point of view is not understood. A common misconception about "Benito Cereno" is that it is told from two narrative perspectives, Delano's limited point of view and the deposition. In fact, there are four, not two, narrative perspectives. At least part of the difficulty in separating out the additional two arises from what may be termed the fallacy of the first reading. Many critics analyze the story from the viewpoint of a reader who has read the story only once. They attempt to show how the point of view functions, how the characters unfold, and how the theme develops within the progression of that single reading.[16] Such a procedure is fallacious because no critic worth his salt reads the story only once and

16. Donald R. Swanson, for example, writes that "the reader's factual knowledge is usually limited to what Delano sees, hears, or knows." "The Exercise of Irony in 'Benito Cereno,'" in Hull, p. 23. See also Mary Rohrberger, "Point of View in 'Benito Cereno': Machinations and Deceptions," *College English* 27 (1966): 541–546.

writes about it, nor is he writing for the one-time reader. A critic may therefore find himself in the impossible position of trying to discuss the initial effects of the story after he has himself read it perhaps several times. It is also fallacious because "Benito Cereno" is clearly the kind of story, pervaded with verbal and dramatic irony, that cannot be fully grasped with a single reading. Meaning changes on later readings. Position and importance of characters shift somewhat. Rereadings also make it clearer that up to the deposition there is not merely one narrative point of view, Delano's, but others as well. The story's four points of view may be conveniently labeled reportorial, official (the deposition), authorial, and individual (Delano).

The reportorial narrative voice is largely neutral in tone and informational in function. It embodies no worldview or any character's viewpoint. It furnishes facts and is nonevaluative. The first paragraph of the story is a good illustration: "In the year 1799, Captain Amasa Delano, of Duxbury, in Massachusetts, commanding a large sealer and general trader, lay at anchor, with a valuable cargo, in the harbor of St. Maria—a small, desert, uninhabited island toward the southern extremity of the long coast of Chili. There he had touched for water" (p. 353). Within the action of the story this voice occurs many times as in the following passage: "At this moment a messenger-boy, a white, hurried by, in the regular performance of his function carrying the last expired half hour forward to the forecastle, from the cabin time-piece, to have it struck at the ship's large bell" (p. 465). Sometimes the reportorial voice relates information which Delano is not even aware of. When Delano speaks encouragingly to a sailor at the tiller, "unperceived by the American . . . two blacks eyed the sailor askance" (p. 472). Delano's boat, a speck in the distance, is first "observed by the blacks," who shout to Benito Cereno, who in turn informs Delano (p. 459). The details of the boarding, when Delano's men defeat the blacks, are also related in the neutral reportorial voice, describing an entire event of which Delano was not a part.

The deposition section, although a statement dictated or at least endorsed by Benito Cereno as embodying his testimony, does not in fact represent his point of view. It is the "official" view of the *San Dominick* affair, the world's final word on it that will go down in the record books and therefore answer satisfactorily every disturbing question about it. It does not dare probe beneath the surface. The world has spoken in the deposition and settled the affair once and for all. It is the official, legal stamp, "case closed."[17] Besides the obvious difference—the use of formal, legal language—the "official" point of view differs from the reportorial in that irony is more prevalent. Both voices, reportorial and official, are seemingly factual in purpose and mostly literal in nature, but Melville's echo technique transforms the deposition from a neutral retrospective commentary on events to a commentary on the vanity and foolishness of ordinary mankind who cannot see or will not see the sameness of all.

Two other points of view must be distinguished in the story— an authorial narrative perspective and that of an individual character, Delano. The authorial voice is both interpretative and evaluative but not through direct, literal language. The vision of similitude that it projects is built up through constant figures of speech. It is permeated with intentional verbal irony, similes, and metaphors. Its style is a metaphor for its message. As Aristotle observed, a talent for effective figurative language "comes from the ability to observe similarities in things."[18]

17. The deposition serves the same function as the public account of Bannadonna's career in "The Bell-Tower." Just before that official view of the mechanician is given, Melville explains it in much the same vein as that in which he introduces the deposition: "In the chain of circumstantial inferences drawn, there may, or may not have been some absent or defective links. But, as the explanation in question is the only one which tradition has explicitly preserved . . . it will here be given" (p. 218).

18. Aristotle, *The Poetics*, trans. G. M. A. Grube (New York: Liberal Arts Press, 1958), p. 49.

Metaphor, his word for all figures of speech, "must be by transference from things that are related, but not obviously so, as it is a sign of sound intuition in a philosopher to see similarities between things that are far apart."[19]

Verbal irony in "Benito Cereno" is clearly authorial, for it is most often directed against Delano, and could not, therefore, represent his own point of view. As the story progresses this voice comes more and more to resemble Mark Antony's description of Caesar as an "honorable man." Delano is termed a "man of such native simplicity as to be incapable of satire or irony" (p. 363). To be simple may be praiseworthy, but to be incapable of using or grasping irony is probably to be incapable of much insight. He is "blunt-thinking" (p. 360), a "person of singularly undistrustful good nature" (p. 353), and a man of "singular guilelessness." Such descriptions are flattering on the most superficial level, but below that level they bite with a sharp irony.

Since Delano is blunt-thinking and incapable of irony, the elaborate similes and metaphors that characterize much of the style of "Benito Cereno" come mostly from the authorial voice. They create the thematic core, the insistence on interrelatedness. The consciousness that links the sea with "waved lead" and the sun with a "Lima intriguante's one sinister eye peering across the Plaza from the Indian loop-hole of her dusk *saya-y-manta*" (p. 354) is not the blunt-thinking American's. Melville depicts what Delano sees, but the *terms* of that depiction, that is, the figures of speech that make the correspondences necessary for the idea of similitude, are usually not Delano's. Melville frequently uses the words *was like* or *seemed*, but seldom adds *to Delano* when figures are used. The "negroes crouched sphinx-like," and Babo in the shaving scene is like "a Nubian sculptor"—these are correspondences that Delano probably would not make.

19. *Rhetoric*, trans. G. M. A. Grube (New York: Liberal Arts Press, 1958), p. 93.

Delano's point of view is, however, an important ingredient in the narrative. Stylistically it possesses three different characteristics: literalness, dead or simplistic figures of speech, and "enchantments." The way Delano's mind works is revealed often in language devoid of metaphor and simile: "Nevertheless, it was not without something of relief that the good seaman presently perceived his whale-boat in the distance" (p. 367). His internal questions are given frequently in the same literal vein: "Had the Spaniard any sinister scheme, it must have reference not so much to him (Captain Delano) as to his ship (the Bachelor's Delight). Hence the present drifting away of the one ship from the other, instead of favoring any such possible scheme, was, for the time at least, opposed to it" (p. 366).

Delano does sometimes use or think metaphorical language. The general difference between the authorial figures and those of Delano is that the latter does not have the insight for what Aristotle called the "right use of metaphors." Delano's figures are shallowly commonplace or dead and thus fail to show the deeper similitudes of the authorial vision. To him the negresses are "unsophisticated as leopardesses; loving as doves" (p. 461). He asks Benito Cereno if the oakum pickers are "shepherds to your flock of black sheep" (p. 361), and he concludes that the Spanish captain did not rise through the ranks, had not "got into command at the hawse-hole, but the cabin-window" (p. 360). His failure to think in fresh metaphors is strongly suggested in two episodes. First, when the sailor throws him the knotted rope and tells him to "undo it, cut it, quick," he does not understand that the knot is a metaphor for the mystery of the *San Dominick*. To the blunt-thinking American, a knot is a knot. Neither does he see anything of the real symbolism involved in the figure of Atufal in chains and lock with the key around Cereno's neck. He says jokingly that they are "truly significant symbols," but he does not grasp their meaning.

Occasionally, however, more meaningful figures of speech do creep into the mind of Delano, but, significantly, when this happens, he is quick to dismiss them. When he has that strange and prophetic feeling in which he compares his setting to the "charred ruin of some summer-house," he breaks the "charm" to be "becharmed anew" by thinking himself "a prisoner in some deserted château" (p. 461). Both these temporary indulgences in correspondences he thinks of as "enchantments." When he imagines Babo a "headsman" and Cereno "a man at the block," he quickly dismisses the metaphor as merely an "antic conceit" (pp. 467–468). He calls his own comparison of the shaving of Cereno to "some juggling play," (the "play of the barber") "whimsy" (p. 469). It is not, therefore, that he is entirely incapable of thinking and seeing metaphorically. He is determined not to, for metaphors, as we shall see when discussing his vision, are a threat to his peace of mind.

Central in "Benito Cereno," then, is the acting of seeing.[20] Delano sees one way, Benito Cereno another, Babo still another way, and against all these is set the authorial vision. The second large image cluster, after images of similitude, involves seeing and the eyes. A character's view of life is suggested by references to his eyes and by descriptions of how he looks about him. Delano, for example, is first seen watching the *San Dominick* through a telescope. He likes to bring everything up close to him. He is disturbed because he cannot distinguish the national origin of the ship—she "showed no colors" (p. 353). His is the vision of colors, of differentiation, and he is troubled when labels of difference cannot be applied to what he sees. His eyes go everywhere, from face to face of those aboard the *San Dominick*, up and down the Spanish captain when he first sees

20. Barry Phillips rightly observes that in Melville's world "the meaning a man induced had to be relative to his own perception." " 'The Good Captain': A Reading of *Benito Cereno*," *Texas Studies in Literature and Language* 4 (1962): 194. The same point is made by William T. Pilkington, " 'Benito Cereno' and the 'Valor-Ruined Man' of *Moby-Dick*," *Texas Studies in Literature and Language* 7 (1965): 201–207. Pilkington warns that each of Melville's characters must be interpreted according to his own individual perception.

him, around the ship to see such strange incidents as the black boy striking the white and the two Negroes jumping on the Spanish sailor. He constantly glances back and forth between Benito Cereno and Babo. He sees a sailor who in turn looks back at him and then to Cereno and Babo as if to relate some hint. His vision, however, is fragmented; he cannot put all the parts together to see that beneath difference is dark similitude.

Paradoxically Delano prides himself on his sense of democracy, his belief in human equality, but this intellectual concept is undercut by his deep-seated need to differentiate. He makes a gesture toward recognizing similitude when he tells himself that "Spaniards in the main are as good folks as any in Duxbury, Massachusetts" (p. 464). He continues, however, to think Spaniards "an odd set." He is very conscious of "relative positions," or rank. What disturbs him most about the *San Dominick* is that an equalization process seems to have taken place which has broken down the hierarchy of captain, officers, crew, and slaves. He is fond of Negroes, but he is ever aware of their difference from whites. In times of anxiety he comforts himself by insisting that he is different. He dismisses the notion, for example, that he is in danger of being murdered on the *San Dominick* because *he* is Amasa Delano—Jack of the Beach, not the kind to be murdered "here at the ends of the earth" (p. 463). He is domestic, a good fellow, a Christian, different from the sort who get themselves killed on pirate ships. When terrible suspicions crowd in on him later and he rushes from the darkness below up to the deck of the *San Dominick*, it is his vision of differentiation that calms him. Characteristically he looks quickly about him, his eye falling on one close object after another: "his trim ship lying peacefully at her anchor, and almost within ordinary call"; down by the *San Dominick's* side "his household boat, with familiar faces in it"; the oakum pickers going about their tasks close by; and the hatchet polishers still working as usual. As he sees all these details and feels the quietness in nature, his "clenched jaw and hand relaxed." All is right because differentiation still holds.

Delano's vision is willfully myopic. He must see things close up where all the details stand out but where similitudes are obscured. Whenever he looks out into the distance, as he does in the beginning to see the *San Dominick* entering the harbor, he is troubled. In another passage he sees his boat approaching at such a great distance that it blends in with the background, and he is uncomfortable. When he sees it close up, distinct and different from the setting, he is cheered: "The less distant sight of that well-known boat—showing it, not as before, half blended with the haze, but with outline defined, so that its individuality, like a man's, was manifest . . . evoked a thousand trustful associations" (p. 463). Details are his security. When he looks, he sees details. When he talks, he likes to give specific details—ne is disturbed when Benito Cereno seems uninterested in hearing the list of services and the costs of materials he is furnishing him with—and when he listens, he likes to hear details. He questions the Spanish captain over and over about the particulars of his alleged troubled voyage. In Delano's way of seeing, Melville represented as he understood it "normal" vision, that of the ordinary man who is humane, liberal, democratic, but who sees in terms of difference. Just how far removed Delano is from the authorial vision of similitude is suggested when he tells Benito Cereno at the end that "the past is passed." His concept of time is linear because he stands so close to the great circle of necessity that any part of it seems a straight line. Perhaps his greatest hidden fear is that he will be forced to step back.

Whereas Delano's eyes go everywhere and constantly differentiate, Benito Cereno's eyes almost never move. They have a "dreary, spiritless look" (p. 356). He closes them often, and when they are not closed, they stare vacantly with "half-lunatic looks" (p. 361) or gaze down at the deck, averted, unseeing. When Delano tries to make him look at the two blacks attacking a sailor, he puts "both hands to his face" (p. 459). Later when Delano tries to call his attention to the ship's keel cutting through the water, he looks with "lack-lustre eye" (p. 473). After his ordeal is over, Cereno does not want to look at Babo; when the court of inquiry insists, he faints. Benito Cereno's vision reveals only terror, so he looks as little as possible. Babo represents to him terror in its unadulterated essence. It is hard for him to look at anything, but the sight of Babo is intolerable. Cereno, therefore, sees neither the variegated and sparkling surface that Delano sees, nor the dark similitude of the authorial vision, for as the descriptions of his eyes suggest, he no longer has a vision of any kind except what may be termed the vision of abject terror.

Babo's eyes as a rule see only one object, Benito Cereno. He keeps his eyes on Cereno "as if to watch for the first sign of complete restoration, or relapse," and as the Spaniard drops his eyes to the deck, Babo turns his face "openly up into his master's downcast one" (p. 364). Time and again Babo "eyed his master" (p. 365), "rested his eye on his master's" (p. 471), or "gazed into his face" (p. 473). The deposition reveals that he told Benito Cereno that his "dagger would be alert as his eye" (p. 640). Even in death, Babo does not stop staring at Cereno: "for many days, the head, that hive of subtlety, fixed on a pole in the Plaza, met unabashed, the gaze of the whites; and across the Plaza looked towards St. Bartholomew's church, in whose vaults slept then, as now, the recovered bones of Aranda; and across the Rimac bridge looked towards the monastery, on Mount Agonia without; where, three months after being dismissed by the court, Benito Cereno, borne on the bier, did, indeed, follow his leader" (p. 644). Babo's, then, is a vision of singularity. Benito Cereno is to him all that enslaves, physical and metaphysical. In his narrowed vision the white figure of authority has ceased to be merely the symbol of what has frustrated him. No distinction remains in his mind between the symbol and the abstract qualities symbolized. They are incarnated, given flesh, in Benito Cereno.

Thus Delano looks about him at just about everything but he makes few connections. Benito Cereno has grown afraid to look at anything. Babo centers his vision steadily and boldly on one subject, Benito Cereno. While all this looking is going on, Melville subtly creates an effect of the characters themselves being watched. At the beginning the rising sun seems a great eye looking down on Delano who is in turn looking at the approaching *San Dominick.* Later Delano puts his trust in the "ever-watchful Providence above" (p. 634). And everything, of course, is being watched by the reader, who is made aware of his role as audience by the numerous references in the story to play-acting. The *San Dominick* seems a stage on which a strange play or masquerade, complete with costumes and mock ceremony, is being acted out. Delano wonders if a real gentleman would "act the part now acted by his host." Cereno seems to be "playing a part above his real level" (p. 364). As Delano looks around the ship, it is as if his eye passes from "a stage-box into the pit" (p. 463). He is himself "ready to play the pilot" and bring the ship in (p. 465). Play nests within play just as layer of appearance covers layer. The shaving incident, for example, is a play within the play, the "play of the barber" (p. 469). After that, Delano encounters Babo in a "wailing soliloquy" (p. 469).

Frequent references to ceremony or ritual enhance the effect of some absurd comedy taking place on a stage.[21] Cereno often acts "with an untimely caprice of punctilio." He affects "Castilian bows" and insists on Delano's "preceding him up the lad-

---

21. Robin Magowan, "Masque and Symbol in Melville's 'Benito Cereno,'" *College English* 23 (1962): 346–351, argues that "Benito Cereno" is a masque through which Melville condemns slavery. Although I do not agree with Magowan's thesis, he does emphasize stage devices in the story.

der" (p. 360). When Delano serves out the water, "Don Benito quaffed not a drop until after several grave bows and salutes" (p. 465). Within this play of the *San Dominick*, with its masks, costumes, and ceremony, more intimate dramas are being acted out. Each of the three main characters is playing his own private role which serves to define him.

Delano's role is much like that unconscious duplicity of the lawyer in "Bartleby." He plays it without realizing what he is doing. He is, like the lawyer, a man of prudence and method forced into a situation in the story where life's terrors are waiting to blind him if his willful myopia fails. Again like the lawyer, he gets through the test and is "saved," but his role playing, carried on as a response to dread, is laid bare to the reader. What Melville is doing with Delano has not, I believe, been well understood. Usually he is seen as a man of great courage whose fault is excessive innocence.[22] He has also been labeled a fool.[23] At least one critic thinks him an out-and-out coward.[24] Others hold that he is neither innocent nor foolish nor cowardly but a representation of the ideals of order and responsibility.[25] Actually he is not a fearless hero nor is he by

22. Ronald Mason, *The Spirit Above the Dust: A Study of Herman Melville* (London: John Lehman, 1951), calls Delano a man "of honesty and courage, but with something more than his fair share of credulity" (p. 185). Max Putzel, "The Source and the Symbols of Melville's 'Benito Cereno,'" *American Literature* 34 (1962): 189–206, argues that Delano's "courage so far outran his perception that he seemed to symbolize a national destiny over which clouds were rapidly gathering" (p. 196).

23. See, for example, Phillips, p. 192, and E. F. Carlisle, "Captain Amasa Delano: Melville's American Fool," *Criticism* 7 (1965): 349–362.

24. Stein argues that Delano shows both "physical and moral cowardice" (p. 226).

25. Widmer sees Delano as "a good, generous, sensitive, thoughtful man" (p. 233). Nicholas Canady, Jr., "A New Reading of Melville's 'Benito Cereno,'" in *Studies in American Literature*, ed. Waldo McNeir and Leo B. Levy, Louisiana State University Studies, No. 8 (Baton Rouge: Louisiana State University Press, 1960), pp. 49–57, writes that Delano combines ideally "authority and power" and thus "illustrates the

ordinary standards a coward. He will act positively when the occasion for spontaneous action arises, as when he attacks both Cereno and Babo after they jump into his boat. At the same time, fears hidden deep within make of him a good-natured innocent. The deeper fears are ill defined, dread of the unknown, dark haunting terrors that he dare not confront directly. He is Melville's ordinary man, who takes whatever psychological steps necessary to avoid open confrontation with these vague intuited terrors.

He can avoid prolonged exposure to the destructiveness of fear because he is a man of prudence and method; his prudence is "good nature" and his method is "good sense." But he nevertheless experiences fear often. He is afraid that Benito Cereno may not be what he seems. He has a "ghostly dread" of the Spaniard (p. 366). He is afraid of the hatchet polishers. He even fears rebuffs and embarrassment. Several different times he fears that he is about to be murdered. He worries that the ship is a "slumbering volcano" about to erupt (p. 366). Once his feeling is described as "panic" (p. 459). But each time fear arises, he is able through mental gymnastics that involve exerting his good nature and good sense to dismiss it. When "fancies" of danger crowd in on him, they come quickly "like hoar frost; yet as soon to vanish as the mild sun of Captain Delano's good-nature regained its meridian" (p. 364). When he cannot rationalize fears away by applying willfully generosity, benevolence, humaneness, and charity, he uses the device of "good sense"· "In short, scarce an uneasiness entered the honest sailor's mind but, by a subsequent spontaneous act of good sense, it was ejected" (p. 366).[26] After more explanation of the role that

---

ease with which command can be exercised under normal conditions" (p. 57).

26. In the version of "Benito Cereno" that appeared in *Piazza Tales*, this sentence was changed to read as follows: "In short, scarce any suspicion or uneasiness, however apparently reasonable at the time, which was not now, with equal apparent reason, dismissed." *Piazza Tales*, ed. Egbert S. Oliver (New York: Hendricks House, 1948), p. 82.

Delano plays, Melville ends on this significant note: "Such were the American's thoughts. They were tranquilizing." To avoid seeing the far-reaching implications of the *San Dominick* situation, Delano, in moments of fear, makes himself dwell on the individual details of what he has seen: "Though ashamed of the relapse [into fear], he could not altogther subdue it; and so, *exerting his good nature to the utmost*, insensibly he came to a compromise. . . . By way of keeping his mind out of mischief . . . he tried to occupy it with turning over and over, in a purely speculative sort of way, some lesser peculiarities of the captain and crew" (p. 464, italics mine). The conclusion that he reaches is "Yes, this is a strange craft; a strange history, too, and strange folks on board. But—nothing more" (p. 464). Such is the language of his role—*strange, odd*, and *queer*, but nothing more.

Delano's then is the "best regulated mind," as he prefers to put it (p. 468). In the deposition an ambiguous passage may well refer to how he uses mental "devices" to contradict what he might otherwise have to conclude. "Fear" in this passage may refer to Delano's as well as the crew's: "During the presence of Captain Amasa Delano on board, some attempts were made by the sailors . . . to convey hints to him of the true state of affairs; but . . . these attempts were ineffectual, *owing to fear of incurring death*, and furthermore *owing to the devices which offered contradictions to the true state of affairs*; as well as owing to the generosity and piety of Amasa Delano incapable of sounding such wickedness" (pp. 641–642, italics mine). Looking back on how he was saved, Delano reveals more than he realizes about the way his mind works: "the temper of my mind that morning was more than commonly pleasant, while the sight of so much suffering . . . added to my good nature, compassion, and charity. . . . Those feelings . . . enabled me to get the better of momentary distrust, at times when acuteness might have cost me my life . . ." (p. 643). It is Delano's pleasantness, good nature, compassion, charity, and good sense that not only keeps him alive but also covers up the gray sameness of the world and makes it appear to him as colorful dissimilitude.

Through most of the story Benito Cereno plays a role forced on him by Babo. Only a few glimpses are seen of him after he is rescued, but those serve mainly to show the terrible effect the blacks have had on him. Whatever estimate the reader makes of him has to come from hints. The "after" picture of him is clear but not the "before." Consequently, critics have widely disagreed on the kind of man he is. For some he is a weakling, lacking in "interior vitality,"[27] who "dies of his own inadequacy."[28] For others, he is "a coward who is capable of the most disgraceful behavior."[29] On the other hand, some critic see him as a martyr figure, the representative of "persecuted goodness,"[30] or as an heroic "exceptional man" confronting the maddening universe.[31] Whatever Cereno once was, he has been broken. His characterization is a study in what happens to a man when he is forcefully denied one role and is made to play another. Literally his new role involves deceiving Delano, but it is far more than that to him.

The end result of this new role is loss of all self-esteem

27. Merlin Bowen, *The Long Encounter: Self and Experience in the Writings of Herman Melville* (Chicago: University of Chicago Press, 1960), p. 203.

28. Guy Cardwell, "Melville's Gray Story: Symbols and Meaning in 'Benito Cereno,'" *Bucknell Review* 8 (1959): 166. James E. Miller, Jr., *A Reader's Guide to Herman Melville* (New York: Farrar, Straus and Cudahy, 1962), sees Benito Cereno as a man who shows "weakness in the face of danger" (p. 157).

29. Pilkington, p. 205. Similarly, Galloway argues that all of the undesirable aspects of the original Benito Cereno were preserved in the story but "presented more subtly" (p. 249).

30. Newton Arvin, *Herman Melville* (New York: Sloane, 1950), p. 240.

31. Marjorie Dew, "Benito Cereno: Melville's Vision and Re-Vision of the Source," in *A Benito Cereno Handbook*, ed. Seymour L. Gross (Belmont, Calif.: Wadsworth, 1965), p. 178.

through forced self-parody. In their final conversation Delano tries to cheer Cereno and ends by asking him what has thrown such a shadow over his whole existence. Cereno's answer "The negro," has been a focal point for interpreting not only the nature of the speaker's problems but also the theme of the story. It is what *follows* Cereno's answer, however, that offers the best clue to his destruction. Here Melville explains that the Spaniard would not speak at all about the things that had bothered him the most: "Pass over the worst, and, only to elucidate, let an item or two of these be cited. The dress so precise and costly, worn by him on the day whose events have been narrated, had not willingly been put on. And that silver-mounted sword, apparent symbol of despotic command, was not, indeed, a sword, but the ghost of one. The scabbard, artifically stiffened, was empty" (p. 643).

As in many of Melville's stories—"Bartleby," "Cock-A-Doodle-Doo!," "The Lightning-Rod Man," and "The Bell-Tower," for example—emasculation, or the dread of it, is an important element in "Benito Cereno." Melville suggests in the passage just quoted two essential factors in the Spaniard's destruction. First, he is forced to attire himself in the trappings of wealth and power knowing that now he is merely wearing a costume like an actor in a play. He is made to parody himself in the play, to make a mockery knowingly of all in the past he has identified himself with, his distinguished family, his wealth, his ship command. Secondly, the wording of the passage suggests that an even more fundamental aspect of his identity has been destroyed, his manhood. His "dress," fancy and costly, "had not willingly been put on." The terms are feminine. The phallic sword, symbolic of his manhood, has disappeared, and only the outward, mocking form remains, an "artifically stiffened" scabbard.

Benito Cereno's is a classic case of brainwashing, a modern term for an ancient practice. The standard definition of brainwashing is as follows: "On the psychological level this process involves the removal of social and perceptual supports . . . the destruction of the person's self-image by humiliation and revilement." [32] Recounting his experiences with mental torture carried out by the Nazis during World War II, a Dutch psychiatrist, Joost A. M. Meerloo, writes: "Even at that time we knew, as did the Nazis themselves, that it was not the direct physical pain that broke people, but the continuous humiliation and mental torture." [33] He goes on to cite the example of a man who was subjected to interrogation and great humiliation. "He refused to answer a single question, and finally the Nazis dismissed him. But he never recovered from this terrifying experience. He hardly spoke even when he returned home. He simply sat—bitter, full of indignation—and in a few weeks he died. It was not his physical wound that had killed him; it was the combination of fear and wounded pride." [34] This could well be a description of Cereno who, similarly, could not recover from his experience in fear.[35] Meerloo insists upon one point: it is not merely the weak who crumble under the pressure of brainwashing. "The spirit of most men can be broken," he writes. "In my opinion hardly anyone can resist such treatment." [36]

32. Edgar Henry Schein, "Brainwashing," *Encyclopaedia Britannica,* 1972.

33. *The Rape of the Mind: The Psychology of Thought Control, Menticide, and Brainwashing* (New York: World, 1956), p. 23.

34. Ibid., p. 23. In "The Reaction to *Benito Cereno* and *Billy Budd* in Germany," *Symposium* 13 (1959): 294–299, Leland R. Phelps writes that during and after World War II many Germans found "Benito Cereno" a poignant reminder of their own situation under Hitler and his systematic crushers of identity.

35. Melville may well have been struck with the real Delano's description of Cereno in *Voyages*: "I saw the man in the situation that I have seen others, frightened at his own shadow. This was probably owing to his having been effectively conquered and his spirits broken" (p. 326).

36. Meerloo, p. 33. Meerloo quotes the New York *Times*, 18 August 1955, on the subject of American prisoners of war during the Korean War: "virtually all American P.O.W.'s collaborated at one time or

The means used by Babo to terrify and control Benito Cereno are identical with the techniques used in brainwashing—removal of social and perceptual supports, the destruction of self-image by humiliation and revilement. Cereno's life has been highly structured. He is a sea captain who has customarily received the obedience and respect that goes with that position. In addition, he is part of a rich and aristocratic family of Old World traditions. Through humiliation and revilement Babo removes these supports, and Cereno is left without a role to play except the mockingly hollow one forced on him. Consequently, on board the *San Dominick* he is depicted as a man about to fall, stumbling and fainting. The only support he has is the hateful new "crutch," Babo, who constantly keeps him on his feet. When Babo is gone, Cereno seems incapable of standing at all. He has to be "carried ashore in arms" at Lima (p. 637). At the official hearing he is brought in on a litter, and in the end he is carried to his burial, borne on a bier.

The brainwashing of Benito Cereno is suggested through imagery of the Spanish Inquisition. This elaborate metaphor involves references to monks, friars, monasteries, crucifixes, friars' girdles, settees that are as "uncomfortable to look at as inquisitors' racks," and a chair for shaving Benito Cereno that "seemed some grotesque middle-age engine of torment."[37] Babo

---

another in one degree or another, lost their identity as Americans. . . . Thousands lost their will to live" (p. 34). Describing the victim of brainwashing, Meerloo seems to describe Cereno, who automatically relates the story Babo drills into him: "Time, fear, and continual pressure are known to create a menticide hypnosis. The conscious part of the personality no longer takes part in the automatic confessions. The brainwashee lives in a trance, repeating the record grooved into his mind by somebody else" (p. 34).

37. The word *middle-age* is omitted from the version of "Benito Cereno" included in the *Piazza Tales*. See Egbert S. Oliver's edition, p. 99. The first critic to trace the development of Inquisition imagery in "Benito Cereno" was John Bernstein, "Benito Cereno and the Spanish Inquisition," *Nineteenth-Century Fiction* 16 (1962): 345–350.

has assumed the role of inquisitor, the expert in mental torture, and the shaving scene depicts him in the act of terrorizing Benito Cereno.[38] Max Putzel has effectively described this scene as having "connotations of ritual murder and human sacrifice and the unspeakable horrors of the torture chamber. It is edged with the threat, nay the promise, of castration. For Don Benito screening his morbid memories under his heavy dark beard it holds threats more fearsome than death. It echoes with the reiteration of ancient torment that has no words, of secret fears deep as the womb."[39]

The "threat more fearsome than death" may well be cannibalism. In Melville's works the fear of being eaten is the greatest terror of all. It suggests not only stark savagery and arch inhumanity but the ultimate in humiliation and revilement. Melville's mind was filled with sharks and whales and other creatures that threaten to eat man's flesh. Ritual cannibalism was widespread in West Africa, home of the Ashantee, when Melville wrote "Benito Cereno," and since he had himself spent some time with cannibals in the South Seas, he was well acquainted with the practice. Tommo's great dread in *Typee* is better understood when it is known that cannibals would frequently capture an infant of the enemy or a stranger and treat him well, even allow him in time to marry into the group, but when a prearranged time came he would be killed and eaten. Tommo, who is constantly fearful that this is to be his fate, physically deteriorates under the pressure. It takes him weeks to recover after he is rescued. Sometimes the victim of cannibalism

38. Bernstein points out that the flag Babo puts around Benito Cereno is suggestive of the colorful *sanbenito* which a victim-heretic wore during the Inquisition (p. 348).

39. Putzell, p. 204. Martin Leonard Pops, *The Melville Archetype* (Kent, Ohio: Kent State University Press, 1970), argues that "Babo not only toys with Benito's life but, no less cruelly, with his sex—for . . . Melville often uses the shorn beard as symbolic of loss of manhood" (p. 152).

was first decapitated and his head hung up as a trophy.[40] When Delano thinks of Babo in the shaving scene as a "headsman," he suggests far more than he realizes. In the horrible practice of cannibalism a man was sometimes sliced to death; choice cuts were whacked off his body while he still lived. The shaving scene, and particularly Babo's cutting of Cereno, takes on new meaning with this specter of cannibalism in mind.[41]

Babo is the exception Meerloo pointed to in his book on brainwashing, the man who could not be broken by terror, physical pressures, humiliation, and revilement. He has conquered fear. But he is not an unselfish and noble leader nor an idealization of the black man fighting for his people.[42] Nor the personification of the principle of absolute evil.[43] Not a Prometheus whose "purpose is to release from bondage his enslaved people,"[44] nor "a monster out of Gothic fiction at its worst,"[45]

40. As part of the circularity of "Benito Cereno," Babo, who had perhaps victimized cannibalistically Aranda, is treated in the end as cannibals treat their victims, for he is decapitated and his head stuck on a stake for all to view.

41. Tom Burns Haber, "A Note on Melville's 'Benito Cereno,'" *Nineteenth-Century Fiction* 6 (1951–52): 146–147, argues that Delano actually cuts Babo after the shaving scene. The theory is effectively refuted by Ward Pafford and Floyd C. Watkins, " 'Benito Cereno': A Note in Rebuttal," *Nineteenth-Century Fiction* 7 (1952–53): 68–71.

42. Several critics interpret Babo this way and many see the story as Melville's attack on slavery. See, for example, Charles I. Glicksberg, "Melville and the Negro Problem,"*Phylon* 11 (1950): 207–215; Joseph Shiffmann, "Critical Problems in Melville's *Benito Cereno*," *Modern Language Quarterly* 11 (1950): 317–324; Warren D'azauedo, "Revolt on the San Dominick," *Phylon* 17 (1956): 129–140; Richard E. Ray, " 'Benito Cereno': Babo as Leader," in Hull, pp. 31–37; Guttmann, p. 188; and Peter Hays, "Slavery and *Benito Cereno:* An Aristotelian View," *Etudes Anglaises* 23 (1970): 38–46. Carolyn L. Karcher finds Babo "on the whole a complimentary portrayal of a black rebel" though Melville does not condone his violence. "Melville and Racial Prejudice: A Re-evaluation," *Southern Review* 12 (1976): 287–310.

43. Fogle, pp. 137–138; Feltenstein, p. 130.

44. Pilkington, p. 203.

45. Arvin, p. 240. Sidney Kaplan, who admits to not liking the story much, sees Babo as thoroughly depraved and the story as antiblack in

nor Melville's version of his critics,[46] nor motiveless malignity.[47] To understand Babo and the play he puts on, he should not be viewed in complete isolation as if he were unique in type but in the context of Melville's post-Pierre rebels through *The Confidence-Man*.

In the characterization of these extraordinary—sometimes almost superhuman—rebels such as Bartleby, the narrators of "Cock-A-Doodle-Doo!" and "The Lightning-Rod Man," Bannadonna, Babo, and the great and mysterious swindler of *The Confidence-Man*, Melville was indulging in what Robert Southey called the writing of "Satanic" literature.[48] After *Pierre* he had reached that emotional dilemma which is so aptly described—as if referring directly to him—in Thomas Carlyle's comment on Teufelsdrockh: "To our less philosophical readers, for example, it is now clear that the so passionate Teufelsdrockh, precipitated through 'a shivered Universe' in this extraordinary way, has only one of three things which he can next do: Establish himself in Bedlam; begin writing Satanic Poetry; or blow-out his brains."[49] The same precise alternatives open

sentiment. For a more balanced view of Melville's attitude toward blacks in the story, see Edward Margolies, "Melville and Blacks," *CLA Journal* 18 (1975): 364–373.

46. Scudder, p. 531.

47. Williams, p. 75. Arthur L. Vogelback, "Shakespeare and Melville's *Benito Cereno*," *Modern Language Notes* 67 (1952): 113–116, sees Babo as Melville's version of Iago.

48. Preface to *A Vision of Judgement* (London: Longman, 1821), pp. xix–xxi: "Men of diseased hearts and depraved imaginations, who, forming a system of opinions to suit their own unhappy course of conduct, have rebelled against the holiest ordinances of human society, and hating that revealed religion which, with all their efforts and bravadoes, they are unable entirely to disbelieve, labour to make others as miserable as themselves, by infecting them with a moral virus that eats into the soul! The school which they have set up may properly be called the Satanic School; for . . . they are more especially characterized by a Satanic spirit of pride and audacious impiety, which still betrays the wretched feeling of hopelessness wherewith it is allied."

49. *Sartor Resartus* (Boston: Ginn, 1896), Book Two, p. 135.

to Melville, he considered all three seriously and wrote "Satanic Poetry."

Melville's deep admiration for Milton's Satan is well documented. It is believed that in his home in Pittsfield hung a drawing by John Martin, "Satan Presiding at the Infernal Council," which depicts that evil figure, as Henry F. Pommer puts it, "in glory above his peers" and illustrating the Satan of *Paradise Lost*, Book Two.[50] In *The Confidence-Man* Melville discusses the qualities of that most extraordinary literary creation, the "original character," and he gives three illustrations: Hamlet, Don Quixote, and Milton's Satan. When he read Shelley's *Essays* he marked approvingly the lines that praise "Milton's Devil." It should be made clear that it was Satan the *literary creation of Milton* as Melville interpreted him and not the Satan of Christian tradition that he admired. Melville was no devil worshiper.

The distinction between Satan and Satanic hero is essential because both kinds of characters appear in Melville's work. The Jacksons, Blands, and Claggarts are soulless, corrupt, hollow, thoroughly evil characters who are often described in Satanic imagery. They may be devils, but they are not Milton's devil. He was a special devil. In discussing the possible influence of Milton's Satan on the creation of Ahab, William Braswell concludes rightly that "Ahab in the ideal is a far nobler character than Satan. Satan is a supernatural being who, though heroic, works by guile to achieve a selfish end."[51] After earlier heroes like Taji, Ahab, and Pierre, Melville went underground, so to speak, in the depiction of his rebels. Milton's Satan, as he saw him, now became a loose model for those more than ordinary and thus heroic but not necessarily noble figures in Melville who work "by guile to achieve a selfish end." The later rebels like

50. *Milton and Melville* (Pittsburgh: University of Pittsburgh Press, 1950), p. 10.
51. *Melville's Religious Thought* (Durham: Duke University Press, 1943), p. 69.

the earlier heroes are concerned mainly with securing complete independence from whatever powers rule them, especially cosmic, supernatural forces. They are rebelling against being mere men, limited, victimized, and enslaved. But the earlier heroes do not direct their energies against other men, though they will smash anyone who gets in the way of their drive toward freedom. With *Pierre* the motivational emphasis begins to shift. The hero still rebels against higher enslaving forces, but misanthropy now becomes a stronger factor, and Pierre's chief antagonist by the end of the novel is ordinary man, the "world."

The Satanic rebels, like the earlier heroes, still desire above all else to be completely free, but many of them are thorough man-haters. This motivation for their actions is often intentionally obscure, and their relative importance in the work has been diminished. Frequently, as in the case of Bannadonna and Babo, they are not center-stage with the limelight on them but more in the shadows. Melville had to take the sharp focus off such Satanic rebels for at least three reasons. He was selling these stories to *Putnam's* and *Harper's* for a public that would never accept bitter man-haters as out-and-out heroes. Secondly, there was danger that he might reveal too much of his own feeling about mankind if he opened the door wide enough for characters like Bannadonna and Babo to be clearly seen and understood. Finally, there was a side of Melville that held him in check, that whispered "hatred destroys" and that kept his ravings quiet and controlled. Consequently, the Satanic rebels are not presented at full length, and they are not idealized as noble searchers after truth. They are heroic in their exceptional will and fortitude, but they work by guile to achieve a selfish end. All of them are, in a sense, confidence men.

Babo is very much a case in point. His goal is sweet revenge; he plays a role that closely resembles that of Bannadonna in "The Bell-Tower." Seemingly a servant, humble and skillful at his job, he is actually a rebel. He leads the blacks in rebellion because he can use them for his own purposes. But perhaps the most important single detail about him in the story is that he was also enslaved by the blacks in his own land. His loyalty is to himself. The elaborate play that he creates and produces on board the *San Dominick* is a ritualistic, hyperbolic, systematic mockery of all those forces that have tried to enslave him. The center of his hatred is of course the white figure of authority, Benito Cereno, but he also controls the black figure of authority, Atufal. It is Babo's idea that Atufal, a king in his land, wear chains. Babo goes far beyond expediency in the play he directs. He savors every minute of such scenes as the shaving and the formal meal. Through guile he is shouting his defiance. He seems to sense that even though he must work under cover, he will never be this free again, never be able to control and mock hated mankind to the same degree. He has, like Bannadonna, forcefully molded with the hands of a sneering sculptor his own rendition of man, the pitiful, helpless Cereno, whom he controls as Bannadonna does Talus. And he flaunts this image of pitiful man before other men without their seeing what he is doing. Delano cannot see that through Cereno Babo is mocking him any more than the people in "The Bell-Tower" can see Banna-donna's insult to them through the creation of Talus. Both rebels take perverse delight in the blindness of the world, in making fools of people without their knowing it. In the end both are destroyed by the creatures they have molded.

Babo's motivation, therefore, is not malignancy so much as archmisanthropy. Since Benito Cereno has become for him the incarnation of all he despises as enslaver and limiter, he must leap after him into Delano's departing boat even though the act leads to his death. Had he been merely a shrewd leader of Ne-groes seeking freedom, he would never have taken this suicidal step. It suggests both the depth of his monomania and the need he has for Cereno. Babo without Cereno is like the Indian hater without an Indian.

Through the use of three large image clusters, then, "Benito

Cereno" projects a pessimistic view of existence.[52] Against the
backdrop of dark similitude, Melville stages a play where the
nature of ordinary man is revealed and where the freedom-
crazed misanthropist, the extraordinary man, is seen in his futile
rebellion. Despite what many critics say, it is not primarily a
story about evil, metaphysical, racial, or individual.[53] In the
central position here, as in a large number of Melville's stories
of this period, is fear. Through the main characters, three responses to fear are developed. Delano survives because he is
able to protect himself by rationalizing and thus to avoid the
full impact of terror. Whether he recognizes the fact or not,
though, he is a slave of fear. Cereno is forced to turn his eyes
full into the face of fear. Through a process we have come to
know as brainwashing, he is not allowed to hold on to any of
those tricks and devices of mind that act as blinders to keep
him stable. Thus he is broken in spirit and body. Babo, the
Satanic rebel, illustrates the heroic response to fear. He has the
extraordinary will and fire to look squarely and openly at fear,
the chief enslaving force of mankind, and to rise above its influence. In Melville's universe of dark similitude, however,
Babo's fate is the same, for he, too, is destroyed. Like Bannadonna and all those who rise above ordinary man, he dies to
mankind. Though physically alive, he no longer has sympathy,
compassion, and understanding for suffering humanity. In the
end he is swept up in the great circle of necessity, his heroic

52. Widmer and Vanderbilt are among the few critics who see the
profound darkness of the story. For Widmer, it is the darkness of
nothingness. For Vanderbilt, it is the darkness that results from Melville's bitter rejection of a God he considered "vengeful and deadly"
(p. 322).

53. See, for example, Lewis Mumford, *Herman Melville* (New York:
Harcourt, Brace, 1929), p. 246; Fogle, pp. 120–121; Yvor Winters, *In
Defense of Reason* (New York: Swallow, 1947), p. 222; and Mason I.
Lowance, Jr., "Veils and Illusion in *Benito Cereno*," *Arizona Quarterly*
26 (1970): 113–126.

rebellion as futile as the life of Delano or Cereno. Echoing through the story are the words chalked on the bow of the *San Dominick*, the name of a children's game, "Follow Your Leader." The words refer directly to Aranda, whose skeleton reminds the whites of their fate if they do not keep faith with the blacks. But everyone has a leader. The mate of the *Bachelor's Delight* tells his boarding party to "follow your leader." As a guest on the *San Dominick*, Delano must follow Cereno's lead. Cereno must follow the lead of Babo on board the ship, and in the end Benito Cereno "did, indeed, follow his leader," Babo, who had already followed the lead of others into death. Theirs is but a game of children, all going round and round, each one both leader and follower, slave and master, victimizer and victim, and none, from the most ordinary and healthy to the broken and feeble to the strongest and most extraordinary can break the control of necessity that carries them all in the end into the abyss of eternal similitude.

Like all of Melville's masterpieces, "Benito Cereno" has multiple dimensions, and like many of the stories he wrote during the period of 1853–56, it can be viewed, among other things, as a personal, if indirect, revelation. Melville's concern for his mental stability is well known.[54] His father died in a state bordering on lunacy, and there were times in his own life when those around him feared for his sanity. During the time he wrote and published "Benito Cereno," he suffered greatly in body and mind. Elizabeth Melville recalled in her reminiscences about her husband that in February 1855 he suffered such a severe backache that he was helpless.[55] The next month his fourth child, Frances, was born. He had a house full of people to feed, but one of the two magazines that had been buying his work, *Putnam's,* seemed to be cooling toward him. George Wil-

54. This problem is discussed in Merton M. Sealts, Jr., "Herman Melville's 'I and My Chimney,' " *American Literature* 13 (1941): 142–151.
55. Jay Leyda, *The Melville Log: A Documentary Life of Herman Melville, 1819–1891* (New York: Harcourt, Brace, 1951), 2: 498.

liam Curtis, reader and literary adviser for the magazine, wrote the editor, J. H. Dix, about the middle of April to "decline any novel from Melville that is not extremely good." [56] In June he was incapacitated by an attack of sciatica and was examined by his neighbor in Pittsfield, Dr. Oliver Wendell Holmes. Friends and neighbors observed that he sometimes said or did strange things. One acquaintance, Maunsell B. Fields, recalled the following incident that occurred in late August: "We found Melville, whom I had always known as the most silent man of my acquaintance, sitting on the porch in front of the door. He took us to a particular spot on his place to show us some superb trees. He told me that he spent much time there *patting them upon the back.*" [57] They then went to visit Dr. Holmes where the taciturn Melville engaged in the most animated conversation. Toward the end of that summer of 1855, J.E.A. Smith wrote in the local newspaper, the Berkshire County *Eagle*, that Melville was "just recovering from a severe illness." [58]

From this period came "Benito Cereno," and many hints in the story suggest that it is a kind of parable of a psychological situation that might well have projected Melville's fears about himself. The action takes place in a hazy setting. A dreamy film seems to cover everything; Melville carefully establishes a distinct impression of unreality, of enchantment. The story seems "a shadowy tableau just emerged from the deep, which directly must receive back what it gave" (p. 355). In this psychological parable, the two ships suggest two people, whom I shall call Bachelor and Dominick, the captains their psyches. Bachelor is a well-ordered person in whom reason, common sense, and discipline rule. Dominick, on the other hand, is a haggard man, and evidently he is in much trouble. Bachelor observes this, and being the friendly, humane, concerned person that he is, he visits Dominick and sees that he clearly needs help. He subse-

56. Ibid., p. 500.
57. Ibid., p. 506.
58. Ibid., p. 507.

quently tries to get Dominick to tell him what the trouble is, what has caused him to become broken in body and spirits. He notices strange things in Dominick, many manifestations of instability. Upon being questioned, Dominick gives erratic answers and tells Bachelor that misfortunes and reverses caused by external conditions have reduced him to this state of physical collapse and extreme nervousness.

Bachelor is greatly puzzled over these answers and Dominick's general behavior, but he is a good-natured man, not generally suspicious. He sees that there is pronounced disorder in Dominick—the man cannot seem to get organized and on the move—but Bachelor nevertheless concludes that Dominick does have control over the darker aspects of his nature, which in any healthy man must be kept down, subservient to reason, common sense, and the other civilized impulses. After some conversation, lunch together, and a few gestures on Bachelor's part aimed at making Dominick more comfortable, Bachelor indicates that he has helped Dominick about all he can for the moment but that he will go even further by making him a loan to get back on his feet. Then he gets ready to conclude his visit. At this moment Dominick almost hysterically confesses that it is not external problems that are responsible for his state of near madness but internal strife, mental disarray. That dark, rebellious side that seemed to be under control has in reality usurped his rule, and his mind has been taken over. He begs Bachelor to purge him of this dark violent usurper.[59] Further, he suggests that this uncivilized side of his nature has gained such control over him that he fears it will destroy him mentally and perhaps even harm others, even Bachelor. He is a split personality, one side violent, strong, and rebellious, the other side humane,

59. Cereno's plea to Delano, and what Delano stands for, is strikingly similar to the speaker's plea to God in the famous sonnet by John Donne "Batter my heart, three person'd God." The speaker has been taken over by a rebellious force within, reason has been conquered, and he has been wedded to the powers of darkness.

reasonable but weak and getting progressively weaker. Soon the dark side will completely take over if something is not done.[60]

In this confession Dominick has taken the first step to help himself. He has torn himself away from that other side which threatens him. He has admitted that he is mentally ill and that he wants to be normal and well like Bachelor. Although Bachelor does not understand at first, he finally sees the real source of Dominick's troubles. With Bachelor's help and the aid of society with its institutions, Dominick is freed from the fiendish second self. Sadly, the exorcising of this dark, rebellious thing in him does not result in a cure for the patient. He continually grows weaker and dies. Looking back over the case history, it is clear that Dominick was doomed no matter what he did. He had too strong a rebellious nature to start with, much stronger than other men. Then he was indulgent with it; he allowed it to gain the upper hand because he was not enough on his guard. Soon reason and the other necessary faculties for mental stability were simply taken over by this madness and it was too late. It was already too late when something was done about it because ironically without this side of his nature, without his fire and rebellion, his iconoclastic nay-saying self, he had no strength, no will, no fight left because those aspects of his being were tied up with the side of him that had been identified and exorcised. So he is left a shell. He could not live with this Siamese twin and could not live without him.

Bachelor has followed all this with puzzlement. He has never had such a problem. He is an ordinary, normal person who

60. Several critics have suggested directly or indirectly that Babo may be Cereno's double. See, for example, Miller, p. 157; Brophy, p. 89; Phillips, pp. 190–191; Mandel, pp. 639–640; Jesse D. Green, "Diabolism, Pessimism, and Democracy: Notes on Melville and Conrad," *Modern Fiction Studies* 8 (1962): 304; and Robert M. Farnsworth, "Slavery and Innocence in 'Benito Cereno,'" *ESQ* 44 (1966): 94–96. Although brief, one of the most provocative arguments on "Benito Cereno" as a double story is in C. F. Keppler, *The Literature of the Second Self* (Tucson: University of Arizona Press, 1972), p. 84.

has never known psychological misrule. What dark side he has has long since been pushed so far back into his mind that it never dares to rear its ugly head. So he remains greatly baffled as to why a mad impulse could gain control over this man in the first place and then why Dominick could not simply snap back and be normal once this illness was diagnosed and the treatment applied.

Whether "Benito Cereno" is seen in this way, with Cereno-Babo projecting Melville's fear of what could happen to him and Delano representing the well-intentioned but blind world around him, or whether the work is seen in a more objective light as one which deals with the theme of dark similitude, or whether viewed, as I prefer to view it, in both ways, the result is the same: a story of rare artistic beauty achieved through complex and highly original techniques on the subject of futility.

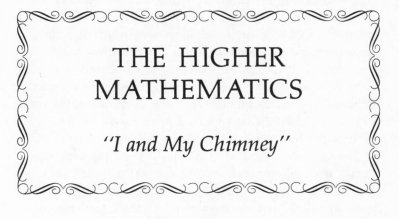

THE HIGHER MATHEMATICS

"I and My Chimney"

Chapter 11

When Melville sent "I and My Chimney" to *Putnam's Monthly Magazine* in July 1855, G. W. Curtis read it for the editor and enthusiastically reported: " 'I & my Chimney' is a capital, genial, humorous sketch by Melville, thoroughly magazinish."[1] Modern critics disagree among themselves about the depth and meaning of the story, but most of them still echo Curtis's description of it as genial and humorous.[2] The narrator of the work is an old

1. Quoted in Jay Leyda, *The Melville Log: A Documentary Life of Herman Melville, 1819–1891* (New York: Harcourt, Brace, 1951), 1: 507. Although Melville submitted the story in July 1855, it was not published until March 1856.
2. William Ellery Sedgwick writes that the story "has an easy-going, sunny quaintness about it that recalls Washington Irving," and he finds it "steeped in sunlight." *Herman Melville: The Tragedy of Mind* (Cambridge: Harvard University Press, 1944), pp. 193, 197. According to Leon Howard, it has an "air of geniality." *Herman Melville: A Biography* (Berkeley: University of California Press, 1951), p. 224. So prevailing is the "good nature" of "I and My Chimney," Richard Harter Fogle states, that it becomes "tiresome." *Melville's Shorter Tales* (Norman: University of Oklahoma Press, 1960), p. 78. Edward H. Rosen-

man who likes to smoke his pipe and sit by his chimney. He is engaged in a domestic squabble with his wife (who acts much younger than he) over the chimney. She wants to remove it from the middle of their house so that a hallway can be constructed and the rooms can be made more accessible. In most respects he seems henpecked, but on the issue of the chimney he stubbornly stands his ground. He recounts this running dispute with his wife with what appears a mature sense of humor, but his cheerful manner is not entirely convincing.

The tone of "I and My Chimney" is not the simple good humor that arises from a mature and well-adjusted man who has made his peace with life. Something unsettling belies his geniality.[3] Both his language and his actions suggest that he is a strange and unusual man. For example, he takes a perverse delight in creating puns and double entendres of such elaboration and with such frequency that they become strained. In the first two brief paragraphs alone he plays upon the words *grey-headed*, *smokers*, *settlers*, and *precedence* to describe himself, his chimney, and his attitude toward it.[4] Shortly thereafter he

---

berry finds the work a "domestic farce" and the narrator "whimsical." *Melville and the Comic Spirit* (Cambridge: Harvard University Press, 1955), p. 180. William G. Crowley believes that "the pervasive good humor of the whole story" indicates that Melville had solved a serious problem in his life. "Melville's Chimney," *Emerson Society Quarterly*, No. 14 (1st Qtr. 1959), 5. Warner Berthoff, in *The Example of Melville* (Princeton: Princeton University Press, 1962), designates it a "charming serio-comic sketch" (p. 175n).

3. Newton Arvin argues that the "lightness of manner" in the story is "convincing enough," but he also perceives—as very few critics have —that all is not right with the narrator, for he communicates "despite the wilful airiness of the form, a real grimness or anger, or extremity of feeling." *Herman Melville* (New York: Sloane, 1950), p. 236. Bert C. Bach also detects a false note in the story, but he comes to a different conclusion. He finds such "excessive joviality" in the work that he feels Melville is taking the narrator "to task" for it. "Melville's Theatrical Mask: The Role of Narrative Perspective in His Short Fiction," *Studies in the Literary Imagination* 2 (1969): 49.

4. Later on in the story the narrator again picks up the word *settling*

puns so much on *behind* and *rear* (and on their opposites *before* and *forward*) that the effect of the passage goes beyond wit into curious silliness:

From this habitual precedence of my chimney over me, some even think that I have got into a sad *rearward* way altogether; in short, from standing *behind* my old-fashioned chimney so much, I have got to be quite *behind* the age, too, as well as running *behind-hand* in everything else. But to tell the truth, I never was a very *forward* old fellow, nor what my farming neighbors call a *forehanded* one. Indeed, those rumors about my *behindhandedness* are so far correct, that I have an odd sauntering way with me sometimes of going about with my hands *behind* my back. As for my belonging to the *rearguard* in general, certain it is, I bring up the *rear* of my chimney—which, by the way, is this moment *before* me—and that, too, both in fancy and fact. (p. 269, italics mine)

His eccentricities are manifold. Humorous as some of his actions seem, they are not those of a normal man. He goes down into his basement to dig with a spade around the foundation of his chimney. He does not have a clear idea of why he is doing it; he admits that he is a little out of his mind. When his neighbor jokingly chides him for digging, he becomes irate and says that he considers his chimney a "personage." He cherishes cobwebs that gather in a narrow gallery over his front door, and he will not allow them to be brushed away. He suspects, he says, that the guests who call do not really come to visit him but his chimney. When he is ready to answer a letter from Hiram Scribe, a master mason and architect who has inspected his chimney for possible removal, he goes in search of a "diabolical-looking old gander," corners him, finds and plucks the "stiffest

---

and uses it repeatedly: "As for its [the chimney's] settling, I like it. I, too, am settling, you know, in my gait. I and my chimney are settling together, and shall keep settling, too, till, as in a great feather-bed, we shall both have settled away clean out of sight." "I and My Chimney," *Putnam's Monthly Magazine* 7 (March 1856): 280. All references to the story are to this, the first printing.

quill," and with this writes Scribe in the name of himself and his chimney. In the final paragraph of the story, he reveals the remarkable fact that he has not "stirred from home" in seven years! These are the ways of a narrator critics have called a genial conservative,[5] a realist,[6] a happy humanitarian,[7] and a sane and mature accepter of things as they are.[8]

In actuality they are the actions of a man who is cutting himself off from the world around him. Despite his facade of pipe-smoking contentment and bemused observance of human folly, he is painfully aware of his isolation. He views his wife as his opposite in every way; he feels that she does not even pretend to understand him. His two daughters, he says, "take after, not me, but their mother" (p. 282). He uses puns and double entendres excessively because he recognizes the futility of trying to communicate straightforwardly with his family and the world. "The truth is," he says in one of his more serious moments, "my wife, *like all the rest of the world*, cares not a fig for my philosophical jabber" (p. 282, italics mine). Lonely as he is, and "in dearth of other philosophical companionship," he dotes obsessively on his chimney. When his wife asks him if he remembers the chimney, meaning, their previous conversation about it, he answers: "It is never out of my house, and never out of my mind" (p. 277). It is before him "in fancy and fact"; that is, in his feeling for the chimney, imagination as well as reality plays a large part.

Significantly the narrator does not love merely the glowing fires in his fireplace or the pleasures of the hearth but the physical structure of the chimney itself. This is an important distinc-

5. Fogle, p. 73.

6. Vicki Halper Litman, "The Cottage and the Temple: Melville's Symbolic Use of Architecture," *American Quarterly* 21 (1969): 638.

7. Judith Slater, "The Domestic Adventurer in Melville's Tales," *American Literature* 37 (1965): 272–274.

8. Stuart C. Woodruff, "Melville and His Chimney," *PMLA* 75 (1960): 283–292. See also John Seelye, *Melville: The Ironic Diagram* (Evanston: Northwestern University Press, 1970), p. 93.

tion because it suggests that the narrator is not simply in search of comfort, quiet, and the good life. What most appeals to him is the size of the chimney and its pyramidical shape. His comments early in the story reveal him as the kind of man who thinks big, who respects largeness and who abhors smallness in any form. He shows this tendency in his impatience with the details of running a farm and household. Among his neighbors he is not thought to be "forehanded," which means thrifty and prudent,[9] but "behindhanded," or backwards in money matters (perhaps even in arrears with his debts). Only after the man who holds a mortgage on his house writes him a stern note of warning that the insurance on the house is about to be cancelled will the narrator do necessary repairwork on the chimney: "The mortgagor cared not, but the mortgagee did" (p. 271). When a new barn is needed, his wife takes charge and orders the lumber. He is not even aware of the purpose of the boards and timbers lying near his orchard until he asks his wife.

His pervasive concern with largeness is apparent everywhere in the early part of the story as he describes his chimney, his house, and his rural setting. He scoffs at city houses, tall and narrow with their several flues "honeycombed into the walls" instead of with one grand central chimney: "Of course, the main reason of this style of chimney building is to economize room. In cities, where lots are sold by the inch, small space is to spare for a chimney constructed on magnanimous principles" (p. 269). Almost as if responding directly to Thoreau's first chapter of *Walden* ("Economy"), the narrator makes it clear that he is against economy in every phase of life. He praises the buildings and grounds of Versailles for their expansiveness: "Any man can buy a square foot of land and plant a liberty-pole on it; but it takes a king to set apart whole acres for a

9. The *Oxford English Dictionary* gives this as an American usage. This important hint about the narrator early in the story should put the reader on notice that the husband is unlike the prudent characters of Melville's works, such as the lawyer-narrator of "Bartleby."

grand Trianon" (p. 270). Those people who build higher and higher houses just to outdo their neighbors "need mountains for neighbors, to take this emulous conceit of soaring out of them" (p. 270). Such people with their tall, skinny buildings know nothing of real soaring. But he does. In his vision economy has no place, as it has no place in nature: "The dandelions in the river-meadows, and the forget-me-nots along the mountain roads, you see at once they are put to no economy in space" (p. 270). He is proud of his setting, his house, and his chimney because they all represent an "abundance of space, and to spare" (p. 270).[10]

The narrator respects only magnitude. Through this preoccupation he becomes recognizable as a type we have seen repeatedly in Melville's short stories. He is the man who does not fit into the world, who feels keenly his difference, who dwells mentally on grandness in all things and scorns the smallness of ordinary men. In their various different ways Bartleby, Merrymusk, the narrator of "Cock-A-Doodle-Doo!," the narrator of "The Lightning-Rod Man," Bannadonna, and Babo all belong to this class. The husband of "I and My Chimney" has much in common with the narrator of "Cock-A-Doodle-Doo!" They live in the same location, they are both at odds with the world, they both dwell so much on greatness that they are somewhat unbalanced, and they both find something concrete to objectify their abstract concept of magnitude. For one, it is a large and awesome rooster; for the other it is a massive chimney.

To decide what the chimney represents in the story, it is necessary to get inside the narrator, for it is scarcely more than

10. He is also proud of his own size. Like his chimney he is large: "As we are both rather obese, we may have to expatiate" (p. 269). This echoes a passage in *Moby-Dick* (chapter 105, "Does the Whale's Magnitude Diminish?—Will He Perish?"), in which Ishmael predicts that the whale will survive "since he has a pasture to expatiate in, which is precisely twice as large as all Asia, both Americas, Europe and Africa, New Holland, and all the Isles of the sea combined" (ed. Harrison Hayford and Hershel Parker, New York: Norton, 1967, p. 384).

just a large chimney outside his consciousness.[11] In his mind it looms huge and mysterious. Since early in his career, Melville had been interested in the obsessed mind and in the process through which obsession comes about. His obsessed characters are men whose mental processes have become focused upon a single abstract notion. But since they cannot see or touch an abstraction, they find some appropriate tangible object to absorb all the qualities of the abstraction and become the idea objectified. In *Mardi*, Taji is preoccupied with the idea of perfection; he is searching for its embodiment to love. When he comes

---

11. Critics disagree so widely on the meaning of the chimney that it has come to be a kind of doubloon, reflecting what is in the eye of the beholder. In one of the most influential and controversial articles on the story—"Melville's 'I and My Chimney,' " *American Literature* 13 (1941–1942): 142–154—Merton M. Sealts, Jr., called it "the heart and soul of Herman Melville" (p. 147). William Ellery Sedwick pronounced it "a symbol of Melville's importunate integrity and of the innate dignity which was his" (p. 195). To William G. Crowley, it is "Melville's talent" and his "inner soul" (p. 2). Richard Harter Fogle finds in the chimney the symbol of the "narrator's conservatism" which "aims at the preservation of organically human values, ties, and relationships" (p. 73). Stuart C. Woodruff seems to agree in large part with Fogle in his assessment of the narrator as a conservative, but he extends Fogle's discussion of the chimney, finding it "an emblem of the empirical reality of time and its manifestation as history" (p. 285). The story is an allegory dealing with the North and South and with the slavery issue, according to William J. Sowder, and the chimney symbolizes slavery, which the southern narrator will not give up (to his credit). "Melville's 'I and My Chimney': A Southern Exposure," *Mississippi Quarterly* 16 (1963): 128–145. William Bysshe Stein sees in the chimney the narrator's faith in God, the "central fire of life-giving faith," which others are trying to destroy. "Melville's Chimney Chivy," *Emerson Society Quarterly*, No. 35 (2nd Qtr. 1964), 64. John Seelye argues that the chimney is a symbol of "All that is best left undisturbed" (p. 92). Ray B. Browne believes the story represents "the conflict between America and England" and that the chimney symbolizes not only the "conservative order, but in fact represents the British constitution," which is a "block to progress." In Hiram Scribe he sees Edmund Burke, in the wife, Tom Paine. The narrator is a Tory, and the home he occupies, the Houses of Parliament. *Melville's Drive to Humanism* (Lafayette: Purdue University Studies, 1971), pp. 259–271.

upon Yillah he thinks he has found it. Ahab is preoccupied with freedom, more particularly with what keeps him from being free. He is looking for something tangible to hate because one cannot hate an abstraction. In the white whale all that he abhors generally, all the enslaving forces in the universe, coalesce. The narrator of "I and My Chimney" is preoccupied with magnitude, and his pyramidical chimney has become its objectification.

Like many of Melville's stories, "I and My Chimney" is a revelatory unfolding of the mind of a single character. Clusters of imagery and allusion all work toward defining the nature of the husband's vision: how he sees. In his perception all of life divides into two broad categories, that which is large and noble and that which is small and petty. His narrative is marked by a continual contrast between the two, developed through the use of several metaphors, the chief of which is that of mathematics. His chimney is the center of this mathematical metaphor. He argues that it can be measured by simple arithmetic, but that it cannot be really comprehended except through what he calls the "higher mathematics":

Even to me, its dimensions, at times, seem incredible. It does not look so big—no, not even in the cellar. By the mere eye, its magnitude can be but imperfectly comprehended, because only one side can be received at one time; and said side can only present twelve feet, linear measure. But then, each other side also is twelve feet long; and the whole obviously forms a square; and twelve times twelve is one hundred and forty-four. And so, an adequate conception of the magnitude of this chimney is only to be got at by a sort of process in the higher mathematics, by a method somewhat akin to those whereby the surprising distances of fixed stars are computed. (p. 272)

What the narrator is saying is again that his chimney is "before" him, is in his vision, "both in fancy and fact." He sees it with the inner eye of the imagination as well as with the "mere eye" of sight.[12] It is both a measurable structure and

12. The relative nature of perception concerns the narrator often in the story. Just as there is a higher and lower mathematics, so is there a

an immeasurable one, or one measurable only by a means far deeper and more complex than the method ordinarily used. Employing the metaphor of mathematics, the narrator articulates in the story one of Melville's most insistent themes, the inadequacy of the world's various dogmas in dealing with the higher mysteries of life. When the narrator says that the chimney can be measured but that its magnitude cannot be comprehended simply through its literal dimensions, he is essentially repeating Ishmael, who is also obsessed with largeness (as well as with ambiguity). Commenting on attempts to understand the massiveness of a whale by applying a ruler to its skeleton, Ishmael says: "How vain and foolish, then, thought I, for timid untravelled man to try to comprehend aright this wondrous whale, by merely poring over his dead attenuated skeleton, stretched in this peaceful wood." [13] To the narrator, the chimney is on the one hand a limited, concrete object; he has himself measured it carefully just as Ishmael does the whale's skeleton. But on the other hand, the chimney has for him (as the whale has for Ishmael) transcendent qualities that can be glimpsed only through a higher perception than ordinary man possesses. He views the people around him as practitioners of a lower mathematics, that is, a shallower perception that relies on dogma. They measure, they calculate, and then they draw rigid and simplistic conclusions.

To the narrator's mind, Hiram Scribe is a perfect example of this type. Melville probably chose the name "Scribe" not to suggest that he is like a certain kind of writer (a mere copier

---

higher and lower perception. When the narrator looks at his house and chimney he sees (as do all "men of cultivated minds") a "goodly old elephant-and-castle" (p. 271). The people of the lower imagination see the chimney as a "brick-kiln" or a "wax nose." The narrator indicates that he can do nothing about their quality of perception: "I will give a traveler a cup of switchel, if he want it; but am I bound to supply him with a sweet taste?" (p. 271).

13. *Moby-Dick*, p. 378.

or hack) but that he is like the biblical Scribes and Pharisees, who rejected the higher mysteries in favor of rigid order and dogma.[14] Scribe is a "master-mason," literally a builder in brick and stone. Melville may also have wanted to associate him with a master mason in the fraternal order of Freemasons, a member of a widespread organization that is built on an elaborate system of orders and dogmas. In the story he functions as the apostle of the lower mathematics. The narrator allows him to survey and measure the chimney three times. During each visit the narrator gives him an opportunity to see the chimney as he does, with his imagination as well as with his eyes, but he fails. When they go down into the basement to view the foundation of the chimney, the narrator imagines that they are in the pyramids, "and I, with one hand holding my lamp over head, and with the other pointing out, in the obscurity, the hoar mass of the chimney, seemed some Arab guide, showing the cobwebbed mausoleum of the great god Apis" (pp. 276–277).[15] As they stand in silence viewing together the base of the massive chimney, the narrator thinks for a moment that his way of perceiving may also be Scribe's, but instead of apprehending any transcendent qualities of the chimney, Scribe begins to use the petty arithmetic of the world to try to convince the narrator to destroy it:

"Look, sir," said he, taking a bit of red chalk from his pocket, and figuring against a whitewashed wall, "twenty times eight is so and so; then forty-two times thirty-nine is so and so—aint it, sir? Well, add those together, and subtract this here, then that makes so and so," still chalking away.

14. William Bysshe Stein argues that the master mason is meant to call up Christ's words, "Beware of the Scribe" (p. 65).

15. The narrator's love for cobwebs is suggestive of his respect for complexity. He likes the cobwebs in his home and he fights to prevent the maid Biddy from removing them for the same reason he admires his house. The house and web of a spider are alike in their maze-like complexity.

To be brief, after no small ciphering, Mr. Scribe informed me that my chimney contained, I am ashamed to say how many thousand and odd valuable bricks.

"No more," said I fidgeting. "Pray now, let us have a look above." (p. 277)

Scribe is not capable of having a look above in the sense the narrator means. He sees by ciphering, and his vision is strongly controlled by the dollar mark. Again revealing his dichotomous way of perceiving, the narrator says: "All the world over, the picturesque yields to the pocketesque" (p. 271). Only those capable of combining fancy with fact, that is, those who "look above" and calculate with the higher mathematics, can perceive the picturesque. Scribe sees the chimney as a "remarkable structure," but only because it constitutes a five-hundred-dollar job for him. His is the "pocketesque" view. The architecture of his own house reflects this vision. It is a horror to the narrator, who respects only what he considers the higher architecture, that which defies the tastes of the world and is magnanimous in its use of space. Scribe's house was built for the purpose of pleasing the world, as "a standing advertisement" for his business. It hideously mirrors with its "ornamental art" and its several skinny chimneys in the shape of "erect dragons spouting smoke from their nostrils," the shallowness and vulgarity so abhorrent to the narrator.[16]

By the time he has described the first two visits of the master mason to his home, the narrator has developed at some length a series of opposites: the higher and lower mathematics, the picturesque vision and the pocketesque, the architecture of his own mind and that of Scribe and the world. The circumstances surrounding Scribe's third and final visit permit the narrator to

16. The name that Scribe has given his home, New Petra, is one of the most biting comments on him in the story. As Melville made clear in *Clarel* (II, xxx), he considered Petra a place of great mystery because of its height, isolation, and antiquity. The buildings of Petra, carved into multicolored rock, are everything Scribe's New Petra is not.

establish still another dichotomy, that between what Scribe and those like him consider to be mysterious and what the narrator thinks of as genuine mystery. References to mystery, secrets, and solutions pervade the final third of the story. After his second survey of the chimney, Scribe writes the narrator suggesting that "there is architectural cause to conjecture that somewhere concealed in your chimney is a reserved space, hermetically closed, in short, a secret chamber, or rather closet" (p. 278). The house was built by a kinsman of the narrator, Captain Julian Dacres, who was thought to be wealthy. Yet when he died, he left only the house and land, which were heavily mortgaged, and a modest sum in stocks. Gossip and rumors spread rapidly about the "mystery involving his will, and, by reflex, himself" (p. 279). Some said that he had been a Borneo pirate, and it was conjectured that he had left a fortune somewhere behind. Knowing that the narrator is aware of these rumors, Scribe (probably with the help of the narrator's wife) concocts his hypothesis of the secret closet, thinking that the stubborn husband will not be able to withstand such an opportunity to satisfy his curiosity (as well as to fatten his pocketbook) and that he will be able to destroy the chimney while ostensibly probing for a secret closet in it.

Scribe soon learns that he cannot sway the narrator through an appeal to personal comfort or financial gain. The master mason is a man of the world; he knows that most men who cannot be moved by dangling in front of them the delicious rewards of self-interest and expediency can almost always be manipulated by pricking their sense of mystery. But the narrator is not an ordinary man. Scribe has none of the higher mathematics, none of the fine spiritual insight, necessary for understanding this strange man he is trying to deal with. He is as unsuccessful as the lawyer of "Bartleby" attempting to reason with the inexplicable scrivener. As the "honest scholar" of *Billy Budd* says: "In an average man of the world, his constant rubbing with it blunts that fine spiritual insight indispensable to the understanding of the essential in certain exceptional characters." [17]

The narrator's refusal to search for a secret closet in the chimney and his wife's apparent fascination with the mysterious chamber have led some critics to label him a realist and her and Scribe flighty idealists. It is true that he sees through Scribe's plot to acquire the lucrative job of removing the chimney, and he realistically reasons that if any secrets had been hidden in his chimney the previous owner of the house, a disciple of the pocketesque, would have spared no pains in trying to uncover them. But the point is not that the wife believes in mysteries and the husband does not. Melville is not contrasting a level-headed husband with a harebrained wife. Unfortunately the story is often read (and misread) that way. The husband rejects the notion of a secret closet not because of any down-to-earth practicality but because of his own deep sense of mystery. He does not believe the secret closet worthy of his consideration. He dwells on the greater mysteries of the chimney. He perceives it in terms of the pyramid of Cheops.[18] He sees it as the means by which he can be put in touch with the higher riddles of the universe. Thus he compares it with "Lord Rosse's monster telescope, swung vertical to hit the meridian moon" (p. 269).[19] Its base in the darkened cellar has to him "a druidical look" (p. 272). To probe the secrets of this chimney, he would need a "witch-hazel wand," whereas Scribe would prefer a "crow-bar" (p. 281). One is the tool of the higher mathematics, the other of simplistic arithmetic.

To the narrator mysteries are not meant for solving but

17. *Billy Budd*, ed. Harrison Hayford and Merton M. Sealts, Jr. (Chicago: University of Chicago Press, 1962), p. 75.

18. For an account of Melville's interest in the pyramids and in the explorer Belzoni, see Dorothee Metlitsky Finkelstein, *Melville's Orienda* (New Haven: Yale University Press, 1961).

19. William Parsons, Third Earl of Rosse (1800–1867), is famous for his great telescope which weighed four tons and was over 58 feet in diameter. He was the discoverer of the spiral nebulae.

merely for perceiving. He objects to a search for the secret closet because it would result in the destruction of his chimney—the objectification of magnitude and mystery—and also because it might actually bring to light such a chamber and thus solve some mystery about Captain Dacres that the narrator does not want solved.[20] When he says that "infinite sad mischief has resulted from the profane bursting open of secret recesses" (p. 282), he means that higher mysteries have been obliterated by blunderers who were determined to solve some shallow puzzle. He feels that "to break into that wall, would be to break into his [Captain Dacres's] breast. And that wall-breaking wish of Momus I account the wish of a church-robbing gossip and knave" (p. 282).[21]

Scribe's failure during his third and final visit to find any real evidence of a secret closet and his errors in measuring and ciphering suggest to the narrator that the master mason has neither a true sense of mystery nor the mental and spiritual means for developing one. The lower mathematics has been put to the test and found wanting. Scribe and the narrator's wife

20. Merton M. Sealts, Jr., is convinced that the name *Dacres* is "simply an anagram for sacred!" (p. 150). Other critics have agreed. See, for example, Richard Chase, *Herman Melville: A Critical Study* (New York: Macmillan, 1949), p. 171, and William Bysshe Stein, p. 65. It has apparently gone unnoticed that the name Melville chose, Captain Julian Dacres, is almost identical with that of an actual person, Captain James Dacres (1788–1853), who gained recognition as the commander of the British ship *Guerriere,* defeated in one of the most famous battles of the War of 1812 by the American ship *Constitution.*

21. The narrator's avid dislike of Momus may derive from two sources. Momus, Jupiter's jester, is said to have criticized the man Vulcan created because no window was made into his breast through which his inner workings could be viewed. Momus also found fault with the house Minerva made because she did not arrange for it to be moveable. Momus would certainly not have admired the narrator's house. Melville may have had Thoreau in mind, for Momus is mentioned in the first chapter of *Walden* as being correct in his approval of small, portable houses. Thoreau, in fact, would like something as simple and economical as a tool box (three by six feet) to sleep in.

and two daughters, Anna and Julia, habitually find and attempt to solve petty pseudomysteries, and in the act they try to destroy the "golden bowl," as the narrator says, that symbol of the true mysteries of existence. The wife never gives up. "Scarce a day I do not find her," the husband relates toward the end of the story, "with her tape-measure, measuring for her grand hall, while Anna holds a yard-stick on one side, and Julia looks approvingly on from the other" (p. 283). Meanwhile, "mysterious intimations" appear in the local newspaper suggesting that the chimney is a "sad blemish to an otherwise lovely landscape" and should be removed (p. 283). Mysterious anonymous letters arrive threatening the narrator unless he tears down the chimney, and his wife awakens in the night claiming to hear ghostly noises coming from what she is convinced is a secret closet in the chimney. What is mystery to them is nonsense to the narrator; what is mystery to him is nonsense to his wife and daughters.

The resultant impression conveyed by the narrator's constant insistence upon polar distinctions—higher mathematics and cyphering, picturesque perception and pocketesque vision, expansive structures and niggardly, vulgar architecture, profound mystery and shallow secrets—is that of his isolation. He sees those around him as so utterly different from himself that practically all real communication has been severed. He has but one link remaining with the world, his wife. Her unreasonable love of change and newness, her shrewish nagging of her husband, and her lack of sympathy with him have made her probably the most roundly condemned of all Melville's women characters.[22]

22. Richard Chase sees her as a "false Prometheus," the "truly 'morbid' person in the story," since she "blithesomely plants her flowers precisely where the north wind will kill them" (pp. 170, 171). Newton Arvin perceives Melville's "deep resentment" against both wife and mother reflected in the wife of the story (p. 204). "In this slightly sardonic portrait of a woman who refuses to act her age," writes Stuart C. Woodruff, "who lacks all reverence for the impact of the past or a chastening sense of 'place,' it is not hard to recognize an implicit criti-

The narrator does portray her largely in negative terms; nevertheless he realizes that she is his last contact with the world.[23] She tells him, "It's I, young I, that keeps you from stagnating." He admits to himself that she has an ordering effect on his life: "Well, I suppose it is so. Yea, after all, these things are well ordered" (p. 275). Keen as his awareness is that she uses the lower mathematics and he the higher, he does not want to leave her. He implies that the penalty would be severe, the "baggage" too heavy to bear. If he becomes completely "stagnant," he will be immobile, unmoving in the world, totally self-absorbed. When she gives him an ultimatum at one time and threatens to leave him unless he agree to her proposal to remove the chimney, he has a perfect opportunity to rid himself of her forever and to live alone with his beloved chimney. If he had felt about her as most of the critics do, no doubt he would have jumped at such a rare chance. But he obviously does not want to lose her; for a time he gives in to her wishes. In a moment of self-revelation he thinks of her as the last principle of health in his life: she is "the salt of my sea, which otherwise were unwholesome" (p. 275). Her role is thus ambivalent. She represents the lower mathematics of the world that would destroy his

---

cism of America itself" (p. 289). Judith Slater feels that the wife has a "perversion" and a "moral deformity" (p. 272). Similarly, Vicki Halper Litman considers the wife as destructively unrealistic (p. 638). She is a "comic counterpart of Ahab," according to John Seelye (p. 93) and to Martin Leonard Pops (*The Melville Archetype*, Kent: Kent State University Press, 1970), who also feels that she "embodies Melville's current notion that sexual energy operates for destructive, not constructive, ends, and although she carries no weapon . . . she wields her finger as if it were one" (p. 175). Only Ray B. Browne finds positive qualities in the wife, who represents to him America and "the urge to change," but he is unhappy generally with the story; he judges it "too long and rambling" (pp. 259, 260).

23. An opposite view of this situation is expressed by Judith Slater, who argues that the wife is threatening to cut the narrator off from humanity by destroying the chimney. Since the husband is losing all touch with society as he guards his chimney, this view is difficult to accept.

means of higher perception, but she is also his final remaining link with a world that he must live in and with.

The narrator therefore seems precariously poised between two destructive alternatives. To break all ties with humanity is to commit a gradual, silent suicide. Yet if he surrenders to his wife's wishes and allows the chimney to be removed from the house, he will collapse as surely as does Benito Cereno when he is rid of Babo. In some odd emotional transference of psychic energy, the chimney is draining the narrator of his strength as Babo drains Cereno. He is channeling his force and masculinity into the chimney. He finds himself stripped of "one masculine prerogative after another" (p. 275). He blames his wife for this loss, but she is not emasculating him; she is merely taking up the slack. He is emasculating himself by projecting his strength into the chimney through an emotional pipeline. He has already gone too far in weakening himself in favor of the chimney. It has become his spine. As he becomes bent over with sciatica, he thinks of his chimney as the only backbone he has left: "To take out the back-bone of anything, wife, is a hazardous affair. . . . No, no, wife, I can't abolish my back-bone" (p. 276). His reason for withstanding the demands of his wife, then, is actually self-preservation. All that is great, deep, and forceful in his nature he has transferred to the chimney. To destroy it now would be to leave him a mere shell. Melville created similar psychological situations earlier with Bartleby, who becomes weaker and weaker as he isolates himself more and more from the world around him; with Merrymusk, who weakens and dies, the cock feeding off his energy as a vampire off another's blood; and with Benito Cereno, who is deprived of his strength and manhood by his dark powerful master, Babo.

Either way, then, whether the narrator continues on his present course of isolating himself from humanity and dwelling obsessively upon his chimney as the essence of magnitude or cedes to the pressure from his wife and allows the chimney to be destroyed, he is doomed because he is obsessed. In one direction lies the fatal and peculiar madness shared by Bartleby and Merrymusk; in the other is the sad plight of Benito Cereno. The narrator is in a sense burning himself out in the chimney, and this is the reason for so many references in the story to fire, smoke, soot, and ashes.[24] As he smokes his pipe with ashes at his feet in the fireplace and ashes all but in his mouth, as he puts it, he is "reminded of the ultimate exhaustion even of the most fiery life" (p. 274). In his words one can hear echoed the passionate cry of Starbuck about Ahab: "Of all this fiery life of thine, what will at length remain but one little heap of ashes!"[25]

The narrator does not consider himself doomed, however. On the contrary, he cheerfully pronounces the prospect of ashes in his mouth "not unwelcome." What appears to be his happy reconciliation with death, his glad acceptance of things as they are, is an attitude derived from his obsession with the chimney, for through it he seems to believe that he will experience a form of immortality. When his family is worried that the chimney might cause the house to burn down, the narrator is not concerned because he knows that the chimney will remain standing. He thinks of himself as he does the house. He is not afraid of becoming "ashy" because he gains permanence through the chimney. Such is not the hopefulness of Christian faith but the optimism of obsession. "In future ages," he tells his wife, "when all the house shall have crumbled from it, this chimney will still survive—a Bunker Hill monument" (p. 276). Behind his frequent references to the chimney as some kind of monument is his conviction of its permanence and consequently his

24. The husband and wife exchange words about the chimney smoke, the wife complaining that the smoke fills her eyes, the husband indicating that he likes to smoke with the chimney (p. 280). This leads to a discussion of the ash-hole in the chimney. Later the narrator speaks again of smoking with his chimney and of his wife's displeasure with soot that comes from the chimney (pp. 282–283). Outsiders refer to the chimney as a "brick-kiln," and the narrator speaks of the secret closet once as a "secret oven."

25. *Moby-Dick*, p. 412.

own immortality through it. At one time he thinks of it as the pile of stones "at Gilgal, which Joshua set up for a memorial of having passed over Jordan" (p. 272).[26] On another occasion it is the pyramid of Cheops, the grandest monument of them all. His wife considers it, the narrator says, the "monument of what she called my broken pledge" (p. 277).[27]

The narrator's appreciation of magnitude through what he calls the higher mathematics, then, is gradually causing him to lose touch with external reality and to give up self-order and self-rule. This situation is plotted through a pattern of imagery and references having to do with rulers. In the mathematical metaphor, rulers are of the sort that measure. The other kind of rulers in the story are leaders of men. The narrator seems to have them much on his mind. He mentions Louis XIV of France; Lajos Kossuth, the Hungarian leader of a famous revolt;[28] the Egyptian builder of the Great Pyramid, Cheops; Oliver Cromwell; Julius Caesar; Brutus; Cassius; Antony; Peter the Great; Nero; the King and Queen of England; King Solomon; Holofernes; Caligula, and others. They are often associated with the chimney, thereby stressing again the narrator's preoccupation with the chimney's greatness. But more importantly he reveals through his talk of kings and emperors what has happened in his life.

That situation is similar to a royal abdication. He is expressing his actual condition when he speaks of what his wife would like: "She is desirous that, domestically, I should abdicate; that, renouncing further rule, like the venerable Charles V., I should retire into some sort of monastery" (p. 275). "Domestically,"

26. The reference is to Josh. 4: 19–24.
27. Related to this pattern of imagery are those references to the chimney as "a kind of soaring tower," a "lighthouse" (p. 273), and as a "sort of belfry" (p. 277).
28. Lajos Kossuth (1802–1894) was a Hungarian patriot and statesman who played an important part in an unsuccessful revolution aimed at gaining Hungarian independence. He visited the United States in the early 1850s and was received warmly.

inwardly, he has abdicated, given up his rule over himself, in favor of what he considers a greater ruler, the chimney. He has become a secondary figure, willingly subservient to his "Harry VIII of a chimney." He makes this abdication clear in the very second paragraph of the story: "Though I always say, *I and my chimney*, as Cardinal Wolsey used to say, *I and my King*, yet this egotistic way of speaking, wherein I take precedence of my chimney, is hardly borne out by the facts; in everything, except the above phrase, my chimney taking precedence of me" (p. 269). And when he says that "it is within doors that the preeminence of my chimney is most manifest" (p. 269), he seems confessionally to mean within himself.

Much of the narrator's language reflects this peculiar stance of one who has known power and authority but has gladly relinquished it to become a subject. He stands behind his chimney because, he says, "in the presence of my betters, I hope I know my place" (p. 269). He calls it "the king of the house" and himself "but a suffered and inferior subject" (p. 272). At times his attitude is positively slavish: "In brief, my chimney is my superior; my superior by I know not how many heads and shoulders; my superior, too, in that humbly bowing over with shovel and tongs, I much minister to it; yet never does it minister, or incline over to me; but, if any thing, in its settlings, rather leans the other way" (p. 269). His chimney is the king, the "grand seignior," his "sacred majesty of Russia," the "Pope of Rome," and the narrator is a former ruler who has abdicated: he is Charles V, who has stepped down from his throne as Emperor of the Holy Roman Empire and is living a cloistered life in isolation from the world; he is a "good-for-nothing, loafing, old Lear," no longer in command, ineffectual but still philosophical.

The narrator treats the subject of psychological abdication lightly, in the same mock heroic vein that characterizes the general tone of the story. But the seriousness of the situation wherein an obsession takes rule over a character is suggested by

Melville's previous handling of it in several earlier works. On the brink of his final madness, Taji cries: "Now, I am my own soul's emperor; and my first act is abdication! Hail! realm of shades!" [29] Melville's interest in Charles V was of long standing, and it is likely that Taji's words were written with Charles in mind.[30] Benito Cereno's abdication of his authority as captain of his ship and his retirement to a monastery parallel generally the case of Charles V.[31] In the story of the great ruler of the Holy Roman Empire who abdicated his throne Melville saw a manifestation of the psychological situation in which a man gives up rule over himself and is driven by a force in his nature thitherto kept in subjugation. Ahab gives up command of himself in this sense. In a moment of deep self-revelation, he says: "What is it, what nameless, inscrutable, unearthly thing is it; what cozzening, hidden lord and master, and cruel, remorseless emperor commands me; that against all natural lovings and longings, I so keep pushing, and crowding, and jamming myself on all the time; recklessly making me ready to do what in my own proper, natural heart, I durst not so much as dare? Is Ahab, Ahab?" [32]

In "I and My Chimney" the narrator does not recognize the full implications of his abdication; the story is far from tragic. But his abdication is as real as that of Taji and Ahab. The chimney is what Melville called in *Moby-Dick* "his forethrown

29. *Mardi*, ed. Harrison Hayford, Hershel Parker, and G. Thomas Tanselle (Evanston and Chicago: Northwestern University Press and the Newberry Library, 1970), p. 654.

30. Hershel Parker traces Melville's references to Charles V in " 'Benito Cereno' and *Cloister-Life:* A Re-Scrutiny of a 'Source,' " *Studies in Short Fiction* 9 (1972): 221–232.

31. In " 'Apparent Symbol of Despotic Command': Melville's *Benito Cereno*," *New England Quarterly* 34 (1961): 462–477, H. Bruce Franklin argues that Melville based that story on William Stirling-Maxwell's *Cloister Life of the Emperor Charles V*. Parker, however, points out that Melville's interest in Charles V predates Stirling-Maxwell's book. The question of sources for "Benito Cereno" is discussed in chapter 10.

32. *Moby-Dick*, p. 445.

shadow . . . his abandoned substance." [33] Only once does the narrator consider overthrowing its rule, when his wife tells him that "either she or the chimney must quit the house" (p. 277). He recounts his momentary agreement to destroy the chimney in terms that suggest a plot to overthrow a king. "In secret" he "conspired" against the chimney. It was almost a "betrayal" and at a time when the chimney's "cause demanded a vigorous vindication" (p. 278). But "better and braver thoughts soon returned," and he remained the faithful, ever-worshipful servant.

Indeed, his regard for the chimney does resemble at times religious fervor. He considers it "the true host" (p. 269). It is the revitalizing force that permeates nature, giving the narrator's wine a delicious flavor by its gentle heat, offering him the warmth and security of its protection, hatching eggs and bringing buds to flower. It is a "grand high alter" worthy "for the celebration of high mass" (p. 272). It is, in a word, his "high mightiness" (p. 273).[34] Through it he is apotheosized.

Melville's concept of apotheosis, it will be remembered, involves a character's lifting of himself (frequently in his own mind only) above ordinary mortals; it is the freeing of himself from the limitations that enthrall most men; it is the victory over those fears that control common people. It is thus ennobling. Unquestionably the narrator of "I and My Chimney" gains sympathy from the reader by his defense of the chimney. Despite the domestic setting and his lightness of manner, he does appear in a sense heroic. But heroism is likely to be flawed in Melville's works. If in the process of reaching for apotheosis a character raises himself to unusual heights, he also kills the humanity within himself—his heroism is accompanied by an

33. Ibid., p. 439. The shadow image is also present in "I and My Chimney," as the narrator describes himself sitting in the "shadow of my chimney" (p. 274).

34. Such references lead William Bysshe Stein to argue that the story is about the narator's unswerving belief in God. The act of worship in Melville, however, does not necessarily imply a deep traditional faith.

"ocean perishing," as Ishmael says in the Bulkington chapter of
Moby-Dick.[35] In freeing himself, the hero becomes a slave; in
discovering a higher realm, he loses the ability to communicate
with ordinary mankind. As Ahab puts it: "Gifted with the high
perception, I lack the low enjoying power."[36] The final words
of the narrator reveal clearly the extent to which his gift of the
higher mathematics, his preoccupation with magnitude, has
made it impossible for him to move as he once did among common humanity: "It is now some seven years since I have stirred
from home. My city friends all wonder why I don't come to see
them, as in former times. They think I am getting sour and
unsocial. Some say that I have become a sort of mossy old
misanthrope, while all the time the fact is, I am simply standing guard over my mossy old chimney; for it is resolved between me and my chimney, that I and my chimney will never
surrender" (p. 283).

The narrator's tone of geniality and humor, as G. W. Curtis
characterized it, is largely a mask that hides what really is at
stake in this story. The work appears to be entirely different in
mood from the dark "Benito Cereno," yet it reveals a similar
deep fear in Melville. It comes from that same bleak summer in
1855 described in the previous chapter, a period when he was
physically ill of sciatica and mentally drained. If "Benito
Cereno" is among other things a psychological parable embodying Melville's fears about himself, "I and My Chimney" is
equally so. This does not mean that it is built on any single event
in his life, such as Oliver Wendell Holmes's physical examination in June of 1855 or the mental examination he underwent a
few years before;[37] rather, it is a disguised, dramatized account

35. *Moby-Dick*, p. 98.
36. Ibid., p. 147.
37. Merton M. Sealts, Jr., was the first to suggest (1941) that Melville was writing about these biographical events in the story. In a later
article, which is among other things an excellent survey of criticism on
"I and My Chimney" up to 1967, Sealts reaffirms his original interpretation, but states: "Were I to write again on the story . . . I should begin

of what was worrying Melville during and shortly after the time when he wrote "The Bell-Tower" and "Benito Cereno." As such it is strikingly similar to the latter.

Certain hints in the story suggest that all the action may be taking place within a single mind, symbolized by the house. It is a large and ample mind of great complexity: "Going through the house, you seem to be forever going somewhere, and getting nowhere. It is like losing one's self in the woods; round and round the chimney you go, and if you arrive at all, it is just where you started, and so you begin again, and again get nowhere. Indeed—though I say it not in the way of fault-finding at all— never was there so labyrinthine an abode" (pp. 275–276). It is thus no ordinary structure. If it seems unbelievable as a literal country house—with its nine doors opening into the dining room causing strangers to commit "the strangest blunders"—it is much more credible as an image of a labyrinthine mind, with rooms "the most rambling conceivable" and "not one mathematically square room among them all" (p. 281).

Just as the complexity and structural disorder of the house is exaggerated in order to make it a symbol, so is the chimney. Both house and chimney are modeled on Melville's residence in Pittsfield, but Arrowhead was no maze, and the chimney was not of the incredible dimensions given in the story. The chimney's size has been made tremendous because it has all but taken over the mind; indeed without it, the mind would collapse. The side of the mind that thinks like the rest of the world (the wife and daughters) would have this massive cause of disorder removed, but its place is central. The ego (the narrator) is willingly giving up control over the mind to this alter ego, this massive, dark other self that isolates the ego from the world and

---

and end with the chimney itself, for it dominates the tale, but pay more attention than before to point of view and tone as provided by Melville's creation of the old narrator." "Melville's Chimney, Reexamined," in *Themes and Directions in American Literature*, ed. Ray B. Browne and Donald Pizer (Lafayette: Purdue University Studies, 1969), p. 100.

will ultimately destroy it. Scribe's role is somewhat like that of Captain Delano in "Benito Cereno." He is invited into this disordered mind to try to help order it. He sees the problem, offers the solution. But as in the case of Cereno, the cure is as severe as the disease. His own mind is so shallow and different from the one he is examining that he has no real understanding of it. If the ego allows Scribe (the world) to exorcise the alter ego, the ego would not have the strength to stand alone. Even if it did, it would then be just like Scribe, a fate perhaps worse than death. If the dark other self remains and continues to sap the self of its psychic energies, disorder, even madness, will reign supreme. In the summer of 1855 Melville was worrying that something like this would happen to him (fortunately it did not). He masked that anxiety so completely that "I and My Chimney" has come to be known as one of his jolliest stories. It is an artificial brightness, but Melville's mood underwent a shift between his writing of "I and My Chimney" in the summer and his next story, "Jimmy Rose," in the fall. He regained control over his house, and if he did not follow the advice of the world and rid himself of the towering inferno within (he respected that side of himself too much to obliterate it), he at least reduced it to what a chimney ought to be before it was too late. By expressing his most intimate fears in "Benito Cereno" and "I and My Chimney," he helped prevent their becoming a reality.

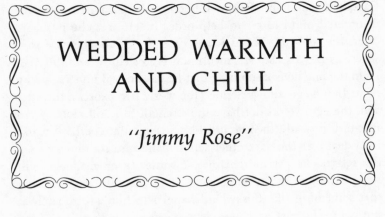

WEDDED WARMTH
AND CHILL

"Jimmy Rose"

Chapter 12

Although Melville did not shift abruptly from pessimism to optimism with "Jimmy Rose," he did arrive at the conclusion that unrelieved pessimism is just as untenable as unqualified optimism. He takes the form of an older man who has reached this philosophical position and who seems determined to retain it. He has had no miraculous religious conversion; he has not suddenly reconciled himself to the world. He is the same Herman Melville who admires the rebel thirsting after independence, who approves of noble fraudulence, and who believes in irony as the chief tool for dealing with a shortsighted world. But in "Jimmy Rose" he has an intensified conviction that unqualified pessimism is not only a sickness but also a dogma, and from the first he had known that dogmas are inadequate in dealing with questions of human existence.

Consequently "Jimmy Rose" has less of a cutting edge than many of the earlier stories. To some this is an indication that Melville has grown old before his time. Newton Arvin observes that Melville "identifies himself with some aged or elderly man, jolly perhaps and bright-cheeked, but with his youth and his hopes left equally far in his wake." [1] Lewis Mumford goes a step further and accuses Melville of being "for the first time downright sentimental" in the story: "One feels tears of self-pity welling into his eyes as he uttered the refrain: 'Poor, poor Jimmy—God guard us all—poor Jimmy Rose!'" [2]

Melville might well have felt old at thirty-six, but "Jimmy Rose" cannot be dismissed as a piece of sentimental indulgence. As Warner Berthoff has recognized, it belongs among several of Melville's stories that are "expert in performance." [3] Nevertheless it is a deceptive story largely because it tempts the reader to focus on the character of Jimmy Rose instead of on the narrator and thus to think of the work in the same terms as others that deal with failures. Richard Harter Fogle, for example, groups "Jimmy Rose" with "The Happy Failure" and "The Fiddler" as "Three Studies in Failure." He feels that they "form a natural trio, since they are all studies in the value of failure." [4] Indeed, much of what has been written on "Jimmy Rose" is based on the assumption that the titular character was Melville's primary interest. [5] In actuality Jimmy Rose is of interest mainly

1. *Herman Melville* (New York: Sloane, 1950), p. 233.

2. *Herman Melville: A Study of His Life and Vision*, rev. ed. (New York: Harcourt, Brace and World, 1962), p. 179. Charles N. Watson, Jr., finds "a residue of self-pity that weakens such stories as 'Jimmy Rose.'" "Melville and the Theme of Timonism: From *Pierre* to *The Confidence-Man*," *American Literature* 44 (1972–73): 406.

3. *The Example of Melville* (Princeton: Princeton University Press, 1962), p. 15.

4. *Melville's Shorter Tales* (Norman: University of Oklahoma Press, 1960), p. 58.

5. See for example Leon Howard (who thinks this a "story of pride going before a fall"), *Herman Melville: A Biography* (Berkeley: University of California Press, 1951), p. 226; John T. Frederick (who argues that the heart of meaning is Jimmy Rose's "bare endurance"), "Symbol and Theme in Melville's *Israel Potter*," *Modern Fiction Studies* 8 (1962): 275; and Vida K. Brack and O. M. Brack, Jr. (who feel

because he is of interest to the narrator of the story, William Ford. It is with the narrator's vision that Melville is chiefly concerned. Whether Jimmy Rose won a "tragic victory"[6] and achieved "a state of inner calm and quiet,"[7] or was a bankrupt spirit[8] and a moral midget[9] is of secondary importance compared to the nature and perception of the narrator.

From the first words of his narrative, William Ford reveals his deep concern with time and change. In the initial three paragraphs alone, he uses the word *old* ten times. He is an old man who has inherited an ancient house in a neighborhood of New York that has changed from a rich and fashionable section to a seedy area devoted mainly to warehouses and counting rooms. Because he is old and dwells on the subject of age, he may seem to resemble the lawyer who narrates "Bartleby," but they are very different men. The lawyer's preoccupation with age results from his fear of death. William Ford thinks of age as a manifestation of that flux which is the only sure aspect of existence.[10] He knows that change is the one unquestionable

---

that Melville is depicting a character who learns nothing from his misfortune), "Weathering Cape Horn: Survivors in Melville's Minor Short Fiction," *Arizona Quarterly* 28 (1972): 61–73.

6. Fogle, p. 61.

7. Richard Chase, *Herman Melville: A Critical Study* (New York: Macmillan, 1949), p. 173.

8. Marvin Fisher argues that Jimmy Rose represents the Christian church in nineteenth-century America, and as such is "servile, self-seeking, and backward-looking, barely tolerated by an increasingly materialistic and mechanistic society." "Melville's 'Jimmy Rose': Truly Risen?" *Studies in Short Fiction* 4 (1966): 11.

9. According to James W. Gargano, "Jimmy Rose" is primarily a "story about a man whose adjustment to failure was made without any essential moral growth." "Melville's 'Jimmy Rose,'" *Western Humanities Review* 16 (1962): 277.

10. The narrator is concerned with change, its nature and inevitability, but there is little if any evidence that he is, as Fisher puts it, "engaged in a quiet crusade against the infidel threats of change" or that he is "fighting a kind of rearguard action against what America is coming to mean" (p. 5).

fact of life. He realizes that he can know nothing beyond that, but in a long lifetime he has observed within the flux both decay *and* bloom. To an open eye, they seem equally matched.

William Ford's view of life is essentially that expressed in Melville's poem "Pontoosuce," which is set near Pittsfield and which may have been composed as early as "Jimmy Rose." [11] The speaker first feels elated as he looks about him at the glories of Lake Pontoosuce in the fall. His mood shifts abruptly, however, as he thinks of change: "Evanescence will not stay! . . . All dies!" [12] While he muses in despair, a vision appears to him, a woman "rose-clear," who chants the message that if decay and death are inevitable in the process of change, so is life. She concludes not on a note of definite optimism or hope or joy, but with the advice to "let go" of bitterness and despair:

> She ceased, and nearer slid, and hung
> In dewey guise; then softlier sung:
> "Since light and shade are equal set
> And all revolves, nor more ye know;
> Ah, why should tears the pale cheek fret
> For aught that waneth here below.
> Let go, let go!"
>
> With that, her warm lips thrilled me through,
> She kissed me, while her chaplet cold
> Its rootlets brushed against my brow
> With all their humid clinging mould.
> She vanished, leaving fragrant breath
> And warmth and chill of wedded life and death.

In William Ford's ruminations on the subject of Jimmy Rose, Melville depicts a character in the act of practicing what the

---

11. William H. Shurr concludes that "the descriptive parts of the poem seem to have an immediacy which would argue for the poem being written during the Pittsfield years, though it seems impossible to date it with any certainty." *The Mystery of Iniquity: Melville as Poet, 1857–1891* (Lexington: University of Kentucky Press, 1972), p. 227.

12. *Collected Poems of Herman Melville*, ed. Howard P. Vincent (Chicago: Packard, 1947), pp. 394–398. All references to Melville's poems are to this edition.

"rose-clear" vision of "Pontoosuce" preaches. He is, as Melville later said about himself, neither optimist nor pessimist[13]—which is not to say that he occupies a place equidistant between the two but rather that by being neither he is both. He observes life alternately with and then without rose-colored glasses, and he knows that both ways of perceiving are equally valid and necessary. He is a further development of the narrators of "Poor Man's Pudding and Rich Man's Crumbs" and "The Paradise of Bachelors and the Tartarus of Maids," who traumatically discover the same truth.

Perceptionally William Ford is an epitomizer. He persistently, even hungrily, seeks out whatever objectifies his worldview. Imaginatively he dwells on these objects because they help him keep his thinking straight; they remind him over and over that "all revolves" but that "light and shade are equal set." In the story it is the old house he inherits and his old acquaintance Jimmy Rose that serve this function of epitomes.

The narrator's subjective response to the house determines its function in the story. It has been seen by various readers as symbolic of such things as the superficiality of American society[14] and the "sensuality and weakness of pre-Revolutionary France."[15] But such attempts to give it symbolic significance

13. Letter to James Billson, 22 January 1885. Melville was commenting on the poetry of James Thomson: "As to his pessimism, altho' neither pessimist nor optimist myself, nevertheless I relish it in the verse if for nothing else than as a counterpoise to the exorbitant hopefulness, juvenile and shallow, that makes such a bluster in these days—at least, in some quarters." *The Letters of Herman Melville*, ed. Merrell R. Davis and William H. Gilman (New Haven: Yale University Press, 1960), p. 277.

14. "Obviously, the description of the house emphasizes the wealth and artificiality of an American society which has borrowed its taste from the supremely mannered and 'overarbored' French aristocracy. Its second-hand elegance clearly suggests a superficiality perhaps as bad as that of the narcissistic class which was eclipsed by the French Revolution" (Gargano, p. 277).

15. Ray B. Browne, *Melville's Drive to Humanism* (Lafayette: Purdue University Studies, 1971), p. 243.

outside the narrator's consciousness miss the mark, since what is important about the house is what William Ford sees in it. He is attracted to the old house because it embodies wedded warmth and chill. His feeling about the wallpaper of the largest parlor is representative of his attitude toward the house in general. For this room he has two names that derive from the wallpaper—"the parlor of the peacocks" and "the room of roses." The colorful birds on the paper, parrots, macaws, but mostly peacocks, suggest to him the evanescence that will not stay. On one side of the room these gorgeous birds have been subjected to decay. A leak in the eaves has changed the "once glowing birds" into faded images. As he pensively regards the peacocks, he might be the poet of "Pontoosuce" murmuring "all dies." But the parlor is also the room of roses, and when he contemplates the great festoons of roses on the wallpaper, he thinks not of death but of bloom, of the ripeness coeval with decay. The wallpaper, then, serves the same function as the "rose-clear" vision in the poem.

It is because the wallpaper epitomizes what William Ford has learned about life that he will not give in to his wife's wishes to replace it with a "beautiful, nice, genteel, cream-colored paper" (p. 804).[16] He does not wish to forget the negative aspects of change such as the inevitable fading of glory and the reality of death and decay; but neither does he wish to forget the warmth of life. "However submissive in other things," he says, "I could not be prevailed upon" to redecorate that room. He is holding on to a vision that saves him from both blindness and bitterness. His family does not understand the painful process through which a man of insight and sensitivity finally develops this way of seeing. It has perhaps taken him a long time. Therefore when he says that he fears his wife is too young

---

16. Herman Melville, "Jimmy Rose," *Harper's New Monthly Magazine* 11 (November 1855): 803–807. All references to "Jimmy Rose" are to this first printing of the story.

for him, he is commenting on her failure to appreciate what he has been through and what he has learned.[17]

For the same reason that he will not give up the house or permit the large parlor to be violated, he will not relinquish the memory of Jimmy Rose. In his mind Jimmy Rose is associated with the house not merely because Rose had once owned it and had retreated there when news of his bankruptcy first broke, but also because through the man and the house Ford verifies his own personal *Weltanschauung*. Still another and more intimate reason makes the old house and its former owner compelling to the narrator. That he inherits the house is a curious detail, though it has not teased critics into speculating much about it. For one critic the fact simply represents "some stroke of fortune which is never explained."[18] A possible explanation is that Jimmy Rose is a relative of William Ford's and that this is a family house passed on from one member to another over the years. If this is true, the narrator's interest in Jimmy Rose and the house takes on added meaning. William Ford's attitude toward Jimmy Rose is that of a wise and mature man as he recalls the life of an older relative, say an uncle or cousin. He is not blind to his falsity and weakness, but neither can he dismiss him as a fool and a failure, for despite the older man's faults, he seemed to create in the younger relative a sense of warmth which he has never forgotten.

Through William Ford's thoughts about Jimmy Rose, Melville was again probing his own life, this time his familial past. The old house is a composite of Melville homes, and Jimmy Rose is a composite of Melville's father, uncle, and grandfather. Jay Leyda points out the similarity between the house in the

17. On Melville's own sense of disappointment in his family see Watson, pp. 398–413.
18. Ralph M. Tutt, " 'Jimmy Rose'—Melville's Displaced Noble," *Emerson Society Quarterly*, No. 33 (4th Qtr. 1963), 30. Tutt confuses the house that the narrator inherits with the house where Jimmy hosts his great dinners. Jimmy owns them both, but they are different houses.

story ("in C—— Street") and the first house Melville probably remembered, at 55 Courtlandt Street, New York City, which his family occupied in his early years.[19] Jimmy Rose's house bears even closer resemblance, as Merton M. Sealts, Jr., has shown, to Broadhall, the great old house in Pittsfield which was occupied for a time by Melville's Uncle Thomas.[20] The parallels are unmistakable. In an essay on his uncle, Melville described Broadhall with some of the same phrases that he employed in the story.[21] Still another house which might have served as a model was that of Melville's grandfather, Major Thomas Melvill, in Boston. As a boy Melville visited his grandparents in their large old wooden house "on the south side of Green Street, between Staniford and the building formerly the Church of the Advent."[22]

Jimmy Rose resembles at least three members of Melville's family. He is both a bankrupt and a man whom time has passed by. Melville had known both types in his own family. His father achieved a measure of success as a merchant before financial reverses overtook him and he withdrew from society in disillusionment to be followed by an early death. Melville himself, as Richard Chase suggested, fits to some extent the same pattern of early success, financial problems, and withdrawal.[23] Sealts believes that Melville's uncle, Thomas Melvill, impressed his nephew so deeply that reflections of him can be seen not only in

19. *The Complete Stories of Herman Melville* (New York: Random, 1949), p. 468.

20. "The Ghost of Major Melvill," *New England Quarterly* 30 (1957): 291–306.

21. In his sketch about his Uncle Thomas, for example, Melville says that Broadhall's "timbers as viewed from the cellar, remind one of the massive gun deck beams of a line-of-battle ship." Quoted in Sealts, p. 297. Of the house in the story, he writes: "So large were those timbers, and so thickly ranked, that to walk in those capacious cellars was much like walking along a line-of-battle ship's gun-deck" (p. 803.)

22. Samuel Adams Drake, *Old Landmarks and Historic Personages of Boston* (Boston: Little, Brown, 1900), p. 372.

23. Chase, p. 200.

"Jimmy Rose" but also in several other works.[24] Strong similarities do exist between his Uncle Thomas, who had been a sparkling social and financial success in France and then a bankrupt trying to eke out a living at Broadhall, and the character Jimmy Rose. But time did not make of his uncle the kind of quaint anachronism that it did of Jimmy Rose, a relic of the old days who still frequents the same places he visited generations before. That aspect of Jimmy Rose is even more pathetic than his financial collapse.

When he stressed this side of Jimmy Rose's fate, Melville was almost certainly writing with his paternal grandfather in mind. Except for Melville himself Major Thomas Melvill has come to be the most famous member of the family, but his possible influence on the writing of "Jimmy Rose" has apparently gone unnoticed. He is remembered chiefly because he took part in the Boston Tea Party, was an intimate of such men as Paul Revere and Samuel Adams, and because Oliver Wendell Holmes made him the subject of probably his most memorable poem, "The Last Leaf."[25] Holmes was a neighbor of Melville's in Pittsfield, and there is little doubt that Melville knew this poem, for it had become something of an American classic by 1855. Looking back on the composition of the poem, first published in 1831, Holmes wrote the following: "The poem was suggested by the sight of a figure well known to Bostonians (in 1831 or 1832), that of Major Thomas Melville, 'the last of the cocked hats,' as he was sometimes called. The Major had been a personable young man, very evidently, and retained evidence of it in 'The monumental pomp of age,'—which had something imposing

24. Sealts, p. 301.
25. For accounts of Major Thomas Melvill, see Drake, pp. 372–373, 406; and Esther Forbes, *Paul Revere and the World He Lived In* (Boston: Houghton Mifflin, 1942), pp. 124, 198, 200, 444, 482. Justin Winsor, ed., *The Memorial History of Boston* (Boston: James R. Osgood, 1881), 4: 197, mentions Major Melvill as being a member of a "committee of merchants" in Boston.

and something odd about it for youthful eyes like mine." [26]
Holmes's poem depicts an old man made eccentric by the forces
of change. The "pruning-knife of Time" has separated him
from others, although he was once surrounded by admiring
friends. Not only his ways but also his clothes mark him as a
queer relic from the past. But the lines that must have impressed
Melville in particular were those that described his cheeks:

> And his cheek was like a rose
> In the snow.

These lines may well have supplied Melville with the title
and chief symbol of the story. He appears to be following
Holmes's description of his grandfather when he writes of
Jimmy Rose: "But the most touching thing of all were those
roses in his cheeks; those ruddy roses in his nipping winter" (p.
806). Just as the poet finds old Major Melvill "so queer" with
his antiquated clothing and the "old three-cornered hat," the
young ladies in the story find the compliments of Jimmy Rose
"smacking of cocked hats and small clothes" (p. 806). Also
like Melville's grandfather, Jimmy Rose has been a military
officer (a general of the state militia), and there lingers in his
"address a subdued sort of martial air" (p. 806).

Through William Ford, then, Melville is pondering the lives
of his paternal relations and responding with complicated emotions. He does not cover up the negative traits in this composite
portrait that he calls Jimmy Rose—the superficiality, the lack of
judgment, the excessive love of good company, the vanity—and
he emphasizes their tragic fates—the bankruptcy that his father
and uncle suffered, the world's scorn that followed, and the
even more terrible plight of his grandfather, who once had
been, as one historian has described him, "a radiant youth . . .
memorable at his club," [27] but who became, as did Jimmy Rose,

26. *The Complete Poetical Works of Oliver Wendell Holmes*, Cambridge Edition (Boston: Houghton Mifflin, 1908), p. 4.
27. Forbes, p. 124.

something of a bore, "tolerated as an old eccentric." This seems to William Ford the worst of all destinies, to be the object of an uneasy tolerance composed of laughter, scorn, and pity. To be placed in this position and to respond as did Jimmy Rose—and as did the aged Major Melvill, tottering about his old haunts in Boston amidst smiles—is to be "bent," as William Ford puts it, "to the lowest deep" (p. 805).

But the negative side of the portrait of Jimmy Rose is not the whole picture any more than Melville's unfavorable feelings about his ancestors were his only emotions. Like the chamber in the old house, Jimmy is to the narrator's eye both a parlor of peacocks and a room of roses. With his "Castilian flourish" and pride in being adored, Jimmy resembles the peacocks, and like them he is to fade and decay. Indeed, the narrator seems to be describing Jimmy Rose as he speaks of the peacocks in the wallpaper: "Most mournfully their starry trains were blurred. Yet so patiently and so pleasantly, nay, here and there so ruddily did they seem to bide their bitter doom, so much of real elegance still lingered in their shapes, and so full, too, seemed they of a sweet engaging pensiveness . . . among their faded bowers . . ." (p. 804). Jimmy is also like the parrots in the wallpaper, colorful but captive birds that echo only what they hear. When he is in the glow of his success, Jimmy Rose is a human parrot. William Ford recognizes that the speech Jimmy makes when presenting a brace of pistols to a famous general is but borrowed wit. He is a mere plagiarizer. In his later years he goes from house to house giving stale compliments and commenting on the latest literature, still a parrot. What Melville had in mind when he chose the name "Jimmy" is difficult to say, but the word was widely used as a slang term, especially in the theater, for an imposter or fraud.[28] But the second part of

28. Eric Partridge lists "jimmy" as meaning "A contrivance; anything faked" from about 1850. *A Dictionary of Slang and Unconventional English*, 5th ed. (New York: Macmillan, 1961). In his discussion of what can happen to a weak person who undergoes sudden hardships,

his name suggests that Melville saw in him not only traits of a showy counterfeit, but also something that reminded him of a rose, the most important symbol of the story and, indeed, one of the most significant symbols in Melville's later writings:

To try to understand "Jimmy Rose" without considering it in the context of Melville's other works where he employs rose symbolism is to labor under a great disadvantage.[29] The story is part of a large and complicated mosaic from which emerges a fundamental vision that informs a great deal of Melville's later writings. As a wide-ranging reader, Melville was familiar with the various associational ways the rose had been used in literature. Its history as a symbol is marked by ambivalence. As Barbara Seward has shown, the rose has been used as a symbol of "beauty, love, spring, joy, festivity, and the afterlife," but also

---

C. G. Jung offers an enlightening explanation of the mind and actions of Jimmy Rose:

"Let us take as an example a businessman who takes too great a risk and consequently becomes bankrupt. If he does not allow himself to be discouraged by this depressing experience, but, undismayed, keeps his former daring, perhaps with a little salutary caution added, his wound will be healed without permanent injury. But if, on the other hand, he goes to pieces, abjures all further risks, and laboriously tries to patch up his social reputation within the confines of a much more limited personality, doing inferior work with the mentality of a scared child, in a post far below him, then, technically speaking, he will have restored his persona in a regressive way. He will as a result of his fright have slipped back to an earlier phase of his personality; he will have demeaned himself, pretending that he is as he was *before* the crucial experience, though utterly unable even to think of repeating such a risk. Formerly perhaps he wanted more than he could accomplish; now he does not even dare to attempt what he has it in him to do." C. G. Jung, *Two Essays On Analytical Psychology*, trans. R. F. C. Hull (New York: Bollingen, 1966), p. 164.

29. Richard Bridgeman rightly observes in his excellent article on "Melville's Roses" that "Jimmy Rose" "marks a significant juncture in Melville's preoccupation with the rose," but he does not perceive the depth and artistry of the story, which, he says, is "not very satisfactory" because "mere proliferation and incantation serve." *Texas Studies in Literature and Language* 8 (1966): 236.

as a "token of death and the sadness of mortality."[30] In his early books Melville used the rose sparingly and then mostly with thoughts of its deceptiveness in mind. In *Mardi* the poet Yoomy finds that roses thrown into his boat by Hautia's heralds have "blighted cores," and he composes the following lines:

> Oh! royal is the rose,
> But barbed with many a dart;
> Beware, beware the rose,
> 'Tis cankered at the heart.[31]

Similarly, in *Moby-Dick* Ishmael says that beneath their beautiful color roses are blank, a part of the "palsied universe."[32]

By the time Melville composed the eleven poems that make up the section entitled "A Rose or Two" in *Weeds and Wildings*, his use of the rose as symbol had become more complex.[33] No single poem in this group reveals by itself the total meaning of the rose to Melville, for roses stand for different and sometimes conflicting ideas in different poems. Taken collectively, however, these eleven poems suggest a cohesive if complicated attitude toward roses that helps to illuminate the earlier "Jimmy Rose." In such poems as "Amoroso" and "Hearth-Roses," the rose suggests an intensive life-force which the speaker values above all else. But in "The New Rosicrucians" the rose is a symbol of shallow optimism. The poet satirically assumes the position of those Christians who see only the rosy side of life, who use their religion to dismiss the darker aspects of existence:

---

30. *The Symbolic Rose* (New York: Columbia University Press, 1960), pp. 16, 19.

31. *Mardi*, ed. Harrison Hayford, Hershel Parker, and G. Thomas Tanselle (Evanston and Chicago: Northwestern Univesity Press, 1970), p. 268.

32. *Moby-Dick*, ed. Harrison Hayford and Hershel Parker (New York: Norton, 1967), p. 170.

33. The poems in *Weeds and Wildings* were not published until 1924, but at his death in 1891 Melville left the collection in publishable order and with a dedication written out (to his wife).

> We let life's billows toss;
> If sorrow come, anew we twine
> The Rose-Vine round the Cross.
>
> (p. 297)

On the other hand, in "Rosary Beads" the speaker admonishes the reader to "adore the roses, nor delay," and he concludes the poem with a frightening image of an ever-encroaching desert, stealthily trying to overtake the garden of roses. Yet in "The Devotion of the Flowers to Their Lady," he seems to feel that the desert cannot ever completely obliterate the garden, and he ends with the "Rose, attesting in spite of the Worm." In two poems he argues the relative values of the blooming rose as opposed to its attar, and he appears to reach opposite conclusions. The speaker in "The Vial of Attar" first tries to reconcile himself to the death of his loved one by rationalizing that he retains her attar, her memory, even though he has lost her bloom, but the argument will not hold as his emotions rebel, and he ends by recognizing that "There is nothing like the bloom; / And the Attar poignant minds me / Of the bloom that's passed away." Although the speaker of "The Rose Farmer" seems to agree with this position, his sincerity is suspect. In this poem, the longest one of the group, the narrator has inherited a large rose farm, apparently in Persia, and he comes to it wondering whether it would be better to raise the flowers to sell or to grow them for attar.[34] He encounters and asks the opinion of an old Persian rose farmer. The Persian is astounded that the speaker, an old man himself, should even have to ask the question. He points out a Parsee who raises roses only for their attar. The Parsee is not well liked; he has little money; he seems to get no pleasure from life. He spends all of his time getting a "mummified quintessence" from the "living rose."

34. For the Persian background of this poem, see Dorothee Metlitsky Finkelstein, *Melville's Orienda* (New Haven: Yale University Press, 1961), pp. 257–259.

309

Then by way of contrast the Persian describes himself, a wealthy, popular, happy man who sells the flowers for their bloom. He advises: "for wise employment, / Repute and profit, health, enjoyment, / I am for roses—sink the Attar!" He echoes a poet Melville knew well, Omar Khayyam, who pointed to the "Bird of Time" on the wing and cried, "Look to the blowing Rose." The Persian's advice sounds much like that of the "Rubaiyat": "Ah, take the Cash, and let the Promise go." [35] The lesson of the Persian rose farmer, though, is too facile to be convincing. And in the contrast which the speaker establishes between the happy rose grower and the unpopular Parsee, we see represented again those two types Melville liked so well to set against each other, the happy bachelor and the preoccupied deep diver. In this poem the man who settles for the bloom rather than the attar is like the "New Rosicrucians."

The position Melville himself seemed to reach was neither that of the prosperous Persian rose farmer nor the Parsee. Nor was it that embodied in any one of the poems in the group, "A Rose or Two." If asked what he saw when he looked at a rose, he might have given something like the following answer: "I see life—the persistent life-force—and beauty, and goodness. And then bleeding through I see ugliness and death and decay, which remains in my vision for a few moments until under that I see color and life again, through which I stare until I see death and decay, but then through that I see the bloom again, and this process goes on and on as long as I look at the rose." He exemplified this paradoxical vision in two poems which were apparently meant to be considered as companion pieces, "Under the Ground" and "The Ambuscade," which he considered calling "Under the Snow." [36] In the first he learns with surprise that roses keep best in the dank atmosphere of a tomb. He observes that a path is cut between a rose garden and a burial vault, sug-

35. *Letters and Literary Remains of Edward FitzGerald*, 2nd ed., 1868 (London: Macmillan, 1903).
36. Shurr, p. 196.

gesting that the bloom of life and the tomb are not to be permanently separated. But if the tomb underlies the rose, the rose underlies the tomb. In the other poem, "The Ambuscade," he insists that a cold existence, a cloistered way of "purity pale passionless," cannot stifle the persistent and exuberant life-force that will ultimately show itself in some way. It is the rose under the snow, a "slumbering germ." In these two poems Melville seems to be saying, "See only the bloom and you are deceiving yourself, for under that is the charnel house. See only gloom, deny life, and the rose underneath will make a fool of you, for it will finally exert itself." Thus from the various and conflicting uses of the rose in the poems of this group in *Weeds and Wildings* emerges the single concept, that "light and shade are equal set," that warmth and chill, life and death are "wedded," not in the sense of being fused into one, but wedded as separate and equal companions.

"Jimmy Rose" is the creation of a mind in which this belief is so firmly held that the very structure and imagery of the work reflect it. After an introductory section that discusses the house, the story divides into two parts of equal length. In the first the narrator describes Jimmy Rose in his prime and society's reaction to his bankruptcy. It ends with the narrator's running away from the old house after Jimmy Rose threatens him with a pistol. The second part depicts Jimmy Rose twenty-five years later, a pitiful old parasite, and ends with his death. Throughout, the narrator seems incapable of sustaining a single view of Jimmy Rose, probably because he does not hold a single view of life, either exclusively optimistic or pessimistic. When he is describing the earlier Jimmy Rose, he stresses his good nature and sheer love of living. But at intervals there creeps into his praise a chilling comment or two, such as that about Jimmy's "borrowed wit." When he moves on to the later life of Jimmy Rose, he emphasizes the pathos of his situation, the depths to which this once successful and beloved man has fallen. Furthermore, he seems appalled that Jimmy Rose could crawl about worm-like among those who had toasted him. He remarks on Jimmy's vanity in connection with his military background. He recounts how Jimmy repaid with peevish complaint the kindness of a young lady who looked after him during his final days. But subtly invading William Ford's attitude of disapproval and sadness— the kind of disapproval that nourishes pessimism—are occasional thoughts about Jimmy Rose's enduring smile and bright cheeks.

The effect that Melville achieves in the two sections of the work that deal with Jimmy Rose is that of a bipartite story, the first part stressing warmth, the second chill. The two sections are like two paintings of the same man, the one portraying him in the glow of youth, health, and success but with just a hint somewhere (say, about the mouth or chin) of weakness— enough to suggest ugliness beneath the bloom—the other picturing him as an old man, poverty stricken, his health flown, but with a spot of color in his cheeks—enough to suggest bloom under ugliness. The effect, then, is much like that derived from examining in juxtaposition the two companion poems on roses, "Under the Ground" and "The Ambuscade"; the first shows chill under warmth, the second warmth under chill.

The motif of warmth which dominates the first section of the story is achieved through an accumulation of images that are related to red roses, red wine, and glowing faces. Jimmy Rose has "bright eyes" and cheeks that seem "painted with carmine." He radiates "health's genuine bloom, deepened by the joy of life" (p. 804). His wit is "sparkling," his welcomes "glowing," and his smile "rosy." At his home with its "radiant chandeliers," wine flows freely and warm compliments fill the air. As a guest toasts the "bloom on his cheek" as well as the "bloom in his heart," Jimmy happily glances around at the scene of "sparkling faces" amidst sparkling decanters. His guests praise the "rare wine" they receive at his house, and some of them consume great quantities. The narrator observes one "wine-bibber" who downs glass after glass while pretending to

talk to "beaming Jimmy" (p. 805). This was a time when "Jimmy's bounteous sun was at meridian" (p. 805).

Underlying this imagery of warmth is a sense of chill, related chiefly through references to snow. The narrator is walking in a snow storm when he hears of Jimmy Rose's financial difficulties. When he goes to the old house on C—— Street, he notices that around it the "snow lay unswept." But perhaps most chilling of all is Jimmy Rose's response to the narrator's visit. Because of Jimmy's hostility, the narrator believes at first that he has come to the wrong house. He cannot believe that this hollow cold voice behind a locked door belongs to the beaming Jimmy Rose. His chill grows as his request to come in is answered by a quivering rejection: "I am afraid of every one." The narrator's recognition is twofold when he says: "It *was* Jimmy Rose!" Literally he now knows the voice to be Jimmy's, but there is a deeper recognition of what Melville called in *Mardi* the "blighted core" of the rose. This insight, more than fear of Jimmy's pistol in the keyhole, causes the narrator to flee.

The sense of chill that is subordinated to warmth in the first section becomes dominant in William Ford's account of the later life of Jimmy Rose. The man of bloom and warmth is now a "shivering gentleman" in a frayed coat. Whereas the glow of health pervaded the first part of his history, now such details as his "white hand" are in the foreground, and the pallor of death is everywhere apparent. For a while after his bankruptcy, Jimmy Rose is pursued "as carrion for jails" (p. 805). Once warmly received by society, he becomes coolly tolerated. The sparkling wine is gone; in its place is milk (and an occasional cup of tea). His has been a "withering change," and Melville skillfully projects it by draining this part of the story of those images of warmth that permeated the first section. This is the cold winter of Jimmy's life, and it ends with the narrator's account of his death. One image of warmth remains, however, the roses in Jimmy's cheeks: "those ruddy roses in his nipping

winter" (p. 806). This image stands out like the "crocus bud-
ding through the snow" in *Clarel* or the "burning rose" beneath the snow in "The Ambuscade."

From this bipartite portrait of Jimmy Rose, then, emerges
the bipartite vision of William Ford. He sees clearly the horrors
that underlie the beauty and warmth of life. Four times in the
story he pauses as if to sigh deeply, and he repeats the same
dark words: "Ah! poor, poor Jimmy—God guard us all—poor
Jimmy Rose!" What he is saying in this refrain is not that Jimmy was a victim of himself and society (although to a large
extent, of course, he was). Nor is he praying that the rest of us
be spared Jimmy's fate. When he says "poor, poor Jimmy," he
is seeing under the rose, seeing mortal man's pathetic frailty
and tragic vulnerability. When he prays that "God guard us
all," he is asking to be delivered from the embittering, destructive pull of this pessimistic vision. He is asking to see the rose
again, and he does see it again. This alternating effect of seeing
the rose and then what is under the rose constitutes the structure
of another of Melville's works, a poem which he left in manuscript at his death, "Naples in the Time of Bomba." The narrator of the poem, Major Jack Gentian, visits Naples during the
reign of the nineteenth-century despot Ferdinand II, better
known as King Bomba. He rides through the crowded city,
stopping here and there for the sights. At one of these stops,
a friendly girl pins a rose on his lapel. Thereafter his mood
vacillates between gloom and hope as he views evidence of the
sad plight of the people and then the rose.[37]

Melville came back to the theme of "Jimmy Rose" many
times in his later life. An unpublished sketch called "Under
the Rose" is of special significance because it adds evidence of
a continuity in Melville's thinking and in his use of the rose
symbol and because it is still another tool for understanding
"Jimmy Rose." Brief and possibly fragmentary, the sketch is

37. In the end, however, the hardness of the world is too severe and
lasts too long, and the petals of the rose finally fall.

narrated by one Geoffry, servant to an English ambassador to Persia. He tells of an amber vase that he first sees filled with roses at a villa of the rich Azem. At this first visit he could see only the roses; at his next visit the roses are gone and he observes the vase itself, made of the rarest amber in which can be seen the skeletons of small insects. Carved into the amber is a strange scene "showing the figure of an angel with a spade under arm like a gardener, and bearing roses in a pot; and a like angel-figure, clad like a cellarer, and with a wine-jar on his shoulder; and these two angels, side by side, pacing toward a meagre wight, very doleful and Job-like, squatted hard by a sepulchre, as meditating thereon."[38] The Job-like figure squatting by a sepulchre represents man contemplating his own mortality. The angel approaching him and bearing a jar represents the reality of death, for the jar contains the wine of the black grape. The other angel represents the life-force, for he carries a rose. By means of the amber vase Melville is saying essentially the same thing as he related in "Jimmy Rose." Man is visited by the angel of death but also by the angel of life.

The sketch derives its title from the fact that dead insects can be seen in the translucent amber of the vase. As long as roses fill the vase this *memento mori* stays hidden, but it is nevertheless always there. The ambassador acquires a book from the Azem in which a Persian poet responded with despair to what he had seen when he pushed aside the roses:

> Specks, tiny specks, in this translucent amber,
> Your leave, bride-roses, may one pry and see?
> How odd! a dainty little skeleton-chamber;
> And—odder yet—sealed walls but windows be!
> Death's open secret.—Well, we are;
> And here comes the jolly angel with the jar![39]

38. "Under the Rose," in *The Works of Herman Melville*, ed. Raymond W. Weaver, 13 (London: Constable, 1924): 340. Finkelstein identifies the two angels as Munkar and Nakir of Islamic tradition (p. 111).

39. "Under the Rose," p. 344.

So shocked is the ambassador when he hears these lines that he cries out to the translator: "And call you that a crushing from the grape? the black grape, I wis."[40] He has been trying to avoid the terrible thought of death, but he has reached the age when both his father and his grandfather died of the same disease. He is like the man on the vase squatting outside a sepulchre and worrying about death. When he listens to these lines, the reality of the "skeleton chamber" overcomes him, and he has to leave the room to cover his fear. He is frightened by a half-blind seer, however, one who does not possess the vision of William Ford. The Persian poet saw the roses, then death beneath them, but he did not see the rose beneath that. He noticed only one of the angels, the one carrying the black wine of death. The other angel, who carries a rose, escapes his view, and he is left murmuring, in effect, "all dies." It remains for a "rose-clear" vision to appear to him as it did to the speaker in "Pontoosuce" and to point out to him that life and death, warmth and chill, are "equal set." The ambassador has that all-consuming fear of death that characterizes the lawyer of "Bartleby," who plays elaborate mental games with himself so that he will not be reminded of his own mortality. Jimmy Rose shows signs of possessing the same fear that is characteristic of a shallow mind. The books that a tenderhearted young lady brings him while he is ill, books that are probably meant to comfort him and prepare him for dying, frighten him in the same way that the poem scares the ambassador. He throws them aside and complains: "Why will she bring me this sad old stuff?" (p. 807). The lawyer of "Bartleby," the ambassador, and Jimmy Rose are all bachelors who possess little vision but much fear.

If William Ford has a fear, it is not so much of dying as of losing his roses while he is still alive. He ends the story by praying that "Jimmy's roses may immortally survive!" (p. 807).

40. Ibid.

But he is not thinking so much of Jimmy (whom he calls a "strange example" of inexplicable behavior) as of himself. What he is asking is that *he* may be allowed to continue to see roses. They do not symbolize for him the immortality of the soul. He does not believe that life will finally conquer death. There is no evidence in the story that he is a really pious man. The roses he sees in Jimmy's cheeks do not affirm to him that Jimmy's soul will survive in eternity. William Ford is not a reconciler of opposites nor a cheerful accepter of mortality, as one critic has put it.[41] Melville himself has not given up an old pessimism. It was not many months after writing "Jimmy Rose" that he told Hawthorne that he had just about made up his mind to be annihilated. The dark view, which came and went, was not lightened by a new optimism like one liquid poured into another to form a new solution. His mental frame as represented in "Jimmy Rose" and in many of his later works is more like that of a chemical suspension than a solution, the separate coexistence of two irreconcilable attitudes rather than their fusion into one.

What the roses in Jimmy's cheeks do represent to William Ford is his own ability to see and feel the bloom of life, to know warmth as well as chill. Melville had come to cherish that spot of color, that experience of the rose. It had not been easy to come by. In "The Rose Farmer" he says, "I came into my roses late," and so he did.[42] "Jimmy Rose" begins with words almost identical with those that open *Moby-Dick*. After naming himself, Ishmael says: "Some years ago—never mind how long precisely. . . ."[43] William Ford opens "Jimmy Rose" with "A time ago, no matter how long precisely . . ." (p. 803). Through

---

41. Judith Slater, "The Domestic Adventurer in Melville's Tales," *American Literature* 37 (1965): 274.

42. He makes essentially the same statement in "L'Envoi," which ends the rose poems: "Wiser in relish, if sedate / Come gray-beards to their roses late" (p. 310).

43. *Moby-Dick*, p. 12.

William Ford, Melville may have wanted to recall his earlier narrator Ishmael and thus to suggest what had happened to the prophet of nothingness, the seer of ambiguity: he has not been converted into Saint Paul, to be sure, but he has made room in his white world for the redness of the rose. That Herman Melville likewise did so may be suggested from the fact that late in his life he turned with great devotion to the raising of roses as a hobby, cultivating them carefully and often presenting them to others as gifts.

ONE SPOT
OF RADIANCE

"The Piazza"

Chapter 13

"The Piazza" is distinctive among Melville's short stories, for it is the only one that was not written for publication in a magazine. Melville composed it (probably during the early weeks of 1856) expressly as an introductory sketch for the *Piazza Tales*, a collection of five stories all previously published in *Putnam's*.[1] The occasion for writing "The Piazza" offered Melville an opportunity to ruminate about his last few years at Pittsfield and about some of the experiences from which the stories had emerged. As an introductory tale, it provided him a chance to bring together in a single work thoughts he had expressed in several separate stories. Consequently, he depicts in it a man in the act of looking backwards, reviewing and recapitulating a painful episode in his life and summing up what he learned from it.

The story makes significant points, as critics have shown,

1. *Piazza Tales* was published in May 1856 and included the following stories: "The Piazza," "Bartleby," "Benito Cereno," "The Lightning-Rod Man," "The Encantadas," and "The Bell-Tower."

about the unreliability of perception,[2] the difference between appearance and reality,[3] the possibilities of the creative imagination,[4] and the falseness of Rousseauean romanticism,[5] but all these subjects are secondary. "The Piazza" is not primarily a fictional treatment of a universal truth but a highly personal account of an emotional crisis, a profoundly provocative crisis of many dimensions. On the literal level the story concerns a weary man who tries and fails to find a spot of brightness in his life. On the symbolic level it deals with a sensitive thinker who seeks enlightening truth but encounters despair. On the autobiographical level it recounts Melville's own search for a radiant savior-friend and his ultimate disappointment. On all three levels the seeker's piazza or porch represents the one viable means of coping with his disappointment and loneliness.

The nature of the narrator's emotional crisis is revealed in the reason he gives for undertaking a journey to a mountain cottage that he has admired from afar.[6] He anticipates that he will find

2. Scott Donaldson, "The Dark Truth of *The Piazza Tales*," *PMLA* 85 (1970): 1082.

3. Richard Harter Fogle, *Melville's Shorter Tales* (Norman: University of Oklahoma Press, 1960), p. 85.

4. Joel Porte, *The Romance in America: Studies in Cooper, Poe, Hawthorne, Melville, and James* (Middletown: Wesleyan University Press, 1969), p. 153.

5. Klaus Poenicke, "A View from the Piazza: Herman Melville and the Legacy of the European Sublime," *Comparative Literature Studies* 4 (1967): 277.

6. Although the narrator gives his reason for wanting to find the cottage, critics have disagreed widely on his motivation. Fogle says that the narrator seeks to "redress the balance" of good and evil (p. 88). Porte feels that the narrator wishes to find the mountain girl who is "the personified spirit of romance" in order that she "might define her meaning to him" (p. 154). According to William Bysshe Stein, the hero is undertaking a "quest for spiritual regeneration." See "Melville's Comedy of Faith," *ELH* 27 (1960): 315. Helmbrecht Breinig argues that the narrator "sets out to find truth." See "The Destruction of Fairyland: Melville's 'Piazza' in the Tradition of the American Imagination," *ELH* 35 (1968): 279. Judith Slater states that he seeks to escape "ambiguity."

"some glad mountain-girl," and that it will do him good to look upon her: "it will cure this weariness" (p. 444).[7] The word *weariness*, as Melville would certainly have recognized, implies more than just physical fatigue. It carries the suggestion of discontentment "at the continuance or continued recurrence of something" and the desire for its cessation. To be weary is to have one's "patience, tolerance, zeal, or energy exhausted," to be "depressed and dispirited through trouble, anxiety, disappointment," to be "sick at heart."[8] Throughout the narrator's account of this episode in his life he repeatedly uses the word *weary* (or *weariness*), first to describe his own mental and physical condition and then that of the mountain girl Marianna.

The narrator's weariness is accompanied by periodic spells of physical illness. He contracts a severe earache from lying on the ground near his house. Later, just when he has started to enjoy the sparkle he sees from a distant cottage, he becomes so ill that he is confined to his chamber "for some time after" (p. 443). During his convalescence his state of mind is still unhealthy. Even the beautiful September weather and the sounds of neighboring children shouting "How sweet a day" cannot cheer him. He believes the fine day to be only a "weather-breeder," a deception because it promises fair weather but is actually followed by foul days. So dreary is his mood after his illness that he cannot bear to look at a lovely flowering vine, a Chinese creeper that he planted near his piazza, for it, like the weather, is deceptive: "if you removed the leaves a little, [it]

See "The Domestic Adventurer in Melville's Tales," *American Literature* 37 (1965–66): 278. John Seelye, in *Melville: The Ironic Diagram* (Evanston: Northwestern University Press, 1970), p. 24, interprets the narrator's motivation for the journey as "curiosity."

7. "The Piazza," in *The Complete Stories of Herman Melville*, ed. Jay Leyda (New York: Random, 1949). All references to "The Piazza" are to this edition.

8. As defined in the *Oxford English Dictionary*.

showed millions of strange, cankerous worms, which, feeding upon those blossoms,[9] so shared their blessed hue, as to make it unblessed evermore—worms, whose germs had doubtless lurked in the very bulb which, so hopefully, I had planted" (p. 443).

This, then, is his emotional state when he undertakes a journey to find the cottage. He is suffering from that pernicious weariness that prevents him from enjoying a flower because he is oppressed with the ugliness that lies under it. He has not yet learned what William Ford of "Jimmy Rose" knew, that the bloom is as real as the worms under it. He regards a beautiful day as a facade for dark days surely to follow and a beautiful flower as disguised corruption. He sums up his condition at that time when looking back on it he calls it "this ingrate peevishness of my weary convalescence" (p. 444). At the very nadir of his despair, he sees anew the reflection of the sun on the distant cottage, and he decides to pursue this "one spot of radiance" in his life in order to cure his dreadful weariness.

What attracts him so strongly to the mountain cottage is its apparent concentration of energy. It is "radiant," "dazzling," "sparkling" like some unknown source of energy in outer space. Above all it is energy that the narrator needs. The "golden sparkle" that he sees in the mountains represents to him a vital life force that he hopes will give him new strength. Its appeal to him is that of a sumptuous meal to a man long without food. Consequently he sets out like a knight searching for a fairy queen because the goal he seeks seems in his present condition as far away and as fantastic as some fairyland.

He describes his journey in a style that projects his weariness. Nowhere in Melville's fiction is there a stranger or more appropriate style than in "The Piazza." It has been described as

9. The narrator has been reading Shakespeare's *A Midsummer Night's Dream,* in which Titania, the Queen of Fairies, commands some in her train "to kill cankers in the musk-rose buds" (II. ii. 3).

"archly ornate" and "dangerously overwrought,"[10] but it suggests the toilsome quality of the journey with rare effectiveness. The sentences are frequently long and laborious; sometimes whole paragraphs consist of a single tangled sentence. Through the inordinate length of the following sentence and the frequent repetition of the word *on*, the narrator conveys his exaggerated sense of the length of the journey and the werinesss with which he proceeds:

By the side of pebbly waters—waters the cheerier for their solitude; beneath swaying fir-boughs, petted by no season, but still green in all, *on* I journeyed—my horse and I; *on*, by an old saw-mill, bound down and hushed with vines, that his grating voice no more was heard; *on*, by a deep flume clove through snowy marble, vernal-tinted, where freshet eddies had, on each side, spun out empty chapels in the living rock; *on*, where Jacks-in-the-pulpit, like their Baptist namesake, preached but to the wilderness; *on*, where a huge, cross-grain block, fern-bedded, showed where, in forgotten times, man after man had tried to split it, but lost his wedges for his pains— which wedges yet rusted in their holes; *on*, where, ages past, in step-like ledges of a cascade, skull-hollow pots had been churned out by ceaseless whirling of a flintstone—ever wearing, but itself unworn; *on*, by wild rapids pouring into a secret pool, but soothed by circling there awhile, issued forth serenely; *on*, to less broken ground, and by a little ring, where, truly, fairies must have danced, or else some wheel-tire been heated—for all was bare; still *on*, and up, and out into a hanging orchard, where maidenly looked down upon me a crescent moon from morning. (p. 445, italics mine)

At times the style reflects so directly the state of mind of the narrator during his journey that it approaches the stream of consciousness technique, as his description of the area surrounding Marianna's cottage illustrates: "Near by—ferns, ferns, ferns; further—woods, woods, woods; beyond—mountains, mountains, mountains; then—sky, sky, sky" (p. 447). A setting of

10. Fogle, p. 85. He goes on to state, however, that the story is "nevertheless a fine piece, with a sustaining core of intense life, like a fine picture in a fantastically decorative frame."

wild and natural beauty, it appears to the tired narrator with a depressing sameness and monotony.

Instead of finding a new source of energy, the narrator discovers in the mountain cottage weariness personified. Of all the women in Melville's fiction Marianna seems the most hopelessly alone. Even Hunilla is rescued at last, and even the pathetic maids of the Devil's Dungeon share each other's company in their misery, but Marianna lives a life of almost complete isolation, suffering a sickness of heart that will not even let her find relief in sleep. She is weary of the view from her window, weary of the heat in summer and the cold in winter. One of the shadows she watches each afternoon reminds her of a weary shaggy dog. Her brother is no company, for he, too, is weary. No birds sing in the woods; no boys shout at play. Berries ripen and wearily fall to the ground to rot. She can neither become insensitive to her loneliness nor overcome it. Hers is a diseased inertia, a "weariness and wakefulness together" (p. 451). The narrator offers her a suggestion for curing her "wakeful weariness," prayer and a hop pillow, but she indicates that she has tried them both without success.

Like all those poor souls whose psychic fatigue has invaded the very marrow of their bones, Marianna yearns to be caught up in some glimmering, radiant, life-giving light. She knows that "the sun is a good sun," but it is not the source of energy she needs. It merely sets "the flies and wasps astir," fades the curtain, and scorches the roof (p. 449). She needs another light, the one she sees shining from the narrator's house far below her. It beckons to her much as her cottage did to the narrator, and she believes, as he did, that if she could just get to that glimmering house and share in the radiance found there she could be cured of her wakeful weariness.

The effect that Marianna has on the narrator is essentially that of a shock treatment. She is an extreme version of himself. With profound shock he recognizes that the nature of her plight is the same as his except that she has reached the very limits of loneliness and despair and he has not. He realizes, therefore, both the similarity of their conditions and the discrepancy between them. In her he sees how much worse his own weariness could be. That he is stunned by seeing her is suggested by his cutting off abruptly his account of the visit. With a meaningful dash and the word "Enough," he breaks off and tells of his life since encountering Marianna. He sticks to his porch now, not able to forget the maiden's face but not drawn either into the abyss of despair that holds her.

In an ironic way Marianna is good for him as shock therapy can be for a depressed person. Psychiatrists have speculated that the positive effects of electroconvulsive shock treatment derive from the "threat of annihilation and death. As a consequence of this death threat the individual experiences an enormous feeling of relief after the convulsion and grasps for close contact with the world, a contact which he greatly desires after his 'revival from psychological death.' "[11] After the trauma of the convulsion, the patient experiences something akin to a feeling of rebirth. In Marianna the narrator sees a paralyzing weariness that is psychological death, and because her situation is so similar to his own he feels the full horror of it.[12] Consequently like a patient who has received shock therapy he experiences a sense of relief in his escape from her and a desire to get back to his world and not to separate himself from it totally.

Although the narrator's journey and his visit with Marianna may be viewed in strictly literal terms, they are described in the

11. Wallace Lockwood, "Some Relations Between Response to Frustration (Punishment) and Outcome of Electric Convulsive Therapy: An Experimental Study in Psychiatric Theory," *Comparative Psychology Monographs* 20 (1950–51): 130. Lockwood is citing the theory of and quoting Paul Schilder.

12. Reminders of death surround Marianna and underscore her condition. Near her house is a woodpile whose sticks are like "the fencing of some sequestered grave" (p. 447). The brother's weariness is compared to that of the grave (p. 448), and Marianna comments that those who built her cottage "are long dead" (p. 449).

story in such a way as to suggest that they are as much symbolic as actual. Much of the unreality surrounding the journey derives from the narrator's frequent references to the world of fantasy and dreams. He has been reading *A Midsummer Night's Dream* so attentively that it occupies much of his time. He enjoys his discovery of the distant spot of radiance only during the time he could "spare" from reading Shakespeare's play about fairy-land. He thinks of the girl he hopes to find as a fairy queen, makes reference to Spenser's great work, and sets out himself for "fairy-land." His description of the journey is marked not only by suggestions of weariness but also by references to sleep, dreams, and enchantment. He comes to a "lone and languid region" where the cattle seem "drowsy" and appear "to walk in sleep." They do not even feed like normal cattle, for "the enchanted never eat" (p. 444). This is an unearthly terrain he is traveling, as if "along a milky-way of white-weed, past dim-clustering Pleides and Hyades," an "astral path" (p. 444).

If he is jolted by what he finds in the mountain cottage, it is not because he has been brought back to everyday reality from dreamland. The rotting cottage is not the fairyland he hoped for and Marianna is not Titania, but neither is she an ordinary girl living under ordinary circumstances in an ordinary place. From the moment when he walks over the threshold and joins Marianna sitting by a window, the account of his visit is pervaded with an air of strangeness and unreality. It seems a fairy tale even though it is not about fairies. Marianna tells the narrator that she and her brother came to the cottage "to cut wood and burn coal" (p. 448) and that they are orphans. But why they chose the loneliest place in the mountains remains a mystery, as do many other things about them.

Marianna functions in the story not only as a real girl living in a real mountain cottage but also as an allegorical figure whom the narrator finds after an allegorical journey. It is a journey that many of the narrators of Melville's short stories make, a deep dive to truth, so deep, in fact, that they have to surface quickly to save themselves. What they see in this dive to truth is often a lonely, weary woman, who represents the human plight. Thus when the narrator of "Poor Man's Pudding and Rich Man's Crumbs" goes on a journey to witness poverty and finds Mrs. Coulter, he is not long with her before he sees in her all the weakness and grief and loneliness inherent in the general human condition. To be exposed to such a truth for long is to become filled either with rebellious bitterness or such woe as can never be cast off. So the narrator leaves quickly in order to retain his stability. Similarly the narrator of "The Paradise of Bachelors and the Tartarus of Maids" reads universal meaning into the deathlike maiden workers in a paper factory. As he views them in their slavish activity, they take on the same meaning to him as Mrs. Coulter had for the earlier narrator. He, too, has to escape lest his mind be unalterably changed by the vision.

Marianna's role in "The Piazza" is twofold. She shocks the narrator into a more healthy state of mind and therefore serves a positive function. But just as shock therapy is dangerous and can be destructive if the shock is prolonged, so is Marianna dangerous to the narrator. His journey is a symbolic representation of his probing for the truth of human existence. In finding her the narrator penetrates deeply into the heart of humankind and to his possible peril, for she symbolizes the hopelessness, the weakness, and the intolerable isolation that is the inner state of Everyman. Too long an exposure to that vision can produce the "woe that is madness."

The narrator's journey has another symbolic dimension that is more personal than is a search to discover the basic human condition. Through various suggestions the narrator indicates that symbolically he is describing a journey within himself, a search to find his *own* innermost principle of being in hopes that the truth he uncovers through introspection will give him new vitality and add new meaning to his weary existence. Thus he finds not only the truth of other human hearts but that of his own as well. Fairyland is that unknown region of the inner self.

The journey is, as the narrator says, his "inland voyage," and his destination is the center of life, which he describes in anatomical imagery that suggests the human heart. It is "in a sort of purpled breast-pocket, high up in a hopper-like hollow" (p. 440).

The mountainous area around the narrator's house, then, is symbolically the deeper recesses of his mind. The outside represents the inside. To develop this unusual metaphor, the narrator refers to the outdoor region that he views from his piazza as some enclosed area or building. It is "a picture-gallery," for "what but picture-galleries are the marble halls of these same limestone hills?—galleries hung, month after month anew, with pictures ever fading into pictures ever fresh" (p. 438). When he describes his place for lounging about outside the house, it is in terms that suggest indoor furniture: "I chose me, on the hill-side bank near by, a royal lounge of turf—a green velvet lounge, with long, moss-padded back" (p. 438). He compares the surrounding area with Westminster Abbey (p. 438), and calls it "this monastery of mountains" (p. 439). On the other hand, he says that "the house was wide" (p. 439), suggesting that in this inside-out metaphor the house represents his outer self, the less hidden, less profound, less mysterious aspects of his being.

When the narrator describes himself sitting on his piazza and viewing the vast area around the house, he is really describing a man poised psychologically between his conscious and unconscious selves. As he looks inward (literally outward toward the mountains), not yet embarked on his journey, he thinks of that unknown and mysterious region (as Melville's introspective characters frequently do) as the sea:

In summer, too, Canute-like; sitting here, one is often reminded of the sea. For not only do long ground-swells roll the slanting grain, and little wavelets of the grass ripple over upon the low piazza, as their beach, and the blown down of dandelions is wafted like the spray, and the purple of the mountains is just the purple of the billows, and a still August moon broods upon the deep meadows, as a calm upon the Line; but the vastness and the lonesomeness are so oceanic, and the silence and the sameness, too, that the first peep of a strange house, rising beyond the trees, is for all the world like spying, on the Barbary coast, an unknown sail. (p. 440)[13]

His journey is a "voyage" into the "vastness and the lonesomeness" of his "oceanic" inner self. Appropriately he dresses for the cruise in what he calls "relics of my tropic sea-going," a "light hat, of yellow sinnet, with white duck trowsers" (p. 447). His destination is what Ishmael terms the "one insular Tahiti": "For as this appalling ocean surrounds the verdant land, so in the soul of man there lies one insular Tahiti, full of peace and joy, but encompassed by all the horrors of the half known life." [14] In search of peace and joy the narrator sets out into the inner sea of the half-known life to find a Tahiti that, as Ishmael warns, is forever lost. The narrator's quest is therefore doomed to failure from the start, and he voyages among the "horrors" of the hidden self at his own risk. He recognizes the danger but not the futility of his journey as he begins it: "None might go but by himself, and only go by daring" (p. 446). Along the way he is periodically warned not to continue. Even the blackberry brakes seem to pluck him back. The scenery of this realm, which is both seascape and landscape, is like that of a vision or a dream—a strange zigzag road, ragged cliffs, and "fantastic rocks" (p. 446).

He disregards all warnings and probes deeper and deeper on his "inland voyage" to the one insular Tahiti. When he first sees Marianna sitting by her window, he describes her as "like some

13. A similar passage describing this oceanic loneliness occurs in *Moby-Dick*: "Now, in calm weather, to swim in the open ocean is as easy to the practiced swimmer as to ride in a spring-carriage ashore. But the awful lonesomeness is intolerable. The intense concentration of self in the middle of such a heartless immensity, my God! who can tell it?" *Moby-Dick*, ed. Harrison Hayford and Hershel Parker (New York: Norton, 1967), p. 347.

14. Ibid., p. 236.

Tahiti girl, secreted for a sacrifice, first catching sight, through palms, of Captain Cook" (p. 447). Rather than a fairyland or a Tahiti, the cottage is but "a bit of wreck in the mid Atlantic,"[15] and Marianna, the hoped-for liberator, is herself enslaved and helpless. Having penetrated to the core of his being, he has found there no happy isle, but a weak, weary, and trapped alter ego, the emasculated inner self. Shocked by this experience in extreme introspection he is (at least for a time) determined to take no more such perilous journeys.

The emotional crisis depicted in "The Piazza" in both literal and symbolic terms is also autobiographical in nature, a disguised treatment of Melville's own frustration during his early years in Pittsfield. The house described in the story is Arrowhead, and the setting is that of the Berkshires with Mount Greylock dominating the scenery. The situation of the narrator is generally similar to Melville's own. He moved to the country from a city, suffered from loneliness, discovered a bright light at a distance, became enthusiastic over it, tried to get to its source, saw that it was not what he had hoped, was gravely disappointed, but learned to live with his disappointment. This dazzling light that so inspired Melville at first was Nathaniel Hawthorne (who like Marianna lived for a while in a cottage, a few miles from Arrowhead), and "The Piazza" is among other things Melville's retrospective musings over this important period in his life when he hoped, tried, and failed to find a godlike friend.

Melville's state of mind at the time he read Hawthorne's *Mosses from an Old Manse* in 1850 is suggested by a passage he later marked in his copy of *Don Quixote*, a book he greatly admired and made reference to in "The Piazza": "A knighterrant without a mistress is like a tree without leaves, a building without cement, a shadow without a body that causes it." Beside these lines he wrote in the margin: "Or as Confucius said,

15. The lawyer's description of Bartleby in "Bartleby, the Scrivener," *Putnam's Monthly Magazine* 2 (1853): 556.

'a dog without a master,' or to drop both Cervantes & Confucius parables—a god-like mind without a God." [16] He was not looking for a mistress in 1850 but for a "master." His was a godlike mind, he was coming to believe, and he yearned for a godlike friend who would understand and inspire him and approve of him. His review of *Mosses from an Old Manse* reveals that in Hawthorne he felt that he had discovered that savior-friend. He calls Hawthorne "Shiloh," which means "messiah," and he gives himself credit for a godlike mind when he speaks of "such a parity of ideas . . . between a man like Hawthorne and a man like me." [17] When Hawthorne wrote him approvingly of *Moby-Dick*, he was overcome with the expectations of such a friendship as theirs promised to be. He calls Hawthorne's a "joy-giving and exultation-breeding letter," claims that "you have now given me the crown of India" and "a sense of unspeakable security." The godlike mind has seemingly found a god. "I feel," he continues, "that the God-head is broken up like the bread at the Supper, and that we are the pieces." [18]

The intensity of Melville's pursuit of Hawthorne is reflected in "The Piazza" through the religious overtones of the narrator's journey. With his interest in enchantment and magic and in the stars, he seems a Magus who sees the star of the Savior and embarks on a journey to find Him. The light that he sees on the mountain dazzles "like a deep-sea dolphin" (p. 444). In Christian symbolism the dolphin is representative of Christ. The spot of radiance is the star of Bethlehem, gleaming and beckoning from among the Milky Way and the "dim-clustering Pleiades and Hyades" (p. 444). To find the place marked by

16. *The Portable Melville*, ed. Jay Leyda (New York: Viking, 1952), p. 551. In "The Piazza" Melville writes that Don Quixote is "that sagest sage that ever lived" (p. 444).

17. "Hawthorne and His Mosses," in *The Works of Herman Melville* (London: Constable, 1924), 13: 142.

18. *The Letters of Herman Melville*, ed. Merrell R. Davis and William H. Gilman (New Haven: Yale University Press, 1960), pp. 141, 142.

this sparkling light, the narrator says, one must travel "with faith" (p. 444). Melville's own journeys to Hawthorne's little red cottage at Lenox were like the pilgrimages of some religious enthusiast to the shrine of his idol.

Hawthorne wrote in "The Old Manse" that his "precincts were like the Enchanted Ground, through which the pilgrim travelled on his way to the Celestial City." He indicated a wish to give this pilgrim peace and rest "in a life of trouble," for "what better could be done for those weary and world-worn spirits?" Melville took him at his word and with a feeling that approached religious fervor tried to come within what Hawthorne called his "magic circle" and "fairy-land."[19] The many references to enchantment and magic in "The Piazza" suggest that Melville had in mind not only Hawthorne's "The Old Manse" but also his own review of *Mosses from an Old Manse* where he writes of the magic spell that Hawthorne's work has cast over him. In "The Piazza" Melville thus returned to the same autobiographical subject that he dealt with in "The Encantadas," the difference between his expectation and his experience with regard to Hawthorne. He expected the friendship to lead, figuratively speaking, to a green enchanted isle, but he found only barren ground. Now as he looks back over this crucial time in his life in "The Piazza," he is not as empty and as bitter as he was when he wrote "The Encantadas" two years earlier, but he still feels keenly how wrong he was to have put such high hopes in Hawthorne and to have raved so enthusiastically in his review of *Mosses*.[20] He claimed there "to be the

19. *Mosses from an Old Manse*, The Centenary Edition of the Works of Nathaniel Hawthorne, general eds. William Charvat, Roy H. Pearce, C. M. Simpson, vol. 10 (Columbus: Ohio State University Press, 1974), pp. 28, 29, 33.

20. The "blue summit" in one of the narrator's comments on the unreliability of perception may refer to Hawthorne. "A blue summit," writes the narrator, "peering up away behind the rest will, as it were, talk to you over their heads, and plainly tell you, that, though he (the blue summit) seems among them, he is not of them (God forbid!), and,

first that has so brayed" about Hawthorne.[21] As if commenting
on that earlier braying, he makes multiple references in "The
Piazza" to *A Midsummer Night's Dream*, even indicating that
the narrator is looking for Titania, the fairy queen of that play.
By implication, therefore, he would be Bottom, the buffoon with
an ass's head.

In his portrayal of Marianna, Melville expressed his most intimate opinion of Hawthorne as he viewed him several years
after they first met. That he had Hawthorne in mind when he
created Marianna is evident from several hints. For example, he
seems to be thinking of Hawthorne's fascination with clouds
and shadows when he has Marianna call a shadow on the landscape a dog. In "The Old Manse" Hawthorne had written:
"Once, as we turned our boat to the bank, there was a cloud in
the shape of an immensely gigantic figure of a hound, couched
above the house, as if keeping guard over it." [22] By creating a
female character to project his concept of Hawthorne, Melville
did not mean to suggest that his old friend was effeminate in
the usual sense of the word. In all ordinary ways Hawthorne's
manhood was, as Melville knew, not a matter for debate. Marianna does not represent the total Hawthorne but only one aspect
of him, his innermost being. Hawthorne's "secret" that Melville

-----

indeed, would have you know that he considers himself—as, to say
truth, he has good right—by several cubits their superior." But, the
narrator adds, "these mountains, somehow, they play at hide-and-seek,
and all before one's eyes" (p. 441).

21. "Hawthorne," p. 140.

22. *Mosses*, pp. 25–26. Melville's use of this image from "The Old
Manse" is pointed out by Helmbrecht Breinig in his provocative article
cited above. Breinig was the first to argue that in "The Piazza" Melville
was writing about Hawthorne. See also Hyatt H. Waggoner, "Hawthorne and Melville Acquaint the Reader with Their Abodes," *Studies
in the Novel* 2 (1970): 420–424. Waggoner points out that " 'The
Piazza' is at once indebted to 'The Old Manse' and constitutes a kind of
'answer' to certain passages in Hawthorne's work that must have struck
Melville, on this new reading, as excessively idealistic" (p. 420). Neither
Breinig nor Waggoner, however, links Marianna directly with Hawthorne.

mentioned to Julian Hawthorne years after Hawthorne was dead, a secret that Melville would not elaborate on, may well be revealed in Marianna. After believing that he had seen the manifestation of no less than a godlike being in Hawthorne, Melville found when he tried worshipfully to get to know him intimately that Hawthorne was not at heart a god at all; in fact he was weary and lonely and somewhat fearful. Later in *Clarel* Melville developed the same characterization of Hawthorne through Vine. Outwardly a serene, mysterious man, Vine proves to have a secret weakness that Clarel discovers when he approaches him unseen: "Could it be Vine, and quivering so? . . . / A trembling over of small throes / In weak swoll'n lips, which to restrain / Desire is none, nor any rein" (III. vii. 16–17, 23–25).[23] Walter E. Bezanson concludes that what Clarel sees is what Melville discovered in Hawthorne: "Clarel has found some ambiguous and discrediting weakness in the noble Vine. If one accepts the Hawthorne identification, then here is Melville's secret conviction: beneath his shy and opulent serenity Hawthorne was scared." Linked with this hidden trembling in Vine is what Bezanson calls "passive ennui," a quality that also characterizes Marianna.[24]

If Melville were disappointed that Hawthorne did not turn out to be a demigod who opened his arms to him, he was also a little disgusted with himself, as "The Encantadas" suggests, for expecting so much, for being such a dreamer, and, in effect, for making such a fool of himself. Nevertheless, the friendship died when Melville discovered that there was a Marianna deep within Hawthorne, for that made him just another man instead of the master he had hoped for.[25] "The Piazza" reviews the whole relationship, Melville's weariness and need of a savior,

23. *Clarel*, ed. Walter E. Bezanson (New York: Hendricks House, 1960).

24. Bezanson, pp. xcvi, xcix.

25. Hawthorne's reserve was also a barrier between them. He must have sensed Melville's hero worship and put him at a distance, for he had none of the arrogance that enables one to enjoy being idolized.

his hope when he caught the glimmer of Hawthorne's brilliance, his attempt to get to know his new friend, his startling discovery of inner weakness and weariness there, and Hawthorne's death as his friend. In the story, of course, Marianna does not die literally, but she dies for the narrator in the sense Hawthorne died for Melville. She ceases to be a vital source of hope and inspiration to him, a possible fountain of energy.

Melville used a quotation from Shakespeare to underscore this point. For an epigram he quoted the following line from *Cymbeline*: "With fairest flowers, / Whilst summer lasts, and I live here, Fidele—" These are the words of Arviragus spoken over the "body" of Imogen (pretending to be a boy, Fidele), who is not actually dead but is thought to be. It is part of one of the most beautiful passages of poetry in Shakespeare's plays, a eulogy of tenderness:

> With fairest flowers
> Whilst summer lasts, and I live here, Fidele,
> I'll sweeten thy sad grave; thou shalt not lack
> The flower that's like thy face, pale primose, nor
> The azur'd harebell, like thy veins: no, nor
> The leaf of eglantine, whom not to slander,
> Out-sweet'ned not thy breath: the ruddock would
> With charitable bill (O bill, sore shaming
> Those rich-left heirs, that let their fathers lie
> Without a monument!) bring thee all this;
> Yea, and furr'd moss besides. When flowers are none
> To winter-ground thy corse—
> (IV. ii. 219–229)[26]

This is a burial speech for a man, Fidele, who is actually a mere girl and who is not literally dead.[27] It is thus highly appropriate for Melville's purpose in "The Piazza" where he recounts the

26. *Cymbeline*, ed. J. M. Nosworthy (Cambridge: Harvard University Press, 1955).
27. As in "The Piazza" references to fairies also occur in *Cymbeline*. About Fidele (really Imogen), Guiderius says: "With female fairies will his tomb be haunted" (IV. ii. 217).

loss of Marianna to the narrator and the loss of Hawthorne as a vital force in his life.

Yet it is not with a sense of resentment that he regards this episode retrospectively in his life, and this is the essential difference between the two treatments of his relationship with Hawthorne, first in "The Encantadas" and then in "The Piazza." The same note of tenderness that is apparent in Arviragus's speech in *Cymbeline* pervades the narrator's attitude toward Marianna. She is not what he had hoped for; she cannot give him new life; but as he looks back on her he does not condemn her because she failed him. Tenderness and pity have outlived disappointment. Melville's moving remembrance of Hawthorne in his poem "Monody" reveals that such was, indeed, his attitude.

The part of Arviragus's speech that Melville chose for his epigram is nearly identical with a line in a similar speech in *Pericles*, which Melville may also have had in mind. Arviragus says: "Whilst summer lasts." The phrase in *Pericles* is "While summer-days doth last." These words are spoken by the girl called Marina, a possible source for the mountain girl in "The Piazza." [28] She like Arviragus is bemoaning the death of a friend, in this case an older woman. The first part of the passage is very much like that in *Cymbeline*, with flower imagery predominant and a tone of devotion:

> No, I will rob Tellus of her weed,
> To strew thy green with flowers; the yellows, blues,
> The purple violets, and marigolds,
> Shall as a carpet hang upon thy grave,
> While summer-days doth last.
> (IV. i. 13–17) [29]

28. Several other possible sources have been mentioned by critics. Breinig, for example, writes: "The lovely mountain girl herself, Marianna, is, of course, Mariana from *Measure for Measure*" (p. 276). According to Fogle, Marianna is "Mariana in the moated grange" and "Tennyson's Mariana, no doubt, as well as Shakespeare's" (p. 89).

29. *Pericles*, ed. F. D. Hoeniger (Cambridge: Harvard University Press, 1963).

The rest of the speech is an indulgence in self-pity, but it is expressed with such poignancy and in such terms as to be pertinent to Melville's own situation and especially to his feelings about the death of a promising friendship:

> Ay me! poor maid,
> Born in a tempest, when my mother died,
> This world to me is as a lasting storm,
> Whirring me from my friends.
>   (IV. i. 17–20)

In a stormy world that whirred him from his friends, Melville had to find a way, as he put it in "The Piazza," of "weathering Cape Horn" (p. 440). His solution was the piazza. It is the central symbol, for it represents a philosophical stance, a way of surviving for an extraordinary mind.

The narrator's deep need for a piazza reveals more about him than any other detail in the story. In the very first sentence he indicates that the house he moved to in the country did not have at that time a piazza and that he regretted this deficiency because a piazza belongs to two worlds, "combining the coziness of in-doors with the freedom of out-doors" (p. 437). Furthermore the piazza is a good place "to inspect your thermometer" (p. 437). The dichotomy Melville established in the opening sentence of "The Piazza" is that of the lee shore and the howling infinite. The cozy inside of his house represents all of the security and craven comfort that Melville had spoken of with contempt in *Moby-Dick*. The area outside the house represents the perilous sea of freedom that calls with a strong voice to the exceptional and the strong but ultimately maddens and destroys.

Melville said in *Moby-Dick* that it was better, more noble, to perish in the howling infinite than to remain always in the sheltered port, but his own lifelong attempt was to find a way to mediate between the two. His group of short stories collectively presents this drama of a man's struggle to build a

337

proper porch, an intermediate point upon which he can remain in contact with the leeward inclined world but overlook at the same time and partake of the wildness and the greatness of the realm of unfettered thinking. He may have admired those who permanently left the piazza, those like Bartleby and Banna-donna, and he may have felt a certain disdain for those who remained always inside the house, those like the lawyer of "Bartleby" and Delano, but he discovered that he must himself stick to the porch. The piazza is not a good place to take the temperature of the world because it is colder or hotter there than on the lee shore, especially when the piazza fronts the north. Neither is it a good place to take the temperature of the howling infinite because the readings in that wild region will always be more extreme. But it is a good place to take one's own tem-perature—that is, to get one's bearings and retain them.

Significantly the narrator tries to do without a piazza at first by going outside and lounging on the ground, but the experi-ence makes him ill, and he decides that "a piazza must be had" (p. 439). The direction he chooses for his piazza further char-acterizes him as an unusual man who needs to retain as much as possible of his Azzageddi impulse, that wild and free inner self of Babbalanja in *Mardi*, while at the same time remaining in touch with the ordinary world. He selects the northern side because it is the most exposed to the severities of winter and because "to the north is Charlemagne" (p. 439). He carefully weighs the advantages of every direction; all of them are tamer in scenery than the north; only there is a view of massive Mount Greylock, which he calls Charlemagne because it towers royally above the other hills. Greylock represents to him the heroic potential, which can be realized only in the howling infinite. Melville knew that by admiring and writing about those excep-tional rebels of life who thirst for freedom and defy all re-straints he could keep alive the Azzageddi impulse within himself without actually following the destructive course of such heroes as Ahab and Bartleby.

But he did not enjoy full peace of mind simply because he worked out this concept of living in two worlds. "The Piazza" reveals that even after he conceived of the importance of an intermediate point upon which to stand and even after trying it out, he suffered from despair and yearned for a new freedom and vitality that he believed he could find only by launching out into a region totally dissociated from the ordinary world. The narrator of the story becomes weary and ill even after he builds and uses his porch, and he leaves it to find a spot of radiance. His experience—whether it be viewed as an actual journey to the mountains, deep probing into the nature of man, extreme introspection, or the search for an idol—taught him that he must "stick to the piazza." [30]

The narrator does not take the coward's way out; he has not fled unpleasantries to return to comfortable domesticity. If he wanted to be a man of prudence and method, a blind accepter of the ways of the world, he would remain inside the house, for that is the lee shore.[31] He prefers his northern piazza, he says, speaking in the present tense and thus describing his state of mind at the time he tells the story: "Even in December, this northern piazza does not repel—nipping cold and gusty though it be, and the north wind, like any miller, bolting by the snow,

30. Although "The Piazza" is not an especially cheerful story it does suggest a way of dealing with life that offers some hope and is thus akin to such stories as "Jimmy Rose." It seems to me somewhat more positive in outlook than is indicated in the following statement by Vida K. Brack and O. M. Brack, Jr.: "The tale has no resolution but irresolution, offers no hope but in the willing suspension of disbelief." "Weathering Cape Horn: Survivors in Melville's Minor Short Fiction," *Arizona Quarterly* 28 (1972): 71.

31. Several critics regard the narrator in a negative light. Stein probably takes the harshest view, seeing him as a moral hypocrite. Indeed, according to Stein, "all the first-person protagonists in *The Piazza Tales* are incorrigible tricksters; and as unregenerate foes of moral order, they merit our scorn, not our respect" (p. 323). Breinig feels that self-mockery is involved in Melville's characterization of the narrator (p. 282). John Seelye regards the narrator as a kind of happy fool, shallow and optimistic (pp. 26–27).

in finest flour—for then, once more, with frosted beard, I pace the sleety deck, weathering Cape Horn" (p. 440). He cannot weather the difficulties of his existence if he deserts the piazza, for it is his ship. Without it he would perish in the wild sea he respects but rightfully fears. The final image of the story is that of a sailor pacing the deck of his ship. During the day the "scenery is magical—the illusion so complete." [32] In the darkness he is haunted by the terrors of the deep, by "Marianna's face, and many as real a story" (p. 453). Thus Melville insisted upon being a sailor rather than a landlubber, but he knew that he could not survive in the howling infinite without a ship, which is in a sense akin to the land but also akin to the sea.

32. The narrator states that the piazza has become his "box-royal; and this amphitheatre, my theatre of San Carlo" (p. 453). He thus reaffirms the theme of "The Two Temples," that acting is a way of surviving with self-respect. The theater and the piazza are the same basic symbol, intermediate points between the "horrors of the half known life" and the world of "prudence and method."

MYSTERY AS MYSTERY

"The Apple-Tree Table"

Chapter 14

In the closing lines of *Walden* Thoreau wrote that "Everyone has heard the story which has gone the rounds of New England, of a strong and beautiful bug which came out of the dry leaf of an old table of apple-tree wood, which had stood in a farmer's kitchen for sixty years, first in Connecticut, and afterward in Massachusetts, —from an egg deposited in the living tree many years earlier still. . . ." [1] Whether everyone had heard the story or not, it was well known, for it had already appeared in print in several places. [2] In using it as an exemplar to argue for man's personal and collective resurrection from the "dead dry life of society," Thoreau relied on its general currency among his readers.

1. *The Variorum Walden*, ed. Walter Harding (New York: Twayne, 1962), p. 266.
2. For accounts of the various uses of the story see Douglas Sackman, "The Original of Melville's Apple-Tree Table," *American Literature* 11 (1939–40): 448–451; Frank Davidson, "Melville, Thoreau, and 'The Apple-Tree Table,'" *American Literature* 25 (1953–54): 479–488; and Walter Harding, pp. 318–319.

When Melville read *A History of the County of Berkshire, Massachusetts* (1829), a copy of which he acquired in July 1850, he marked a passage that recounts the same event.[3] But unlike Thoreau's version this one (which was written by the Reverend Chester Dewey) was not offered as an illustration of man's immortality or as anything else other than a curious natural fact. Calculating the probable age of the table and describing the appearance of the bug, Dewey is careful to avoid any suggestion of transcendence. Nor does he speculate in any way about the implications of the incident. His is an empirical observation, supported by details and by eyewitness evidence.[4] "These *facts*," he writes, italicizing *facts*, "were given by Mr. Putnam, in whose possession the table still remains, and were first published in the *Repertory* at Middlebury, Vt., in 1816."[5]

Melville would also have seen the story in Timothy Dwight's *Travels in New England and New York* (1821). In his review of Hawthorne's *Mosses from an Old Manse* he claims that he had been reading Dwight when he discovered *Mosses*.[6] Although Dwight gives substantially the same facts as Dewey, his represents a third way the story of the bug was treated, for he speculates about the meaning of the phenomenon in rational terms. For him it offers rational answers to previously unsolved

---

3. The passage reads in part: "In 1806, a strong and beautiful *bug* eat out of a table made from an apple-tree, which grew on the farm of Maj. Gen. Putnam, in Brooklyn, Conn., and which was brought to Williamstown when his son, Mr. P. S. Putnam, removed to that town. It was cut down in 1786, sixty-five years after it was transplanted, and if the tree was then fifteen years old, it was 80 years old when cut down. . . ." *A History of the County of Berkshire, Massachusetts* (Pittsfield, 1829), p. 39.

4. Of the three bugs that emerged from the table, one was preserved for posterity by the Reverend Dr. Fitch. Dewey describes it with precision: it "was an inch and one forth long, and one third inch in diameter; colour, dark glistening brown, with tints of yellow."

5. *A History of the County of Berkshire*, p. 39.

6. "Hawthorne and His Mosses," in *The Works of Herman Melville* (London: Constable, 1924), 13: 125.

mysteries. He takes it as proof that the eggs of insects are, like seeds, "vivacious." Whereas it had been a mystery how certain insects were seen only once in a lifetime, now it is all clear to him: "What was true of this insect is in all probability true of many other species. It ceases then to be strange that various tribes appear once during the life of man, or during the existence of several generations. Every such tribe must ordinarily be new to the existing generation, because no account of its appearance has been recorded. The want of a regular cause of their existence cannot any longer be alleged. . . ." Because the eggs of some insects have such a long period of dormancy the species seems to disappear only to reappear in a new generation of man. Dwight finds "inexplicableness" no longer applies to these seemingly new insects. Because of the apple-tree table and its bug, "there can be nothing perplexing in the periods of the locust, nor any further necessity of inquiring whence new species of insects are derived, or what has become of those which are apparently extinct."[7]

The source of the central episode in "The Apple-Tree Table," then, was not some obscure and trivial natural curiosity that Melville had encountered just once but an incident that had been talked and written about in New England for a generation. Many of Melville's readers would have known both the story of the table and the various ways the phenomenon had been interpreted. Melville's own interest in the episode derived from both the inherent appeal and mystery of the strange occurrence and from what the conflicting opinions of it revealed of human nature and the relativity of perception. Melville repeatedly sought out puzzling occurrences that had become well known because public response to them was poignantly illuminating.

---

7. *Travels in New England and New York*, ed. Barbara Miller Solomon (Cambridge: Harvard University Press, 1969), pp. 277, 278. The "Author of the World," concludes Dwight, has ordered nature with infinite wisdom and foresight. To perceive this "conduct of Providence" man need only exercise his powers of reason.

He reacted with obvious interest to a much talked about experiment of the English writer G.P.R. James, who planted near Stockbridge, Massachusetts, some ancient wheat that had been taken from an Egyptian pyramid. James's son, Charles Leigh James, many years later described the unusual event (but without much enthusiasm): "At Stockbridge I remember something very curious. We had received and planted some Egyptian wheat taken from the inside of a mummy case. It came up, and I saw it growing; but it did not seed 'worth a continental.' "[8] Others saw much more in the incident than "something very curious." No doubt it furnished the occasion for inspirational messages of rebirth as well as rational and scientific opinions on what it all meant. It made a lasting impression on Melville. He wrote Hawthorne: "My development has been all within a few years past. I am like one of those seeds taken out of the Egyptian Pyramids, which, after being three thousand years a seed and nothing but a seed, being planted in English soil, it developed itself, grew to greenness, and then fell to mould."[9] The story of a bug emerging from its egg in a table is of course similar to that of the seed in the pyramid; consequently, Melville may have been writing about himself and his artistic career in "The Apple-Tree Table," as one critic argues.[10]

More often than not, however, Melville was interested in such incidents for what they revealed about other people, about mankind in its varieties, rather than for what they reflected of himself. The title he chose for the second chapter of *The Confidence-Man* restates one of the principal themes of "The Apple-Tree Table": "Showing That Many Men Have Many Minds." The chapter begins with comments by passengers aboard a riverboat about an inexplicable fellow traveler, a deaf-mute dressed

8. Quoted in S. M. Ellis, *The Solitary Horseman or The Life and Adventures of G.P.R. James* (Kensington: Cayme Press, 1927), p. 164.

9. *The Letters of Herman Melville*, ed. Merrell R. Davis and William H. Gilman (New Haven: Yale University Press, 1960), p. 130.

10. Edward H. Rosenberry, *Melville and the Comic Spirit* (Cambridge: Harvard University Press, 1955), p. 183.

in cream colors. By some he is believed to be a fraud, a "humbug," but others call him a "Jacob dreaming at Luz." Another passenger thinks him Casper Hauser.[11] Still another accuses him of being a "spirit-rapper." He is appealing to some, frightening to others. Some say that he "means something"; others find him merely an "odd fish" or an "escaped convict."[12] The Confidence Man in his several disguises (of which the man in cream colors is but one) is an "original character," inexplicable in himself but a Drummond light in illuminating the natures of those people who respond to him. They are as they see him.

In a sense Melville's last short story, published in *Putnam's* in May 1856, is a rehearsal for *The Confidence-Man*, his next work. "The Apple-Tree Table" does not have an original character, but it does have an original incident, as the subtitle suggests ("Original Spiritual Manifestations"). An original incident is a mysterious occurrence that catches the attention of various kinds of people, who reveal themselves while trying to solve the mystery. Melville recognized that the marvelous bug in the table constituted just such an incident. When some people examined the strange occurrence they, like Thoreau, optimistically saw hope for mankind. The insect's emergence from the table suggested resurrection to them. Others, like Dewey, were content to consider the entire phenomenon as just some queer happening and to let it go at that. Still others drew rational conclusions as did Timothy Dwight.

An original incident that Melville found equally revealing was that involving the Fox girls, who are mentioned in "The

11. The sudden appearance of Casper Hauser in 1828 in the Nuremberg marketplace caused worldwide excitement. He was a "wild boy" who had lived his early years in a hole and could not even stand until taught by a man who later deserted him. The case of Casper Hauser was still another example of the kind of puzzling and unusual incident that interested Melville, for people interpreted the phenomenon of Casper Hauser according to their own predilections.

12. *The Confidence-Man: His Masquerade*, ed. Hershel Parker (New York: Norton, 1971), pp. 4–5.

Apple-Tree Table." The narrator states that "the incident now about to be given," the story of the table and its two insects, "happened long before the time of the 'Fox girls' " (p. 467).[13] In February 1848 the Fox family, who had recently occupied a house in Hydesville, New York, began hearing strange rapping noises. The sounds continued without any apparent pattern until March, when the older of the two Fox sisters living at home, Margaret, began communication with what appeared to be the spirits doing the rappings. News spread swiftly of the phenomenon and soon the entire country knew of it. The cult of spiritualism in America had its origins in this incident.[14] Critics have responded to the reference to the Fox sisters in "The Apple-Tree Table" with opinions that are almost diametrically opposite. Marvin Fisher, for example, feels that "the mention of the 'Fox girls' in the story" is "like a red herring to lead those readers least interested in Melville's main concerns off in a different direction."[15] Carolyn L. Karcher, on the other hand, finds that the reference to the Fox sisters sounds the keynote of the story, which is "a topical satire on a current religious movement: the Spiritualist cult of the 1850s."[16]

Melville was genuinely interested in the spirit-rapping phenomenon; his allusion to the Fox girls is not merely a red herring to throw readers off the track. But neither is the incident that occurred in Hydesville (and its aftermath) the center of his story. He makes reference to it because it is similar to the story of the table. Both are original incidents. Both serve to

13. "The Apple-Tree Table: or, Original Spiritual Manifestations," *Putnam's Monthly Magazine* 7 (May 1856), 465–475. All references to "The Apple-Tree Table" are to this, the first printing of the story.

14. For an excellent treatment of the Fox girls as well as the broader subject of nineteenth-century spiritualism, see Earl Wesley Fornell, *The Unhappy Medium: Spiritualism and the Life of Margaret Fox* (Austin: University of Texas Press, 1964).

15. "Bug and Humbug in Melville's 'Apple-Tree Table,' " *Studies in Short Fiction* 8 (1971): 460.

16. "The 'Spiritual Lesson' of Melville's 'The Apple-Tree Table,' " *American Quarterly* 23 (1971): 101.

show that, as Melville said in *The Confidence-Man,* "many men have many minds." The public response to spirit rapping was very similar in kind to the reactions evoked by Mr. Putnam's table of apple wood.[17] Some people believed that the noises were actually made by spirits of the departed. Whether these were evil or good spirits, they were spirits, and thus the grave was not the end for man. Others offered scientific and rational explanations (such as animal magnetism) for the phenomenon.[18] Still others muttered "Humbug" and refused to believe anything at all about it. The devotees of transcendence, reason, and empiricism made themselves known through their responses just as they did in the case of the apple-tree table.

During the time when the controversy over spirit rapping and the Fox sisters was most intense, a prominent New York minister, the Reverend Samuel Byron Brittan, gave a lecture on "Spiritual Manifestations" at Hope Chapel in Manhattan that was attended, as the New York *Daily Tribune* reported, "by a crowded and deeply interested assemblage, among whom we noticed many of our most respectable citizens."[19] The point of Brittan's lecture was that spirit rapping should not be dismissed lightly but should be considered as further evidence of the truths of the Bible. Before he presented this view, however, he described three common types of people, characterized by how they respond to phenomena. The *Daily Tribune* reported this part of his lecture as follows:

The lecturer commenced with a statement of the threefold plane or sphere which was occupied by human beings, namely, the sphere of sensation, of reason, and of intuition. The plane of sensation, which

17. For a discussion of the public response see Earl Wesley Fornell and also Howard Kerr, *Mediums, and Spirit-Rappers, and Roaring Radicals: Spiritualism in American Literature, 1850–1900* (Urbana: University of Illinois Press, 1972).

18. Current explanations for spirit rappings and table movements are discussed in the "Editor's Table" section of *Harper's* 7 (1853): 127–129.

19. New York *Daily Tribune,* 8 March 1852, p. 7, col. 2. Cited by Earl Wesley Fornell.

was common to man with the lower animals . . . was often the only one attained by an individual in his mental developement. Many persons had no ideas beyond the impressions made on the organs of sense. They lived entirely in the province of the material. No evidence in their view was valid but what was addressed to the sensual nature. . . . Men often place themselves in the plane of sensation by their own confession. We daily hear it said by numerous persons, that they will believe only what they have seen with their own eyes or heard with their own ears. But there is a higher sphere, a higher source of evidence than sensation. That is reason. Here is the province of argument, of logical deduction, of inference from cause and effect. This is the foundation of the physical sciences. A still higher sphere is that of intuition, by which we have cognizance of spiritual realities.[20]

Melville may or may not have known of Brittan's lecture, but it is pertinent here at any rate because Brittan expressed systematically and succinctly the same observation that Melville made in "The Apple-Tree Table." Brittan described the three principal ways people react to any original incident. In "The Apple-Tree Table" Melville presents a group that is a cross section of humanity. They respond to a phenomenon in precisely the three ways Brittan outlined: on the level of sensation (the narrator), reason (the wife and Professor Johnson), and intuition (the two daughters and the maid). Melville's theme is that all three ways are inadequate for explaining or solving the mystery, which remains after all is said and done still a mystery.

The family in "The Apple-Tree Table" seems at first glance to be the same one that appears in "I and My Chimney."[21]

20. Ibid.
21. Frank Davidson feels that "The Apple-Tree Table" is "a companion piece to 'I and My Chimney'" partly because "the setting, characters, and tone of the two stories are essentially the same" (p. 481). Edward H. Rosenberry sees "The same cast of characters" in both stories (p. 182). Richard Harter Fogle writes that "the characters of 'The Apple-Tree Table' are about the same people as the principals of 'Jimmy Rose' and 'I and My Chimney.'" *Melville's Shorter Fiction* (Norman: University of Oklahoma Press, 1960), p. 78. Marvin Fisher agrees that "the characters in 'The Apple-Tree Table' are members of the same family that figures in 'Jimmy Rose' and 'I and My Chimney'" (p. 460),

Both works depict a family of four: a husband, his wife, and two daughters named Julia and Anna. Both stories have a maid named Biddy. "The Apple-Tree Table" and "I and My Chimney" are not so much companion pieces, however, as they are counterstories. Their contrasts are more fundamental than their similarities with respect to characterization. In both stories the narrator is the main character.[22] But the two men are as different as the narrators of "Bartleby" and "Cock-A-Doodle-Doo!" The narrator of "The Apple-Tree Table" does not have the unsettling preoccupation with magnitude that marks the other narrator. Both stories deal with mystery, but the two husbands respond to it in entirely different fashions. The narrator of "The Apple-Tree Table" is a married version of the lawyer of "Bartleby." They are kindly, intelligent, and personable, but they are also weak and shallow men who camouflage their fear with a slight but disarming self-mockery and an ingratiating sense of humor that gives a decidedly comic tone to both stories. Into the ordered life of each man comes a mysterious phenomenon. In the case of the lawyer it is an original character, Bartleby. In the case of the husband of "The Apple-Tree Table" it is an

---

and Ray B. Browne argues that these three stories involve "substantially the same characters." *Melville's Drive to Humanism* (Lafayette: Purdue University Studies, 1971), p. 272. Like "I and My Chimney" and "The Apple-Tree Table," "Jimmy Rose" has a family of husband, wife, and two daughters (who are nameless) and a maid named Biddy. The husband and wife are not the same as those in either of the other stories, however, and the settings of the three works are different. The house in "I and My Chimney" is in the country, that in "Jimmy Rose" in the city. The house in "The Apple-Tree Table" is also in a city, but it could not be the same dwelling occupied by the same person as in "Jimmy Rose" because William Ford inherited his home whereas the other narrator states that he purchased his.

22. That the personality of the narrator has not been previously analyzed with care is one of the more puzzling aspects of criticism on "The Apple-Tree Table." Malcolm O. Magaw calls him a "skeptic," but since the focus of his argument is elsewhere, offers no real proof. "Apocalyptic Imagery in Melville's 'The Apple-Tree Table,'" *Midwest Quarterly* 8 (1967): 366.

original incident, that involving the table and its insects. Both characters are delineated through their responses to the phenomena.

One reason the narrator of "The Apple-Tree Table" may seem at first more like the husband in "I and My Chimney" than he does the bachelor lawyer of "Bartleby" is that both the family men stress their interest in old things. They begin their two stories with paragraphs that repeat and thus emphasize the word *old*.[23] If this seems a quirky diversionary tactic on Melville's part intended to fool the reader into believing that the same man is speaking in both stories, it may well be. But once the personalities of the two speakers begin to unfold, their differences not only become apparent but are underscored by the narrators' common use of the word *old*.

A genuine sense of the past is usually one indication of depth in a person. Therefore when the narrator of "The Apple-Tree Table" describes his old garret and the ancient table that he found there, he begins on a note of what seems civilized maturity. It soon becomes clear, however, that his references to the past reveal no deep sense of history but a superficial antiquarianism, his allusions to ancient practices of magic no feeling for true mystery but a shallow fascination with the odd and curious. His garret is "hopper-shaped," and it contains relics of the past, but he does not link it in his mind with the Great Pyramid of Egypt as does the narrator of "I and My Chimney" his hopper-shaped chimney. He says that the table might have belonged to Friar Bacon, and he describes the "broken, becrusted old purple vials and flasks" he sees on it, but his tone is that of a bemused antiquary, not that of one who has some understanding of what Bacon and the vials suggest—alchemy. Melville knew well the

23. William Ford in "Jimmy Rose" also loves ancient things and begins his narrative with a paragraph that repeats the word *old*. But he is a far deeper character than the narrator of "The Apple-Tree Table." It should also be remembered that "Bartleby" begins on a note of age: "I am a rather elderly man."

complexity and profound aims of the mystical practice of alchemy. The suggestions of alchemy in "The Apple-Tree Table" form a backdrop just as they do in "The Happy Failure" to point up by contrast the shallowness of the character being depicted. The narrator is well educated; he recognizes the outward signs of alchemy, but he is insensitive to the mysteries that gave rise to it. He knows traditional symbols when he sees them, but he does not participate emotionally in the symbolic process. For example, he says that the table had two features "significant of conjurations and charms—the circle and tripod" (p. 465), but this is purely an intellectual and empirical observation. He makes associations but without felt insight.[24]

The narrator brings the old table down from his garret for two reasons: he is charmed with it and he thinks it might be useful. In these two responses to the table he reveals his dominant traits. His reaction to anything out of the ordinary is usually superficial: the ancient table with its circular top and cloven feet merely charms him. If it suggests to him necromancy or the universal presence of evil or anything else, it does so only in the shallowest sense. "A very satanic-looking little old table, indeed," he says in a tone of approval. It is for him a piece of virtu, a curio, not a true symbol in any profound sense. That he is incapable of profound response to mystery is indicated by his favorite words *strange* and *curious*. When Melville puts these words and their synonym *queer* repeatedly into the mouth of a character, he is subtly condemning him. Such words are symptomatic of a character who cannot or will not dive deeply. Thus the lawyer in "Bartleby" describes his scrivener in the first paragraph of the story as "the strangest I ever saw, or heard of," and thereafter he often uses the word *strange* in his narration. The superficial minister Derwent in *Clarel* calls a grotesque rock

24. When he bursts open the scuttle of his garret and thrusts his head into fresh air, he says that he is reminded of man's resurrection from the grave, but the statement carries little conviction; it is expressed in clichés of superficial piety.

on the landscape "queer" and promptly receives a rebuke from
the more profound Rolfe:

> "*Queer?*" muttered Rolfe as Derwent went;
> "*Queer*" is the furthest he will go
> In phrase of a disparagement.
> But—ominous, with haggard rent—
> To me yon crag's brow-beating brow
> Looks horrible—and I *say* so."
>   (II. xxx. 72–77)

Melville reveals the shallowness of Stubb in *Moby-Dick* when
he has him say in response to Ahab: "It's queer, very queer;
and he's queer too; aye, take him fore and aft, he's about the
queerest old man Stubb ever sailed with." Then he adds:
"Damn me, but all things are queer, come to think of 'em." [25]
There is no reason to believe that Melville is being any less severe in his judgment of the narrator of "The Apple-Tree
Table," for he has him refer to the tattered copy of Cotton
Mather's *Magnalia Christi Americana*, which he discovers in his
garret, as a "queer old book" (p. 467), and after the mysterious
ticking has started he says of the table: "It's a queer table, wife;
there's no blinking it" (p. 472). Similarly he uses *strange* and
curious at every turn. The insects in his garret are "strange," as
are the carvings on the old chairs he finds there. The *Magnalia*
looks "strangely" as it sits in the middle of the apple-tree
table.[26] His daughter Julia's emotions upon first seeing the table
are "strange." The first sounds that come from the table are
"strange." The bug is a "strange object." The rusted key that
he discovers in his garden is "curious." When he first peers into
the garret he says: "A curious scene was presented" (p. 465).
On another page he uses the word *curious* four times (p. 473)

25. *Moby-Dick*, ed. Harrison Hayford and Hershel Parker (New
York: Norton, 1967), p. 113.
26. The narrator calls it the "Magnolia." Since this spelling is used
in both places where the volume is mentioned by name, this is possibly
the narrator's comic mistake rather than a misprint.

to describe what he calls "coincidences" and his desire to see the second bug emerge from the table.

His language alone is enough to indicate that he is not Melville's spokesman or a projection of the author, but his second reason for bringing the table down from his garret offers still further proof. He is a disciple of utility. "I thought it would make a nice little breakfast and tea-table," he says. "It was just the thing for a whist table, too. And I also pleased myself with the idea that it would make a famous reading-table" (p. 466). Utility is not always an ignoble or petty aim, and this one instance where it motivates the narrator does not by itself mark him negatively. But his thoughts about how he can *use* the table are characteristic of his general makeup.

In every phase of his life he is guided by utility. One of the earliest bits of information that he gives about himself is that he considered the rumor that his garret was haunted "absurd" but that he did not at the time of purchasing the house contradict it since, as he puts it, "it tended to place the property more conveniently within my means" (p. 465). He did not enter his garret for five years after buying the house because "there was no special inducement," that is, he "had no special *use* for it" (p. 465, italics mine). Besides, there was a lock on the door for which he had no key, and to call a locksmith would have been "an unnecessary trouble" (p. 465). When he finds the key to the lock and decides to enter the garret, he is acutely aware that he is doing something unusual for him: he is taking an action "irrespective of any particular benefit to accrue" (p. 465).

For coping with the everyday problems of life, the narrator's philosophy of utility is adequate. When he encounters a mystery, however, the thinness of his utilitarianism is apparent. It gives way under the slightest weight and panic comes crashing through. Ironically the narrator's devotion to utility is sometimes instrumental in making it useless as a protective armor, as his response to Cotton Mather indicates. "A thousand times," he says, he had "laughed at such stories" as those found in

Mather's *Magnalia*. "Old wives' fables, I thought, however entertaining" (p. 467). But he had never read Mather before. Mather was no old wife; nor was he a "romantic Mrs. Radcliffe." He was a "practical, hardworking, earnest, upright man, a learned doctor, too, as well as a good Christian and orthodox clergyman" (p. 467). What he is saying is that Mather may have been a preacher but that he was also a man of utility, a practical man, a doctor. If *he* believed in spirits and witches, then maybe they exist after all. He also remembers that "Dr. Johnson, the matter-of-fact compiler of a dictionary, had been a believer in ghosts" (p. 467). His respect for Johnson is not derived from his having been a poet or a man of profound intellect and feeling but a man of utility, a compiler of a dictionary. He considers Mather and Johnson practical people; consequently their opinions carry a great weight with him, and his own philosophy of utility no longer guards him against panic.

His barrier against fear has already crumbled, then, when he hears the sound of the first insect working its way out of the table. He retreats in confusion, waking his wife as he tremblingly makes his way to the safety of his bed. His fear is comic as he recounts it, but it is none the less real and revealing. The next morning he is somewhat embarrassed "at having been thrown into such a panic" (p. 468), but his fear returns when he rises and discovers that the ticking continues. First he wants to abandon the table and eat breakfast in another room, but his wife insists upon remaining. Then when the table has been taken out and his wife wants him to bring it back, he replies: "My dear . . . we have plenty of other tables; why be so particular?" (p. 469). He makes it a point to be out of the house that day. During the morning, fear and uncertainties still dominate him, but gradually he regains composure through contact with other people like himself: "But, towards noon, this sort of feeling began to wear off. The continual rubbing against so many prac-

tical people in the street, brushed such chimeras away from me"
(p. 470).

Realizing that his philosophy of utility must somehow be
buttressed if it is to protect him against panic, he dreams up a
hero whose example he can follow. He remembers the story of
how Democritus responded to some mischievous boys who tried
to frighten him in the tombs of Abdera. Democritus reportedly
said in answer to the weird sounds he heard, "Boys, little boys,
go home. This is no place for you. You will catch cold here"
(p. 470). Here was a practical man, the narrator concludes, one
who like himself had been confronted with the frightening possibility of a spiritual phenomenon. The "worthy old gentleman
had set a good example to all times in his conduct on that occasion" (p. 470). Henceforth, the narrator determines that he
will not allow the sounds from the table to frighten him, that
the "philosophy" behind Democritus's words will be his own.
Those words "imply the foregone conclusion, that any possible
investigation of any possible spiritual phenomena was absurd;
that upon the first face of such things, the mind of a sane man
instinctively affirmed them a humbug, unworthy the least attention" (p. 470). Nevertheless, when the ticking resumes on
the second night, "the contest between panic and philosophy
remained not wholly decided" (p. 470). Trying to calm himself he says, again revealing his high regard for utility, "For
shame . . . what is the *use* of so fine an example of philosophy,
if it cannot be followed?" (p. 471, italics mine).

He flatters himself when after three nights of hearing the
ticking he says that he "oscillated between Democritus and Cotton Mather" (p. 473). In reality he has very little in common
with either one of these men of substance. His oscillation is between his shallow utilitarianism on the one hand (which he
fancies to be the philosophy of Democritus) and his fear of
mystery (which he associates with Cotton Mather) on the other.
His shifts between the two are strikingly like those experienced

355

by the lawyer in "Bartleby." Both characters are men of prudence and method who confront a phenomenon that they cannot
explain with their practical philosophy. They make up their
minds that they are going to follow a calm and sensible approach to this phenomenon only to be caught up again and
again in the grip of fear. One indication of their close similarity
is their common use of the words "I resolved." Both men are
constantly resolving to do this or that. The lawyer *resolves* to
give Turkey less work in the afternoons that he can spoil, to put
Bartleby in a corner near the folding doors, to question his
silent scrivener about his past, to dismiss him because of his
"strangeness," to argue with him again about his preferring not
to, to get his own wits together and once and for all rid himself of Bartleby, and so on. The narrator of "The Apple-Tree
Table" *resolves* to make the table a part of his home, to quit
reading the *Magnalia* after it scares him, to get back in his wife's
good graces, to imitate Democritus in his bravery, to address the
ticking in the table in an offhand manner, to "keep cool," to get
some benefit from having discovered the first bug in the table,
and to catch the second bug when it emerges. Their repeated
use of this same expression, "I resolved," points up their common weakness of character. The more they use these words of
strong decisiveness the more ironic becomes the expression in
their mouths.[27] They are also alike in that lacking a true self-
esteem they crave the approval of others to feed their vanity. To
reap "credit" the narrator of "The Apple-Tree Table" implies to
his wife that he knows the source of the ticking and that he has

27. Melville also links the two narrators by other terms they use.
The lawyer uses the expression "for the very soul of me" when he says
that he could not help being cross with Bartleby. The narrator of "The
Apple-Tree Table" says about the ticking, "for the soul of me, I could
not, at that time, comprehend the phenomenon" (p. 471). The lawyer
describes his feelings of melancholy over Bartleby as "chimeras," and
the other narrator uses the same word to describe his anxiety over the
ticking table.

put an end to it. "It was a sort of innocent deceit by implication," he says, "quite harmless, and, I thought, of utility" (p. 471).

This man of utility is a clear illustration of the sensationalist, the first type Samuel Byron Brittan defined in his lecture on "Spiritual Manifestations," a person who lives chiefly on the plane of the senses, who relies on what he sees with his own eyes and hears with his own ears. When he sees the first bug, he raises what is for him the most crucial question imaginable: "Could I believe my senses?" (p. 471). If he cannot, then he does not know what he can believe. He is greatly influenced (and frightened) when he realizes that the stories of witchcraft in the *Magnalia* had been "corroborated by respectable townsfolk" and that "of not a few of the most surprising, he himself [Cotton Mather] had been eye-witness. Cotton Mather testified whereof he had seen" (p. 467). He likes the sensuous life, comforts of home, his reading cushion that he bought at a ladies' fair, his cup of punch on Saturday night, the warmth of a good fire, and a "deliberate and agreeable toilet" performed with flesh-brush and nail trimmers. That he is a true sensationalist is indicated when he says that he is "aware that most disorders of the mind might have their origin in the state of the body" (p. 468).[28]

To say that the narrator is a sensationalist, however, is not to say that he is unintelligent or animalistic but simply that he places full credence in the validity of sense perceptions. He is the higher type sensationalist. Just weeks before "The Apple-Tree Table" appeared in *Putnam's,* Melville published in *Harper's* a sketch called "The 'Gees," which delineates the lower

---

28. Sensationalism can be defined as "the theory that all knowledge originates in sensations; that all cognitions, even reflective ideas and so-called intuitions, can be traced to elementary sensations." *Dictionary of Philosophy and Psychology*, ed. James Mark Baldwin (New York: Peter Smith, 1940), 2: 515–516.

type sensationalist. Despite its having gone almost unnoticed, "The 'Gees" is highly revealing.[29] A brief and deceptive sketch, it amounts to a major definition of one of Melville's most important character types. Though ostensibly describing the descendants of "certain Portuguese convicts" who were sent to Fogo in the Cape Verde Islands off the northwestern coast of Africa, the sketch is in reality a veiled depiction of the rudementary average man as Melville conceived him, the lower sensationalist. The only difference between a higher and lower sensationalist is one of degree; consequently, to know a 'Gee is also to know the essential self of men like the narrator of "The Apple-Tree Table."

Melville begins "The 'Gees" by indicating that he has known many of the people he is describing, "sometimes as casual acquaintances, sometimes as shipmates" (p. 507).[30] He has repeatedly referred to them, he says, in his "stories," and "being myself so familiar with 'Gees, it seemed as if all the rest of the world must be" (p. 507). But his stories, he implies, have not been fully understood because his "auditors" have not known what 'Gees are. The speaker is a seaman (or ex-seaman) referring here to the yarns he tells, but the voice of Melville commenting on his own stories is unmistakable. In describing these much maligned inhabitants of Fogo, he assumes the stance of a bigot and racist of the first water. To him 'Gees are little more than animals—they smell like "haglets," and they kick like "a wild zebra." Furthermore they have to be judged as one

29. R. Bruce Bickley, Jr., discusses the sketch briefly in "The Triple Thrust of Satire in Melville's Short Stories: Society, the Narrator, and the Reader," *Studies in American Humor* 1 (1975): 172–174. A more extended discussion is to be found in Carolyn L. Karcher's "Melville's 'The 'Gees': A Forgotten Satire on Scientific Racism," *American Quarterly* 27 (1975): 421–442, which argues that Melville is parodying in format and style certain antebellum ethnologists who attempted to use science as a means of justifying Negro slavery in the South.

30. "The 'Gees," *Harper's New Monthly Magazine* 12 (March 1856): 507–509. Other references to "The 'Gees" are to this edition.

would a horse. "Simple as for the most part are both horse and 'Gee, in neither case can knowledge of the creature come by intuition" (p. 508). He then proceeds to instruct the "inexperienced" in the best methods to tell a good 'Gee from a poor one. From beginning to end, the sketch is a hoax, a joke played upon the 'Gees of the world who will read it and not recognize themselves, people (as Melville defines 'Gees) of "great appetite, but little imagination; a large eyeball, but small insight" (p. 508). If Melville was a racist he did not direct his bias against an oppressed minority but against the majority of the human race, for which the 'Gees are a metaphor.[31]

The narrator of "The Apple-Tree Table" is a man of "large eyeball, but small insight." He is what the speaker in "The 'Gees" terms a "sophisticated 'Gee." After depicting the animalistic qualities of the stupid lower sensationalists, the "green 'Gees," the narrator ends the sketch with a highly suggestive paragraph that points toward the higher sensationalist. This form of 'Gee, he says, is to be found in many places: "The above account may, perhaps, among the ethnologists, raise some curiosity to see a 'Gee. But to see a 'Gee there is no need to go all the way to Fogo, no more than to see a Chinaman to go all the way to China" (p. 509). Those found throughout the world, however, are apt to be "sophisticated 'Gees" and "hence liable to be taken for naturalized citizens badly sunburnt," so that "a stranger need to have a sharp eye to know a 'Gee, even if he see him" (p. 509). On the heels of "The 'Gees," as if to point

31. Like the mass of ordinary men, the 'Gees do not possess the strength and dignity that Melville associated with true manhood. Yet like the emasculated mass, they yearn for even the trappings of masculinity: "There is no call to which the 'Gee will with more alacrity respond than the word 'Man!' Is there any hard work to be done, and the 'Gees stand round in sulks? 'Here, my men!' cries the mate. How they jump" (p. 509). Emasculation and the futile desire for manhood are almost always characteristics of Melville's average men. The narrator of "The Apple-Tree Table" is no exception. "Upon occasion," he says, "my wife was mistress in her house" (p. 469), but she is *always* the dominant force.

out a sophisticated 'Gee to that stranger who can recognize him for what he is, Melville wrote "The Apple-Tree Table." Unfortunately, most of the time the utilitarian husband of that story is mistaken for something else, like a "Chinaman, in new coat and pantaloons, his long queue coiled out of sight in one of Genin's hats" promenading Broadway and being "taken merely for an eccentric Georgia planter" (p. 509).

If the husband reacts to the mystery of the bug as most people would (Melville was not an admirer of most people), the wife's response is also a fairly common one to mystery. He is a sensationalist, she a rationalist, the second type that Brittan defined in his lecture. Although she may appear to be the same wife as in "I and My Chimney," she is not—unless she drastically changed her attitude on certain matters between stories! The wife in "I and My Chimney" has an "itch after recently-discovered fine prospects" and pursues "Swedenborgianism, and the Spirit Rapping philosophy, with other new views, alike in things natural and unnatural." [32] The wife in "The Apple-Tree Table," on the other hand, scoffs at the spirit rapping philosophy: "For that spirits should tick . . . was, to my wife," the narrator comments, "the most foolish of all foolish imaginations" (p. 473). To her daughter Anna's claim that spirits could enter into tables, she scornfully replies, "Pshaw!" (p. 474). And when her husband suggests calling in an expert for an opinion of the bug, she sends him for Professor Johnson, a scientist, not for Madame Pazzi, a medium that the girls wish to have come.

Mysteries do not frighten her as they do her husband because she has faith in the power of reason to solve every puzzle. About the mysterious ticking the husband says: "True, she could not account for the thing; but she had all confidence that it could be, and would yet be, somehow explained, and that to

32. "I and My Chimney," *Putnam's Monthly Magazine* 7 (March 1856): 274.

her entire satisfaction" (p. 473). She does not put her full trust in sense perception because she knows that the senses can become unreliable as she believes her husband's have because of the punch he has been drinking. Neither is she inclined toward intuitions, which she considers generally humbug. With a commanding presence and a sense of authority that only an unshakable advocate of reason possesses, she says to her daughters: "Go to your chamber till you can behave more like *reasonable* creatures. Is it a bug—a bug that can frighten you out of what little wits you ever had" (p. 472, italics mine). Her hero and guide is not Democritus (though her husband believes her to be a "female Democritus") but the man of science, Professor Johnson. He speaks for her (and like her) when he comments on Julia's theory that spirits were doing the ticking in the table: " 'Why, now, she did not *really* associate this purely natural phenomenon with any crude, spiritual hypothesis, did she?' observed the learned professor, with a slight sneer" (p. 475). She is completely satisfied with the professor's rational explanations; for her the mystery has been solved.

It is also solved in the end for Anna and Julia, but theirs is a different conclusion because they are neither sensationalists nor rationalists. In their makeup intuition is the strongest force. The Reverend Brittan would have thoroughly approved of them, for they represent that segment of humanity that relies most on "intuition, by which we have cognizance of spiritual realities. This opens to the rapt vision a world beyond our own, connects us with a superior order of intelligences, reveals to us the fact of our immortality. . . ." [33] They are ready to believe first that the table is evil because of its satanic appearance, then that evil spirits are causing the ticking, and finally that the bug is a symbol of man's immortal soul. "Say what you will," preaches Julia in triumph, "if this beauteous creature be not a spirit, it yet teaches a spiritual lesson. For if, after one hundred and fifty

---

33. *Tribune*, p. 7, col. 2.

years' entombment, a mere insect comes forth at last into light, itself an effulgence, shall there be no glorified resurrection for the spirit of man?" (p. 475). What Julia ignores is that the bug's emergence is not a rebirth at all, for it has never existed before except as an egg, but a birth, and after it is born it "expired the next day" (p. 475). That is hardly cause for transcendent joy, except to those among us—and their number is substantial—like Anna and Julia.

In "The Apple-Tree Table" Melville has presented the three most common ways in which the human race responds to a mystery, the three reactions that he had noted in connection with such phenomena as the bug in Mr. Putnam's table and the Fox girls' spirit rappings. With penetrating indirectness he proves the inadequacy of each response to account for the mystery, which is more profound than any of the characters in the story realize. Mystery underlies mystery; the greater mystery they never even sense.

As most readers of the story immediately notice, "The Apple-Tree Table" is one of Melville's most humorous tales. It has all the ingredients of a light domestic comedy: a much imposed-upon husband who wants nothing more than to enjoy the simple sensuous comforts of home; a stern, no-nonsense wife, who is not only "upon occasion . . . mistress of her house," as the husband confesses, but very much in charge all the time; two flighty, superstitious daughters ready to swoon upon command; a confused and scary maid; and a know-it-all professor. Something close to slapstick comedy erupts when these characters—as a group inherently funny anyway because of their contrasts—are placed in a situation of the haunted house tradition. No analysis of the story should overlook this pervasive element of humor. But Melville has built in a second pervasive effect that works against the humor—we have a tendency to grin and to frown at the same time.

Comedy wafts lightly across the surface of the story; just beneath it is its antithesis, irony. It becomes explicit chiefly through the effects of symbolism. Melville has saturated the work with some of the richest and most ancient symbols in man's history. Irony results when the reader responds to these symbols and realizes that the characters in the story do not. The narrator, of course, communicates the symbols, but he does so without grasping their deeper significance. For example, the key is a traditional symbol of knowledge. The finding of a key suggests the first step toward insight into a mystery or enigma. Irony results in the story when the narrator finds and uses a large old key that fits the locked door of his "haunted garret," for no initiation into knowledge, no insight, comes from his having discovered the key. He does not wish to unlock mystery but to clap a tumbler over it when he runs across it and then to retreat. He unwittingly reveals this tendency in himself when during the third night of hearing the ticking he locks the door of the cedar parlor, puts the key in his pocket, and goes to bed.

When the narrator is describing how the bug made its way out of the table, he is suggesting through his choice of words the miracle of human birth. The ticking in the table corresponds to a heartbeat. After the first bug struggles from the "crack" in the table, the narrator's wife suggests that perhaps a second insect might later emerge. The husband says that he had not thought of the possibility of "twins" or even "triplets." He perceives a "heaving up, or bulging of the wood," and his wife proposes "taking a knife and cutting into the wood there," but he suggests that they "sit up with the table" and await a more natural birth, which, he says, "from present symptoms" would be before morning (p. 473). Although the narrator may be aware that he is using anatomical imagery, his aim is not symbolism but wit. Notwithstanding, a strong current of mystery flows as always beneath his humor. The birth of the bug suggests the birth of a human, which in turn suggests the birth of Christ. The narrator refers to his awaiting the "advent," and the time of year is December.[34] The ticking is that of a bug, but it also is like the sound of a clock (the narrator at first thinks it *is* his clock or watch), which in turn suggests the phenomenon of time. The bug is merely an insect, part of the lower order of life in the universe. But its appearance recalls a scarab, symbolic of the Egyptian sun god Chapers and for centuries an emblem of immortality. The applewood table superficially reminds the narrator of necromancy because of its orb and tripod, but this combination is also an ancient symbol of the solar system,[35] which is also suggested by the celestial globe that the narrator finds in his garret.[36] The garret is hopper shaped and consequently one of Melville's numerous images of a pyramid, which is symbolic of "the whole of the work of creation."[37]

The effect of such symbolism—and one could go on enumerating other examples of it—is that of a series of concentric circles. Each circle in itself represents all the profound mysteries of existence: for example, God, Satan, birth, time, death, immortality, the universe. The same enigmas are in every circle whether it is a small circle or a large one. The bug, a very small circle, is in a table, a larger circle, that is in "a very old garret of a very old house . . . of one of the oldest towns in America" (p. 465), and so forth. The circles could be drawn ever larger and larger, but the totality of mystery is present everywhere, even in the smallest circle, the insect in the table. At the end of the story each character believes that he has found a solution to the mystery he has witnessed. Ironically, they have not even perceived how deep the mystery is, much less solved it.

34. Ray B. Browne makes the observation that the language the narrator uses to describe the bug's birth suggests the birth of Christ, but the conclusion he draws is different from my own (p. 277).

35. J. E. Cirlot, *A Dictionary of Symbols*, 2nd ed., trans. Jack Sage (London: Routledge and Kegan Paul, 1971), p. 352.

36. Ironically the narator also finds the means for perceiving the solar system, a telescope, but in keeping with his lack of insight the telescope is broken.

37. Cirlot, p. 268.

A central point of Melville's in "The Apple-Tree Table" could be put this way: manifestations of the fundamental mysteries of existence are real, though most people cannot read them for what they are; solutions to these mysteries are unreal, though most people believe in the illusion of evidence. Anna and Julia preserve as evidence the second bug that comes from the table. "Embalmed in a silver vinaigrette, it lies on the little apple-tree table in the pier of the cedar-parlor" (p. 475). It is for them a relic, like a chip from the cross, proving to them that their own view is the answer to life. "And whatever lady doubts this story," writes the narrator in his final paragraph, "my daughters will be happy to show her both the bug and the table, and point out to her . . . the two sealing-wax drops designating the exact place of the two holes made by the two bugs, something in the same way in which are marked the spots where the cannon balls struck the Brattle street church" (p. 475).[38] The dead bug is in reality no more evidence of the immortality of the soul than the cannon ball and the hole it made in the Brattle Street Church are evidence of the rightness of the American colonists' cause against the British.

38. During the period when the American colonies were rebelling against England, the British general Thomas Gage quartered his troops in the Brattle Street Church in Boston. It was a sturdy brick structure, not likely, he felt, to be attacked by the colonists. Nevertheless a 24-pound cannon ball fired from Cambridge struck the church, awakening the British both to the boldness of the Americans and to their own vulnerability. Later the ball was made a permanent part of the church wall, embedded where it had struck. Until the Brattle Street Church was torn down in 1872, Americans pointed proudly to the hole and to the cannon ball as relics of a noble cause, as evidence of the rightness of their belief in independence. See Samuel Adams Drake, *Old Landmarks and Historic Personages of Boston* (Boston: Little, Brown, 1900), pp. 122–124. Marvin Fisher and Frank Davidson both argue that through the symbolism of the cannon ball striking the church Melville is commenting on the demise of Calvinism, but it seems to me more likely that he is simply showing again the inadequacy of relics to reveal the truth. This was in Melville's view probably another original incident. Many people would interpret a cannon ball hitting a church in these particular circumstances in many ways.

Throughout the story what is taken for proof—evidence derived from the senses, evidence derived from reason, evidence derived from intuition—is shown to be erroneous or inadequate. One of the most glaringly defective bits of evidence comes from the man of science, Professor Johnson. He calculates that the egg of the insect must have been laid in the table 150 years previously. The process by which he arrives at this figure may appear reasonable at first, but it is suppositional and defective to the point of comedy. What he offers for evidence is guesswork of the worst order. By "reasonable conjecture," the professor figures that the eggs were laid in the table ninety years "more or less, before the tree could have been felled." Then he calculates by some unknown means that the table is eighty years old. He adds ninety and eighty and arrives at 150! Whether the error is Professor Johnson's or Melville's or the narrator's, the effect is precisely the same, to underscore the idea that runs throughout the work that the proofs men present to support their own answers are not proofs at all because while mankind (or at least a segment of it) may have the facility for discerning mystery, it does not have the facility for deciphering it.

"The Apple-Tree Table" ends Melville's career as a writer of short stories, but it is as much an introduction to his later fiction, *The Confidence-Man* and *Billy Budd*, as it is a conclusion to his shorter works. Some aspects of "The Apple-Tree Table" and *Billy Budd* are especially striking. *Billy Budd*, which is about the killing of an inherently evil man by an inherently good man, like the "Apple-Tree Table" turns upon an original incident. Melville's purpose is the same in both works, to study the varieties of humanity by examining the ways they respond to an original incident and to make the reader feel that when all the explanations for the mystery are in—after the sensationalists, the rationalists, and the intuitists have all presented their conclusions and their evidence—mystery remains mystery, unsolved and unsolvable.

CONCLUSION

In his short fiction Melville studied closely two opposing ways of life, the one dominated by fear, the other by anger. These are the poles around which many of his characters cluster because, as he saw it, these were the strongest and most compelling of human emotions. He believed that fear, manifested in a hundred different ways, controlled the thoughts and the actions of the majority of people, making them slaves groveling at the feet of fate for petty favors. One favor came in the form of rose-colored spectacles to protect the eyes from blankness. Another was skill at rationalization and self-justification to protect the mind from meaninglessness. The lawyer of "Bartleby" is Melville's most probing and most extensive portrait of the fear-marked man, but the type is almost omnipresent in the short stories. He examines these people, most of them no better or worse than those encountered every day in life, not with sneering bitterness but with an intense interest born of personal anxiety. He did not want to be one of them. He did not want to trade his insights, his sensitivity, even his melancholy for the fear-spawned gladness of the average man. But the pressures on him to join the world were so great at this period of his life that he must have felt at times that he might ultimately end up like the husband in "The Apple-Tree Table," a sane, solid citizen, to be sure, but mentally emasculated and deficient in that commodity Melville so highly prized, a profound awareness of mystery. By analyzing so closely and so constantly the nature of ordinary humanity with particular reference to the subtle effects of fear, Melville was like a man studying the causes and symptoms of a dread disease in order to assure himself that he has not caught it and will not catch it.

What keeps the fearful man "eminently safe," as the lawyer in "Bartleby" puts it, is his superficial vision through which he perceives a life-sustaining variety of forms and colors. Paradoxically his fear is his protection; it prevents him from seeing that below the surface of varied appearances is only a blank, white sameness. That horrible sameness is what torments and maddens the rebellious characters. They willfully refuse to attach any reality to the infinite variety of phenomena that fills the vision of ordinary humanity. They focus with heroic but destructive resentment upon the meaningless similitude of the palsied universe. If the fear-ridden man does not truly see, the angry man sees too much, for it is his penetrating vision that creates and feeds his rebellious anger. The characters of Melville's stories dominated by anger are thus never average people; the capacity for all-absorbing rage is rare. These are the extraordinary beings, set apart from the everyday world by their defiance of it and of all else that would enslave them. Melville of course depicted such heroes long before he wrote his short fiction; among them are his great cosmic warmongers, Taji, Ahab, Pierre. Their flame, if not their heat, has diminished by the time of the short stories. Now anger is more likely to be submerged and reflected in actions that either totally puzzle or mislead the ordinary world. Bartleby's employer speculates frequently about his scrivener's silence, but he never understands the reason for it, obsessive resentment. The rage of Bannadonna in "The Bell-Tower" is channeled into his art, where he attempts to mock both man and God, but the city fathers who commission him to construct a great tower believe him to be merely an eccentric mechanician who is killed in a tragic accident. The narrator of "The Lightning-Rod Man" seethes beneath his alternating wit and pseudo-piety, but the salesman, target of his scorn, thinks him a common fool. Babo is decapitated in "Benito Cereno" for his part in a bloody slave rebellion, but his rage is directed at far more than his white masters—they simply typify. The anger of silence, which the world almost always misinterprets, is no less heroic and at the same time no less wrongheaded and destructive than the deafeningly loud roar of Ahab's rebellion. It is simply another form of the same disease, a disease that Melville dreaded perhaps even more than that of fear, for he was born with its germ in his soul. Through anger came the dignity and exhilaration of arrogance, but on the other hand it led to solitude, to a loss of compassionate human feelings, and finally to insanity and self-destruction. Melville admired the defiance that anger creates, but by depicting its negative results in his rebellious characters he kept himself aware that it cannot coexist with love.

Between these two extremes of character there emerges in Melville's short fiction a third type representing the synthesis in his dialectic. This position is fundamentally the one Melville worked out in his own life, a kind of emotional middle state, dominated by neither fear nor anger, and made possible through an oscillating vision, a willful changing of view whenever the inner eye began to stare too long at the white world that underlies life's variety and color. Each character who exemplifies this alternating vision is, as was Melville himself, an ironist, that is, a person who realizes that sense perception is deceptive but who never loses faith in it completely. He is like an actor who performs his part—even at times enjoying it—but who never confuses the play with life. An ironist perceives a level beneath the surface, but he does not separate himself from either; he functions in both realms.

The central experience of the ironist in Melville's stories is one first of dangerous encounter and then withdrawal to safety, submersion into himself or into the nature of existence so deeply as to almost drown and emergence back to the surface of ordinary life. The narrator of "Poor Man's Pudding and Rich Man's Crumbs" encounters the poverty and then the bestiality of human existence. In both episodes his physical discomfort or danger signifies the psychological peril of such insights; so he does not remain among the poor. In other works the same pattern emerges where the narrator goes on a journey, as in "The Paradise of Bachelors and the Tartarus of Maids," experiences some deep and disturbing insight into the nature of human existence, and realizing his danger returns quickly to his former position, not precisely the same as he was before his traumatic revelation but, as "The Piazza" makes clear, with a renewed sense of the need to keep his hold on ordinary life while never forgetting what he has seen. The ability of such characters to do this, to survive among the unseeing without losing their own insight, to retain both their self-esteem and their human attributes, is reflected in their practice of the art of irony, which is not only their stylistic method and tone in the stories they narrate but also a metaphor for their *Weltanschauung*.

The ironists of Melville's stories are not happy, well-adjusted characters who have found the answer to all life's problems. As was the case with Melville himself, they barely manage to hang on, to keep themselves together. There is something deeply moving in their attempts to do that, to avoid the indignity and cravenness of the lee shore without perishing in the howling infinite. This body of writing, completed between the years 1853 and 1856, consists of several works of short fiction, but it is also a disguised journal of Melville's plague years and a record of noble survival from the ravages of fear and anger.

INDEX

Characters from Melville's fiction are listed separately and the works in which they appear identified in parentheses and in the following abbreviated form:

Nicol, Charles, 229n
Nippers (BS), 23, 25, 26, 27–28,
33, 36, 46, 50n
Norman, Liane, 19n

Oberlus (TE), 79, 80, 86, 90, 91,
102
O'Brien, Fitz-James, 143n, 209n
*Observations on the Effects of the
Corn Laws* (Malthus), 132n
"Old Burton." *See* Burton, Robert
"Old Manse, The" (Hawthorne),
92–93, 332, 333
Oliver, Egbert S., 50n, 56n, 172n,
201n
Omar Khayyam, 310
Omoo, 4, 75, 76
Orpheus, myth of, 158n, 165
Our Old Home (Hawthorne), 99n

Pafford, Ward, 260n
Paine, Thomas, 277n
Pandora, myth of, 155n–156n
Paracelsus, 145n
Paradise Lost (Milton), 262
"Paradise of Bachelors and the
Tartarus of Maids, The": as bipartite story, 8, 104, 183, 185,
206; autobiographical details in,
16; bachelors and bachelorhood
in, 184, 187, 188, 190, 195, 198,
199, 200, 206; Dantean setting
in, 184–85; imagery of envelopment in, 184, 189, 190, 199, 205;
health as subject in, 184, 194–
95; contrasts in, 185; whiteness
in, 185, 186, 198, 206–7; sameness as theme in, 185–86, 189,
190, 196–98; narrator of compared to narrator of "Poor
Man's Pudding and Rich Man's
Crumbs," 187; maids and maidenhood in, 187, 205, 324; benedict as type in, 188–89, 206;
wedded man as type in, 188,
206; law as subject in, 189, 200;

slavery as subject in, 189, 200,
202, 203; decorum as subject in,
190, 193–94; irony in, 190, 206–
7, 370; battle imagery in, 191;
meal as metaphor in, 191–92;
wine as measuring instrument
in, 192–93; Jericho horn in, 193–
94; walls as subject in, 194, 200;
déjà vu in, 195; as dream or
vision, 195, 196; narrator's danger in, 196, 204; narrator as
seedsman in, 198; emasculation
as subject in, 198, 200; sexual
symbolism in, 198, 201–2; narrator's way of seeing in, 199;
narrator as diver in, 199, 204;
narrator's central experience in,
200; paper machine as symbol
in, 200–205; industrialism as
subject in, 200, 210; mystery of
nature as subject in, 202–3; narrator's revelation in, 203, 205,
327; myth of Actaeon in, 204;
narrator's vacillations in, 206
"Paradise of Children, The"
(Hawthorne), 155n–156n
Parker, Hershel: on "Bartleby,"
53n; on "The Fiddler," 163; on
"The Lightning-Rod Man," 168–
69, 170n; on "Benito Cereno,"
229n; on Charles V, 291n
Parsons, William (Third Earl of
Rosse), 283n
Patrick, Walton R., 40n, 54n
Pazzi, Madame (ATT), 360
Pearce, Howard D., 85n
Pericles (Shakespeare), 336
Peter the Great, 289
Phelps, Leland R., 257n
Phillips, Barry, 247n, 269n
Piazza Tales, 10, 221, 253n
"Piazza, The": common reactions
to, 6; writing and publication
of, 10, 319; autobiographical
details in, 16, 320, 330–37;
Hawthorne in, 17, 330–37; as